ADVENTURES
ON THE FREEDOM ROAD

The French Intellectuals in the 20th Century

Bernard-Henri Lévy

ADVENTURES ON THE FREEDOM ROAD

The French Intellectuals in the 20th Century

*Translated from the French and edited
by Richard Veasey*

THE HARVILL PRESS

LONDON

First published in France in 1991
with the title *Les Aventures de la liberté*
by Editions Bernard Grasset, Paris

First published in Great Britain in 1995 by
The Harvill Press
84 Thornhill Road,
London N1 1RD

Second impression

This edition has been published with the
assistance of the
French Ministère de la Culture
et de la Communication, whose support is
gratefully acknowledged

Bernard-Henri Lévy asserts the moral right
to be identified as the author of this work

A CIP catalogue record for this book is
available from the British Library

ISBN 1 86046 035 6

Set in 11/13pt Janson by
Rowland Phototypesetting Limited,
Bury St Edmunds, Suffolk

Printed and bound in Great Britain by
Butler & Tanner Ltd, Frome, Somerset

For Arielle

Table of Contents

Preface

For five years I have nurtured the project of telling in my own way the story of French intellectuals from the time of the Dreyfus Affair. I have done this with mixed feelings of uncertainty and conviction.

I have made investigations and tracked down documents as well as unpublished or rare pictures. Since my initial idea was to make a film, I visited – we visited – the film archives of Europe to find a particular photo of Gide in Berlin, of Aragon in Leningrad, an early shot of the surrealists, and a scrap of film of the young Drieu La Rochelle, believed lost.

I met a number of survivors of the period and pressed them endlessly to tell their story, to repeat things, to be specific, even though I risked trying their patience and straining their memories. What impression did Malraux make in Spain or Josette Clotis in the Maquis? How did Eluard and Benjamin Péret strike those who saw them on the platform at an anti-fascist rally? What were Cocteau's last words? How did Althusser spend his final hours? What really happened when Breton and Bataille came face to face again and tested each other's influence as intellectuals? I accumulated details, a mass of details. I realised very quickly that only details count in a project of this sort. During the five years I spent on it, I was often struck by the thought that perhaps all that remains of a person's life is an accumulation of details.

I travelled a great deal. I went to Berlin on the trail of Brasillach and Crevel, to Moscow to retrace the steps of Aragon and Nizan, and to Algiers on account of Camus. I wasn't able to film in Peking, but I did re-read Malraux's *Antimémoires* and Claudel's *Connaissance de l'Est*. The whole enterprise was a long peregrination in space and time and led me to delve into books and into people's minds. In the course of it, I suddenly came to realise something I had sensed in advance. Though the undertaking itself had been enjoyable, however disconcerting I found the style, the rhetoric and syntax of a visual medium, I was left with a sense of unfinished business, and this, for a writer, can only be resolved by means of a book. Those with experience of such projects already know this well enough.

The book can therefore be read, first of all, as an apologia for an undertaking which, by its very nature, was unlikely to satisfy the demands of rigour and scholarship or to respect shades of meaning.

I

How, for example, do you represent visually the literary tradition initiated by Barrès, or the way in which countless works survive, or the moment when Althusser's life effectively came to an end? How can you film a meeting which never took place, like the one which might have occurred between Malraux and Drieu, or Sartre and Camus? How can you show these things on the screen? Initially, I conceived my book as an ordered series of scenes and portraits. I constructed it as a counterpoint to the film commentaries which are to be found in an annexe.[1] The complexity of the book contrasts with the simplicity of the film, just as the nuances of literature may be contrasted with the reductive nature of visual images.

Above all, it will be read as a text which, by the very nature of the genre and because of the particular qualities of language, inevitably acquired its own rhythms and its own cohesion. Its sources too were different, as were the connections made between various issues and ideas. Indeed, the book freed itself totally from its original model. It offered another representation of the same material, another route through it. Though its narrative line was originally to have echoed that of the film, in the end it acquired its own peculiar logic. It was as if the act of writing a historical survey of intellectuals could not but challenge and correct the firmly established conclusions I had previously drawn. Discovering this came as quite a surprise to me. When I had completed these two accounts (the film and the book), which covered the same material, I gave up trying to decide whether the one had inspired, shaped, or simply repeated the other.

In the end, I would like the book to be read as an exploration of my own convictions as I survey the lives of other people. Equally, it is an attempt to sketch in the genealogies of those who have made me what I am, however unsavoury they may have been. It is unfortunate if my methodology offends those who champion a more "objective" approach to history. It has, after all, been tried and tested: from Baudelaire to Malraux and Borges, countless writers have only been able to define their identity by calling to mind the "invisible band" of fellow writers who were crucial to their development, whether or not they were their true contemporaries. For my part, and with appropriate humility, I can think of no other way of making my confession. I have chosen to write this book to mark my coming of age.

In conclusion, perhaps I might add that this quest was begun several years ago when the signs of collapse of the communist world were already perceptible. They were completed just as new regimes were coming into being in a rather disorderly fashion. We move therefore from the death throes of communism to the reawakening of Islam; from one all-embracing regime to another. One period of history ends and another begins. During all the years I was writing, in the shadow of Aragon, Zola, Eluard and Cocteau, I couldn't get the idea out of my mind that the whole saga was at the same time very remote and very close, involving as it did numerous quarrels as well as absurd and bloody wars in which so many destinies were wagered and lost.

Have we thus reached the point where former passions have come to seem like the multiple symptoms of a state of mind which no longer exists? This is doubtless true in part, as the simple fact of re-telling a story is in a sense proof enough that it is over and done with. For the rest, we should be more cautious and take care not to forget that the realm of ideas is a privileged one. The same issues and obsessions are endlessly reworked, as are the forces which underpin them, though at different times different ones hold sway. But the most important of them relate to war and peace, passion and weariness, great fears and right-thinking people.[2] On reflection, I am glad that I chose this moment to share with interested readers a particular segment of our collective memory and the passions which stirred the French nation during that period. Whether we are friends or enemies, our inheritance is the same. Whichever of us can come to terms with it will perhaps be set free.

Bernard-Henri Lévy,
January 1991

NOTES

1. The annexe in the original French edition features in this edition as the Introduction.

2. An allusion to *La Grande Peur des* *bien-pensants* (1931), a polemical essay by Georges Bernanos in praise of the anti-semitic politician and journalist Edouard Drumont.

INTRODUCTION

[The numbers in square brackets refer to the
appropriate chapters in each section of the main text.]

I

Great Hopes

I

The scene opens in Paris, at the beginning of the eighties, with the funeral cortège of a famous person – but whose? Could it really be that of Jean-Paul Sartre, as the official announcement suggested? Could it not also be Michel Foucault or Maurice Clavel, two other philosophers who died almost at the same time? Perhaps it was Doctor Jacques Lacan, in his own way an intellectual mentor, or even Roland Barthes. Finally, what is there to say about Louis Althusser, who entered the realm of darkness before he actually died?

We undertook our investigation with a view to unravelling the mystery of this group of people, all now deceased. It took us to the USSR, to various strange towns which held some bizarre fascination for Gide and caused Aragon to go astray. It took us also to Algiers and to the poor quarter of Belcourt. It was there that Camus grew up, one of the nobler figures in our gallery of portraits. We went to Berlin, where it was even more difficult to get our bearings, and spent a long time listening for echoes of distant voices. For it was there that Malraux challenged Nazism and there too that others, such as Drieu, came to sing its praises. We followed in the footsteps of Georges Bataille and the arrogant André Breton, who was the most extreme example of intellectual seriousness. In Tiananmen Square, in Prague, and at the Berlin Wall, we looked for signs of an epoch drawing to a close, an epoch in which intellectuals had perhaps enjoyed their greatest influence.

Our story begins in fact at the end of the last century,[1] in the France of Zola, Péguy and Marcel Proust. Why then, one might ask, rather than at the time of Voltaire or of Lamartine and Hugo? Because it was at that particular point that the term "intellectual" was first used. Another current idea of the period was that a writer or an artist could and should on occasion give up creative writing[2] and put his talent to the service of some great cause. All this came about in connection with a quite extraordinary affair which I think I ought to outline before going any further.

Paris was a happy, radiant city at the end of the nineteenth century.

It was preparing to celebrate its great exhibition of 1900 and bathing in the glow of what came to be referred to as the Belle Epoque. But then from the depths of the city and from the darkest corners of the collective consciousness a strange rumour began to emanate. A French officer called Alfred Dreyfus was accused of spying for the Germans. As he was Jewish and had the effrontery to proclaim his innocence, thereby calling into question the authority of the judicial system and the French army, he became the target of a powerful campaign of anti-semitic hatred. Amongst the throng of people who hounded him were a number who belonged to the France of the ancien régime which had never really accepted the creation of the Republic; behind Dreyfus, they believed, there existed a dark conspiracy to sully the nation's honour. There were certain members of the French Academy who emerged from their headquarters on the Quai de Conti. There were also traditionalist and patriotic writers who were far keener to accept injustice than disorder. There were sculptors at the height of their fame and painters of genius in the anti-Dreyfus camp. There were also younger polemicists who were prepared to cross swords for their ideas: men like Léon Daudet and the young Maurras, who fumed and raged against conventional thinking in the famous *Cahiers gris* of the early "Action française" movement.[1] Then there was Drumont. Something which is too often forgotten is that his anti-semitic pamphlets were in commercial terms amongst the most successful works not only of the period but of the century as a whole. Nor must we forget Valéry, who, when he wasn't conversing with Gide, was not above joining that theoretician of racism Vacher de Lapouge in a Montpellier cemetery[3] where they dug up hundreds of skulls in order to measure and classify them. There was that other great writer as well, Maurice Barrès, idol of the young, and intellectual mentor of Blum, Proust[4] and all up-to-date thinkers. He inveighed against "the ethnic nose", "the racially different face"[5] of the condemned man on Devil's Island. It was Barrès whose mixture of nationalism and socialism, cult of brute force, and repeated attacks on Jewish politicians and financiers awakened some disturbing echoes, to put it mildly. At the same time, the majority of the Left started out by thinking that less attention would have been paid to Dreyfus had he been poor; they took the view that it was merely a confrontation between two sections of the bourgeoisie and no concern of the working class. That included even Jaurès[6] who at the end of '97 was still hesitating to declare himself and who had been able to write two years earlier about the situation in the French Departments of Algeria: "The revolution-

ary mentality spreads in the somewhat narrow form of anti-semitism."
He went on: "Why doesn't a serious anti-Jewish movement exist over
there in the face of the extortion practised by colonialist Jews?" The
confusion of thought which existed at the time and almost reduced
the country to open warfare[7] also created the "big bang" from which
the intellectual emerged.

II

There was, of course, the other France as well. It stood for courage
and honour and the fight for justice and truth, which was already on
the march. High-minded, indomitable, democratic Frenchmen took
Dreyfus's part and rebelled against what they took to be an outrage.
At first, they were isolated, a minority. But gradually with the passing
of the years (and the Affair lasted years), that minority cohered into
a group and the group became a small band, which in time grew into a
huge army. Organised or not, they were the heroes of the pro-Dreyfus
campaign.

They included artists as diverse as Paul Signac, an anarchist by
nature and on principle, Vuillard who was connected with the *Revue
Blanche*,[2] and also Bonnard and Vallotton. They were great painters,
whose only authority was derived from their work, yet they forsook
their easels in order to defend justice. There were also writers and
poets who dropped everything to move into the public arena and
make themselves intermediaries between the concerns of the moment
and the timeless values of truth, goodness and right. Intellectual mentors signed petitions along with their disciples and immoralists took
up the cause of morality. Some of the disciples, like the young Blum,
went round collecting signatures, thereby running the risk of making
errors of judgment which gave the conflict a touch of farce.

There were, however, four leaders whose names stand out from
the rest. First, there was Bernard Lazare,[8] then Péguy, who was
always in the forefront of the student battles which shook the Latin
Quarter. With his fiery rallying cries and the cane which he brandished like a truncheon, he led the young supporters of Dreyfus at
the Sorbonne. The third was, of course, Zola who had always said:
"I detest politics because it offers competition to novelists." But he
threw himself into the battle and brought down on his own head the
thunderous might of the law. This helped turn the Affair into a public
scandal. The great Zola, a rich and celebrated writer, saw himself
vilified and persecuted for years because he had been prepared to

defend an innocent man or an idea, which amounted to the same thing. Finally, there was Lucien Herr, a more discreet and enigmatic individual, who operated from his office as Librarian at the Ecole normale supérieure[9] in the Rue d'Ulm and was in many respects the inspiration behind the movement. To some people he was simply a source of information; others, such as Blum, Péguy, and finally Jaurès as well, he convinced with the force of his arguments and won over to the cause. Subsequently, he attempted to convert the whole university to socialism.

Far away, on Devil's Island, the man who had been condemned, who was exhausted and in a state of despair, confessed in letters to his wife that he felt as if he were already in his grave. Then, suddenly, Dreyfus learned that his friends had carried the day. Justice had triumphed and he was freed. Intellectuals could raise their banner high because they had won, but also because, in the heat of battle, they had invented a new character: "the intellectual".

III

Not that this was the end of the matter; it would be quite false to imagine that France had calmed down, that a mood of reconciliation prevailed and that overnight the same values were shared by all. First, and most obviously, this was because those who had been defeated did not lay down their arms. Also, Barrès, Maurras and their friends still enjoyed a large following. Secondly, the victors who, as fraternal and zealous militants, had fought shoulder to shoulder in defence of their martyr, rediscovered their old differences, once victory was achieved, and reverted to the most implacable disputes.

On the one side were those intellectuals who had adopted a bourgeois lifestyle and become ministers. Just a short while before they had been combative writers but had subsequently taken on the manner and appearance of good old patriots who had stepped back into line. They were, in other words, men who had furthered their careers by supporting Dreyfus and who ruled over the Sorbonne as they did over the Republic, which had truly become "the Republic of the Professors".

On the other side were intractable and uncompromising individuals such as Sorel, his disciple Edouard Berth, and above all the socialist bookseller, Charles Péguy. They were angry that the noble mystique surrounding the Dreyfus cause had descended to mere politics and were bent on keeping the original flame alive. Unfortunately, they were carried away by their hatred of their former friends who had become rulers in the land and started to talk like their erstwhile enemies, especially Maurice Barrès. Péguy began to decry democracy and universal suffrage, to voice his support for such things as national energy and the instinct of race, and to issue a clarion call in defence of war which had, he said, become the hope of all true Frenchmen. Poor old Lieutenant Péguy went off to war, like Apollinaire, with a flower in the barrel of his gun, convinced, as he put it, that "the greatest glory was the glory achieved in war." But having longed for war with an insane nationalistic fervour, he found himself in an exposed position at the head of his small company, under fire in the mud. Then one September afternoon on the Plain of Brie he suddenly realised how different the landscape was from the sun-drenched wheat fields of which he had dreamed where French soldiers of olden times had achieved such renown.

What took place in those modern killing fields? How did the men react and what thoughts did they have before they died? What lessons did the survivors learn, the intellectuals who lived long enough to tell of their experiences at Verdun and the Chemin des Dames? What new thoughts were forged and tempered under that frightful onslaught of bullets and shells?

The first reaction was one of pacifism, expressed by writers like Barbusse, who had volunteered in '14 and then become a stretcher-bearer. There were others, too, such as Genevoix but especially Romain Rolland,[10] who didn't fight because of his age but immediately felt excluded from the bloody communion the others shared. Horrified by the killing,[11] these writers sought to persuade future generations that it should "never happen again." More important than them, in my view, were the young men who began to realise that it was the older generation as a whole, pacifist and anti-pacifist, pro- and anti-Dreyfus alike, which had led them to the slaughter. In their anger and absolute despair, they had something in common with the young soldier who had been driven mad by the war: Antonin Artaud.

Whether they were half-crazed like Jacques Vaché who, though not well-known, was the inspiration of the group, or sickened by what had happened like Breton, Aragon, Eluard and Soupault, these young men proclaimed themselves "spiritual deserters" and "European defeatists".[12] Surrealism emerged from the carnage of war with its black, nihilistic view of things, its conviction that the old world had disappeared taking western culture with it, and its belief that science, philosophy, art and literature had been rendered meaningless by the slaughter.

Yet there was joy and elation too. What a sense of jubilation those "Paris peasants" felt when they were able to get back to the cafés where they truly belonged and dance on the ruins of the old world, once the war was over. "Art is nonsense," said one. "Criminals, parricides, hooligans, and madmen of every kind are far more admirable than your Republican heroes," declared another. With what gusto and delight they attacked all those things that French officialdom revered, which in their eyes had been totally discredited. They attacked the poet Claudel, who prided himself on having brought substantial benefit to France. At the end of an unprecedented mock trial with terroristic overtones, they condemned Barrès for "crimes against sanity". They were equally condemnatory of that splendid humanist Anatole France, who had been given a state funeral in recognition of his achievements. In Eluard's opinion, he was just another old man, whereas Soupault saw him as an empty husk, a figure of fun, and Breton and Aragon thought of him as a sceptical old scoundrel surrounded by worthless books which deserved to be ridiculed to extinction. The virulence of what they wrote has been forgotten[13] and it is difficult to imagine the vehemence with which they sought to sweep away the *ancien régime* of the intellect.[14] At the same time, they saw surrealism as a way of totally liberating the human mind and all its works through the macabre happenings which they staged, their highly disquieting practical jokes, and their glorification of the body, of eroticism, and wild passion. We have indeed forgotten the extraordinary vehemence of this group, which was exemplified in the physical convulsions of the actor, Antonin Artaud.

Various things immediately come to mind when one thinks of the surrealists: their love of the ridiculous and the fantastic, their delight in black humour, their awareness of cruelty and of the fatal forces governing human destiny which challenged the very notion of the wild passion they extolled. Then there was their view of suicide as perhaps the soundest and the most decisive solution. This new young generation of intellectuals had wiped the slate clean. Yet they still hesitated as to what part they should play in the new order in the making and which they knew would fill the void they had created.

IV

It was precisely at that moment, of course, on the other side of Europe and almost at the edge of the world, that a revolution was taking place which would fulfil all these people's expectations, and more. Only the echoes of that distant revolution reached them, and it would be a number of years, decades even, before they could measure its importance. But in the event itself, in the spectacle of huge crowds breaking their chains and seeking to fulfil their dreams, there was something which aroused the enthusiasm of French intellectuals and which seemed to respond to their misery and their hopes. This was the "October Revolution": it was like a great beacon in the East and was to alter the course of history radically for some time to come.

One must try to imagine the effect it had on the France of Clemenceau and Poincaré when the Tsars were overthrown, the army mutinied, and the old idols fell. Suddenly, all the bonds were broken which until that point had in fact or in theory shackled people's hearts and minds. Similarly, they had to come to terms with strange new masters preaching revolt. The world had been turned upside down and a new epoch dawned, as it did in France. But here the horizons were defined by interminable debate and the quest for stable government. The Revolution was a real-life epic, a poem of heroism and fraternity, scripted by Eisenstein and his friends. Emmanuel Levinas,[3] who witnessed those events and subsequently became one of the greatest philosophers of his day, commented that history, having run out of steam and ground to a halt, relaunched itself on an uncertain course in circumstances which were totally chaotic.

Some people also made a slightly forced parallel with the French Revolution, comparing Lenin with Robespierre and Trotsky, the leader of the Red Army, with Danton. Everyone, however, marvelled at a regime which could make Chagall its Minister of Fine Arts and use the great Mayakovsky as an actor in a splendid propaganda film illustrating the success of the Bolshevik literacy campaign. In fact all propaganda films are splendid. French intellectuals could only wonder at a regime in which propagandists, proselytisers, orators and theoreticians had real tasks to perform. They themselves had no such tasks and were dazzled at the spectacle of those who were directly involved in the real world.

Jacques Sadoul, a French military attaché, decided to stay in Moscow. He, like the young writer, Raymond Lefebvre, who mysteriously disappeared in the North Sea and whose legend Drieu La Rochelle kept alive, was fascinated by the austerity of the new Russia, by its asceticism and purity. The first major intellectual who gave his support to the USSR and also joined the French Communist Party was Charles Rappoport. Alongside him was Boris Souvarine, a Russian who had become a naturalised Frenchman. He was a rather haughty aristocrat of communism, but at the same time was the key figure amongst those acting as propagandists for the Bolsheviks. Also seeking to revive the spirit of the supporters of Dreyfus was a group of young philosophers[15] who expressed their idealism in small reviews. They were only Marxists in name, or seeking to become Marxists. The most remarkable and colourful of them was Georges Politzer. Though he is almost forgotten today, he left the most lasting impression on those who survived him. Nizan, a friend of Politzer and also of Sartre – who kept his distance from the group – was one of those individuals who seemed to have entered the world cursing and raging, as Barrès said one should. It is not clear whether he became a communist at the Ecole normale supérieure, in Aden, or like Rosenthal, the hero of one of his novels, whilst following the ashes of Jaurès through the streets of Paris to the Panthéon. One thing is, however, clear to me: Nizan, the enemy of traditional philosophy, of well-rehearsed ideas, and of those who taught them, was more of a romantic in revolt than a pure, hard-line Marxist. He was an adventurer, who penned the following memorable line: "I was twenty, and let no one try to tell me it's the best time of one's life." Then there was Aragon. He had recently claimed that, in the history of ideas, the October Revolution was scarcely more significant than a ministerial crisis. But along with Breton, Eluard, Benjamin Péret and René Crevel, he joined the Communist Party. They did so cautiously, with a degree of misgiving, but they did so all the same, believing that it was in the USSR that the future was being defined.

It was also around that time that the French army was sent to Morocco to fight a war against a people whose only crime lay in their struggle for freedom. That war has long been forgotten. For the surrealists, however, who had sworn they would never again put on military uniform and who as internationalists wanted their country to be open and fraternal in its dealings with other nations, it represented an injustice which they opposed with all their might. So they joined Nizan, Politzer, the young philosophers, as well as those involved with the review *Clarté* in a sort of common front. For them, idealism and instinctive anti-colonialism were more important than scientific socialism.

Finally, I almost forgot the young adventurer who read Barrès and was involved in the theft of Khmer statues. André Malraux, the future writer, was still thought of as a man who had just returned from China where he had been fighting. Though that too was a dream and a lie. Yet one surely must believe what he said when he maintained that his only motive for supporting the revolution stemmed from the fact that he had seen the police ruthlessly attacking people, had witnessed the suffering of the oppressed and watched them rise up in revolt against it.

V

In the end, I don't believe that was the only reason so many of our intellectuals became Stalinist communists. But however carefully one tries to understand their true motives and strives above all not to judge the past in terms of current prejudices,[16] I don't think one should idealise a story which contained its fair share of horrors and dark deeds. If we look more closely and try to get inside their hearts and minds, we shall discover that they had other more disturbing and complex feelings which played a part in shaping their enthusiasm.

For example, I'm convinced that we shall completely misunderstand their allegiance to communism if we fail to take into account the dream of creating a new man, of regenerating people, the purpose of which was also to repudiate and eliminate real people in the new Russia. Just listen to Barbusse who, on reaching Moscow, prophesied "that Lenin, and Stalin as well, would one day be seen as the messiahs of humanity renewed" (he spoke of them as messiahs!). Now listen to Romain Rolland: "In spite of one's disgust," he said, ". . . in spite of the horror, the terrible errors and crimes, I look to the child, the new-born babe; they are the hope of the future." At the heart of the communist dream, overriding any reservations and intellectual misgivings they may have had, there was a fascination with youth which, for a while, was a great source of inspiration, though it caused no little embarrassment to other intellectuals. For better or worse, these men were obsessed with life above all else, with life in all its vigour, with life as Barrès had glorified it and as it was depicted in the films they saw. These were strange, almost obscene images, yet they were the ones Rolland had in mind when his Soviet friends extolled the virtues of their regime and when he uttered the magic formula which, in his eyes, excused every crime: "Life, life forever, one mustn't halt the surge of life, because whatever stops dies and putrefies." What he said didn't, of course, detract from the nobility of his spirit but it did add significantly to his capacity to turn a blind eye. The man who, in his last novels, revealed his admiration for strength, for forceful rogues and brutes, and who had one of his heroines say that she felt free as she lay beneath the iron weight of dictatorship, such a man needed to look no further than socialism to justify his cult of vital energy and all-conquering power.

Aragon, who had rallied to the cause somewhat noncommittally, also made the trip to Moscow as a penitent communist in order to learn about the cult of youth, strength and life. In so doing, he broke with those of his friends whose more reasonable concern was limited to the war in Morocco.

The truth is that all these people sounded like converts and resembled their new-found comrades in Moscow who were destroying churches, smashing the old idols, and chasing out the wicked priests of a dead religion, even as they embraced their new religion in a show of faith which remained inviolate and which was transferred undiminished to the "Montagnard in the Kremlin".[4] Thus the commitment of Rolland, Barbusse, Gide, and even Aragon was more religious than political. The high priest of the new religion[17] may have been Maurice Thorez, but the gods were Marx, Engels, Lenin and Stalin.

I should also point out here that it was due to Alexandre Kojève, the supreme intellectual leader of his day, that the texts, if not of Marx himself at least of his illustrious predecessor, Hegel, became known in philosophical circles in France.

VI

Then there was the horror;[18] the crimes and the camps, the State lies and the massacres. There were trials, piles of corpses, an archipelago of suffering, which most of the major intellectuals came to accept in the end. Were these things known about? Did they know about them? Did they go on believing, in the full knowledge of what was happening, whilst their dream turned into a nightmare before their very eyes? There is only one terrible answer to that equally terrible question. It is to be found in a succession of images.

There were arrests, for example, in the Russian Republic, but in the other Republics as well. There were telegrams signed by Lenin, couched in the same cold-blooded language that the leading exponents of terror had used towards the end of the French Revolution. There were summary executions and shootings which began immediately after the events of October, the number and the savagery of which everyone knows were not justified by the war, the fact that they were surrounded by hostile forces, or by the counter-revolution of the

White Russians. Then there were the travellers who made their definitive journey to the monastery of Solovki which had been turned into a camp. The processions of prisoners, seen in a new propaganda film, were intended to prove the delights and the virtues of re-education through work. These revolutionaries made it totally clear what their intentions were. Did the Nazis make their intentions equally clear, relatively speaking? Was there ever a despotism which showed its colours so clearly? Quantities of books were published in London, Berlin, and in Paris too of course, with respectable publishers, and the information they provided was not contested. Everything was said and brought out in the open, and those intellectuals who had eyes to read, a head with which to think, and perhaps a heart which could be moved were confronted with the most terrible images and scenes. Even though they didn't refuse to read these books, their faith and religion saw to it that they literally didn't understand what they were reading. Everyone knew about the trials. Most of our intellectuals had in fact been taken to the pillared hall where those strange and terrifying ceremonies took place which were impudently referred to as trials. All of them who visited this place were shown the splendours of the Soviet regime.

After Kirov was murdered, the people as a whole were duped by the masquerade of his funeral and a great show of mourning. And, as happens in bad novels, his murderer returned to prowl around the scene of his crime. As if absolutely nothing had happened, Aragon returned to Paris.

The trials continued, and the ranks of revolutionaries were decimated by the use of terror. The world's press reported them and the whole world learned what was happening. As at the time of the Dreyfus Affair, there were many who proclaimed their innocence. But where were those who had supported Dreyfus? Where were the heirs of Zola and Jaurès? Where were the disciples of truth militant? They were certainly there, but on the wrong side. Aragon went back to Moscow.

And still the trials continued, as if they would never end. How many did they need? How many victims and innocent martyrs did the regime require? How many Devil's Islands? Picture our heroes, with their splendid consciences, piously listening to the one whom they saw as their ideal representative of liberty, referring to "traitors and spies who had betrayed their country". The ghost of Dreyfus hovered in the wings! And Aragon returned to Paris.

What did the high priest have to say? What was he so sure about?

In what new trial was he about to act as prosecutor? Where were all these men and women heading? Where was Georges Politzer going, and Jean-Richard Bloch, Paul Nizan and André Gide, men who, we recall, had set out on the road to freedom? Hold on! Aragon set off again for the USSR.

NOTES

1. An influential nationalist group and newspaper founded in 1899. Its propaganda was monarchist and anti-semitic.

2. A literary and dramatic review which numbered Debussy and the future Socialist leader Léon Blum amongst its critics.

3. Professor of philosophy at the University of Paris IV until his retirement, he helped introduce Heidegger into France.

4. So-called because they occupied the high benches in the National Convention. They were extreme revolutionaries.

2

Days of Contempt

(THE 1920S TO 1945)

I

Back to the twenties and another revolution is taking shape. Another terrible upheaval is about to plunge the whole of Europe into grief and horror. I know the word revolution will surprise some people as it isn't often used to describe what I want to talk about. But, sadly, it's a fact, and the testimonies of the time bear it out. Furthermore, if I'm to remain faithful to the principles underlying this account, and to describe things as the actors themselves experienced them, trying to discover their state of mind, their illusions, their motives, one thing must be made clear. Before it turned into a dictatorship, a regime of terror, and became the most appalling and infamous killing machine ever conceived, fascism was first of all a revolutionary upheaval. Whether rightly or wrongly, some people saw it as a sequel to what had happened in Moscow in October 1917.

The upheaval began in Italy with the bands of Blackshirts who set out to achieve power. At their head was a former socialist and revolutionary syndicalist, Benito Mussolini. They had a rather curious ideology which took a number of its elements from Sorel.[1] He was author of *Réflexions sur la violence*, a believer in the national strike, and an admirer of Lenin and the Soviet Revolution. There was something of the clown about Mussolini, but he soon revealed himself unscrupulous as a dictator. Initially, however, he seemed perhaps more of a *condottiere* and an opponent of the established order.

The shock waves which emanated from Rome then reached Germany, where another leader emerged on the streets. Hitler was carried along on a wave of popular support, a charismatic figure who soon won an election, creating a synthesis of Left and Right, of nationalists and socialists, of conservative-revolutionaries like Hermann Rauschning and Bolshevik-nationalists such as Strasser.[2] He too appeared to be a total nonconformist, but was also a barbarian, a sinister and grotesque dictator, who, on occasions, seemed to mimic Chaplin's caricature of him. To his contemporaries, and especially to the French who observed him at a distance, he was the miraculous inventor of a new political order.

What was happening in France during that period? What had become of the intellectuals who had escaped the slaughter of the Great War, but had not succumbed to the siren call of communism, remaining faithful instead to the political legacy of Barrès? They too were disgusted and shared the common view that the old values had foundered, but what distinguished them from the rest was their questioning why all those men had withstood what they did, why they had made that prodigious act of self-sacrifice. These intellectuals were obsessed by the mysterious docility of the ordinary soldiers who had been so brave under fire. The only explanation they could find was that, like puppets, they were controlled by an age-old instinct which bound them to their race, their kin, their soil. This was the generation of Montherlant and his young warriors, who had the same pride as the characters in Plutarch. Céline might have been one of them, had he not been so gloomy, so utterly despairing. Drieu La Rochelle, who achieved considerable literary success with his *Comédie de Charleroi*, was, however, of their number.

None of them could stomach the times in which they lived; they loathed the France of the small shopkeeper, the evening apéritif, of bogus governments with their string of intrigues, manipulations and false promises, not to mention their scandals. These lent their bitterness an air of virtue, a necessary ingredient in genuine fascism. Even if only in thought, they were on the side of the rioters who took to the streets on the famous night of February 6th, 1934 and, fired up by the smell of gunpowder and the memory of "Boulangisme",[3] almost overthrew the government. The uprising failed, of course, and when morning came and it was time to count the dead and determine which symbols of the old France had been trampled under foot, they had to face the facts. France was not going to go the same way as its neighbours.

What's more, they knew that, in place of Stormtroopers and Blackshirts, all they could rely on to lead the assault were the somewhat pathetic Leagues,[4] the rather stale extreme Right; bowler-hatted patriots still enjoying the past glories of the Dreyfus Affair, or the weary figure of Maurras – who, it has to be said, still retained something of his old aura.

Robert Brasillach was one of those disappointed followers of Maurras[1] who went to Nuremberg. There is a picture of him standing in the window of Goering's bedroom, enraptured by the flags and the second-rate theatre of the Nazi Party Congress. He longed for something similar to take place in his own country. Another picture, taken between two parades – which he referred to as two "ceremonies" or "mystical acts of communion" – shows him in the workshop of the sculptor Arno Brecker. He was admiring the naked bodies, the exaltation of youth and strength, in which he found echoes of the Graeco-Roman culture which had so delighted him as a young student. He wandered about the German countryside, dazzled by an image of man which was at once very old and very new, struck by the fact that these people posed no questions about their kinship or their soil. Back in a sort of scout camp in Nuremberg, he discovered "the young fascists, rooted in their race, proud of their vigorous bodies, disdaining the coarse pleasures of the world. There they were, surrounded by their friends, and full of joy whether they were marching, working, or dreaming." Robert Brasillach saw Nazism as "the poetry of the twentieth century".

Another individual of a similar kind was Pierre Drieu La Rochelle,[2] the socialist fascist. He too was haunted by the idea of decadence and angry at having to live in what he thought of as the most reactionary country in Europe. He too made a trip to Germany and was given a conducted tour of the concentration camp at Dachau which had been open for two years. "Visiting the camp was an astonishing experience," he wrote. "I don't think they hid much from me. The predominant atmosphere was one of splendid comfort and simple austerity. Even if," he added, "one sadly deplored the persistent and determined resistance of certain elements." We retraced his footsteps to the old stadium in Nuremberg to try to understand how a refined and really quite subtle writer could take it into his head to describe the Congress of the Nazi Party as "an overwhelmingly beautiful spectacle, worthy of an ancient tragedy", or as an "impeccable ceremony with wonderful songs and choruses". "What are we in the face of all that?" he exclaimed; "it is the most beautiful thing I have seen since the Acropolis; my heart grieves that such things are unknown in France." Strangely (but was it really so strange?), he then went on to Moscow, where he was also quite well received and, thanks to his friends Nizan and Malraux, was given a guided tour of the city. "I really made the right decision in coming here," he said. In the end, however, aesthetics won the day, as he declared his preference for the poetry of Berlin and its "most tasteful" torchlit tattoos.

Not many years later, during the Occupation, there were two or three organised visits of artists. Berlin had come to Paris.[3] Then there were the fervent apologists of total collaboration. After the aesthetes had expressed their admiration, it was the turn of the fanatical believers in a Europe dominated by Germany to come to the fore, though in some cases they were the same people. Before the war, of course, first Berlin and then other cities had witnessed lynchings, the Kristallnacht,[4] the burning of synagogues, the persecution of Jews, which those sensitive souls must have been aware of. The most radical of them had their own papers, their own style, their own obsessions. There were films which they found acceptable and exhibitions to which they gave their backing. Céline, a writer of no mean talent, was not content just to give his tacit approval but contributed to the climate of madness both before and during the war with his own hair-raising texts. But the most unforgivable – and incomprehensible – suggestion was the one made by Brasillach that we should "part company with the Jews and not even keep the children."

II

But one shouldn't think that those roaring, blood-and-thunder fascists were the only ones, the hard-liners who had completely sold out to the Germans and were almost Brownshirts. I sometimes wonder if, by systematically drawing attention to the most guilty such as Céline and Drieu, Brasillach and Rebatet, we're not being too indulgent towards those individuals who seemed better mannered and more acceptable. Their language was more civil, less controversial, which made them perhaps more representative figures. I'm aware that, here again, I'm touching on sensitive areas of the collective memory. But what would be the value of a survey such as this, what is the point of going back to basic sources, unless the object is to try to get to the truth?

The Catholic journal which the young Thierry Maulnier contributed to was certainly not fascist. Nor was *Esprit*, that nonconformist review which denounced communism and capitalism with equal vigour, and which was edited by the Christian philosopher, Emmanuel Mounier, who was to join the Resistance. As early as 1933 it took a stand against Hitler's anti-semitism, and in 1940 it distanced itself from the Germans. Yet one is bound to shudder at the comment made in all these reviews that, from the ashes and devastation of war, France would be regenerated and become a new country. The contributors to *Esprit*, for example, might not have used the expression "national revolution", but they did remind their readers that they had "for years been deepening and disseminating" the slogans of the new regime. In their own words again, they claimed that they couldn't help recognising "the main features of their own movement" and that it would be churlish on their part "to avoid involvement in the vital adventure which had been initiated by the Vichy regime".[5]

The truth is that in this case as in others their whole drift was intended to differentiate what they said from Hitlerism. It was French in style and inspiration, sunny and full of contrasts in tone: rustic and almost bucolic, and yet modern, indeed modernistic. It is usually forgotten that systematic planning began under the Vichy regime and, even more unbelievably, the cult of the technocrat. There was an appeal to the family, too, with the institution of Mother's Day. Pétainism was also keen on promoting patriotism and on being anti-Boche. At the same time, it helped to cultivate sport with its "city of muscles", the French version of the youth camps referred to a moment ago. This enabled Montherlant, the author of works such as *Les Olympiques* and *L'Angélus sur le stade*, to give free rein to his Roman, pagan, and virile proclivities. Finally, like all forms of totalitarianism, Pétainism was fascinated by the idea of youth and attributed to it all sorts of virtues as well as considerable prestige. Then in 1940 there was the creation of the famous leadership school at Uriage, near Grenoble, the aim of which was to produce future intellectuals for the regime. It is important to point out, however, that not everyone considers it to have been a fascist institution. We, in fact, went back to the place and interviewed someone who knew it at the time. Jacques Baumel told us that when the Germans entered the Free Zone and thus destroyed the illusion of a French version of fascism, the young intellectuals at Uriage bravely took to the Maquis. Yet they had, in the intervening period, thought about what one would have to call a French model of the European revolution. This certainly had considerably more support amongst writers of some reputation[6] than the tactlessly harsh German model.

III

Not that we should forget the other France. I still refer to it as the other France, because I like the idea of France being divided into two camps, two value systems, with neither pity nor compromise being possible, as was the case at the time of the Dreyfus Affair. It rejected both versions of fascism, having nothing to do with either the Germans or Vichy. Those concerned maintained the dignity and nobility of France, yet they shouldn't be idealised, because they too had their dark side. They were, however, responsible for handing on to us something of considerable worth, which, for convenience sake, can be referred to as "an anti-fascist culture".

All sorts of people belonged to the anti-fascist coalition in France. There were some like those we've already come across who weren't especially concerned about freedom as such. I'm thinking of Romain Rolland, for example, of Henri Barbusse,[5] the founder of *Clarté*, as well as of young writers like Albert Cohen,[6] who founded a review which published articles by Freud, Einstein, Werfel and Proust and who definitely belonged with those who sought to defend culture and intellectual values. There was Julien Benda,[7] the author of *La Trahison des clercs*, and quieter, more traditional humanists. Then there were people like Gide and Malraux: at the beginning of '34, when the Germans were trying to pin the blame for the Reichstag fire on the communist Dimitrov, they decided to go to Germany to plead his innocence. Their biographers, oddly enough, have nothing to say about this journey. So we tried to retrace their steps as we set out from the station in Berlin which is now completely destroyed, and where they had arrived arm in arm, the young author of *La Condition humaine* and the old immoralist. Let's try to picture this well-known pair, out on the spree in the streets of the city where they were killing time as they waited for the interview they had sought with Hitler. I presume they went to the Reichstag to look at the scene of the crime and also to the Moabit prison to stand under the window of the cell where their hero was being held. Forty years later, be it noted in passing, legendary Prussian discipline was manifestly no longer what it had been. They must have walked to the river Spree, which flows through the city, and found the exact spot where Rosa Luxembourg, another communist in their pantheon, had been bludgeoned to death. Then they went back and prowled around the station. At the same time, it must have gone through Malraux's mind that he might well come across his friend Drieu who, within a few days of his own visit, was also in Berlin but already on the other side. What would they have said to each other? Would they have stuck to their principle of never discussing politics? Those were the days of contempt and of summary executions. But even if our two friends didn't meet Hitler, they returned home with invaluable information about the barbaric regime which was taking shape and they made use of it in fine speeches to anti-fascist congresses.

For this was the era of congresses. The famous Anti-Fascist Vigilance Committee of Intellectuals was active, though its founders were dead. We were lucky enough to meet one of its surviving members.

It's a little difficult to believe that this French Academician and special-ist in pre-Columbian cultures, who was subsequently associated with the extremist movement, the OAS,[8] could have been one of the earliest anti-fascists. His name was Jacques Soustelle.

I wouldn't want to finish without saying a word about the surrealist poets who threw themselves into the struggle and were, in some respects, the founders of the Popular Front. These exceptional writers with their heads in the clouds, who found inspiration in Nietzsche and nurtured a passion for theology; who believed neither in Progress, nor in Goodness, nor in Mankind, and yet were proposing to "save the world from carnage", were the only ones at the time to be thinking through the implications of fascism. They did so in little coteries, I was going to say sects, which ranged from the group "Contre-Attaque", founded by Breton and Bataille,[7] to "Acéphale"[8] – that strange secret society[9] about which very little is known[10] – to the "Collège de Sociologie",[11] where in '38–'39 the young Roger Caillois joined forces with Pierre Klossowski and Walter Benjamin; in which a rather more sceptical Michel Leiris rubbed shoulders with the future founder of the first Resistance network in free France; and where Georges Bataille threw down the gauntlet against the "spirit of Munich".

IV

The war on this front, though, was for the moment no more than a war of words. Insults were exchanged, people fought and sometimes killed each other, but essentially it all took place on paper. Then history intervened again on a grand scale and provided a real-life battlefield for what up until then had been no more than manoeuvres in the mind. The arid and desolate battleground was of course Spain – that lyrical country, which had given the world so many saints and mystics, was indeed a place of suffering. During three long years it was to influence the fate of our heroes and turn some of them into soldier-poets, aviator-novelists.

Let us summarise the situation. A Popular Front government had been in power for almost five months in Spain as well. A section of the army refused to accept its authority and this included the majority of the generals, amongst whom were the professional butchers who had led the repression in the Rif ten years earlier. So that when, in July '36, these generals rebelled, a new war broke out, a horrible war and yet one which was sufficiently "clear-cut" for very different writers immediately to take sides.

This was true in Mauriac's case, for example, a man one would scarcely associate with the Popular Front. It was also true of Bernanos, a fellow-Catholic, but in addition a royalist and a disciple of Drumont.[9] However, he quickly realised that behind the pro-Franco slogan "long live death" lurked the figures of Mussolini and Hitler, and all that was shameful in Europe. There were numerous other writers whose backgrounds were totally different and who, if they didn't actually sign up for the International Brigades, acted as war correspondents for major newspapers. Besides Saint-Exupéry and Benjamin Péret, John Dos Passos and Arthur Koestler, George Orwell, Anna Seghers and Jean-Richard Bloch, there was the Russian novelist and war correspondent of *Izvestiya*, Ilya Ehrenburg. When Ernest Hemingway returned to the United States from Spain, he too became a tireless propagandist for the Republican cause. But the truly symbolic figure amongst this new breed of writers,[12] who lent them style and legendary status, was none other than André Malraux. Barely four days after the putsch occurred, he hurried off to Madrid, his fist raised in salute, already thinking of his future squadron of pilots and machine-gunners. Paul Nothomb,[13] who looked like a hero out of *L'Espoir* or *Les Conquérants*, was allegedly the political commissar of the squadron and is today one of its few surviving members. If you're one of those who suspected Malraux of being a bluffer and a mythomaniac and who thought that a writer couldn't also be a man of action, take careful note of what Nothomb had to say. Even with his broken-down bombers and his Latécoère, from which he'd removed the machine-guns in order to install cameras, Malraux the dreamer had an influence on the course of the war.

Not everything about the war was this admirable, of course, and the brave airmen were sadly not always beyond reproach. The militants who belonged to the POUM[10] and other anarchists in the province of Aragon, who were undisciplined but courageous fighters, discovered this for themselves. When their Stalinist "allies" led them into the prison cellars of the GPU[11] and they realised they were going to be destroyed like dogs, they were astonished – though a little late in the day – that our high-minded intellectuals casually closed their eyes to what was happening. Apart from this crime which cast its shadow across events,[14] the war in Spain remains one of the high points of my story. At any rate, it was the moment when most of our heroes abandoned their cult of pacifism, which had been their religion until that point. What lingers in our memory and what haunted subsequent generations, like a piece of music or a fine poem, are the images of the film which André Malraux hurriedly shot and never completed. He had to pack up the reels very quickly, one day in January 1938, when Franco's troops entered Barcelona. Yet, for years to come, through the magic of art, that film was to remain the embodiment of hope.

V

Then the real war began, which made the events in Spain seem like the dress rehearsal for the much wider conflict which left France utterly humiliated. A whole section of the intelligentsia was, as we've already seen, profoundly disturbed by it. For the moment, I want to concentrate on the other faction, the anti-fascists; they realised that culture could be defended sword in hand and that the Goncourt Prize was no bar to involvement in aerial combat over Teruel before taking up ministerial office. The choices and the conflicts were again tough, affecting the Left and the Right, those who believed in heaven and those who didn't, and they led the bravest amongst them to enter the Resistance.

What could an intellectual do faced with the scandal of the German occupation? He could express his indignation and rebel, as Mauriac did. Georges Bernanos, on the other hand, went into exile in Brazil immediately after Munich; from exile he bombarded the Vichy government with inspired and often deadly denunciations. The surrealists withdrew to the sunny Air-Bel villa in Marseilles where they passed the time playing Consequences or organising Max Ernst exhibitions in the garden. There too Breton formed another of those fantastic groups for which he had a knack. The intellectual might also take off for the West Indies and go on to New York, again like the surrealists,[15] and there meet up with other exiles, notably Claude Lévi-Strauss. In New York, he could maintain a high profile publishing Gaullist texts or a low profile, as did Breton, who engaged in literary tourism, made trips to Canada, gave lectures on surrealism at Yale, or did the occasional broadcast. He might go to London, as Aron did, where again there was a choice between writing and fighting. Or he could return to Paris, as Aron's friend Sartre did, once he was freed from captivity.[16] There, he became embroiled in the issue surrounding *Les Mouches*.[12] Clearly, it wasn't a very judicious decision to put on a play during the Occupation with the approval of the German censor. But one shouldn't be too hard on someone who was scarcely back in Paris before joining Desanti and others to set up the clandestine organisation "Socialism and Liberty".

If he were in Paris, the intellectual might have climbed the winding staircase to Paulhan's office in the Rue Sébastien-Bottin, which was also a Resistance cell. Paulhan, former director of the *Nouvelle Revue Française*, who claimed he would have been a "bastard" to go on writing for it, took enormous risks, as he was just a few steps away from the office occupied by Drieu, the man put in by the Germans to replace him. What's more, Paulhan didn't completely break off his longstanding friendship with Drieu. What a strange pair they made! Pierre Seghers, meanwhile, published the poems of a former surrealist turned communist. One risked censorship and torture maintaining the dignity of poets. Besides Aragon, who was called François la Colère, and Elsa Triolet, who was known as Laurent Daniel, he published Eluard and François Mauriac, alias Forez. One could, as Vercors did, create Les Editions de Minuit, or follow the great tradition of the International Brigades and decide that liberty had to be defended with something other than books. In that case, one took to the Maquis, having laid down one's pen which had become an ineffectual weapon, and resorted to weapons of a different temper. Amongst others, this is what Georges Politzer did, whose strength of character was described by Henri Lefebvre. It was also the path chosen by the historian of the "Annales" school, Marc Bloch, by René Char, alias Captain Alexander, and Jean Cavaillès, who, when asked by his torturers: "Do you realise you're going to die?" answered, with the impeccable logic of a mathematician, "Truth never dies." André Malraux, though a latecomer to the Resistance,[17] displayed his customary bravery and panache. First of all, he was in the Dordogne and then he went to Alsace, where he took the name of one of his own characters, Berger, and commanded the legendary Alsace-Lorraine Brigade which liberated Strasbourg. Thus Malraux played his full part in the final victory. Lastly, the intellectual could grieve for his fellows who sadly didn't live to witness the triumph of those values for which they had been prepared to die.

VI

But what happened to the others, the ones who, with varying degrees of misgiving, had thrown in their lot with the murderers? What was their experience at the end of the war, given the confidence they had shown that they would be on the winning side? Here they were once again, true to form – they had learnt nothing, understood nothing. They reached the end of the road in a ghost town, depicted by Céline as an absurd, lugubrious charade.

I went to Sigmaringen and, as I've done at each stage of this survey, I tried to discover what traces they'd left behind. This time, strangely, nothing had changed. I tried to imagine what those peaceful houses had been like when they were taken over by the fleeing collaborators. There was the Schöen cake shop where they drank ersatz coffee, the Loëwen Inn, where they claimed to remember a strange doctor who always had his cat Bébert with him and who had occupied room 11; and there was the castle, a truly elaborate building that towered above the small town and had belonged to Prince Hohenzollern's family for centuries. It was there that the Vichy government in miniature set itself up. Pétain had a floor to himself. Laval and his ex-ministers were also present, as were former members of the political police. Others passed through, like Rebatet, Abel Bonnard, Châteaubriant, and the actor Le Vigan, who always had a scarf around his neck. These were the hard-core collaborators. Then there was Céline, of course, who seemed to have gone there simply in order to paint a hilarious picture of Hitler's regime under siege. He described how he got lost amongst the network of passages, wall-hangings, stylish sitting rooms, and false exits. That was in August 1944, and the masquerade lasted eight months. For eight whole months those pathetic characters lived on red cabbage and swedes whilst waiting for the arrival of the Wehrmacht's famous secret weapons. They waited in fact until the Allies came and finally shattered their day-dream.

In Paris, the game was up and purges had begun. They were less brutal than has been claimed, more controlled, but even so excesses were committed and old scores settled. The whole climate of violence caused Paulhan to say: "Why are you so excessive? A sincere patriot is calmer and more modest." The trials of Pétain and above all Laval were conducted in a curiously rushed manner in the High Court, leaving the witnesses feeling rather uncomfortable. At the same time, a fundamental debate took place amongst intellectuals who had belonged to the Resistance. On one side were Camus and the partisans of uncompromising justice, on the other François Mauriac, who was referred to as Saint Francis of the Assizes, and who pleaded for a more charitable approach. The thirty-five-year-old writer, Robert Brasillach, who was caught between these two factions, was astonished by what happened. His became a test case as people debated whether a writer was responsible (and if so as a capital offence) for crimes which he had not committed, but which he'd applauded or merely tolerated.[18]

A petition with fifty-nine signatures, including that of Albert Camus who wrestled painfully with his own conscience, landed on General de Gaulle's desk. Brasillach was, however, executed on February 6th, 1945, which recalled that other February 6th when everything had started.

Drieu La Rochelle had known for a long time that it was all over. Embittered and alone, he went back to the flat of his first wife, Colette Jeramec, to hide. You will remember that the surrealists, whom Drieu frequented as a young man, had asked themselves whether suicide was a final solution. The answer seemed to be yes. Having ruined his life in such a carefully contrived way, the only thing left was to try to make a success of his death.

NOTES

1. A philosopher and revolutionary syndicalist who believed that social reform was achieved through violent action.

2. Rauschning was a member of Hitler's intimate circle in the mid-thirties. He became disillusioned and exposed the nihilism of the Nazi movement in two books published in 1938 and 1939. Strasser was the leader of the left-wing faction in the Nazi Party.

3. A late nineteenth-century movement associated with General Georges Boulanger, supported from the Left and the Right, which sought to end the abuses of parliamentary government.

4. Anti-parliamentary groupings active in the twenties and thirties. Some were more overtly fascist than others.

5. A journalist and novelist who achieved fame with his novel *Le Feu* (1916) depicting life in the trenches.

6. He published four novels about Sephardic Jews as well as some volumes of autobiography.

7. An essayist who championed reason. In *La Trahison des clercs* (1927) he attacked intellectuals for betraying their true calling by concerning themselves with social and political issues.

8. The Organisation de l'Armée Secrète was an insurrectional organisation formed in February 1961. Supported by civilians and military personnel, it engaged in acts of terrorism in Algeria and France.

9. A polemical and violently anti-semitic journalist who founded an anti-Dreyfus paper.

10. The Workers' Party of Marxist Unity, a revolutionary group under Trotskyist influence in the Spanish Civil War.

11. The Soviet state security agency which took over from the Cheka and subsequently became the OGPU.

12. A reworking of the story of Orestes and Electra; the play was well-received by the German occupation paper, *Pariser Zeitung*, and by the underground *Lettres françaises*. Interpreted by some as an anti-Vichy play, it was also popular with German officers.

3

Lost Illusions

(1945 TO THE 1960s)

I

So, the goodies won and the baddies bit the dust. As a consequence, the intelligentsia of the extreme Right disappeared from the scene for a number of years. And everything would have been for the best in the best of all possible worlds if, in the euphoria of victory or the excitement associated with the anti-fascist struggles of the thirties, our intellectuals hadn't chosen completely to ignore a certain "detail" of the day. What they seemed not to notice was the fact that Stalin's concentration camps continued to exist alongside their Nazi counterparts, that they resembled them in certain respects and were outliving them.

"Chosen completely to ignore" is perhaps overstating things, since from the thirties on certain men and women had swum against the tide and warned against being taken in. This they did whilst the cult of personality was in full swing in Moscow and the requirements of the anti-fascist struggle in Paris drew most intellectuals into Stalin's fold. At the time, the Soviet regime took care to show only smiling, radiant images of Stalin. They had that almost lyrical and mystical quality of Eisenstein's films celebrating the October Revolution.

One such man was Boris Souvarine. He had been one of the proto-communists, you will remember. In a sense, he became the first anti-communist, the first at any rate to use his knowledge of the system to analyse its perverse intricacies in his books and in his magazine. This he did whilst living with Colette Peignot,[1] the legendary beauty who had been Bataille's companion and Jean Bernier's[1] before becoming his.

Then there were the Trotskyists. Not that Trotsky, the man who had organised the Red Army and massacred the sailors at Kronstadt, had any title to offer lessons in democracy. But his panache, his legend, the aura he acquired in exile all helped to make him a sort of rallying point for those marginal figures like Breton who wanted to remain faithful to their dream, without prostrating themselves before those in power in Moscow and above all without accepting the scandal of the rigged trials.

The famous Congress for the Defence of Culture was held in 1935. Guéhenno was later to describe it in the following terms: "A congress organised in Paris by the Communist Party and the Soviet Embassy, on orders received from Moscow." It took place in an atmosphere of great excitement at the Mutualité which was jam-packed for the occasion. The meeting was dominated by fellow-travellers, and the fiercest battle was for the microphone. Madeleine Paz spoke of Victor Serge,[2] Breton read a poem by Eluard,[3] Benda praised bourgeois literature, and Pasternak dumbfounded his audience by saying: 'Beware! whatever you do, don't organise!' Huxley and Musil were also there."

On the fringes of that Congress in '35, there was the tragedy of Crevel's[4] death. The author of *La Mort difficile*, who had close links with Breton, had in fact been one of the organisers of that event and had battled for his right to address the meeting in person. Was it despair at having failed, the sense that art and Revolution just didn't mix, or were there more private reasons for his feeling of helplessness? Whatever it was, he came out of a final meeting, where he had pleaded yet again in favour of a version of communism which would still allow the voice of the poet to be heard, and turned on the gas tap.

Later still, in August 1939, there was the incredible meeting between Molotov and Ribbentrop which led to the Nazi-Soviet pact, and which flabbergasted many an intellectual who watched his party suddenly go down the road to Munich. Nizan went off to war feeling completely isolated. The courageously clear-sighted line he took, albeit a little late in the day, caused him to be thrown out of the Party. When he died from a stray bullet on the first floor of a castle near Dunkirk, was he aware that he had already been referred to as a "frightened and abject police informer" in an article by Thorez entitled "Traitors in the pillory"? This was inevitable if you claimed you were trying to avoid telling further lies about the USSR. Then there was Gide's account of the famous trip he made to the Soviet Union in 1936, which he wrote on his return and which caused such a stir. We went back over the same ground that he had covered, place by place and detail by detail.

We went to Leningrad, where the great writer arrived by plane and met up with his friends Eugène Dabit and Louis Guillou, who had travelled by sea. He clearly enjoyed Leningrad: it seemed to him like a town dreamed up by Baudelaire and Pushkin. He loved what he called the marriage of stone, metal and water. He visited the Hermitage, of course, describing it as a "phenomenal museum". But the first sour note was struck and he felt shocked when he came across a museum of atheism within the walls of the Cathedral of Saint Isaac.

The second leg of our trip took us to Moscow where intellectuals associated with Perestroïka were keen to show us the room in the Metropole Hotel where he stayed. Though he didn't refer to it in his book, it may have been here that he met Bukharin[2] who was already on the defensive. From here it was only a few hundred metres to Red Square; this was where Gide, paralysed by fear and by the presence at his side of the "father of the people", made his speech of homage to Gorky, who had just died.

When he was at a loose end, he would walk in the "Park of Culture". It was a place, he said, where one could "have fun" and he claimed to have only "pleasant memories" of it. There was an atmosphere of "joyful enthusiasm" about it. The children were "handsome and well-fed". The grown-ups too were "handsome and strong". People had a bright look in their eye and laughed without malice. On the banks of the Moskva, beside the walks which have clearly changed a great deal, the glorious youth of the country frolicked in the swimming pools. The amusement park is still there, which he compared to a huge "Luna Park". He went on to comment that there was never any sign of "stupid and vulgar pranks" being played, of flirtation, womanising, or indecent behaviour. Dear old Gide was amazed by these new, "perfectly dressed" Russians who were "the epitome of honesty, dignity and decency"; not to mention the sporting youngsters whose "sturdiness" and "grace" he never stopped admiring.

Things deteriorated at Sochi, in Georgia. The beauty of the beaches certainly impressed him but he went on to say that it pained him to see the workers so appallingly treated. Happily, things got better, because it was in Sochi as well, surrounded by flowers, that he visited the Stalinist writer Ostrovski, author of *How the Steel was Tempered*. Ostrovski was blind and paralysed following an accident and never left the room in which he dictated his memoirs night and day. Gide spent an hour at the bedside of this emaciated young hero, whose "thin fingers ceaselessly transmitted a vibrant message of support to his fellow citizens". On leaving him, he was delighted to discover that someone had thoughtfully produced posters of him in his honour.

From there we went to Gori, Stalin's birthplace, and visited the little post office, which hadn't changed at all in fifty years. It was from there that Gide decided to send birthday greetings to Stalin, which gave rise to another incident. He dictated the following message to the official: "As I was passing through Gori, I felt I ought to send you . . ." The official said to him: "What? One doesn't simply address Stalin as 'you'! one says, 'you, the people's master' or 'you, leader of all the workers'!" Gide pleaded and argued in vain. His telegram was not accepted until he agreed to accept one of the phrases.

He had time enough in Moscow to wander round and see, not the garden of Eden he had imagined in Paris, but the shortages in the shops, and the resigned faces of the people who were leaden-eyed with worries. "I would like to take back memories to my friends," he noted, "everything is frightful." On the collective farm he visited he found the dullest uniformity rather than any signs of enthusiasm or of the new man. Finally, he went to Bolchevo, which had been described to him as a model town where former criminals lived who had been rehabilitated by communism. He was extremely disappointed to discover that the only people there were informers of the GPU. Despite its naivety, its superficiality and its comical side, his *Retour de l'URSS* remains one of the first works to have exposed certain illusions about communism.

II

That was the truly anti-totalitarian culture that intellectuals in the Resistance had or might have inherited in the immediate aftermath of the Liberation. Instead, most of them chose to wipe the slate clean. As a consequence, in the immediate post-war years when one would have liked to hear only of valour, heroism and liberty, one was left with a vague sense of disquiet.

To understand what, with hindsight, may seem like a strange regression,[3] you have to try and recapture the climate of the period. It was the time of Stalingrad, then of heroic, hard-fought battles for the liberation of Berlin and the capitulation of the Third Reich. It was a time when the Red Army – now invariably referred to as "the glorious Red Army" – was striving inch by inch and house by house to get rid of the remnants of Hitler's retreating army. The truth is, when Europeans, weakened and shattered by war, saw Russian soldiers climb on to the roof of the Reichstag and plant the red flag, it suddenly appeared to them as a symbol of freedom. They simply didn't think about the show-trials and the Gulag or the subtleties of the surrealist and Trotskyist alternatives; and the Nazi-Soviet pact was dead. When Thorez returned to Paris, the man who had insulted Blum and slandered Nizan was welcomed as a hero, just as Aragon was, whose reputation was further enhanced by his participation in the Resistance.

It was a period when communists applauded the simple and edifying displays put on at the festival organised by *L'Humanité*, which resembled the mystery plays performed in church squares during the Middle Ages. At the same time Aragon[4] reigned supreme in the committees of writers which had emerged from the Resistance. The war had matured and even aged him a little and he was accepted without challenge by his peers. Paulhan, also a prominent member of the Resistance, was concerned that the Party appeared to have achieved a dominant position in the common struggle and in shaping the new order. He felt that everyone who had contributed to the victory should have played a part. But in various parades as in the newspapers which he controlled, Aragon presided over a veritable court. His word was law and his decision final. He could make or break the reputation of anyone, whether they were in the Party or not. This too was the period when Eluard made a film celebrating Stalin's birth, a film at once witless and hilarious, a classic of its kind. This was the same Eluard who was still close enough to Breton at the Congress in 1935 to read out his speech for him, since the Soviets wouldn't allow Breton to read it himself. It was a period too when great peace gatherings were taking place in the aftermath of Hiroshima. People had finally come to realise that they were mortal and that the world was perhaps in the process of dying. Yet again, it was the communists who set themselves up as the vanguard of this consciousness-raising movement. Joliot-Curie[5] said no to the bomb and to the threat of the third world war. "Long live peace!" he cried, as did Picasso, Amado, and of course Aragon. Who could resist these slogans, which the communists made their own, as they moved to the fore on every front? Who could resist the Doves, even though their creator, Picasso, kept reminding everyone, jokingly, that the dove was a bird of war?

When a Soviet scientist, a member of the establishment, announced to his people and, through them, to the world at large that science should be in the Party's control, that furthermore there was bourgeois and proletarian science and that bourgeois scientists should change sides, keep their mouths shut, and in some instances die, there were philosophers who approved of every word he said. When a gallery put on an exhibition of extreme socialist-realist paintings by Fougeron, glorifying miners of the Nord and Pas-de-Calais, a number of critics, led by Aragon, praised them to the skies. And when Stalin died in 1953, a scandal broke which revealed a great deal about the aesthetic obscurantism of the Party.[5] Of course, not all intellectuals were communists in the aftermath of the war. But the prestige of the Party was such, its reign of terror so strong that even the existentialist community, for instance, had to fall into line. Take the case of Sartre. He might visit the ageing Gide and pay him homage, but the one thought on his mind during that period was that Billancourt[6] shouldn't be driven to despair.[6] In his view, Marxism was the inescapable system of thought of the century and was starting afresh.

III

How long did this period last? How long did Sartre close his eyes to the horrors of totalitarianism? It is of course difficult to give a precise answer. As with the fight against fascism, it was a slow, complex task, with failures, betrayals, much to-ing and fro-ing, and a number of volte-faces. Quite early on there was, however, a handful of men who, almost alone in the face of widespread indifference and hatred, began to break the silence. They were greeted with a chorus of slander and insults which was perhaps even more terrible than that which Souvarine and Nizan had experienced.

The most prominent of these was Malraux who appeared to turn his back on the ideals of his youth[7] when, to everyone's surprise, he became a Gaullist and the star speaker alongside the General at the great rallies of the Rassemblement du peuple français. But a closer look at what he said, in the article of February 1949 for example, will show that his denunciations of totalitarianism were couched in almost the same language as his earlier anti-fascist speeches. Then there was Aron, who was a friend of Malraux as well as of Sartre, with whom he had recently founded *Les Temps modernes*, the major review of the intellectual Left. In this instance, he sided with Malraux against Sartre and opted for uncompromising resistance to Soviet imperialism. With Claude Mauriac and others, he sponsored *Liberté de l'esprit*, which was a Gaullist review.

If one is to believe the communists, Kravchenko was a "fascist" because he had had the effrontery to flee the Stalinist paradise and to reveal its murderous face to the West. He brought a libel action against Aragon's paper, but people were so deaf to what he had to say that one might have thought *he* was on trial. Despite the "good faith" of the lawyer, Maître Nordmann, and the near riot outside the Law Courts, Kravchenko produced a whole succession of witnesses who had survived the Gulag and, for the first time, told the world the unbearable truth.

Almost immediately after this, the Rousset affair hit the headlines. Rousset was a former inmate of the Nazi camps and, with other former prisoners, he had the idea of setting up a commission of inquiry to go to the USSR and verify Kravchenko's claims. It prompted the same reaction, the same psycho-drama involving the same actors, but once again the party of truth emerged victorious. David Rousset had joined Sartre the previous year in founding a short-lived party, wanting it to be a third force between an American world order and the Soviet nightmare; he certainly deserves to be counted amongst the pre-cursors.

Finally, we come to that curious intellectual, Camus. He spent half his life in the streets of Belcourt, the poor quarter of Algiers. It was here that he got his first schooling and here too that his mother worked as a charwoman in order to bring him up. There is something disturbing about the house where he lived, with its decor unchanged and its walls slightly flaking. Children played on the staircase and the same air of poverty prevailed which had been his initial source of inspiration. Camus was an outsider; from the beginning he adopted a line that ran counter to the accepted thought of the day. His refusal to accept definitive solutions, his sense of the fortuitousness and the fragility of things, and that measured humanism which may well have been conceived at Tipasa, amidst Roman ruins overlooking the sea, these were the themes of his great book *L'Homme révolté*. When it appeared in 1952 and became part of the already rather rigid landscape of existentialism, its author immediately became a key figure on the philosophical and political scene.

Already in 1952, Camus's views were at variance with Sartre's. In the polemic which was taking shape, in the battle which the book provoked by challenging not only historical messianism in general but Marxism in particular, the supporters of Sartre, after remaining silent, finally committed themselves. Not Sartre himself, of course! That would have honoured the traitor too much! Instead, a young disciple was charged with the job of performing the execution, which, forty years later, he accepted without regret. Did Camus win or lose in his polemic with Sartre's supporters? That was of little consequence, since, within a short time, history was to come down on his side. The following year, in East Berlin, the people rose up against their revolutionary leaders who had become despots, and the despots retali-ated by sending in tanks, supposedly defending the cause of socialism.

37

Then, in 1956, from the very citadel of communism in Moscow came the famous report on Stalin's crimes. Also in that year, there was the uprising in Budapest, where the same idols were shattered and the same red flag was burnt in celebrations of joy. This was followed by the same sort of repression, undertaken in the name of liberty. As a consequence, misgivings began to grow amongst hard-line French intellectuals and those who had attacked Camus. As for the rest, the more sceptical communists and fellow-travellers and those who accepted the Soviet line without altogether believing in it simply because they were prepared to accord it a basic infallibility, something was irreversibly destroyed in the regime to which they had subscribed. Camus died too soon to see his ideas triumph. But other intellectuals appeared on the scene who, like Michel Foucault (the author of *Histoire de la folie* which some realised opened a new era in history and thought), never forgot the lessons of '56.

IV

During the same period, whilst Aragon began to have doubts, Sartre kept talking, and Marxism started to disintegrate as a result of the uprisings in Eastern Europe, the Algerian people had been in a state of rebellion for two years. I'd like to place particular emphasis on the Algerian affair, first because it was one of the darker chapters in our national life and has been too systematically ignored. Secondly, because it played a greater part than has sometimes been recognised in the process of divorcing our intellectuals from communism.

The setting for the war was the Massif of Aurès – but also Kabylie, the Plain of Mitidja and North Constantine. The army reacted with Jacobin firmness, and perhaps even with the same savagery witnessed in the massacres of the Rif War, to the insurrection which was started by an unknown organisation, the Front de Libération Nationale, on All Saints Night, November 1st, 1954.[8]

For eight years, different governments of the Republic waged the most bitter war in those French Departments, because in law that is what they were. It was a shameful war, not referred to as such, because right to the end words such as "events", "situation", "pacification", "operations" and "maintenance of order" were preferred. Nonetheless, it was a war, with all that this entailed: extortion, napalm, terror-tactics.

The war was also waged in a pretty Moorish villa in the residential quarter of Algiers where the formidable Intelligence Service (DST) had its headquarters. In the same building was one of the well-known screening centres to which Algerians suspected of having contacts with the FLN were sent. In one of those ironies of history, we met an Algerian who had passed through the centre and remained in the building when it became the offices of the ministry for which he worked. We asked him if he would recall his memories for the film, even though, thirty-five years later, they were still intensely painful. We asked to visit the cellars where the sinister bath tubs had been. We also went into the cells where those who were to be tortured or executed were crammed in total darkness. One could still see the bullet marks on the walls.

We mustn't forget either the left-wing governments – because until de Gaulle returned to power they were mainly left-wing – which quickly adopted a resolute militaristic tone sufficient to reassure and even condone the torturers and the bullies. Initially, they had been criticised by lower-class Whites for their lack of firmness. When it came to the question of voting for or against the special powers sought by Guy Mollet, even the Communist Party abstained. In effect this was to vote for them, which cut the Party off from those in its own ranks who wished to remain loyal to their anti-colonialist principles. One such was Fernand Yveton, a communist worker who lived in the Clos Salambier quarter of Algiers, and whose house we discovered. No one remembered his tragic but edifying story. He was picked up carrying a bomb and charged with aiding those who were still referred to as "terrorists" or "rebels". He was condemned, jailed and beheaded in the yard of the Barberousse prison, whilst the party of the workers, his party, far from coming to his defence, repudiated him and thereby denied support to the cause of Algerian independence.

So where did the intellectuals stand? Malraux was caught up in his ministerial duties and less inspired than usual. Aron, on the other hand, declared himself in favour of independence[9] very early on. He said and wrote that the time for empires had passed; that a colony was a burden, and that France should therefore rid itself of Algeria since it served no purpose. It was a lucid and courageous position, but one dictated less by moral solidarity with a people that had been attacked, crushed, indeed tortured, than by a cold and rational calculation.

In the quiet of his house in Malagar, Mauriac was getting ready to speak out, as he had done so vehemently in the Spanish Civil War. He compared the torturers with those who had crucified Christ and the victims of torture with Christ himself. He even made use of his

Nobel prize in this new crusade.[10] Alongside him was the great Camus, whose views everyone was keen to know. One thing that should be pointed out, is that, long before Aron or Mauriac had made their views known, back in 1938, Camus had published in the newspaper *Alger républicain* excellent reports on the poverty in Kabylie. Both at the time and more generally they represented the most damning indictment of French colonialism. What he said as he arrived in the Kabylie village of Tizi-Ouzou, and climbed the hill above it is worth listening to: "The poverty of this village is like a denial of the world's beauty." Coming from him, this was a powerful cry of revolt. However, twenty years had elapsed since that time and revolt was no longer on his lips but taking place in the streets. He was in Algiers again in January '56, the day before a gathering was to be held in connection with the civil truce which he had initiated. Those who saw him remembered how fragile, how perplexed and ambivalent he appeared to be. The following year, when he was awarded the Nobel Prize, he made the now famous remark which everyone took as a sign that he was abandoning any forthright, unconditional moral stand. In choosing between justice and his mother, he chose his mother.[11]

Others at this time were choosing justice, such as certain young philosophers on the fringes of the Communist Party. They realised that, to some degree, their honour was at stake in the Algerian conflict. They were French intellectuals who sided with the Algerian liberation movement and appeared therefore to be in conflict with their own army. Alongside Jeanson, were writers, teachers and actors who took the risk of hiding those engaged in the struggle, collecting and transporting funds, and setting up a whole propaganda and support network. As at the time of the Dreyfus Affair, there were pamphlets, demonstrations, and the sense that truth was on the march. As at the time of the anti-fascist movement,[12] individuals knowingly ran the risk of being imprisoned or outlawed by a nation which seemed to waver once again between universal values (liberty for all including the Algerians) and those of nationalism (hang justice so long as the high command prevails). They used the tried and tested methods of fellow-travellers, who remobilised in a flash on behalf of this cause; these included meetings and demonstrations. Sartre was involved as usual, but this time he was on the right side. Finally, as the surrealists had done at an earlier stage, 121 rebellious intellectuals[13] signed a call to disobedience. Let us remind ourselves that their action was at odds with the Party which might have been expected to give them its support (and for the purposes of this survey that fact is of crucial importance).

V

Clavel and Foucault were right. The great schism not only with the Party but with the Soviet model of socialism undoubtedly dated from that time. What they didn't mention, however, which might have tempered their optimism, was the price which had to be paid for that emancipation. This is something we have seen elsewhere in our story. The fact was, a new kind of ideology was taking shape at the time, in relation to the Algerian War. Intellectuals were completely taken up with it and were to be led astray in wholly new directions. It can be described either in terms of a hatred of Europe or a turning towards the Third World.

The truth is, however, that a hatred of Europe was a well-established phenomenon. At the time of the Colonial Exhibition in 1925, the surrealists had expressed their disgust at France for treating those peoples like insects or some rare flora, whereas in the eyes of Breton and Aragon they represented the future of humanity. A similar attitude was adopted by another great writer, Jean Genet, who had loathed white Europe throughout his life; this was evident in his questionable response to the virility of the SS and in his more recent support for the Black Panthers. He could have echoed Aragon's words: "I am a European defeatist. Let this earth be set ablaze." At any rate, he shared the total disdain for Western values, which he considered criminal and false.

It was during this same period that Zionism was in the ascendant and that the State of Israel was created in the promised land,[14] the outcome of a successful war of liberation. Far from being denied, democracy and European values were thereby given a new lease of life.

But though intellectuals looked favourably upon the birth of Israel and though, in their eyes, the young Jewish nation had a certain prestige, born as it was of infinite suffering, and though Sartre was (and remained) almost indestructibly loyal to it, the fact remains that the dominant spirit of the times was more associated with Bandung. It was in this Indonesian town that the first great conference of Afro-Asian States was held in 1955. Proletarian nations began to achieve their freedom and in so doing sounded the death knell of their infamous European masters.

If one had to name a single individual who symbolised the feelings of remorse and expectation and the desire for a new sense of direction via the Third World, it would be Fanon. His books were a source of inspiration for a whole generation. He was a strange person whose influence was equally strange. Yet I've always felt that part of his secret was to be found in the hospital at Blida, near Algiers, where he was a psychiatrist and where we met some of the nurses he had trained. Before concerning himself with the victims of oppression, the damned of the earth, he dealt with the victims of madness and tried to liberate them. Fanon was a psychiatrist and a revolutionary. Someone who knew him and arranged his historic meeting with Sartre spoke of his desire for "regeneration", for the "creation of a new world", his desire for people to have "the sky above their heads". Everyone could agree with such a benign programme, and most of the idealists of the age did. Yet it was in his name and in the name of that same will to purity that our intellectuals once again went astray and alienated their freedom in one final adventure.

NOTES

1. One of the editors of the independent Marxist review *Clarté*.

2. He was in turn a revolutionary anarchist, a supporter of the Russian Revolution, and a Trotskyist. He was also one of the first to condemn the USSR as a totalitarian state.

3. An influential poet and founder-member of the surrealist movement who explored dreams and the unconscious in several early volumes. Subsequently, he joined the Communist Party and became a more committed writer.

4. A fervent surrealist who acted as a mediator between the group and the communists at the first International Writers' Congress for the Defence of Culture in 1935.

5. A distinguished nuclear physicist who joined the Communist Party in 1942. He campaigned against nuclear war and wanted science to be used for peaceful and social purposes.

6. A Paris suburb where the main Renault factory is situated.

4

The Demise of the Prophets

(THE 1960S TO THE 1990S)

I

As you've already guessed, our intellectuals had still not been cured. Certainly, they no longer cared for the Soviet Union or believed in Stalin. But their faith in genuine, authentic revolution, which would put an end to the ills of the West, remained intact. They were constantly on the look-out for a new field of experience, something they could believe in to replace their fallen idols. This was at the beginning of the sixties, when Third-World issues were to the fore, and Cuba became the incarnation of their new communist dream.

There was something unique about Cuban communism. For a start, it was cheerful. There was an air of exhilaration and excitement about it, something carnivalesque and slightly mad. "We have no soap," shouted the jubilant crowds, "but we have courage." Their bravado and defiance, their uprising with its accompaniment of rumbas and salsa, had an air of freedom which reminded our oldest intellectuals of the October Revolution. It was a form of communism which intended to combine democracy and heroism: a workers' movement, which also claimed it would bring knowledge and culture to the peasants who had been denied them by dictatorship; and this was something new. It was a youthful communism. There was still that same incurable fascination with youth.[1] Fidel Castro was only thirty-three! He was so different from the elderly hierarchy in power in the Kremlin. "I am not a professional military man," he explained; "when I have completed my task I shall withdraw. I have other ambitions." At the time, no one doubted his sincerity. When Sartre arrived in Havana in February 1960, he was elated, overwhelmed even, and he returned to France with a series of articles which matched the eulogies of Barbusse and Rolland in their praise for the vigour, vital strength and youthfulness of what he had seen. Other, younger intellectuals, who felt stifled by Gaullist France and the most reactionary Communist Party in Europe, not surprisingly made the trip as well; they hoped to find, in the shadow or wake of this tropical version of communism, the principles of a revolutionary movement which would break out of the impasse in which it had been trapped by Stalinism.

Here, mention should be made of Régis Debray, a friend of Fidel but also of Che Guevara, another young bourgeois, who had become a symbol of armed struggle in Latin America. The young scholar Debray, his head no doubt filled with images of Nizan in Aden, Malraux in Spain, perhaps even of Lawrence in Arabia and Byron in Missolonghi, intended to take part in the revolution while still elaborating its theory. Under the *nom de guerre* of Danton (what a claim!),[2] he was to become one of the select band of adventurer-writers. Che died of course, but became a legend as a romantic revolutionary with his khaki tunic, his beret, his long hair, his image as a secular saint caring for lepers in Cordoba and teaching literature to poor peasants in Peru. Debray was arrested and imprisoned. He was interrogated, tortured then tried at Camiri, and through his trial the whole adventure was condemned in Bolivia. In Paris, however, it was glorified on the platform of the Mutualité. "I was with Che . . ." boasted Danton, who realised that his adventure ended there. "I would like to have been with him when he died and to have died alongside him." The tribunal contented itself with a thirty-year prison sentence, of which he served the first three. He was still in jail that morning in August 1968, when left-wing intellectuals were amazed to learn that their fabulous Fidel applauded the arrival of Russian tanks in Prague, thereby destroying the hope they had placed in him. It was the death of a legend, the collapse of a myth. It was not in Cuba that history was to be refashioned.

II

Vietnam became the next focus of attention. To be more precise, it was the spectacle of a small people taking on, almost with their bare hands, or so it was thought, the mightiest army in the world. The violence of the war, the nature of the resistance, the image of these simple people fighting the symbol of Western power, like David against Goliath, made an impact on people's minds. On top of that, China had its Cultural Revolution. Together, these events were to change the character of the intellectual. He was no longer the just man of the Dreyfus Affair, the adventurer of the thirties, or the Stalinist of the fifties. The Maoist intellectual had been born.

I remember the images we saw in the films of Joris Ivens. I remember the bombs, the sheets of napalm. I remember the B52s engaging in saturation bombing of the country north of the 17th parallel. I remember the pilots, stock characters no doubt, but in my eyes they were the incarnation of evil. I remember a film made by Jean-Luc Godard, which, whatever one said, expressed our revulsion and our anger. I remember the demonstrations in the streets, where we felt we were following in the footsteps of those who had fought against fascism and identifying ourselves with the Vietnamese communists, who were essentially victims and martyrs. Never mind if future generations laugh at us and our naivety. I remember the emotion I felt when these splendid, barefoot people filled in the craters and dug new trenches after every air-raid, and unflaggingly rebuilt the basis of their resistance with limited means, with courage and tenacity. I remember Sartre, in the forefront as always, presiding over the Russell tribunal which judged American war crimes. Above all, I remember other intellectuals, our true mentors, who, each in his own way, undermined the basis of Western humanism which in our eyes was becoming a gigantic sham. What a joke these concepts were – man, the soul, the individual, hope; what a sinister and grotesque farce, if everything was to end in a hail of shells. Certainly, that wasn't the only aspect of the structural revolution[3] which occurred. But if it has its place as part of this long story, it is because, in its own way, it had something in common with surrealism. You will recall that, in the wake of what happened in World War I, surrealism had challenged all aspects of the culture and the value systems of the day.

I remember there was a curious mixture of theory and anarchy, of dogmatism derived from Althusser, and naked revolt in the lycées.[4] I remember terrifying young men[5] in "khâgne"[1] at the Lycée Louis-le-Grand who, as if they had suddenly been inspired by some mysterious force, abandoned their Greek and Latin exercises overnight. They completely forgot their lessons and their career plans, to turn into experts on guerrilla warfare and to immerse themselves in the strategy of Giap and Chairman Mao.

I remember too that China, with its Red Guards and Cultural Revolution, was, in everyone's view, at the eye of the storm. China was the new Mecca, which invited us to make a clean break with the past and to transform man so as to reveal his true depths. How absurd! you will say. The intellectuals were falling into the same trap as their elders had done who had first visited the Soviet Union. The China they so admired was, in fact, a terrible, savage country where every leap forward was paid for in millions of deaths. That may well have been true, but in recalling the climate of the times, I want people to grasp what we then understood by China. All right, it was a violent country; it was terroristic and totalitarian; people were re-educated and the intellectuals were sent into the fields. But that's the way of history, and, however shocking it may seem, China came to replace the last remnants of our attachment to Stalinism. Whether that China was real or imagined, an actual place or a myth created by propaganda, is in the end of little importance – at this point in our story. The essential point I wish to make is that a new way of thinking was beginning to take shape. Furthermore, the revolution itself had nothing whatsoever to do with the one which Nizan, Breton, Barbusse, Aragon, and even Sartre in his classic fellow-traveller period talked to us about.

The events of May '68 are meaningless, if one fails to realise that the target of those who took to the streets, other than the police and the Gaullists, were the revisionists or, in plainer language, the communists. In addition, if the intellectual currents which contributed to May '68 and the emergence of the "Situationists"[2] are to be understood, it must be recognised that Marxism was a borrowed language, a straitjacket within which a new type of discourse was being created. Finally, the incredible mental conversion which took place during this whole period is only comprehensible if one bears in mind that when our young intellectuals in Paris were talking about China, they were less hostile to those old war-horses François Mauriac and André Malraux than they were to the official Left. They denied all connection with it.

Sartre is a case in point. I've already ridiculed his desire to latch on to young people's movements, but I have to recognise that he realised better than anyone that a page had been turned in the history of ideas. He knew that the Maoists were beginning to write the new agenda in books and in the streets and that they would soon do so in the factories as well. Modestly, therefore, and a bit the boy-scout, he took to selling the paper of one of these groups just as they were in the process of jettisoning some of the false problems that he felt he'd wasted his life on. Though what they achieved may not have marked a new departure in the history of the world, it did represent a clean break as far as the Left was concerned.

III

This is not, of course, to deny that Maoism had its dark side, its excesses and its tendency to go off the rails. Indeed the remarkable thing is the way the same ideas, the same dreams, the same utopian vision of a break with the past leading to a desire for saintliness,[6] and the same terrible aberrations – all of this brought these men and women very close to what has to be described as terrorism. It's not the first time we have seen such unfortunate reversals turning the best intentions and the most splendid appeals for the liberation of mankind into something entirely different. But inasmuch as they pushed the desire for purity further than anyone else and dreamed of achieving the most radical revolution, the Maoists were an exemplary case.

It all began with the murder of a young Maoist worker, Pierre Overney, by a nightwatchman at the gates of the Renault factory. This was in 1972, at the height of the movement. The affair caused a great stir. Subsequently, in the Maoist group which formed part of the procession behind the body of the murdered militant, there was a handful of zealots who decided to avenge the victim's death by seizing a foreman. Doubtless, he had nothing at all to do with the murder, but by seizing him they were demonstrating that the new form of resistance was going over to the attack. It was a faultless tactic, an imitation of terrorism. It was also a symbolic act which, on closer inspection, had little or nothing to do with democratic humanism. Seeing pictures of those serried ranks of helmeted, left-wing militants, one recalls that their leaders, like Geismar and Serge July, had not waited for the death of Overney before prophesying "civil war" and hoping for it. Godard's film, *La Chinoise*, had foreshadowed violence, and now it seemed to be coming to pass. It was a time, too, when a strange debate began, as Foucault questioned whether traditional justice, with its rituals, its verbal sparring, the separation of the litigants, the lawyers in robes, in short, the whole apparatus in which the democrat sees the guarantee of its fairness, was not in fact an institution that had been invented to stifle the sacred violence of the people. Simultaneously, Sartre called on the miners in the Département du Nord to take their revenge on their criminal bosses, believing that the people saw things with a clearer eye than the judges. It was also a time when Ulrike Meinhoff and Andreas Baader were active; when real terrorism brought bloodshed to Germany. It is not altogether clear by what miracle France was spared,[7] though some people claim it was because major intellectuals wisely restrained the Maoists. I know one at least, Jean Genet, who supported violence in a famous article which would have come as no surprise to those who remembered his violent outbursts against white man's laws, democracy, and Europe. The terrorists' lawyer, Klaus Croissant, on the other hand, did not mind admitting that he had been inspired in part by Genet. And when Croissant was charged as an accomplice of his bizarre clients, I recall

47

that Michel Foucault didn't hesitate for a second to lend him his support. And let's not forget Sartre again: he found Baader "interesting, revolutionary, uncorrupted". Baader's only mistake was, he said, that "he was right a little too soon." Sartre kept his distance and doubtless expressed his reservations, but two years earlier he had not expressed them, the day after a commando group massacred Israeli athletes in the Olympic Village in Munich. On that occasion, he wrote an unforgivable article which came down unequivocally on the side of the terrorists.

IV

Worse still were the terrible events in Cambodia and Iran. There again, some accepted what was going on with an enthusiasm matched only by their insane will to believe in it. In lending their support to such barbarity, their judgment was clouded once again by their hope in a revolution reduced to its purest state.[8] On this occasion, however, things went so far and the disaster was on such a scale that, by a new quirk of history – a happy and positive quirk this time – their whole system collapsed and for the first time the revolutionary ideal fizzled out.

So far as the Iranian affair was concerned, the central figure was, yet again, Michel Foucault. He visited Teheran several times and watched these men with increasingly passionate interest who, he said, relied on and embodied "the most modern expression of revolt". He returned with a series of articles which Jean Daniel[3] and others believed were an integral part of his philosophical opus. In fact he produced several series of articles, which can be interpreted as an expression of his admiration for Khomeini, referring as he did to the "mythical dimension of the prophet of Qum". Elsewhere, he spoke of that "mysterious current which passed between the exiled old man and his people who called upon him". In certain of these texts – some of which were published in Italy but strangely not in France – it is clear he was trying to reflect on "something which, since the Renaissance and the great upheavals which beset Christianity, we have tended to deem impossible: a politicised form of spirituality." My own view is that Foucault's error – for error it was – represented a more or less obligatory stage on this journey of the mind. Indeed, the will to purity and the revolutionary ideal pushed to its limits were bound to be part of that insane, extremist revolt. Above all, I believe in the end that, confronted by the evidence of those upheavals and convulsions, soon to be followed by terror, the will to purity was bound to turn on itself and come to doubt both the notion of purity and the revolutionary ideal. Put another way, Foucault followed the path of error to the point at which he was able to pose the question: "What if the revolutionary dream was an intrinsically barbaric one?";[9] and this was of the utmost importance.

A similar pattern of thought developed in relation to Cambodia. A whole generation looked at what the Khmer Rouge had done in forcing the people out of Phnom Penh[10] and made it a key element of their own philosophical programme before taking fright at the mass murder which ensued. One of our slogans was that towns and townspeople should be brought into contact with the countryside. There was a hatred of thought and a criticism of books and culture. Moreover, both Freud and Lacan believed that books were a repository of painful experience, and this belief was shared by their disciples. One of our dreams was that teachers would be sent to work in the fields and that there would no longer be a division between intellectuals and manual workers. According to Christian Jambet this "was the ultimate basis of oppression." In addition, the banal notion that sex was a mechanism of power and the theory that human beings were the slaves of their basic desires found an echo in those state-arranged marriages in Cambodia. Yet again, the state took its mania for purity to extremes.

V

After that, everything collapsed, and our whole mental landscape was gradually rebuilt. Now that the revolutionary star was on the wane and the Marxist galaxy fading fast, French intellectuals suddenly rediscovered ideas which, until recently, had appeared outdated and absurd; concepts such as morality, the Rights of Man, and even the old idea of democracy. For the first time in a century, people started to think about democracy; after a century, freedom was being reconsidered.

To fill in the picture a little, it should be pointed out that earlier on, whilst the children of '68 were totally preoccupied with the sanctity of the Red Guards and whilst Sartre was perched on his soapbox haranguing his ideal audience, a whole series of movements had begun to develop which were in tune with the democratic spirit. Those in the women's movement, for example, had a simple and cheery demand to make. They wanted equal rights and they wanted them straightaway, rather than waiting for the great social upheaval promised by ideologues. There was also the painful, vital fight for abortion. Other minority groups struggled to achieve their identity and their dignity without waiting for some larger revolution to embrace their cause. There were modest and specific battles waged against racism, with precise targets such as the appalling shanty towns and the scandal of those lethal dormitories, into which workers from Mali and Senegal were crammed in their hundreds. Militants still sang the Internationale merely because they had nothing better to replace it, and as if out of habit. But when they came face to face with abject poverty, they seemed less concerned to reorder the world than to make it a somewhat less hostile place.

In this connection, the crucial event was the arrival in our midst of a mathematician who had been freed from a Soviet asylum for the insane. Another Soviet citizen, a writer this time, was swapped for a Chilean communist, a victim of fascist tyranny. When he landed at Zurich and recalled the grim years he had spent in communist concentration camps, he observed: "Arrangements should now be made for Brezhnev to be swapped for his double, Pinochet." Above all, there was the towering, the exemplary figure of Alexander Solzhenitsyn,[11] who became known to the French public through a television programme. Various dissidents were greeted by Sartre and Michel Foucault at the Récamier theatre in Paris. They were also a source of inspiration for the work of Maurice Clavel, a Christian, a Gaullist and a left-winger. When his friend, André Glucksmann, stated that the Gulag was as much a creation of Marxism as Auschwitz had been a creation of the Nazis, and when I myself tried to appeal to morality as opposed to ideology, the voice of those same dissidents was speaking through us.

When Michel Foucault's conversion was complete and he took up the cause of the Polish people, he again owed his understanding of the issues to the dissidents. The result of all this was a renewed concern for the Rights of Man – without limits or frontiers. As one of the advocates of that movement I am dealing here with its prehistory. It was also the moment when Bernard Kouchmer launched the idea of rescuing the boat-people who had fled Vietnam and were sailing in the China Sea. This was done without any consideration as to their colour or their political views and would have been unthinkable ten years earlier. Two brothers, who had been on opposite sides of the ideological divide for thirty years, now worked side by side for these boat-people, trying to get them simple entry visas into France. People could be mobilised in vast numbers in support of an idea, which, however banal or unremarkable, had been completely lost sight of, namely that of saving individual human beings on a global scale.

Intellectuals were involved in this, in spirit at least. Moreover, when very young people reminded them that man's only obligation to his fellow man was that he should not kill him but treat him as a brother, they took it in their stride, which was a remarkable turnabout. These same young people were not in the least bit interested in either "making a clean break with history" or in "changing man so as to bring out the deepest aspects of his nature". The intellectuals could accept this – those of them who survived, for one couldn't help being struck by the fact that this new, more sober, democratic era was witnessing the wholesale demise of the intellectual.[12] With no one to replace them, it was as if the species itself was dying out. In the case of Louis Althusser, one might have said that he suffered a double death; once at the Ecole normale when, in a fit of madness, he strangled his wife Hélène, and then ten years later when he actually died. Those who liked him were left with a very disturbing image of this enigmatic man. In his early life he had been something of a mystic and a disciple of Saint Theresa. He then achieved renown as an orthodox Marxist and taught a whole generation of philosophers the hard business of how to think. At the end of his life, he seemed like one of the possessed in Dostoevsky. He was weary and gloomy; he had gone through the dark night of the soul and, one might add, of the century.

Those intellectuals who remained, then, were there in thought, in June 1989, when a young man stood alone and defiantly halted a tank in Tiananmen Square, right where the crowds had once so clamorously expressed their insane adulation of Chairman Mao. They were stupefied by what had become of the monster communism which had held them in its spell and which they had believed immortal. They had worshipped then hated it. It had been the fixed point around which their debates, their battles, their enthusiasm and their regrets had revolved. Now it was crumbling and would leave not a trace behind,[13] and they, as might have been expected, no longer possessed a voice, nor a guiding star. Was it not significant that the last of those intellectual leaders, Louis Althusser,[14] died within a year of the collapse of the last symbol of that defunct political order?

Our adventure has come to an end, and the intellectual, whose fate was linked to that of ideologies which are now defunct, has not emerged unscathed. Looking at these enfeebled thinkers, displaying caution and pragmatism in place of a message, one hesitates between two feelings. On the one hand, there is the sense of relief, doubtless shared by everyone, that a more measured, tolerant manner has come to replace the fanaticism of those who have been parading before us from the outset. On the other hand, one is bound to feel uneasy, since their gentler form of philosophy is unlikely to measure up to challenges which history will continue to offer. With the return of nationalism and the upsurge of diehard attitudes, of populism and tribalism, a further metamorphosis of the intellectual may well occur, which would restore his status and his role as a spokesman.

NOTES

1. The second-year class for those preparing to take the entrance exam to the Ecole normale supérieure.

2. A group of nihilistic, surrealist students who were responsible for a lot of posters, slogans and graffiti in May '68.

3. A political speech-writer who became a journalist and then editor of the influential weekly the *Nouvel Observateur*.

I

GREAT HOPES
(The 1890s to the 1920s)

"Our story begins in fact at the end of the last century"

THE BIRTH OF THE INTELLECTUAL

The question always asked is, why *then*, why at the end of the last century? Why not begin with Voltaire or Victor Hugo? Didn't they fight? Didn't they also put their pen and their talent to the service of "great causes"? Doesn't that entitle them to open an account such as this, which sets out to trace the history of the intellectual?

The initial answer lies in the word itself: it did not exist before the Dreyfus Affair. Or if it did, if it was to be found in the dictionaries, it was less as a noun (the intellectual, an intellectual) than as an adjective (and generally with a derogatory connotation). If a judgment was referred to as "intellectual", it denoted woolliness and superficiality. When one spoke of an "intellectual" tendency in a writer, it denoted a certain rigidity of mind as distinct from genuine thinking. Thus it was not until the Dreyfus Affair that a group of men and women took the adjective, transformed its meaning, and used it not merely as a noun but as a veritable title of distinction. "We are the intellectuals." There was something provocative, something arrogant in such a claim; something daring about taking a derogatory epithet and waving it like a banner. That's exactly what Zola did, and those who backed him did the same. It was Georges Clemenceau who initiated the famous "manifesto" – referred to as the manifesto of "the intellectuals" – published from January 14th, 1898 in *L'Aurore littéraire, artistique, sociale*. The initial answer is therefore a nominalist one, and since I strive to be a consistent nominalist, it's a true one.

The second answer relates to numbers, the countless number who rallied to the cause of Dreyfus and then Zola. Basically, Voltaire had stood alone, and Hugo had been exiled. In those times, writers who adopted a political and even a moral stance seemed to stand out as exceptions to the norms of intellectual life. The Dreyfusards, however, were a group; they formed a crowd. There were poets by the score, writers, painters, and professors who took up the title of intellectual and considered it their duty to lay down their pen or their paintbrush and come down officially into the arena. Even those who opposed them, those who insulted Dreyfus or who accepted the arguments of the State, adopted the same kind of language, the same tactics, and formed themselves into various leagues and associations. Thus, instead of sulking or quietly restraining their sense of indignation and keeping their beliefs to themselves, instead of maintaining the tradition of academic silence in the face of the troublemakers, they challenged them. It was a sign of the times. It may perhaps have been that they were imitating their opponents or that they enjoyed what they were doing. Whatever the reason, there appeared on the intellectual scene an entirely new character, who was as original and distinctive as the scholar, the scribe, the sophist, and the polymath had been in earlier times. Barrès, after all, proclaimed that his "Culte du moi" novels depicted the apprenticeship of a "young French intellectual".

The third explanation of the phenomenon is to be found in certain values. Voltaire and Hugo had, of course, fought for values; they believed they were defending Right when they battled on behalf of Calas or Lally Tolendal[1] or denounced the Second Empire and Napoleon III. There is, however, one idea of which they had no conception; or had they conceived of it, they would have considered it crazy and naive. It was the idea that the quasi-ontological vocation of a writer might be to act as an intermediary between, on the one hand, the values of Justice, Truth, and Right and, on the other, the body politic; between the spiritual and the temporal; between the realm of the ideal and the domain of things secular. Like the new priesthood of a religion which had been revived, there appeared between these two orders or spheres a body of intellectuals who sought to act as mediators of those spiritual values, which seemed to represent a debased form of transcendence. The conditions were, of course, right for the concept itself to take hold. For instance, Neo-Kantianism prevailed in the universities at the time. Similarly, there was a great upheaval in theological circles, predicted by those who had spoken of "the death of God". Nor should one underestimate the importance of the separation of Church and State which preoccupied the politicians of the day. As far as the media were concerned, the birth of great newspapers gave intellectuals the possibility of participating in public debate which writers of the Enlightenment or the Romantic period did not enjoy to the same extent. The fact is, a combination of forces of that order was necessary for individuals to find the courage to proclaim themselves intermediaries between universal values and the everyday world. Hitherto, the notion of the intellectual as a kind of priest had been unheard of in the history of ideas.

NOTES

1. Both these men were tried and executed on false charges. Calas was a Protestant accused of having murdered his son because the latter wished to become a Roman Catholic. Lally Tolendal was accused of treason in the war against England which broke out in 1755.

"A writer could and should on occasion give up creative writing"

A CONVERSATION WITH CLAUDE SIMON

The whole issue is summed up in those words "could" and "should". There are, however, writers who cannot give up and others who do not wish to. There are respectable, even admirable, writers who consider the one thing they can and must do is to write their books the way they need to be written. Yet, from time to time, without any sense of obligation and certainly at irregular intervals, they also speak their mind. Does that make them "intellectuals"? Are they in the tradition of Zola and Herr? I wanted to put these questions to one such writer at the very beginning of this book. As Beckett and Michaux are no longer with us, I turned naturally to Claude Simon.

Most of the writers I'm concerned with in this book have continually taken up positions, engaged in polemics and so on. What is striking about you is that you have steered clear of these kinds of antics, apart from two or three occasions, beginning with the war when you were, of course, actively involved.

I didn't enlist in 1940. I was mobilised like all the other young men of my age. But during my military service, which I served as a private, I applied to join the cavalry. I didn't do so out of heroism, but simply because I'd been riding since the age of twelve, had enjoyed it, and considered it preferable to foot-slogging. That's all. To talk of my "commitment" to the Resistance would be to exaggerate. I escaped with my life from the massacre in Belgium, into which the cretinous French High Command had hurled the cavalry, and I also escaped from a prisoner-of-war camp in the depths of Germany, where I had been denounced to the guards as a Jew by a French fellow-prisoner. I have to admit that after these experiences I wasn't burning with patriotic zeal. But I had friends in the Resistance, and you know how it is. One day, someone asks you to hide a case, then to give someone a bed, and one thing leads to another and you find you've got four chaps lodging with you who are coordinating military information and transmitting it to London every evening. My part in it was simply to open my door to them.

Where was this?

At 148 Boulevard Montparnasse, where I had a flat at the time. The block was ideal for these purposes. If I didn't pin an agreed sign on my door in the morning, or if the Germans arrested me or set a trap, the guys had only to go quite casually on up the stairs, follow the corridor leading to the maids' rooms, and slip down the other staircase.

There was also your involvement in Spain in 1936.

Here again, one mustn't exaggerate. I was, of course, on the "right" side. It was a question of youthful rebellion against my family and against the social and religious order of the day. But when I think back on it now and try to be honest with myself, I believe I went to Barcelona more out of curiosity, as a kind of spectator more than as an active participant. I unconsciously applied one of Descartes's principles, without having read him (I was almost totally uneducated).

All the same, there was the story of the unloading of a shipment of arms which you organised.

We didn't land arms – it was a transfer at Sète on to an old tub from Barcelona; the cargo had been loaded at Marseilles on to a Norwegian freighter. Norway had signed the famous Non-intervention Pact, and the captain was forbidden to go to Spain. The captain of the old tub – it was called the *Carmen* (I've still got a photo of the two boats side by side in the outer harbour at Sète) – took his orders from a rather strange Italian adventurer, who was referred to as the "Comandante". He was holed up in a hotel in Perpignan, and I still wonder if he wasn't a double-agent. The crew were a silent bunch of anarchists. I'll spare you the details of the whole story, it would take too long to tell.

Would it?

Well, as I say, I was a youngster. It was an adventure, it involved breaking the law, handling contraband, false documents and so on. I discovered all sorts of types I knew nothing about: arms dealers, a rich provincial pharmacist with a double-life as an anarchist, customs officers who were more or less privy to what was going on, people who could be bribed, that sort of thing . . .

But in Spain?

I'm not particularly bright, but it took me just two weeks in Barcelona in September '36 to grasp what it took Orwell six months to realise.

Meaning what?

That what was taking place was insurgency rather than revolution, and that it was doomed to failure. The communists hated the Trotskyists more than anyone else, and the anarchists hated the middle-classes and the Civil Guard with whom the communists were in league. Do you know what they called Largo Caballero? "The rabble-rouser". OK, it was certainly very exciting, but frankly it was all pretty pathetic.

There was a third occasion when you rallied to a cause: the Manifesto of the 121[1] during the Algerian War.

Well, the situation was clear-cut; it wasn't difficult making up one's mind.

How did it come about? How was it organised?

Jérôme Lindon spoke to me about it. I was staying with him at the time in Etretat. He got me to read the manifesto which hadn't yet been published and asked if I'd agree to sign it. I said yes at once . . . as a matter of course.

You'd done nothing up till then?

No. But from the outset I'd found the whole Algerian business appalling.

From the outset?

Absolutely.

The official Left took quite a different view, didn't it?

We were pretty much on our own, it's true. Things changed dramatically when deferment for students was suspended. Till then . . .

Who made the first move?

A few intellectuals. Amongst them, I knew Lindon, Vidal-Naquet and Nadeau. I also knew that Blanchot was involved.

Yes, that's true. Blanchot was very active.

Now it can be said: he and Nadeau drafted the Manifesto. I don't know who gave them away, but they were charged. Then someone had the idea that we should all write to the examining magistrate, and say that we'd all contributed to the drafting of the Manifesto, that one or another of us had added or deleted a word, an adjective, a comma. Imagine the poor magistrate, whose usual task is to try to prove the guilt of someone who claims he's innocent. On this occasion, his role had been reversed. He was now trying to prove the innocence of those who claimed they were guilty. Rather amusing, in a way.

One can't imagine Blanchot as a militant.

I didn't know him very well. I've only got one memory of him. We'd all gathered at the Mutualité[2] where a meeting we were to have held was banned. We were talking quietly outside on the pavement in front of the closed doors, when a few cops came up quite nonchalantly and mingled with us in a peaceful manner. Suddenly, they began hitting people with their truncheons. Blanchot and Nadeau were quite seriously hurt.

Alright, so those were three occasions when you took sides. Apart from that, you've done nothing, or almost nothing. Why?

Not exactly nothing. I was subsequently charged on the initiative of Messmer[3] with insulting the army. During an interview with Madeleine Chapsal about *La Route des Flandres*, I'd remarked that the French army was engaged in murder in Algeria, not in a war. But that's a detail. After that, there didn't seem to be any compelling reason to "take sides", as you put it. Oh yes, three years ago, I called for people to vote for Mitterrand. But writing itself is already a commitment.

Agreed. But like everyone else, you're constantly being asked to sign one petition or another. So how do you react?

I don't answer. The ability to put words together in a more or less expressive and eloquent manner (and that's all I try to do) doesn't qualify you to act as a guru and pontificate on every issue. Having said that, a writer has a right to his opinions as an ordinary citizen. He has his likes and dislikes and can make them known when certain limits are exceeded, as in the Algerian War. As far as "committed literature" or "committed science" are concerned, one knows what they have led to: Stalin's socialist realism, Michurin, Lysenko, and to the total economic and spiritual collapse of a country which had enormous economic and intellectual potential. One only has to think of Dostoevsky, Chekhov, the Leningrad school of linguistics, Russian mathematicians and so on.

There are, however, writers who sign petitions.

That's their business. I don't tell anyone else what to do. I speak only for myself. I'd simply repeat that a writer who thinks he can act as a guru shows signs of misplaced self-importance.

Why do you think it is no longer appropriate?

It can be precisely dated as a historical phenomenon. Broadly speaking, it goes from Voltaire to Sartre and takes in Zola.

How do you react to Sartre, for example?

Can you imagine Proust on the platform at a meeting or on his soap-box in Billancourt?[4] Yet that didn't prevent him from supporting Dreyfus. It's just occurred to me that he offered an early portrait of Sartre and committed literature. Do you remember what the old reactionary diplomat, M. de Norpois said when talking to the young

Marcel? It's got everything, including a condemnation of "mandarin" literature.

You're not very kind!

Why should I be? Listen, you said you didn't have a lot of space to devote to this interview. Well, if you don't mind, let's talk about something more interesting than Sartre and his ineffable Castor.[5]

So, to sum up, you don't accept at all the idea that it's a writer's social duty to be committed?

But of course I do, absolutely. There was a Nobel symposium at the Elysée Palace a few years ago, and someone asked what the writer's duty was. My answer was very simple, as it all seemed so obvious to me. The overriding duty of a writer is to produce the best literature possible, just as a scientist's duty is to produce the best science. "Bourgeois" literature no more exists than "proletarian" science. In a world which is being perpetually transformed, each time a writer, an artist, or a scientist discovers a new form, that is to say new relationships (between words, colours, sounds, physical or chemical phenomena), he contributes to this "trans-formation", according to his own limited abilities. I use the word "discover" because my friend Léon Cooper, the inventor of the computer who won the Nobel prize at the age of forty, drew my attention the other day to the fact that these relationships (whether in the realm of nature or language) exist before they are "dis-covered".

All the same, can one talk about criminal writers who have written criminal books?

Who, for example?

Céline, or at least the Céline who wrote the pamphlets.

Morality and finer feelings have nothing to do with literature any more than with science. Einstein was the father of the Atom Bomb; was he a criminal? Not that I've ever been a great admirer of Céline. But for reasons other than moral ones. I'm not attracted by his "imprecatory" style of writing. His best works are *D'un château l'autre* and *Nord*. It's as if he had been saved by his own baseness. His description of bomb-damaged Berlin with balconies hanging like festoons of lace is superb, as are the final pages, and the journey across a devastated German landscape in a freezing train.

And what d'you make of a book like Rigodon?

I don't remember it very well. *Guignol's Band*, on the other hand, is supremely boring. I couldn't take more than three pages of it.

What about someone on the other side like Malraux?

There are only two sides in literature, to adopt your terminology: the good and the bad. I find Malraux mediocre.

Is it that you find his vision of the world too simplistic, too Manichaean?

Yes, that's partly it. For instance, in *L'Espoir* the way he suggests "everyone's noble, everyone's good". For Heaven's sake! When you think of the murder of Nin, for example, the prisons of the NKVD, the events of May '37. And then there are the people who philosophise for pages on end (they always occupy important positions, if you've noticed; they'll be officers, officials, airmen and so on). From a literary point of view, it adds nothing at all.

In other words, you're against what is conventionally known as the novel of ideas?

Why would I read a novel to get ideas? It seems to me that the work of philosophers, essayists, sociologists, theologians serves that purpose exactly.

Why then does anyone write novels?

Ah! That's a very good question. But its scope is rather too large for such a short interview as this. All the same, I'll try to give you a brief answer. Firstly, why does anyone write? Why does anyone paint pictures, compose string quartets; why do architects design palaces, squares, gardens? For a long time (up to the time of Proust and Joyce in fact, but excluding Dostoevsky whose stories and characters are both totally ambiguous), people have written novels modelled on the didactic tale, but which have been embellished and developed to a certain extent. (There are other kinds of writing as well: municipal decrees, treatises on law, economics, and cookery). As you know, Balzac wanted his own work to provide readers with "a complete social study". What's more, this style of writing is far from being exhausted. But what value does a fictional narrative have which has been wholly invented and in which everything, including the way all the events hang together right up to the dénouement, depends solely on the whim and pleasure of the author? That's why some people approach literature from a different angle. For example, Valéry wrote: "If I'm asked what I meant to say, my answer is that I wanted to do rather than to say something". The difference between the traditional novel and a novel of a wholly different type is summed up in that statement. In the first case, the ideas (the meaning) precede the act of writing, whereas in the second case meaning is produced in and through the act of writing.

In that case, what do you think of writers like Musil and Broch, who tell us that one of the functions of the novel is to provide us with knowledge?

63

One would have to agree what one means by the word "knowledge". Let me answer you with another quotation. This time it's Novalis speaking: "Language, like mathematics, is nothing but the expression of its own extraordinary nature, which explains why it expresses so well the strange relationships which exist between things." As someone else also put it very neatly: "Language says things before we do, and only the individual who is aware of its propositions, its rhythms, and its music will become a prophet."

There are novels which generate thought and knowledge.

A negro mask is just as much a product of thought as a page of Pascal. However, in contrast to meaning which precedes the act of writing, meaning "produced" is not made explicit. It is "open", multi-dimensional.

Has literature given you a greater knowledge of certain things?

Absolutely: the pleasure of reading and of trying to write.

I realise that. Is there anything else?

Forgive me if I return to mathematics. With literature and art in general (painting, music, etc.), it's the one thing which really interests me. The title of the first chapter one studies in "Math' Sup'"[6] is "Arrangements, combinations, permutations". That's all I do with words. Flaubert said: "One has only to look at something long enough for it to become interesting." That's a formulation which frequently recurs in maths. "Let us study this figure (square, circle, triangle, etc.) and try to discover its properties." By properties, one understands the other figures it may contain or give rise to; for example, the square on the hypotenuse, the circumference, an ellipse or parabola produced by the section of a cone or a plane, depending on the angle of attack. It was Lacan who said "a word is not simply a sign but a node of possible meanings." Each one of them carries its own powerful metaphoric charge. So, it's a question of examining the multiple properties of a word, including its musical ones and the way they can be harmoniously combined in the composition of a phrase, a paragraph, a chapter, a whole book . . .

So composition is the main thing?

It's everything.

You know what Gide's reaction was when Bernard Lazare went to see him and asked him to sign something in support of Dreyfus. When Lazare had gone, he exclaimed: "There's a man who values something more highly than literature!"

I wouldn't use the terms more or less highly. I would say on the same level.

Another possibility is to treat literature as something sacred.

I don't consider anything sacred. I don't like the word. I'm too profoundly materialistic.

Alright. But the fact remains that there is no great cause which you would consider superior to that of literature.

Sartre has uttered countless inanities ("We mustn't drive Billancourt to despair", "every anti-communist is a swine"), but I came across a real gem the other day in an anthology: "It's a question of knowing whether one would rather talk about the condition of the Jews or the flight of butterflies". Really! The great philosopher would doubtless turn in his grave if one pointed out to him that Nathalie Sarraute (who has never talked about the condition of the Jews) is herself Jewish, or that Louise Nevelson (who has never depicted a concentration camp) is Jewish. He might also have reacted equally strongly had he learnt that Rauschenberg's teacher, who suggested he assemble pieces of wood, tar-lined paper, old material, and streaks of paint in his compositions, was Schwitters, a Jew who had fled from Nazi Germany. Or perhaps they have all spoken about the condition of the Jews in their own particular way. Everything interconnects in history. The "black hole" of Auschwitz (not to mention the Gulag) has rendered all "humanist" discourse obscene, which no doubt explains the relentless pursuit of the concrete.

Are you writing at the moment?

"It's all I'm fit for," as Beckett said.

What might stop you writing?

Death. After all, it's getting nearer.

What else?

Old age and lack of strength. Writing is very difficult. It's very tiring. So, to stop myself from getting bored, perhaps I'll go back to mathematics. I've taken it up again a little (oh, at a very elementary level. Sadly, I've forgotten almost everything I knew). But the other day, the simple demonstration of Pythagoras's theorem gave me infinitely more pleasure than reading a poem by Baudelaire. It gets one closer to the absolute perfection of the mind.

NOTES

1. A document signed in 1960 by French intellectuals who were opposed to French Government policy in Algeria and which had a significant impact on public opinion.

2. A large meeting hall in Paris.

3. He became Minister of the Armed Forces in 1960.

4. A Paris suburb where the main Renault factory is situated.

5. The French word for "beaver" and the nickname by which Simone de Beauvoir was known.

6. The first-year advanced maths class for students preparing the entrance exam to the Grandes Ecoles.

3

"In a Montpellier cemetery"

AN OBSESSION WITH PAUL VALÉRY

The scene, one must admit was pretty stark.

Picture on one side Paul Valéry, the young Paul Valéry. He had just turned twenty and as yet published nothing. However, he enjoyed poetry, admired Mallarmé, and was friends with Gide and Pierre Louÿs. When in Paris, he frequented Symbolist circles, in which he already enjoyed a reputation for his courteousness, his intelligence, and the cigarettes he rolled himself and smoked from dusk to dawn. He was a keen conversationalist, liked strolling around, and was fond of remarking: "Tobacco, coffee, and friendship are gifts from the gods." He was in Montpellier that summer because it was the holidays and his brother owned a house there.

Opposite him was Georges Vacher de Lapouge. Actually, I have no idea what Georges Vacher de Lapouge looked like, but I do know that he was thirty-five, and an "agrégé" in law. He was one of those encyclopaedists who were interested in everything yet who knew very little about anything and who dazzled those around them, but were suspect to the truly learned. Until a few years previously, he had been a lawyer, or to be more precise a public prosecutor. That was now behind him and he preferred his more modest post as Deputy-Director of the Arts Faculty Library in the University of Montpellier. It was, he claimed, a post which gave him more free time for the one thing which interested him, the comparative study of races. He believed in the existence of races and that the evolution of history was dependent upon the struggle between them, and on that alone. In order to study the subject, he had perfected techniques which involved the measurement of the cranium. He was soon to publish *L'Aryen* and *Les Sélections sociales*, but his doctrine had already been formulated in its essentials, as had his methodology. Indeed, they were quite well known in the area, as they formed the basis of a course he gave in the Arts Faculty. As a consequence, everyone in Montpellier was aware of his theories concerning the superiority of the Nordic over the damnable Semitic races.

There the two men were, face to face; the congenial poet and the scholarly savant, the pupil before his master, the holidaymaker in the presence of the local celebrity. First they went to the cemetery where they had been given permission – in the name of science! – to unearth six hundred skulls. Subsequently, they moved to a laboratory in order to examine at their leisure all the material which had been transported there for them. Then it was down to work and full steam ahead, measuring this one, sizing that. They put the long-heads on the right, the short-heads on the left, and sorted out the flat, the round, the mixed, and those which were unclassifiable. Some specimens matched or complemented each other, whilst others were at variance. What a perfect Aryan this fat chap was with his enlarged frontal bone, his jutting chin, and slightly rounded upper jaw! Didn't this young fellow look slightly Jewish with his narrow forehead and over-arched eyebrows? As for this third specimen with his deformed parietal bone and sunken temples, didn't he look like your typical manic depressive? Vacher de Lapouge's chief advantage was that he had read and seen everything. Moreover, he dazzled his pupil with craniometric ideas he had gathered together from England, Poland and Germany, as well as from other regions of France. This was real knowledge, he told him, which came from the true International of scholars. It represented real progress in the sciences and the arts. Yes, Valéry was there in that room with a madman, not to mention the six hundred skulls they were sorting and labelling.

My first interpretation of Vacher de Lapouge is that he was a racist, the quintessential racist. He believed, for example, that the Jews were the sworn enemies of the Aryans and that they deserved the persecution they suffered "because of their bad faith, their cupidity, and their domineering attitude." It should, however, be noted that he was also a leftist, a revolutionary even. He had known Guesde[1] and been a militant in various workers' parties. In these circles, he had earned himself a solid reputation as a propagandist and a scholar. Perhaps more unusually, he had Marxist ideas as well, which led him to believe in particular that racial conflict was the ultimate stage of the class struggle. Yet again, it's that old story of left-wing anti-semitism, to which I shall return in due course. One is struck by the same old mixture of progressive ideas coupled with infamy, of socialism and ignominy which was characteristic of the period which preceded and followed the Dreyfus Affair. This measurer of skulls and fanatical believer in the inequality of the races had the reputation of being an upright man, indeed passed for a man devoted to justice, equality, and liberty, which doubtless explains the feeling of affinity he inspired in the young poet.

My second interpretation concerns craniology itself. It is clear that it was a pseudo-science and, on the evidence, simply anthropology for the half-witted. But to whom exactly was this obvious and since when? Remember, this was 1891, when another genial racist, Jules Soury, was teaching at the Sorbonne. He was not just a scholar, but a philosopher as well, who was considered by thinking Parisians to be at least the equal of Bergson. It was a period too in which a number of great minds, from Taine to Renan and from Barrès to Bourget, considered it natural to distinguish Aryans from Semites and blond long-heads from short brown-heads. One only has to read selected extracts from Taine's *Histoire de la littérature anglaise*, in which he established scientifically, as one might have expected, that "there are types of men just as there are types of bulls or horses." He also pointed out that the "Aryan races", devoted to the "beautiful" and the "sublime", could be contrasted with the "Semitic races". These were characterised by the "myopic fanaticism in which they indulge". Unfortunately, the pseudo-scientific does not betray itself as such or to everyone at large. The idiotic and downright criminal in science can for years on end produce commonplaces and convictions for whole generations of people. This is true in the case of Paul Valéry, boringly, stupidly true. He was one of the countless intellectuals at the time who believed that it was possible in all innocence to measure the skull of a negro and compare it with that of an inhabitant of Rodez, in order to deduce, not surprisingly, the former's congenital inferiority.

My third interpretation concerns Valéry himself and his passionate thirst for learning and knowledge. He had sworn that he would unlock the secrets of the soul and the mystery of thought in all its sublimity, and he never gave up trying. In a poem inspired by Huysmans, written when he was just fifteen, the youthful Valéry proclaimed a trifle pompously: "I take endless delight in my own mind." He was still a young man and had not yet created Teste.[2] But what one can surmise about his life (and especially what one knows about his precocious preoccupations) suggest that the essential outline of his project was already in place. Science was in the air and positive thinking formed part of the intellectual landscape. When he learned of a possible new system of classification, Valéry was immediately eager to find out about it and to embark upon a voyage of discovery into the sphere that interested him above all others. This he referred to as "the mind and all its processes". He would have sold his soul to the Devil – not to mention to Vacher de Lapouge! – for the pleasure and excitement of delving a little deeper into the soul of man. I think that Balzac must have been like that. Surely those were his feelings, as he spent whole nights dreaming about Lavater's work on physiognomy. Imagine if Balzac had had at his disposal a reasoned theory concerning not just faces, but facial types, and even brains, when he wrote the *Comédie humaine*. Imagine the joy and exhilaration he would have experienced. I'd be willing to wager it was the same brutal and mephistophelean pleasure which Valéry experienced when he was surrounded by six hundred skulls in that Montpellier cemetery.

Make no mistake, these are interpretations, not justifications: they excuse nothing. The images which linger in the mind are sinister and horrible; they might have been taken from a crime novel involving real characters. My main reason for coming out with all this is to provide a framework, a perspective; or rather to set it all alongside other images of Valéry which are more conventional and better known; images which are more in keeping with what we know from other sources about one of the most eminent writers of the first half of the twentieth century. There is, for example, the image of the man of letters chatting with Gide in the Luxembourg Gardens or that of the coldly dispassionate poet, the disciple of Edgar Allan Poe. The image of the mature writer with fevered lips and a frenzied expression, who had learnt to control his passions and whose handsome forehead rather more than the look in his eyes seemed to illuminate the rest of his face. The image of his long, slender hands. The image of the democrat also comes to mind, the true democrat (were there ever that many?), who understood in the thirties that "if the State is strong it crushes us, if it is weak we perish." The image of the great European for whom Europe was synonymous with the spirit and the mind. The image of the humanist who calmly asserted that "man is intelligent just as the tiger is strong and the pigeon flies" (which was not so easy at a time when there was a cult of strength and instinct, of nationhood and war). The image of the Academician who gave the funeral oration for Bergson in 1941. The image of the upper middle-class conservative who quickly understood that Marshal Pétain's "assuaging tones" would cost his country dear. Images of his mind, his pure mind, which alone deserve to be remembered. Didn't he remark: "Beyond the mind the body, but beyond the body the mind"? Lastly, there is the image of him as an old man nearing death, who said, with reference to Degas: "The long and gloomy twilight of life, with eyes dimmed that had laboured so hard, his mind somewhere between absence and despair." I wish they had been my own words recalling the poet whom I consider the true successor of Baudelaire.

NOTES

1. Jules Guesde was one of the main followers in France of Marx. He became the editor of a socialist weekly and a Deputy.

2. A character created by Valéry in *La Soirée avec Monsieur Teste* who is the embodiment of intellectual introspection.

4

"The intellectual mentor of Blum and Proust"

THE INTELLECTUAL LEGACY OF MAURICE BARRÈS

There are biographies of Maurice Barrès as well as essays and studies on his life and work. Yet no one has produced a history of the influence and effect he has had in France; they would certainly be fascinating. Drieu would be included, of course, also Malraux, for whom Barrès was a formative influence, and even Aragon, of whom Rivière said in 1923 that he reminded him of "the young Barrès". Much later on, in the darkest days of extreme sectarian Stalinism, Aragon himself always mentioned Barrès as an important influence whom he still revered. One would also have to include Nizan's *La Conspiration*, the early writings of Camus, and *La Rencontre* of Mauriac: imagine the young writer from Bordeaux on the point of sending Barrès a copy of his first book and quite transfixed with admiration for the man he still considered to be the prince of youth and an eternal source of inspiration. This was in 1911! Montherlant, Cocteau and Morand would also have to figure in such a work. In addition, one might examine a little more closely the strange case of André Breton who organised the celebrated "trial"[1] of Barrès in 1921 and who delivered, or had someone else deliver, an extremely violent indictment of him. In the end, however, he confessed that what had given rise to the ceremony and lay at the heart of the violence and of his desire to distance himself from Barrès was a longstanding fascination with the man and the sense of complicity that attracted him. There would have to be at least one chapter devoted to the Jews, or rather to those Jewish intellectuals who paradoxically were captivated by this declared anti-semite. Even more paradoxically, it was from him that they sometimes derived a sense of their own identity. There is, for example, the story of Blum, who demonstrated his admiration for Barrès by going to ask him to sign a declaration in support of Dreyfus at the beginning of the Affair, even though his anti-Judaism was common knowledge. Less well known perhaps was the admiration shown him by the young Marcel Proust, who was greatly moved when he read *Colette Baudoche* and praised its author to the skies. From his deathbed, he sent Barrès a first edition of *Sodome et Gomorrhe* with the following dedication: "To M. Barrès with humble and profound respect". There was also a little band of aesthetes, which included Robert Dreyfus and Fernand Gregh as well as Proust, who were grouped around the review *Le Banquet* and who claimed to have been inspired by Barrès's ideas and by *L'Ennemi des lois*. It is not widely known that Bernard Lazare, the first of those who rallied to the defence of Dreyfus, was also a fanatical admirer of *Sous l'oeil des Barbares*. Furthermore, almost nothing is known about that like-minded group of thinkers – André Spire, Edmond Fleg – who, according to Levinas, were the "Jewish followers of Barrès". His was a strange story, it must be said. And given that he was the first national-socialist in France and perhaps in Europe, it is equally strange that he should have had such a following, though the one does not exclude the other. Barrès simply represents a paradox.

NOTES

1. The mock trial conducted in 1921 by the Dadaists, many of whom had idealised Barrès in their youth.

5

"The racially different face"

THE ENIGMA OF BARRÈS

There is a mystery concerning Barrès. He was a dandy. He was also a subtle and refined egoist. Indeed, he was a writer whose whole concern, whose entire art were tirelessly devoted to the study of his own self in its multiple facets. Young people who had responded to the survey conducted by Agathon[1] as well as the more demanding avant-gardists associated with the *Revue Blanche* and the *Revue Bleue* were immediately delighted to recognise themselves in the hesitant, decadent, and subtly epicurean characters of *Jardin de Bérénice* and *L'Ennemi des lois*. Was he a role model? He was more than that. A leader? More than that too. Proust wrote to him: "You were what perhaps no one else has ever been." You were what Chateaubriand himself "never remotely was". And to convince oneself of this fact, one need only think of Proust who, as I've said, never missed an opportunity of expressing his great esteem for Barrès. In addition, one only has to think of the surveys that appeared at the beginning of the nineties in which lycéens and undergraduates placed him, together with Verlaine, way above the other intellectual leaders of the day. Above all, one should re-read Blum who was overcome at the idea of spending a week in Charmes, the writer's birthplace, and who thus had "the singular honour during a whole week of breathing the same air as Maurice Barrès". It was Blum again who described Barrès as a "prince", in his account of the famous visit and who was manifestly captivated and won over by his qualities, as was a whole generation. The qualities of Barrès to which he referred were his "stately charm and grace", his "natural nobility", his "heady mixture of masterful activity, philosophy, and sensuality" and finally his thought which "though seemingly dry, was as dry as a feverish hand, had a metaphysical and provocatively poetic charge and pulsated with pride and a sense of domination". In short, he enjoyed unique prestige and had incredible panache. On top of that, he had the traces of a working-class accent and a certain rebelliousness which were to the liking of the contemporaries of Ravachol.[2] All in all, I don't think there was anyone before him who had enjoyed a similar position. The real mystery, however, is that this star, this idol, the writer most sought after by eminent Parisian thinkers of the day and, not surprisingly, by the progressive ones as well, took the no less extraordinary – and in Blum's view – unforeseen risk of turning his back on all that. In so doing, he disappointed his little court of admirers by taking sides not for, as had been expected, but against Alfred Dreyfus.

His vision of the world changed at that moment. Or, at least, his admirers had the feeling that it changed. He had been hedonistic, individualistic, and inclined to anarchism, and had sworn by his "cult of the self" which, depending on his mood, he situated in the tradition of either Amiel or Stendhal.[3] He was now to become patriotic, mindlessly patriotic, and chauvinistic, and to claim he believed only in the dead, in roots, in the race, and in blood. Furthermore, in the quarrel that set "nationalists" against "cosmopolitans" to use his own terms, the man who until the previous day had sided with the latter against the former and had unhesitatingly championed "American and Russian" writers against those minor figures we would term "typically French" caused a great stir among the young: overnight, they discovered their hero had become the leader of the "Ligue de la Patrie française",[4] the very incarnation of conservatism. True, there had already been Boulangism[5] and the campaign in Nancy. It's also true that our dilettante friend had been responsible for some of the most colourful anti-semitic language, but young people hadn't taken that too seriously. In his attacks against "Jewish bankers" they detected a hint of impatience and rebelliousness, which indicated that his remarks could be seen as belonging to so-called left-wing anti-semitism, which doubtless was reassuring. The fact is that at the time little attention was paid to young Jewish intellectuals – Blum, Proust, Bernard Lazare and others – who were not greatly troubled by the political outbursts of Barrès. His new-found stance was however somewhat different. Certainly, they sensed or had a foreboding that things had changed. So that when on this occasion their leader dared to write that Dreyfus's guilt could be explained in terms of his race and the shape of his nose, they felt he had perhaps betrayed them.

This was all the more the case since the world, the landscape in which his books were set also changed at that point, which was no less remarkable in the eyes of those young aesthetes. A writer always has his own landscape, the places he has selected from amongst the countless possible ones and which serve as the stage-set of his intimate dramas. Yet they are not always or even often associated with the place where fate decreed he should be born. Barrès's places were Venice and Toledo; "the garden on the Oronte", Bérénice's garden.

They were certainly tormented, slightly tragic landscapes, which seemed haunted by decadence and death. Yet there was intensity and magic in the light which surrounded them, in the very colour of their dust and ashes, in the tomb of the Escurial, as well as in the "cool marble" of the Doge's Palace, which made them the ideal setting for the trilogy devoted to the "cult of the self". Then, suddenly everything was overturned, everything shifted and became more complex. Not that he renounced his former places, forgot Toledo, Cordoba and the inestimable sensual delight they evoked. But what was it he dreamed of when he returned to these places and moved once again into his red-and-gold room in the Hôtel Saint-Marc in Venice? He dreamed of Lorraine, of Charmes, the town of his childhood! He dreamed of Sion, Domrémy, the Château of Gerbéviller, the Lac des Corbeaux, and of Les Moraines! Similarly, when he returned to the Orient, when, on the eve of war, he set off back to Beirut, Alexandria, Antioch and Constantinople, when he meditated on the banks of the Euphrates or in the ruins of the Castle at Masyaf, as he had done in the past, he still had images of Lorraine running through his mind. As he stood in front of the gilded mosques where previously he had had such daydreams, he thought only of village churches, the glory of our native land, and was distressed by their decay. New settings were required for new ideas and new inner landscapes for a new vision of the world. Instead of the glorious images of his dandyish period, there was a return to the rather dull and predictable countryside around Nancy, to its fertile earth and dampness, in which devotees of *Sous l'oeil des barbares* found it difficult to get their bearings. His early novels needed the light of Cordoba and the languid atmosphere of Toledo. But *Les Bastions de l'Est* and the trilogy, *L'Energie nationale*, had to be anchored, rooted in the sod and soil, though at the cost of denying part of himself. This again left his former rivals flabbergasted.

Perhaps less clear-cut and less spectacular but almost as significant was the slow metamorphosis which affected his personal bearing and appearance. He seemed to age well and to keep his body in good shape without any coarsening of his features. On the day of his election to the Académie française, his youthfulness and upright stance, as he entered the domed hall dressed in his new green jacket, caused poor old Gide to turn pale with jealousy: "Of all of us [he protested] he has changed the least. I do like his thin face, his straight hair, and even the sound of his working-class voice." But on a close inspection, one would see there was something Venetian or Spanish about the man. In the end he came to resemble one of those passionate figures of El Greco which so enthralled him when he looked at them. One became truly aware of that studied blend of melancholy and dandyism, of sensuality and insolence which created his charm and his success, especially in the portrait by Jacques-Emile Blanche (the famous portrait which was exhibited in the Salon of 1891 and which shows him full-face, very pale, with the already celebrated tuft of hair slightly swept up on his forehead, the disdainful curl of the lip, the mocking eyelids, a carnation in his button-hole, and a white tie adorning his wing collar). But that image had been abandoned. He had renounced his casual air and the arrogance of the poet who was the enemy of the law. Gone were the carnations, the white ties, the discreetly raffish look of someone whose whole project could be summed up in the word "freedom". What was striking in most of the later portraits and photos was, rather, his official, almost formal appearance. They are images of the patriot-writer draped in the tricolour. With a cane in one hand and a cocked hat in the other, he struck poses as an Academician. In a thousand and one photos, as the result of an imperceptible but decisive transformation, insolence had given way to haughtiness, disdain to bitterness, and his ironic look had been replaced by the dull self-satisfaction of a libertarian who has achieved success. François Mauriac referred with some acuity to this "rich and ambitious man who got his hands on everything that the world makes available to winners". Much later, he was to refer to his "solitary watchfulness, half absorbed by the shadow of death". I myself would add that it was no longer geography which was the servant of philosophy, but physiology and physiognomy which conformed with the one and the other. Barrès created for himself, if you like, a nationalistic cast of mind and based his appearance on a landscape. He adjusted his look, the set of his chin, his moustache to the new inner world which turned him away from Toledo. In Vailland's very apt phrase: "From the age of forty, a man is responsible for the way he looks." Barrès was just forty when he completed the second trilogy and adopted permanently the air of a right-thinking man.

The question of course is why he did this. What happened? What determined such an astounding metamorphosis? How does it come about that a man gives up his flattering role as conscience of the nation, in favour of a role as champion of church-buildings in disrepair? His contemporaries, as one might expect, became lost in conjecture. The most indulgent referred to him having suffered a painful wound in his private life, intensified by "metaphysical despair", for which the robust and simple convictions of nationalism provided a remedy. The harshest, and perhaps the most observant, spoke of an earlier and maybe innate temptation, the warning signs of which might have been detected in his first novels. The shrewdest and most clear-sighted, who were not to be taken in, claimed to detect the classic ploy of the old actor who fears he is no longer a success and tries to find something new to hold his audience's attention. It was rumoured that, when the trembling young Mauriac went to present him with a copy of *Les Mains jointes*, Barrès said: "What a bore, I've got to leave him with an impression of me which will live up to his expectations!" For Mauriac himself, the true Barrès was to be found in the first trilogy. But later in his life, in his *Rencontre*, he wavered over three possible explanations of the change in Barrès: cynicism, cold calcu-lation, and the almost strategic analysis of the person who has come to realise that there is nothing like a new part to rejuvenate an old actor. "The second Barrès," he said, "moved me as if he had been a god in disguise." Then there was his *world-weariness*, the straightfor-ward and dizzying world-weariness of a man who believed in nothing and especially not the slogans of the Parliament in which he feigned an interest. Politics was a mere distraction; it bemused him. Mauriac was correct when he said that it "occupied him", "sustained" him, because it was "a duty he took extremely seriously" – "what would have happened to him without the Chamber of Deputies?" Finally, there was his *work*, the profound chemistry of his work which deter-mined everything else, as is the case for all writers. "I was unaware," wrote Mauriac, "that an artist, even without realising it, almost always obeys the dictates of his creative processes, and that, at the age he had reached, Barrès couldn't have managed without the great themes afforded him by the burial grounds of Lorraine." This was Mauriac's own preferred explanation.

The truth, one realises, is that none of these arguments carries conviction. One hesitates and gropes around. One might perhaps incline towards cynicism as the explanation, were it not for the fact that in Barrès's late writings there are splendid moments full of feeling which remind us of the early works. Soon after the death of Jaurès, for example, there was the letter of condolence which he delivered personally to the dead man's daughter, Madeleine. One would be inclined to accept the hypothesis of despair, of ultimate weariness; one might even believe him when he sighed: "I no longer enjoy life's feast, I have lost my appetite in the middle of the banquet," were it not that at the critical moment when he was thought to be grieving over the death of Jean de Tinan he'd come out with that mocking snigger of his that used to be his hallmark. One might have accepted that it was his writing, the unfathomable chemistry of that writing, but as an explanation it explains nothing, because one would still want to know why at the age "he'd reached", as Mauriac put it, he became enslaved by those burial grounds and by the cult of the dead. As for the clues which he himself gave, the half-secrets which he scattered throughout his writings, they suggest first one thing then another. One has scarcely got used to the idea of the charitable and pious Barrès whose heart truly bled for the dynamited church towers of Cinqueux and Mont-Chauvet, when one comes upon a confession which seems to justify those who detected calculation on his part, in short, the stage-managing of his transformation from young man into a belligerent old bourgeois: "It's not very hard being marvellous at twenty, the difficult thing is being prepared to learn from life's experiences and to draw on them when her first gifts are taken from us." In short, we are left uncertain and in the dark. The issues are clouded since they are all equally likely and plausible. Thus there is no way, I believe, to come to any conclusions. One is confronted with a genuine enigma, almost as fascinating as that of Malraux (and basically of a similar nature), when he announced at the end of the war that he had joined the Gaullist cause.

I shall return to Malraux, as I shall also return in some detail to the mystery of the multi-faceted nature of certain intellectuals and to the even greater mystery of the facets which posterity fixes upon. Which is the true face of a writer? Which one is remembered? How is it that everything is resolved and frozen in one particular face? How is it that in the case of Malraux, for instance, neither the Gaullist, nor the minister, nor the poor old demonstrator stuck between Michel Debré and Maurice Schumann in that well-known photo have obliterated the much older image of him as a young adventurer with his fist raised? How is it that even on the day he died, when the collective memory made its first selection, it was that image which carried the day over all the others and which was displayed, as if by magic, on the front page of every newspaper and magazine? Basically, there are two issues. One concerns the shift from one face to another. The other has to do with the choice made between the two faces by those who live on. But it was the author of *Bastions de l'Est* who had the honour, albeit unwittingly, of being the one to raise these two issues for us in the first place, as well as a third issue. The terms of this third issue can be appropriately applied to the case of Drieu La Rochelle and may be stated as follows: how is it that a writer who has betrayed himself, denied what he stood for, and, not content with that, has countenanced the utmost villainy, how can he continue to enjoy part of his former prestige with those who are in the opposing camp? In Drieu's case, it raises the puzzle of the loyalty shown by Nizan and Benda before the war and of that shown by Malraux and D'Astier de la Vigerie during his last moments and beyond. In Barrès's case, it is the puzzle of a following which, as I've said, embraced all shades of political and literary opinion.

Barrès–Malraux. Barrès–Drieu. The adventurer who became a public figure and the fascist who, despite his fascism, continued to enjoy a flattering, paradoxical, and contradictory following. It is all very strange, and these recurrences are disconcerting. But I must make it clear that I don't subscribe to the notion of providence affecting the course of history, and nothing is more alien to me than the idea of some invisible hand guiding everything towards its predestined future. Yet with the sense of *déjà-vu* that I have, and confronted by such coincidences and the impression of events and fate repeating themselves, it is difficult for me to discount completely the idea, not of inevitability, but of some sort of regular pulse at work. For that is what appears to give shape to this whole story, to distribute the major roles, and to assign to some the formidable privilege of being the incarnation for all time of certain great choices of the human Mind. Imagine a piece of Commedia dell'arte and within it a finite range of stances, poses and gestures. Then imagine that it falls to some individuals to try out – in the language of the theatre to "rehearse" or "create" – certain roles which others will subsequently take up, reinterpret, and eventually perfect either through their clowning or their seriousness. This is, of course, an image, something fictitious. At the present moment, however, as I deal with the case of Barrès, it fits best with my notion of the "adventures" I am describing.

NOTES

1. The joint pseudonym of Henri Massis and Alfred de Tarde who published enquiries into the attitudes of young people in 1911 and 1912.

2. A revolutionary and anarchist who was guillotined in 1892.

3. Both these nineteenth-century writers kept diaries.

4. A body formed in 1899 during the Dreyfus Affair which expressed anti-semitic and reactionary views.

5. See Note 3, page 30.

6

"That included even Jaurès"

AN ANSWER TO THE QUESTION: WHAT IS LEFT-WING ANTI-SEMITISM?

Strictly speaking, Jaurès is not what I'd call an intellectual. On the other hand, he was a major symbol of the humanist and liberal left. The Dreyfus Affair both served as a pretext and was the occasion for an astonishing groundswell of anti-semitic fervour, but I wouldn't wish to leave that subject without making clear that the groundswell was not limited to one section only of the French population. It was not to be found exclusively in the châteaux, amongst the hunting fraternity, the bishops, in the newspaper *La Croix*, and the Academy; that's to say on the conservative right. It undeniably contaminated the other side as well. Jaurès's text, for instance, dates from 1895. It was part of an article written after an anti-semitic demonstration in Algeria and was published in *La Dépêche de Toulouse*. It was subsequently quoted in *Le Dix-neuvième siècle à travers les âges* by Philippe Muray. These were Jaurès's precise words: "Under the rather restrictive guise of anti-semitism a truly revolutionary spirit was spreading in Algeria." He went on: "Why isn't there a serious anti-semitic movement in Algeria, since the Jews are practising their methods of appropriation and extortion on the Arabs?" Doesn't it seem unbelievable, unthinkable, coming as it does from the pen of the representative par excellence of democratic humanism? It certainly is unimaginable, unless one remembers that ways of reading texts have changed over a century and that frenzied anti-semitism, a strange passion which some would like to think was confined to neo-fascist circles, had solid roots in other areas at the time.

Whilst considering the subject from this angle, one ought to mention – and never cease mentioning – the seminal texts of Marx in which he identifies Judaism with capital and usury. There are also the texts by our own national socialist, Auguste Blanqui, in which he justified his mistrust of parliamentary and bourgeois democracy on the grounds that it might lead to "the permanent establishment of the Rothschilds" and "the accession of the Jews". The texts of Toussenel, who was also a socialist, a disciple of Fourier,[1] and the author of a cult book – yes forty years later it became a cult book in progressive Parisian circles – under the rather suggestive title, *Juifs, rois de la République*, set out principally to demonstrate that the "Jew" possessed at that time all the privileges which were formerly "the prerogative of royalty", and that "their brazen money-making" could and would "only be achieved by ruining the people". Finally, among the major precursors, one ought also to mention Proudhon who could write: "Hatred of the Jew, as of the Englishman, must be an article of our political faith" and "The task in hand: that which the people of the Middle Ages hated instinctively, I hate studiedly and irrevocably." He also went on to say: "The Jew is the enemy of the human race; he must be sent back to Asia or exterminated." And again, "By the sword, by assimilation, or by expulsion the Jew must be made to disappear; only old men incapable of begetting children can be tolerated."

For our purposes, the outcome was certainly very clear. When, in 1886, Drumont published his book *France juive*, it was hailed by the Left and well received in the *Revue socialiste*. It was discussed and criticised in certain revolutionary circles, but accepted as a work of reference that raised essential questions. So much so that when the author introduced himself as an "enfant terrible" of the revolutionary fraternity, when he claimed it was obvious he belonged to the socialist Left, and when he recalled that he always joined forces with the Left in the Assembly, no one challenged him on this, quite simply because what he said was right. When, for his part, Barrès went on to the attack, notably in his electoral campaigns, against "the Jewish party", the "servants of high finance", and public servants who "came out of the synagogue", when he attacked "shady German/Hebrew dealers on the Stock Exchange", and when he accused "the filthy yids" of being speculators and driving the country to ruin, he also seemed on the whole closer to the "Left" than to the "reactionaries" and the "Right". What's more, that's how leading lights of the Socialist Party saw him up to the time of the Dreyfus Affair. So that when the Affair erupted, when it was a question of coming or not coming to the aid of a Jewish officer unjustly accused of being in the pay of the Germans, it was quite natural that the "Guesdists", the "Broussists" and other "Possibilists"[2] either turned a deaf ear or lined up quite explicitly behind the anti-Dreyfus banner. Moreover, they did this without having the least sense of going back on what they'd said or of denying their principles. Jaurès was, admittedly, the first to turn. Influenced by Herr, it's said, he led the campaign, and did so splendidly, for the quashing of the verdict. However, it would really be rewriting history if we failed to observe that, in so doing, he did not conform to but denied a culture which, at least as much as that of the conservatives, was steeped in infamy.

For the truth – in general terms and in this case fundamentally – is that anti-semitism in France has never had a simple or constant set of expressions. It has changed them, just as it has had to change its ways of justifying itself. The professed anti-semite has for centuries been asking himself how to be an anti-semite. Why? In the name of what and of whom? What can possibly justify and therefore reinforce this extraordinary hatred? And where does one find the words with which to convince the crowds who would feel more at ease if they were given solid reasons for their hatred? There was a time when it was enough to say: "The Jews are to be hated because they killed Christ," and Christian people took up this easy refrain as if with a single voice and with joy in their hearts. At another period, the trend was reversed and the idea turned inside out: "If the Jews are to be condemned, it's not because they killed Christ but because they invented him." That was what Voltaire, d'Holbach, and the Encyclo-paedists thought, and the anti-semitism of these Enlightenment figures was anti-clerical and anti-Christian, just as their concern was to get rid of priests, eliminate religions, and thus eradicate their Judaic roots. There was a third and much later phase when suddenly what one was expected to say was: "If it is right to detest these people, if it is acceptable to kill them, it's because they are an 'impure race' and this impurity clearly hinders the 'regeneration of Europe'." This was the new and differently argued version of anti-semitism produced by "scientific" racists and "doctrinaire" Nazis. At the time of the Affair, a different line of argument held sway. What it shared with those just outlined was the desire to establish a kind of hatred which was most effective when it seemed to be inspired by a concern for purity, indeed for justice and good. "No", declare the anti-semites, "the Jews are not hateful by nature; yes, we would be ready, if necessary, to like them; but you are only too well aware that they are unrivalled in their enslavement of the humble and their willingness to starve the poor, and because these humble folk inspire love and compassion in us and because it is our duty to defend them, we have to fight against the 'Jewish bank' and get rid of it." This represents then a fourth kind of anti-semitism: anti-capitalist, social, "progressive" even. It's the kind from which Jaurès managed to escape but of which the Left, I fear, remained a prisoner for a long time.

What about anti-semitism today? I don't believe I'm mistaken in suggesting that yet another version is perhaps in the process of

83

developing before our very eyes, though we may be unaware of it. Unless, that is, one imagines a world freed for the first time from this scourge and dreams of a planet restored to peace and reason or considers anti-semitism a childhood sickness of which the world might be cured. Alas, these are hypotheses which are incompatible with what we know of the deep-rooted nature of a hatred which extends beyond bodies and souls and targets the claim of Jewish law to govern the affairs of the Jewish race and to direct its ways of thinking. This is certainly not the place to discuss these issues, all the more so since it would take us beyond the limits for even a subjective historical account of intellectuals. Yet I find it difficult to resist the temptation to extrapolate what I've just said about the birth – the persistence? – of a firmly entrenched left-wing anti-semitism. The fact that we are almost at the end of another century offers too many pretexts – occasions? – for such an extrapolation for me to shy away from it.

Think of the Jewish people being restored to the land of their collective memory. Think then of another people which, rightly or wrongly, considers itself an injured party on account of their return. Think how our own socialists, the heirs, though perhaps also the critics, of Marx, Blanqui and Proudhon, would be inclined to side with that proletarian people. Imagine what they might say: "We are not anti-semitic, we have nothing against the Jews as such, but we feel obliged to point out that yet again they are causing suffering amongst the poor and the humble. It is therefore on behalf of their just struggle against oppression and the oppressors that we are forced – justifiably – to fight against them." There was precisely the same campaign of "social" anti-semitism at the time of the Dreyfus Affair. It was similarly motivated and used the same arguments. The same wrongs were committed in the name of right, the same hatred was shown in the name of love. The only difference is that the Palestinian people have become martyrs in place of poor Frenchmen who, according to Drumont, were crushed by "Jewish financiers", and that Israel has replaced the Rothschilds as the persecutor. If there is to be anti-semitism in the future, serious anti-semitism capable of rousing great masses, then it will be anti-Zionist or nothing at all.

NOTES

1. The founder of a doctrine of economic and social reform.

2. The supporters of the socialists Jules Guesde and Paul Brousse as well as those of the moderate workers' movement.

7

". . . almost reduced the country to open warfare"

THE VOICE OF FRANÇOIS MAURIAC

Here is Mauriac in the fifties calling to mind the Dreyfus Affair.

Mauriac had a croaking, husky voice and spoke in a conniving and sibilant whisper, which reminded one of the wheezing and wheedling voice of a priest in the confessional. It was a suffering and exhausted voice, toneless, colourless, and of unvaried pitch. But it had triumphed over pain and was, one felt, secretly exultant. In fact, I've got two hypotheses about Mauriac's damaged voice. He had, of course, suffered from cancer and received radiation treatment. One of his vocal chords had also been removed which, until then, had given him a lilting intonation. But one can't explain in purely physiological terms one of the most remarkable voices in French literature.

To my first hypothesis then. As a writer, Mauriac had most serious, scandalous, and provocative things to say. He was aware that his books were heretical and poisonous, to say nothing of the subsequent stances he adopted. He also knew his own people too well, the feelings, fears and reactions of the right-minded who read him, to be unaware that they would forgive neither the pessimism of *Le Noeud de vipères* nor the insolent audacity of the support he was about to give to communists in Spain. Then, sensibly, he changed his tune, as if he were relying on his body – or to be more precise his illness – to tone down his overstated message.

My second hypothesis is the converse of the first. Nothing is more powerful than a voice which sounds worn-out. Nothing carries as effectively as a voice which is muffled. If you want to be heard, if you want above all to have an attentive audience hanging on your every word, there is no better way than to speak in a faint voice which one has to strain to catch. Mauriac knew that of course. Had he been tempted to forget it, he would have remembered just a few days or weeks after the operation, when he entered the French Academy. There he was confronted by a crowd quietly gathered under the dome, intent on hearing every inflexion of his inaugural address. Thereafter, from one platform to another, at meetings and lectures alike, he used his weakness as if it were a powerful megaphone. Thus, the body, instead of acting as a mute, served as an unexpected echo to the soul.

If these hypotheses contradict each other, they do so necessarily, as befits the person concerned.

8

"First, there was Bernard Lazare"

The following anecdote was recounted by Malraux in his *Antimémoires*. Bernard Lazare went to see Gide, just as Blum had gone to see Barrès and the young supporters of Dreyfus went to see various important people whose signature they sought.

Gide greeted him, listened to what he had to say, but was not especially polite as he studied this over-eager young journalist who had come to tell him that there were times and circumstances when a novelist such as he should lay down his pen for the moment and make common cause with humble militants. Did he accept straight away. eagerly and enthusiastically? Or did he weigh up the pros and cons? Did he, as was usually the case, wonder what the great writer Gide would have done in his place? All that is known – and recounted by Malraux – is what happened once the interview had ended and the young hothead had gone. Disturbed and wearied by his words and arguments, Gide reacted as follows: "I'm appalled! I've just met a man who values something more highly than literature!"

I like this anecdote because it puts the whole issue in a nutshell. The scene was set, and there they were face to face. On the one hand, the unalloyed writer who would have risked damnation for the sake of a book, a phrase, a word. At any rate, he valued literature above all else (even the defence of an innocent man) and considered it something sacred. Opposite him was someone who was certainly a good writer, who doubtless loved books, and who displayed his talents in avant-garde reviews, where he frequently stated that he too valued the finer points of language. Yet in certain circumstances, confronted by injustice, for example, or the misfortune of an innocent man imprisoned on Devil's Island, language was suddenly of secondary importance to him.

I've devoted pages and pages to the definition of the intellectual and expended enormous amounts of energy attempting to distinguish him notably from the related figure of the writer. Then lo and behold, there it was in all its simplicity. But Gide wasn't always on the side of literature. More frequently, he acted as Lazare suggested he should on that occasion (I'm thinking not only of the manifesto in favour of Dreyfus, but also of the voyage to the Congo and his return from the USSR).[1] Yet the fact remains that in the two views expressed there exists the basis for making the distinction between them. Thus the intellectual can be described as someone who believes in values; or someone who seeks or claims to mediate between the realm of values and the real world; or someone who occasionally stops writing to devote himself in a practical way to mediation. There is a way of saying all that in a single phrase, which is how Gide put it when he expressed amazement that someone should value "something" more highly than literature.

NOTES

1. After a trip to French Equatorial Africa, Gide published his *Voyage au Congo* in 1927, adopting a marked anti-colonialist stance. *Retour de l'URSS* (1936) expressed his disillusionment with the Soviet Union.

9

"From his office as Librarian at the Ecole normale"

THE MEDIATORS

What is fascinating, as I've already said, in this account of intellectuals is that their role and function seems to have been defined once and for all. There are and always will be the reformed anarchists like Barrès and Malraux. There are and always will be the "men of conscience" like Zola and Sartre. There is and always will be the just man, one against the rest, resisting the forces of history and its alleged diktats, like Camus and Julien Benda. In a word, it's like a comedy which, instead of Columbine, Harlequin and Pantaloon, would have a set number of stock figures that had been defined and distributed even before specific individuals came along to embody them. There is, however, one role within the whole range which also seems to have been permanently fixed, though it is scarcely ever given much consideration and those who take it on are for the most part unknown. Yet it is an essential role and can be defined in different ways: escort, link man, facilitator, or mediator.

What exactly are mediators? They are those intellectuals who, though they fit the original definition and believe in values, universality, and mediation, consider, unlike Claude Simon, that it is not only their right but their duty to devote their time on earth to the defence of the said values; but they do so not in their own name but under someone else's banner. They act as advisers, confidants, instigators, prompters of all kinds, professors and publishers. There are a whole number of practical ways of playing the part, but the role itself always remains the same. It always involves choosing influence over power, and the pleasure of expressing one's own anger and passions via someone else's as well as passing off one's own work as theirs. It always involves the same feigned humility, the same desire to stay out of the limelight and to act furtively. It requires silence, but an active silence, unlike that of those masters of silence, Beckett and Michaux, who remained quiet because worldly affairs were insufficiently important to them to interrupt the pleasures of literature. My reason for referring at this juncture to the role these people have played is because it is at the same time a very ancient and a very modern one. Mediators have in fact taken over the role formerly played by the king's confessor, and the first intellectual to have made it his own in modern times was Lucien Herr.

Who was Lucien Herr? He had an Alsatian name – Herr – which in itself raises a number of issues. It was a name which evoked a particular region and thus made him an intermediary between France and Germany, between two intellectual worlds to which his life was devoted. The least one can say about the position he held as librarian at the Ecole normale supérieure in the Rue d'Ulm is that it was an eminently strategic one at the time. From Péguy to Blum and Jaurès, everyone, or almost everyone, was at the Ecole and it proved to be a place where various currents of thought came together and were argued out. In philosophical terms, Herr straddled two different worlds: that of the old French spiritualistic tradition, which came down from Victor Cousin, and that of German philosophy which the university strove to keep at bay. Herr, on the other hand, knew about German philosophy and promoted it, and this resulted in his becoming a gentle but insistent expert on the subject. In the contacts and conversations he had, he would reorientate one person's way of thinking and suggest to another what he might read. "Why don't you have a look at this text of Spinoza? What if you tried that bit of Hegel? Have you read the reports of Zola's trial? Spinoza and Zola were involved in similar struggles. Hegel and Dreyfus are equally relevant to us. Can't you see that everything hangs together and that the same old issues constantly recur?" Herr was the soul of discretion, a veritable saint. Never any show or fuss. He never pushed himself forward or gave the impression that he was doing anything in his own name. It was so much more important to be moulding the minds of the future élite of the Republic, much more essential to shape Jaurès's arguments and to bring him step by step towards support for Dreyfus. Blum, the dandy of the *Revue Blanche* who scarcely knew anything about the world of politics, had his eyes opened by Herr. After the first meeting with his mentor, he said: "It's like having an operation for a cataract," which was both witty and original coming from someone who was himself so short-sighted.

There are other mediators one might also mention; Bernard Groethuysen,[1] for example, whose role was so crucial in the political development of Gide and Malraux. Malraux, there's an oddball novelist for you! An adventurer, too, who was more stimulated by the legend of the Queen of Sheba and by his escapade to Cambodia than by all the theories and niceties of metaphysical speculation put together. Malraux had his intellectual mentors, of course, Lawrence and

Nietzsche, Dostoievsky and Pascal. Then Groethuysen arrived unexpectedly out of nowhere. People weren't sure at first whether he was a Russian, a German or what. He was in fact a total cosmopolitan with a good knowledge of German philosophy – he introduced Kafka to the French. He installed himself in the Rue Sébastien-Bottin,[2] and became a modern Socrates who claimed, too, that his only talent was that of a conversationalist. How did Malraux react to him? "Of all the men I've ever known, he was surely the one who most compelled recognition as an intellectual genius. He's the only oral genius I've ever met and the man I've perhaps admired the most." What was his effect *on* Malraux? He was responsible for his interest in communism, Marxism, revolution, his involvement in the Spanish Civil War, as well as his contact with German émigrés and his friendship with Sperber. Jean Lacouture insisted that, had it not been for Groethuysen – a jovial, placid and learned fellow who spoke with equal authority about *The Brothers Karamazov*, *Das Kapital*, the offensive against Teruel, and a detail of translation in *The Trial* – the author of *La Condition humaine* would be quite unintelligible to us. What was Groethuysen like? Look at Gisors.[3]

Yet another example would be Bernier.[4] No one has heard of Bernier and no one remembers the man who was a key figure at the time of the surrealist movement. He tried his hand at one or two novels and immediately after the First World War was a member of several war veterans' associations which he might have headed. He had charm and charisma, the figure of an athlete, and was attractive to women. There was an easy-going side to his nature allied to a natural authority which might have made him a group leader. But, as always, posterity has provided its own version of events, or, to be more accurate, his role was determined by the vagaries of the literary scene, as is again always the case. Bernier was the man who initiated the contacts between surrealists and communists, welcoming the former as contributors to *Clarté* and pleading their cause to the latter. He was there when they split, there when they came together again. There was no one who could speak as he did of the new figure now emerging, that of the "revolutionary poet". He took part in all the secret meetings and those between top officials. He kept his links with Souvarine[5] and was responsible for the contact with Bataille. Subsequently, he was one of the first to become aware of the existence of a surrealist with an interest in psychiatry, namely Jacques Lacan. One perhaps gets the measure of the man and of the position he occupied when one learns that he was one of the rare friends mentioned in Drieu's will and whose presence he requested at his funeral.

A further example would be that of Kojève,[6] who was apparently better known and had a higher profile. But what exactly was the role of this mediator par excellence? His influence derived from his double life; as a philosopher, of course, and as a rather strange top civil servant, which is what he became after the Second World War. Imagine Cagliostro as a philosopher or the Comte de Saint-Germain as a Hegelian. Or think of one of those Jesuits who so alarmed Michelet because they would worm their way into a family and, in the process of teaching the daughters and dominating the sons, would gain control over their minds. I am, of course, exaggerating and distorting the truth on purpose. But Kojève was somewhat like that; or at least that's how he behaved in part during the second period of his life. There was a certain side to him as if he were thinking: "I make myself at home . . . become one of the family . . . give a few lessons to the children . . . seduce the mistress of the house . . . make use of the chauffeur . . . and they end up by giving me a small allowance . . . but, most important of all, I win the trust of the head of the house and start to shape his ideas." It's true, however, that more is known about the first part of his life. His famous course on Hegel, attended in the thirties by Sartre and Merleau-Ponty, Breton and Bataille, Lacan and Levinas, has been talked of a great deal, especially since Dominique Auffret published her biography of him. He was first and foremost a mediator and that's what he remained. Though his life altered radically in 1945, there was one thing about this enigmatic figure which never changed and that was his desire to achieve something by influencing the way people thought. Kojève was the archetype of the eternal mediator.

NOTES

1. A Marxist philosopher of German-Dutch extraction who had been Professor of Sociology at the University of Berlin and worked for the literary review, the *Nouvelle Revue Française*. Malraux met him in 1928.

2. The address of Gallimard, the publishers of the *Nouvelle Revue Française*.

3. A sage-like figure in Malraux's novel *La Condition humaine*.

4. One of the editors of the independent Marxist review *Clarté*.

5. Born in Kiev, he was a journalist and one of the founders of the French Communist Party. He backed Trotsky against Stalin and was expelled from the Party.

6. A Russian émigré who lectured on philosophy at the Ecole Pratique des Hautes Etudes, 1933–39.

"Others, too, such as Genevoix, but especially Romain Rolland"

CONCERNING AN INJUSTICE, FOLLOWED BY A CONVERSATION WITH ROMAIN GARY

I have the impression that in using the phrase "especially Rolland" I'm not only repeating a well-worn remark but also acting badly. There is no doubt that Romain Rolland was an intellectual who deceived and disgraced himself. He was one of those who most vehemently denied the truth about the tragedy of the Soviet system and exonerated the murderers associated with it. Maurice Genevoix was also an intellectual, but he never lost his way or compromised himself. Nor was he a supporter either of Stalin or Hitler. He was one of those rare writers who avoided any implication in the perversions which have defiled the century in which we live. And yet, of the two, it is about Romain Rolland that I want to say something "especially". As I wanted to include a writer who had echoed the great cry of horror which the French uttered against the First World War, I chose the (mediocre) author of *Au-dessus de la mêlée* rather than the one who wrote *Ceux de 14* (though he was superior from a literary point of view).

I did it without thinking and without sensing in any way that I might be making a mistake. If someone were to ask me why, if I had to explain my reason for choosing images of the one rather than the other for this particular sequence, I would be inclined to reply that the work itself necessitated the choice of individuals one would be likely to come across again. With that aim in mind, Rolland suited my purposes better than Genevoix. Rolland was a Stalinist whose life was inextricably bound up with all the upheavals of the day, even the blackest and most horrendous events, whereas Genevoix was a reasonable and moderate democrat who had none of the excessive enthusiasms which make for an interesting biography. But the plain fact is I've committed a grave injustice. In making my choice, I was aware that a writer's glaring mistakes had a retroactive effect, imbuing his past with a certain relief and colour and conferring on him an apparent destiny.

One comes across the same thing over and over again. Consider, for example, the inspired errors of Sartre as opposed to the totally boring reasonableness of Aron, or the panache of Aragon in contrast with the sententious logic of Julien Benda. Look at Barrès and Zola, or take the case of Camus, a mere philosopher for sixth-formers, and compare him with Céline who achieved considerable fame. France is a funny country, where one achieves renown by straying from the straight and narrow, adds to one's mythology by being associated with evil, and enhances one's stature by indulging in minor betrayal. Infamy is rewarded, just as an act of treachery opens the doors to the Panthéon. This explains why everyone always says "Genevoix and especially Rolland" and why, in terms of literary classification, certain writers are gradually forgotten. For example, Genevoix has been confined to the rather dull backwater of "regionalist writers". One should, however, bear in mind from the outset that history is always written from a certain standpoint.

ROMAIN GARY

In 1977, I had a conversation with a writer I liked, called Romain Gary, about ways of writing history. We met in his flat in the Rue du Bac. It was very bright, as if flooded with light, and the bronze supports of his bookcases, which he claimed had been sculpted by Giacometti, appeared to hold up the walls and the ceiling. For once, we talked about politics, as well as literature and all sorts of other things, including life, women, the make of his cigars and hats, his wife, their son and his allowance (which was too big), and the nanny and her wages (which he had to increase). It's amazing how much Gary liked talking about money, and how his voice changed when he did so, becoming suddenly distant and a touch vulgar as he adopted a nasal intonation! But finally we got round to talking about literature. He wanted to show – to show me – that he had views and theories about it. Malraux wasn't the only one who enjoyed expounding his ideas about things. Heavens no! Gary did too. He was more than just an ex-consul and the former husband of Jean Seberg, which was the way I was inclined to think of him whenever we met. To start with, our conversation revolved around the wrong done to him by those who, like me, saw him only in terms of those unhelpful and narrow biographical details. There was a particular pathos about this since it is now known that he had embarked on a crazy adventure. "Here, have a look at this . . . Yes, it's *Pour Sganarelle* . . . You don't know it ... But it's my best book ... My *Noyers de L'Altenburg*[1] ... It's different from that new criticism stuff your friends write, you'll see." And in a shaky hand, which seemed out of character, he wrote the following strange dedication I find moving every time I read it: "To B.H.L. A brief survey of literature against authority. For a culture free from ultimate goals – and since our paths have re-crossed, fraternally."

Our conversation lasted half an hour to an hour, but my memory is of having participated in a dialogue of the deaf. My sole wish was to get him to talk once more about Los Angeles, his mother, the RAF, actresses, *La Promesse de l'aube*[2] and "Les Compagnons",[3] in short the somewhat glitzy legend which interested me above all else. He wanted to impress me, or simply gain my interest, by explaining the errors Sartre had made, the stupidity of St Exupéry, the difference between nationalism and patriotism, the total idiocy of engaged literature, Lukács, Lucien Goldmann, and his own liking for picaresque narratives. What I remember especially is that he suddenly fell into a gloomy silence and adopted a sulky and defeated air, without my having said a word or objected to what he had said. (Why should I have objected, as what he told me was neither true nor false, interesting or boring. It simply had very little to do with literature as I understood it from my reading of *Le Degré zéro de l'écriture*[4] or the review *Tel Quel*[5]). It was as if he'd come to realise that there was nothing to defend, no one to convince, that no one would read *Pour Sganarelle*, certainly not me, and that, irrespective of Sganarelle, we had entered upon a new "ice age" (another of his themes). No one would be read and books would just pile up unopened. He concluded by saying: "The only thing that counts is whether or not one is quoted, and I'm one of the truly damned who isn't." I must have appeared somewhat at a loss for words, as he went on: "Perhaps you think that what matters is being good or high-powered, having something to say or writing because one has nothing to say; that's a joke! The only true distinction is between those who are quoted and those who aren't. Take my own case, I can say what I like, write something really good, dazzle your 'Trissotins'[6] at the Ecole normale supérieure, yet no one ever takes any notice of me. You never see anyone write: Gary says this ... Gary thinks that ... according to Gary ... People plagiarise me, pinch bits from what I've written. I constantly have the nasty feeling I'm being robbed. But will anyone quote me? Oh no! That would be impossible. The person who borrowed something from me and went on to say that Gary had said this or that would look a total idiot."

Poor old Gary! He had such a high opinion of himself. He would have renounced there and then his fame, his hats, his cigars, his memories of Jean Seberg and Dolores del Rio, his war service, his heroism, the duels he had fought with pistols, not to mention the unwarranted admiration of those very things by young people such as me. All he sought in return was a tribute, a mention, a footnote even, in one of those learned studies which were proliferating at the time around new criticism. Though occasionally pedantic they were very topical, and he was greatly impressed by them. He referred to them as "those structuralist books of yours," with a bogus air of disdain that betrayed his disappointment. I genuinely don't know whether *Pour Sganarelle* deserved better than the indifference with which it was greeted when it first appeared and which has dogged it ever since. But on the basic issue, on the mystery as to why a writer is or is not worthy of being taken up, discussed, referred to (Gary's word was "quoted"), how right he was! There are the writers one chooses, from whom one borrows a theme, a concept, a turn of phrase, and one says so. One eagerly admits it, because one feels that, far from weakening one's argument, the quotation will lend it greater legitimacy. There are also those one draws on from time to time or borrows from a lot without mentioning the fact. One takes care not to and even denies it. Whatever one owes them, however much one is in their debt, merely to admit it, to write or mention their name would mar one's whole argument and give it a hint of frivolity. Lastly, there is the rather pathetic but important case of those to whom nothing is owed and no one need refer, yet who are mentioned quite gratuitously. But the fact that they are cited isn't wholly gratuitous, as one detects an advantage to be gained by using their name in support of an argument they didn't inspire. The whole piece will somehow be miraculously enhanced. It is not a question of honesty or dishonesty, nor is the practice itself unjust. It's quite simply the way things are, a law. Moreover, it's a law which governs who will be talked about, and which therefore determines a writer's destiny, as Gary was only too well aware.

Though I have to admit we've lost sight of the distinction between Genevoix and Rolland, we have moved on to a subject which interests and concerns me just as much, as you have doubtless become aware. What is it that causes works of literature to disappear from view? Look around you and have a go yourself. Pick a name at random and do as Gary asked me to. Just write down: "As so and so says", "as so and so thinks", "to judge from X's argument", "as Y has shown". You will see how the phrase takes shape, how it encompasses or embraces a name, surrounds it like a precious stone. Or you will see it retract and resist, you will observe how that wretched name unravels or dissolves the sentence, how it literally stops it from being formed or written. Stendhal claimed that introducing a real person into a work of fiction made it totally unreal. Well, a name can have the same effect. It can be like one of those viruses which wipe out computer programmes. What then distinguishes one set of names from another, the good from the bad? What makes one name comforting and reassuring, an utterly safe bet, which will always look good though it may not carry much weight? Why, on the other hand, are some names thought less well of, considered disreputable? Why are they avoided? It's not that they are forbidden or scandalous (scandal wouldn't matter too much), but rather that they are totally unsuitable; names that can be neither mentioned nor written down. That is the crux of the whole matter. But sadly I'm no more capable of resolving it than Gary. What is not in dispute is that the problem exists, that distinctions are made between writers, and that intellectual life is shaped as much by this as by great quarrels. And in the final analysis, it determines whether books survive or not. That's what I learnt from Gary that day.

Each time I think of this law, each time I come across a case either close at hand or at some remove, I am reminded of Gary with his overlong hair, his moustache like that of an old Mongol, and the curious gait of a "tonton macoute" looking for trouble. I think of his bitterness, his sadness, and the weary look he had. Nothing seemed to take his mind off it, and certainly not the fame he'd achieved which he blamed for the mess he was in. Nothing distracted him, not even the pleasures of life. Moreover, if one pointed to the fact that he had produced a body of work which was of value, whether or not he was "quoted", and that God would recognise his own, he couldn't accept it. He would imply that writers couldn't rely on God and that providence played no part in literature. There would not even be a judgment day for those who had been found wanting in their earthly life. Everything was determined in the cruel lottery of names and quotations. In any case, why should he care? Was he expecting some reward or advantage? One might as well suggest he was looking for honour and respect. Being in their papers was like being in the great book of the dead . . . one could cease mentioning a name and obliterate it . . . one could register it quite casually in the happy band of the famous who were smiled on by fame and fortune, but who wouldn't be attacked or quoted to again . . . How convenient it was! One could

97

have fame and fortune, but the process of obliteration had already been set in motion, nicely, of course, with flowers and wreaths! There would be no appeal, no second chance. All at once, you and I would cease to exist.

NOTES

1. Malraux's last novel in which he explores the concept of Man.

2. A volume of autobiography published in 1960.

3. A reference to the fact that he was made a "Compagnon de la Libération", a limited and special order established by De Gaulle.

4. Roland Barthes's influential study of the nature of literary language.

5. A literary review which first appeared in 1960 in which several of the "new novelists" published extracts of their work in progress.

6. A pretentious poet and wit ridiculed by Molière in *Les Femmes savantes*.

"Horrified by the killing"

ALAIN AND HIS DISCIPLES

I'm thinking here of Alain, of Emile-Auguste Chartier, who was better known as Alain and whose authority as a legendary teacher in "khâgne"[1] dated precisely from the time of the Dreyfus Affair. If ever there was an intellectual leader, it was him. He was also an educator, a seeker-out of minds, a spiritual guide, a shaper of ideals, as well as being the indefatigable author of countless remarks, maxims, and other sorts of aphorism. The list of those who were influenced by his books and lectures either at the time or in the years that followed would indeed be endless.

Alain went to great lengths to defend freedom and the individual, and he was equally vigorous in his criticism of the herd instinct. He was also a man who praised modesty and restraint. A whole series of words and values – good sense, temperance, etc. – which recurred frequently both in his speech and in his articles perhaps make one smile when one reflects on them today. Yet there are less outmoded, bolder concepts as well, such as his view that fervour, enthusiasm and ideals were dangerous in politics, or that the duty of a politician was not to rouse the passions of the people but rather to help to cool them. He also thought that politics itself was a form of religion, with its superstitions, its mysteries, its emotional charge, and that the job of any sensible man was to deritualise it.

In fact everything about his thought makes it appealing and valuable to me – to us. One could say that the *Propos* represented some of the most effective writing of the period, to the extent that it discredited totalitarian ideology of all kinds and undermined its prestige. Yet you have to be on your guard, as things are never as simple as they seem. Indeed, Alain's thought might be construed as having encouraged resignation in the face of those very ideologies. You have only to read *Mars ou la guerre jugée* or the opening pages of *Citoyen contre les pouvoirs* to realise that they provide a justification for the most radical form of pacifism. In addition, you might look again at his critique of power, of all forms of political power and ask yourself how, on the basis of such a critique, it would be in any way possible to draw a distinction between a totalitarian power and one that was not.

Some of his disciples tried to do just this when the moment came in 1940, but they only entered the Resistance (I'm thinking here of Canguilhem) once they had broken with their mentor. Others remained faithful to him, but at the cost of rallying to the cause of Pétainism (Claude Jamet, for example). Obviously, neither one side nor the other offered a judgment on Alain's thought. Thus, the praise he received from Gracq (who continued to think of him as a "splendid awakener" of people's intelligence) seems to me no more decisive than Jean-Toussaint Desanti's post-war judgment (that Alain was a "teacher of cowardice"). May I simply add a warning to those looking for a new, secular, and democratic culture who might be tempted to find it ready-made in Alain's defence of moderation. One should beware of weak ideas. Paradoxically, they are often imbued with the greatest ambiguity.

NOTES

1. The second-year class for those preparing to take the entrance exam to the Ecole normale supérieure.

12

"Spiritual deserters, European defeatists"

A CONVERSATION WITH PIERRE NAVILLE

Naville had the figure of a young man, a keen eye beneath his bushy eyebrows, and a sardonic smile. He looked something like Fred Astaire dressed in his green-checked woollen jacket. But his tone was vulgar, and at times he became slightly heated, an echo no doubt of his militant past. He laid his cards on the table in a somewhat blasé manner, but he was friendly all the same: "Oh yes, I know what kind of interview this is . . . you'll keep me talking for a couple of hours, and in the end you'll use two minutes' worth . . ." There were shelves everywhere, papers, books inscribed to him by Trotsky, photos of the twenties, all within a surprisingly comfortable flat that seemed at odds with the tough, hard-line militant I'd been expecting. The man sitting opposite me was the last remaining witness of the great surrealist adventure, apart that is from Michel Leiris, whom I'd not yet met. He was the only person still alive who had known Breton in '23, Trotsky in '27, Aragon before he became a communist, and Artaud before *Le Pèse-Nerfs*. It was an emotional moment for me.

Let's talk about surrealism and the moment when you joined the movement. When did you meet Breton?

I met Breton in 1924, or rather at the end of 1923. I was taken to see him by Aragon, whom I'd met at a meeting to do with a journal which was published at the time by a theatre manager whose name I forget. When I met Aragon, he said to me: "I'll take you to see Breton." I'd already read a lot of what he'd published. So he took me, and that's how I got to know him. We quickly became close friends, though he didn't like the way I reacted to literature and various other things.

What, for example?

Oh, I used to make jokes which he didn't think were wholly acceptable. Breton was a curious mixture, you know. He was both serious and ironic. He'd burst out laughing all of a sudden or he'd comment on something in a funny way. And then immediately after, he'd adopt a much more serious attitude. That sometimes created difficulties. For example, when he decided that someone had just said something absolutely fundamental and decisive. He didn't like jokes that were merely superficial, that's all. He wasn't the only person in the surrealist movement to react in that way.

Could one be friends with Breton? He gave the impression of being such a solemn and pontificating character.

One certainly could. I think I was a friend and that we remained friends despite our differences. Actually, I met him in a café two or three weeks before his death. I'd brought some photos of Benjamin Péret[1] for an edition of his works which was being put together. Breton was there with his wife. I believe he was very pleased to see me. He said to me: "You know, Naville, it was strong feelings which were at the root of our disagreements, not moral and intellectual issues. They didn't enter into it." I can give you another example. When he returned from the United States after the war, he came to see me and we talked in a very friendly manner about what was happening and what might happen. Another example would be what he said to me as we stood by Péret's grave: "You know, we have to concern ourselves with him now because he never showed any concern for himself." That's how a committee was formed which also looked after the publication of his works. Breton had organised a meeting of this committee in a café on the Place Saint-Sulpice. Twenty to twenty-five of his friends were there. Breton said: "We must vote on the setting-up of a committee, then appoint four or five people to supervise the publication of Péret's works." He put forward a few names and finally mine. When he asked who was in favour of Naville, just a few put up their hand. There were a lot more, when he asked who was against! At that point, he burst out laughing and said to me: "Things don't change much!"

So you remained a friend of Breton. That wasn't the case with Aragon.

True, but you can't say we exactly had a row. It was simply a matter of going our separate ways. We stopped seeing each other. The last time I talked to him must have been before my trip to Moscow. Yet, believe it or not, it was Aragon who introduced me to Boris Souvarine. I'd already joined the Communist Party, but I'd had no dealings with Souvarine, as he'd been expelled. I'd got to know Alfred Rosmer, Monate, the Syndicalists. Then one day I met Aragon who said to me: "I'm going to see Boris Souvarine, would you like to come with me?" That's how I met Souvarine, with whom I had quite friendly relations for a while. I'm not sure what Aragon found particularly interesting about Souvarine. He just enjoyed meeting people in general.

Do you remember your first meeting with Souvarine?

Yes, quite clearly. I ought to say that during this period, up to 1929 when Trotsky was expelled from the USSR, it was Souvarine who told me a great deal about the Soviet Union. He had, of course, spent several years there and had learnt Russian. He knew several top Soviet officials and opened my eyes about a number of things. When I went to Moscow in 1927, I had in my pocket the proofs of a copy of the *Bulletin communiste* which he published and which he'd asked me to give to dissident comrades in Moscow. It was later on that we disagreed about the political line to adopt. Souvarine thought there was nothing to be done, that one couldn't count on what might happen in the USSR, and certainly not along the lines which Trotsky hoped. On the other hand, I was wedded to the idea that, whatever happened in the USSR or elsewhere, it was important to take a stand on the line adopted and expressed by Trotsky. I didn't meet him or see him again after that, as I didn't much like the direction he followed. It seemed to me that he more or less totally abandoned his original ideas. One mustn't forget that in January 1924 he wrote an article on Lenin's death which ended with this phrase: "To have worked for Lenin is the greatest honour of our lives."

When you met Souvarine, is that how he came across? Did he strike you as the person who had known Lenin, belonged to the Komintern, as someone who had lived and worked in Moscow?

He was a man who had moved in the upper echelons of the Communist International, not so much with the Soviets who were preoccupied with internal affairs of their country, but with those who belonged to the International. However, at a much later date, Trotsky said to me: "Oh, he was small fry. One scarcely ever saw him at the meetings of the Committee, and he didn't say much."

May I return for a moment to what you were saying about Breton? When Breton said to you: basically what separated us was the strong feelings we had about things . . .

Yes . . .

Is that what you think today?

Yes, it's partly true as far as he was concerned, but not so true in my case. He was capable of exploding in great outbursts of emotion – of jealousy, for example. I tried to operate in a more rational way. For instance, he didn't like music. OK, music didn't interest him. He both said so and wrote about it on several occasions. On the other hand, I really loved it, as did Aragon incidentally. He was the only one who would turn up at a café with a musical score under his arm. That created a conflict, an aesthetic conflict, if you like.

When you joined the Communist Party, did you have the impression that you were breaking with your surrealist past, that it was a form of conversion?

Not at all. In the first place, I felt I was doing something which fitted in with the perspectives opened up by the surrealists. You're aware of all the declarations which stated that Marxism was the path we should follow. At the same time, I said to myself that it wouldn't stop me from enjoying works of surrealism. Whilst I was a member of the Party and subject to the disciplines of a political organisation, I could continue to enjoy surrealist works.

In fact, you were the first to take the decision to join.

Perhaps I was in terms of the actual date, but Péret, Breton and Aragon all made a symbolic gesture of joining. They then withdrew again quite quickly, except for Aragon who stayed. I joined the Communist Party not as a surrealist, of course, but as a militant who was committed one hundred per cent. I changed my life, my life-style completely. But as I've already said, it didn't prevent me from enjoying the poems of Eluard and Péret, for example. Even today, I have to admit, my greatest moments of pleasure are to be had reading Lautréamont and the real "luminaries" of the surrealist movement. Personally, I've never felt that it conflicted with strongly held political convictions.

That's not the view everyone took!

It's one of the reasons I quarrelled with Breton as well as with various Trotskyist groups. I had enemies who told Trotsky: "Naville used to run *La Révolution surréaliste*. What's that got to do with our ideas!" Once or twice Trotsky asked me what my thoughts were on the subject. We were in the dinghy he went fishing in and we exchanged odd scraps of conversation. Then all of a sudden he said to me, in the nicest possible way: "What's the surrealist movement all about?" I said: "Listen, you won't get me on to that subject again. It's not worth it, and anyway I don't want to talk about it at the moment." Then he said: "At least say something about the pictures, tell me what they mean!" So I replied: "We're not even going to discuss painting; it's better that way, it's better that way." In fact, we never spoke of it again. But he didn't reproach me for that.

I'd like to discuss briefly your quarrel with Breton.

Alright, I'll tell you about it. First of all, we'd had rather general discussions about the need to join the Communist Party and become militants. Then at a certain point, together with Marcel Fourrier, we published articles about the principles of surrealism in the review *Clarté*. I wanted to show that my militant activity within the Communist Party in no way implied hostility towards surrealist activities. So I published articles by Eluard and Aragon. Two pieces by Aragon, entitled "Le prix de l'esprit", were quite remarkable. There were also articles by Leiris, Desnos and Péret. That annoyed Breton who thought to himself: "Naville is going to pinch all these people and get them into the communist movement. We'd better see what it's all about." Then one day there was a gathering at the villa where Péret lived. The conversation was fairly random, until Breton suddenly said: "I don't understand what you're doing in *Clarté*. Why have you published that article on Brest-Litovsk by Victor Serge? It's intolerable!" I replied: "It's an article which Victor Serge himself sent me and which reveals the truth about that particular episode in the Russian Revolution and about the end of the war. It's very important, and I felt we had to publish it." "It's scandalous, it won't do," Breton retorted. Then, to everyone else who was there, he said: "I think you know what I mean." At that point, I exploded: "I understand very well what you mean. To hell with you! I'm off!" I left the room, and we didn't see each other again for ten years. That's precisely what happened. He hoped I wouldn't get over that incident. But I did.

You didn't see each other again?

Yes, we did. One day, our political organisation was holding a small meeting in a café, and I saw Breton walk in with some chap, a friend of his whom I didn't know. They sat down almost in front of me in the front row of the audience. One of my comrades spoke first, and then I gave my spiel. At the end of the meeting we put forward a resolution, and I asked who was in favour. Almost everyone put up their hand. I asked who was against. One hand, one finger went up. It was Breton. He didn't say a word. That was it, and he left. Funny little scenes like that show you what relations with Breton could sometimes be like. Why did he come to that meeting to see me? Perhaps he thought it would upset me. He was, of course, greatly mistaken.

Listening to you, one certainly has the impression that relations were very emotional, but that they also had something to do with power. Did problems arise when one tried to take power from him?

His idea of power was always tinged with emotion. It wasn't power as such, since there was no organisation. What he really wanted was cultural or aesthetic domination. He was obsessed with betrayal. He kept a close eye on everyone. He didn't want it to be possible for someone to leave, saying: "I'm fed up with Breton. It's stupid. Surrealism is a lot of nonsense." That's how I see things. It's not a simple question of power. That's meaningless, because there wasn't any organisation, no statutes in the surrealist movement.

What about Bataille? The least one can say about their relationship was that it was quarrelsome. Wasn't there a problem of power in their case? Didn't Breton himself fear Bataille's influence as well as that which he had over his former friends? When Bataille took the initiative over the second "Cadavre",[2] the one against Breton, wasn't Breton worried that things were slipping from his grasp?

He thought that Bataille's ideas were indecisive, therefore dangerous; that he had no real convictions. That's what jarred with him. Breton's convictions certainly changed, and sometimes radically, but they were still convictions and they retained an emotional charge. He considered that if he adopted a position at a given moment, he should follow it through to its logical conclusion. Whereas Bataille was totally different. If he had an idea he thought: "I might have a different one in three or six months time." Breton disliked that. He said to himself: "We'll see where a brief attempt at understanding with Bataille's group will lead us. But if he takes a negative line where surrealist ideas are concerned, I won't go along with it." That's what Breton thought.

Let me change the subject. Something that has always seemed strange to me is the presence of Drieu La Rochelle in the earliest surrealist gatherings. At the time of the Anatole France affair, the Barrès trial, etc. . . .

What do you mean? We got the impression early on that Drieu was quite close to us. I remember reading his first two slim volumes of verse on the '14–'18 war. He was a young man who'd been directly involved in the war, had got out, and was against it. It disgusted him. The poems in no way glorify what happened, as opposed to those of Apollinaire, for example, (which is one of the paradoxes of the avant-garde milieu of the period, by the way). I'd read those two collections of Drieu, published by the NRF, and I'd greatly enjoyed them. Then with his friend – whose name I forget – he produced a journal . . .

Berl?

Berl, that's it. Berl said to him: "You ought to speak to those chaps, to Breton and Aragon, and to the younger ones, like Desnos, you really should." So he sometimes came to the café. But not often! Not often! He was always in an indecisive rather than a critical frame of mind. He never offered any criticism. He didn't know what to do.

He wanted to write, of course. I didn't much care for his novels. I had ... Let's just say I had insulted him in a pamphlet in '27. One day I met him in the street, having forgotten what I'd said about him. He suddenly stopped and said to me: "Hey, you dragged my name in the mud." So I replied: "What did you expect, that's what polemics are all about."

And Breton, how did he view him? Did he respect him?

I don't know. I don't think so. He was a bit distant. Breton needed to have very close, very special friends and acquaintances. It would be difficult to say what the criteria were which led him to establish a new relationship. People sometimes disappointed him, and Drieu was a disappointment.

To finish with, can you say a word or two about Artaud?

Listen, Antonin Artaud was someone who had pushed his exploration of physical unease to limits hitherto unknown and then tried to give expression to those feelings of uncertainty in his writing and in the way he spoke. When I first got to know him, that's to say when he had just arrived from Marseilles, his violent and brutal way of rejecting all fashionable ideas greatly appealed to me. He attended surrealist meetings we held and would thump the table with his fist, saying: "Bravo, that's just what we need! We'll shake these people up a bit!" And that's exactly what he started to do. Breton was somewhat horrified. The famous letters that had been sent to the leading authorities of various institutions were published,[3] which didn't please everyone. Oh no! Not all the surrealists were happy about it. Even Breton was beginning to be a little alarmed. My view, however, was that it was a form of revolt which should be taken as far as possible. But then Artaud started to write things against some of the more "dogmatic" tenets of surrealism and a quarrel was inevitable. In the end, I stopped seeing him. I met him once after the war in Adrienne Monnier's boutique. That's when I realised he wasn't as sick or as mad as people made out. He was discussing publishing matters with two people in a very technical way. He'd always been like that. He wasn't an amateur writer. Oh no! He corrected his texts with great care, including those written in a language that suggested madness. I believe Artaud was one of the rare surrealists to extend the bounds of his mental and physical experience as far as he could. He'd never retrace his steps.

One last thing. How could one be close to Breton, to Artaud and people like that and at the same time remain close to Gide? Because that's what you did, isn't it?

Gide is a totally different story. I got to know him when I was very young because my father knew him and had been at the Ecole Alsacienne with him. They kept in touch with each other and that involved the whole family. My father collected Gide's works and corresponded with him. He met him from time to time and talked to us about him. I have a memory – I was fourteen at the time – of my father reading aloud to us a text by Gide with such enthusiasm that I thought to myself: "Does my father write things like this?" This is simply to say that, from a literary point of view, my youth began with this association with Gide's work and things related to it. My father sent him letters which I wrote about his novels. He sometimes came to look at paintings I'd done as well. Subsequently, at the time of the surrealist movement, I had somehow to break with him, so in 1923 I criticised him in an article in a little review called *L'Oeuf dur*. It was polite. I didn't indulge in crude insults. Anyway, Gide loved people who were critical of him, and especially people he liked.

What were his relations with Breton?

I never heard Breton speak ill of Gide, not once. Gide was of course the one who encouraged Gallimard to publish Eluard's collections of poems and Breton's books too. There was that side to Gide: "One has to give these young people their chance." I remember it very well because I was well in with the Gallimard publishing house and was astonished that they accepted one of Breton's first collections of essays. Well it was Gide who had set things in motion. He introduced Gide to the people at the NRF.

NOTES

1. A poet and founder member of the surrealist group. He joined the Communist Party and then became a Trotskyist.

2. The original "Cadavre" was an extremely insulting pamphlet produced collectively by the surrealists on the death of Anatole France. The second "Cadavre", modelled on the first, was hostile to Breton. It was signed by dissident surrealists and published as a riposte to the "Second Manifesto".

3. Letters addressed to the Rectors of universities, the Pope, the Dalai Lama, those in charge of mental asylums which appeared in *La Révolution Surréaliste* in 1925. They were expressions of revolt and alienation.

13

"The virulence of what they wrote has been forgotten"

THE EXECUTIONERS

There is a certain literary "tone" typical of that will to purity, hatred of thought, and cult of youth which are symptomatic of the totalitarianism we now appear to be outgrowing. The tone itself might perhaps be labelled savage, terroristic or bloodthirsty. One might even evoke anachronistically the image of the Khmer Rouge as a term of comparison. At any rate, it has been virtually the dominant tone adopted by intellectuals in the twentieth century.

One thinks, for example, of the young Nizan. Here's what he was writing at the age of twenty, when he decided to take on "petit bourgeois" France, with its guard dogs and glass-topped walls: "One mustn't be afraid to hate, one mustn't be afraid of being fanatical" and "It's a matter not of simple victory over the enemy, but of destroying them totally; we are no longer living in the age of feudal wars with their God-given truces. This war cannot be expiated," and again "If you discover that your parents or your wife are in the enemy camp, you must drop them."

One thinks also of the mature Sartre. When he was just over fifty, and interestingly in the preface to that book of Nizan's,[1] he himself adopted the tone which his dead friend had used and depicted "the Left" of that period as "a great worm-ridden corpse," childishly observing "this corpse stinks." Subsequently, after meeting Fanon, he was, if anything, more unbridled in his remarks about killing a white man; eliminating a European: "It's a matter of killing two birds with one stone," as one gets rid of "the oppressor and the oppressed" at the same time. After the murder, one was simply left with "a dead man and a free man". Later still, as the editor of two or three papers which grew out of the events of '68 and which had the honour of printing the most overtly barbaric headlines in the history of the French press, he wrote: "Bosses should be locked up ... deputies lynched ... three cheers for the people's war ... three cheers for the extermination of the bourgeoisie." Finally, he was the actual author, never mind contributing a preface or an endorsement, of a text which approved the celebrated Palestinian attack on the Israeli athletes at Munich. This little known text appeared in *La Cause du peuple* of

October 15th, 1972. The vehemence of the language he used again leaves one speechless. As for the content, I repeat, it offers wholesale support for the principle itself of the massacre: "The only weapon the Palestinians have at their disposal is terrorism; it is a terrible weapon, but the poor and oppressed have no other. The French who approved FLN terrorism when it was directed against their own countrymen can only approve, in turn, of the terrorist action of the Palestinians."

One thinks of the earliest writings of Aragon, for instance as co-author of the collective pamphlet *Un Cadavre*, a work of unbelievable violence produced by the surrealists in 1924 on the death of Anatole France. "Have you slapped a dead man's face? I consider any admirer of Anatole France as utterly debased. I have on various occasions dreamed of a rubber which would erase human filth." These were the words of the young Aragon, who wore a black cape and a permanently conspiratorial smile. Some weeks later, intensifying his rage still further, he wrote: "Politicians" [you should be aware that] revolution-aries will expect you to account for every aspect of your life. They will delve into your conscience, fully armed, and will judge you in the clear light of day with the incisive weapon of terror." Then, on April 18th, 1925, in an outburst which was no more dispassionate or con-trolled, he addressed the students of Madrid: "We shall destroy the civilisation that is dear to your hearts and which formed you like fossils in schist; we, the defeatists of Europe, condemn the western world to death. This land is tinder dry and ready to be set ablaze. You may laugh, but we shall always lend the enemy a helping hand."

One thinks of the surrealists in general, the leaders and the led, the major and the minor figures. One thinks of their insults, their anathemas, their lampoons. One thinks of the trials they endlessly set in motion and the chief targets of which were always those closest to them, as terrorist logic required. Read the trial of the "Grand jeu" group, the condemnation of Vailland. Look at the welter of insults in the *Second Manifeste* intended to confound their chosen targets. Delteil was referred to as "vile", Gérard as an "imbecile", Masson a "megalo-maniac", Soupault as the "infamous friend of blackmailing papers", Vitrac as having "the ideas of a slut", Picabia as "rubbish", Artaud as having a "taste for filthy lucre". Read the piece about Artaud in which Thirion evoked the punitive raid led by his former friends on a lecture he was giving. Nor should we forget, whilst we're on the subject of Thirion, his splendidly violent denunciation: "As for that carcass Artaud and that slug Vitrac, may they crawl from dung heap to dung heap." Finally, read the second "Cadavre", which took the old title but this time was used to dispose of Breton. It was a collective pamphlet and perhaps the high-point of the genre. Baron called him a "rotten worm", Desnos referred to him as "a phantom", destined to "rot for ever in the stench of paradise", and Prévert described him as "useless" and "a dupe" and who could only attract "women in labour who were crying out for ugly brutes". As for Bataille, who was to some extent the initiator of the whole thing (and who, by the way, met up with Breton five years later as if nothing had happened in order to found the anti-fascist group "Contre-attaque"), he described his enemy as "a religious old gas-bag" as well as "a soft belly-button and a great hairy animal with a head like a spittoon". He belonged, he concluded, to an unspeakable race which wasn't quite human.

You could go on and on, piling up examples and quotations, working your way through most of the movements which have come to prominence and had some impact this century. But contrary to what one might think, it was not the least significant, the genuinely second-rate who were involved in all this. These frenzied writers, who were supposedly men of letters but expressed themselves like barbarians, were neither the worst nor the most bitter of our predecessors. Moreover, they were certainly not people who had scores to settle either with those who had talent or with a society that might have denied them fame and success, as the anti-intellectual mood of the times would have us believe. One is forced to admit, in other words, that even the greatest (Breton) as well as those most favoured by fame and fortune (Sartre, Aragon) succumbed to the temptation and were quite prepared to adopt a bellicose tone. The way they raised their voices, crushed their opponents, slaughtered those who disagreed with them, and thereby aped the very methods and style which were being created at that moment by totalitarian militants, you might have thought there was an idiom, a certain norm of behaviour. It seemed as if only a handful of "quiet types" were spared from adopting these rituals because they had withdrawn from the public arena, apart, that is, from the inevitable "classics".

There are several possible reactions to this phenomenon, though in my case they tend to merge. First of all, I have to confess that it frightens me. The texts are so harsh; one senses that the desire to kill was so much on their mind, such a tempting possibility, that it would have taken very little for the "rubber which would erase human filth" to become the reality it was at the time in certain dictatorships. Then an irresistible urge to laugh comes over me because it *was* all so unreal, so desperately literary! One realises it's precisely because Aragon didn't have any power at all that he dreamed of his "rubber". There was such an air of childishness surrounding these crazy ideas. Thirdly, the dominant feeling I have is one of incredulity; I was going to say of incomprehension. In one respect, these texts are very close to us and their authors are almost our contemporaries. We ourselves, at least I'm speaking for myself, might have thought and written as Aragon, Nizan or Sartre did, had we been surrealists in 1928, just returned from Aden in '24, or read Fanon in '60. Yet despite the closeness we might feel, there is something which inevitably distances them from us.

When historians of science attempt to date great scientific revolutions – or, to be more precise, the moment when one scientific era gives way to another – they say there is a sure sign. It is to be seen in the fact that the very words and language scientists use, which are like a code or a means of determining things, suddenly appear not just old-fashioned or inadequate (which would at most suggest that the discipline had progressed) but incomprehensible (like a dead language that has only distant links with the one currently in use). Well that's what has happened to intellectuals like us. We are confronted with a revolutionary change of that order. If one needed proof that one era has ended and another begun, to which I referred at the outset, or if one needed some indication that we had irrevocably moved out of the totalitarian era, I would point to a change of language. I would see it in the fact that the language Breton used to insult Bataille, or Bataille used to abuse Breton, or that both used to revile most of their contemporaries, had suddenly become almost a foreign language.

Some people will keep an eye on the popularity of communism and of Marxist studies in the West to make sure that the change is indeed irrevocable, and they will be right to do so. They will make sure that our democratic reflexes are in good order and will watch what happens to Gorbachev, to Havel, Walesa and others [written in 1991]. They will permit me to add that we intellectuals have our own personal monitoring devices. The day it again seems quite natural for a writer to refer to a fellow writer as "rubbish", a "worm", "a phantom, destined to rot for ever in the stench of paradise", the day when insults such as these are heard once more, it will be a sure sign that the counter-revolution is under way.

NOTES

1. Sartre wrote the preface to a new edition of Nizan's essay *Aden Arabie* which was published in 1960. The essay, originally published in 1932 on Nizan's return from a stay in Aden, is a vehement condemnation of bourgeois France.

14

"The ancien régime of the intellect"

FINAL THOUGHTS ON THE SURREALISTS

The surrealists. The surrealists again.

As "executioners", one has to admit they certainly were past masters and models too.

Not that Nizan was a surrealist or Sartre, or the stream of Stalinist and crypto-Stalinist writers who sadly needed no one else to create their own kind of terror. But the surrealists were the first. They initiated it as a way of writing and gave literary authority to a particular verbal style of brutalising and destroying their adversaries. I now want to know why.

I'll ignore the obvious reasons which are always given in histories of surrealism. I'll ignore too the explanation which goes something like this: it was "the war . . . the trenches . . . a generation which had just left the trenches and was filled with an immense hatred against the entire universe". I'll come, therefore, to what seems to me to be the crucial explanation and which has to do with the link they created between literature and politics.

Let's be clear about one thing. The surrealists obviously didn't invent political literature. Before them, there had been Lamartine and the Revolution of '48, Hugo and Napoleon III ("Little Napoleon").[1] Much closer to them in time, the Dreyfus Affair had been a great mobilising force for writers. Thus it wasn't by chance that the first thing the group did when it came into being was to attack Anatole France ("Un Cadavre") and Maurice Barrès (the subject of the famous mock trial held in the "Salle des Sociétés savantes"), that's to say, the two most celebrated representatives of a certain kind of intellectual produced by the Affair. What the surrealists invented was something else – another type or model. There were four aspects of their originality.

1. The Romantics, like the intellectuals who came to prominence as a result of the Affair, were already writers before they became politically active. They had produced a body of work, acquired a reputation, and had in some cases achieved fame, all of which they used in the service

of the cause which they took up. The surrealists, on the other hand, never missed an opportunity of reminding people that they became writers as a result of the impact on them of two things, though it is hard to say which was the more important. The first was the effect of certain books and a particular concept of the mind and culture (that's to say of Dadaism, Lautréamont and Rimbaud as well as the discovery of the unconscious, the significance of dreams and automatic writing). Secondly, there was the strictly contemporary and equally powerful impact of a certain view of politics and of the intellectual's role in relation to it, which was also a crucial factor in their decision to write. In this instance, the influence was Russian or rather Soviet, encouraging those who were still a little sceptical of the October Revolution that it was the moment to foster revolution outside Russia. The absolute necessity was thus to transform man and the world through the medium of poetry.

2. Does this mean that the surrealists were committed or militant poets, that in their eyes literature was inseparable from politics and should therefore carry a political message? Does it mean they were the precursors of "socialist realism", which was to develop ten years later? Heavens no! Certainly not! Because the second original feature of surrealism was that the two concepts (culture and politics) were not only distinct but independent, and heterogeneous into the bargain. The surrealists experienced in a fundamentally different way what they inherited from Lautréamont as opposed to what they inherited from Lenin. Yet they were not in the least perturbed to discover that the two tones of voice were largely at odds with each other. Nor were they bothered by the fact that the sophistication of their poetry, its reputation for nihilism, elitism, and decadence might also seem at odds with the martial aspect of communism, its constructive and militant side. Thus, nothing was pared down or simplified. These young men were guided by a single overriding idea, namely that they were the heirs of two histories, two traditions, each of which had to preserve its own rhythm and develop in its own way, without their trying to bring them together. When, in January 1921, Breton and Aragon first considered taking the step of joining the Communist Party, they went together to the headquarters of the Paris Federation in the Rue de Bretagne. They were received by a large man called Georges Pioch, a journalist by profession. (Incidentally, they invited him three months later to act as a witness in the trial of Barrès). On that day, however,

they were unable to make up their minds and finally withdrew, all because M. Pioch told them more or less that: "Literature is all very fine, but there comes a time when one has to throw in one's lot with the masses, join their struggle, and sweat alongside them." Aragon's reaction was: "We looked at this large man and decided we had no desire to sweat with him," which was his way of saying: we were ready to do anything except renounce the autonomy of literature and thereby accept that one of these histories was subordinate to the other.

3. Does this mean to say that the two histories had nothing, absolutely nothing in common? Did the surrealists lead double lives? Were they schizophrenic? Were their twin preoccupations not only at variance but also developing along different lines? Wasn't it simply that they found themselves in the classic situation of the intellectual who, on the one hand quietly gets on with writing his books in his own little corner and then on the other, when necessary, stops writing and gets involved in politics? No, of course it wasn't! Certainly not! Because they clung to their belief that there was a link between the two. They liked to remind people that they had become writers in part because of the events of October and the Revolution. But they went even further than that. They maintained that their books, pieces of pure literature, which had no connections with explicitly political concerns and which someone like Georges Pioch would never understand, would, in their own way, help to bring about a happier society. So there was a link, but it was a secret or invisible one. It was a postulated, predetermined link which would ultimately bring about a reconciliation between the surrealist revolution and the revolution proper, without one having to worry about it. There is a famous passage in the *Deuxième Manifeste*, in which Breton proclaimed in that half-reasoned, half-inspired manner which he usually adopted when defining points of doctrine: "Everything leads one to believe that a certain state of mind exists in which life and death, real and imaginary, past and future, communicable and incommunicable, high and low, no longer appear contradictory." I myself would add (Breton might have continued): Everything leads one to believe that there is a certain social or mental state in which Aragon and Pioch, surrealism and revolution will also be reconciled. It would be a state in which the most refined and gratuitously sophisticated literature and the need to join the struggle on behalf of rebellious Moroccans or French workers would

no longer appear contradictory. All one had to do was locate it and, having done so, achieve it for oneself.

4. That's all well and good, but the idea is doubtless somewhat naive and a little fanciful. Yet it's almost as plausible as Leibniz's theory concerning monads, which have no contact with each other but which communicate via their "position" – comparable perhaps to a sort of a satellite – which is a form of divine understanding which surpasses them all. However, one might object that it isn't totally clear what made the system a perverse one and its adherents the executioners I've already described. That's what I now want to come on to. Everything would be fine if the system worked. Everything would be for the best in the best of all surrealist worlds if one really could believe in the "satellite", and in that alone, as a means of reconciling ultimately the revolution as Marx (Pioch) understood it and the revolution as seen by Rimbaud (Aragon). But it's impossible to believe in it. Is it due to a lack of self-confidence or the need to provide proof? Is it a flaw associated with the period in which we live or an error of language, something in the air which insinuates itself between the lines? The fact remains, I'm afraid, that there is a point where the two worlds meet and contaminate each other, where the Pioch line and the Breton-Aragon line come together, despite all the efforts made to keep them apart. The point where they meet might be defined in terms of tone and style. In the case of the surrealists, it was the tone or style which made it possible for them to use such terms as "hyena", "rotten worm", "rubber to erase human filth". Nonetheless, I have to admit they were not the exclusive property of Breton and his friends. But one also has to admit that they were being used at a time when, in the real world of totalitarian revolutions, actual machines were being perfected to eliminate human filth in a quite explicit sense. Thus, literature was betrayed and infected. It became inseparable from politics and was, in extremis, hijacked by it. Basically, it was as if surrealist language was nothing more than a transcription of another language that was being invented by the *real* executioners as they went about their business.

The theory that cultural and political revolutions might evolve side by side at the same speed and the belief that writers, fully devoted to their task, are automatically plugged in to the central powerhouse are

both ideas which characterise and define the avant-garde; a phenomenon which goes beyond surrealism itself. One might add to that the
error which certain individuals seem in the end incapable of avoiding,
which consists in aping the most grotesque contortions of the totalitarian "new man". All these things, which contribute to a collection
of principles, avowals and beliefs, as well as to an ultimate blindness,
characterise and define what one thinks of as the avant-garde. What
a term that is! What a confession one makes in using it! For it suggests
that ideas are a form of warfare, that writers are combatants, and that
the best amongst them are manning the frontier posts as part of some
crusade or other. To think that we went along with that, believed in
it, and accepted without the slightest reservation the terrorist implications of the word! I am in no way a believer in a return to the classics
and I would be the last person to decry what was achieved in the field
of the novel in the fifties and sixties which opened our eyes to new
things. Nonetheless, there is about the very term and all that it suggests an aura which is no longer acceptable and which emanated –
emanates still – from surrealist declarations of principle. Have we seen
the last of various avant-gardes? Is the fact that they have recently
been discredited merely an eclipse, a shortlived disappearance from
the scene? One thing is sure. Were the totalitarian mentality by any
chance ever to return, it would use the avant-garde as an extremely
seductive, harmless and banal channel of communication. For that
reason, I myself would be inclined to suggest that what looks like a
demise may not in fact be irreversible. The task in the coming years
will be to aid the emergence of a modern mentality (over which there
can be no giving way), owing nothing to the themes, phraseology and
vacuity of the avant-garde.

FINAL THOUGHTS ON SURREALISM – CONTINUED

Surrealism again. Still surrealism.

I seemed to imply that terrorism had invaded surrealism, almost
by accident, as a result of an unforeseen breakdown of its automatic
mechanisms for achieving harmonisation.

Unfortunately, things are more complicated than that.

The ills go deeper.

All I need to cite as proof of this are the famous trials which were
instigated by our executioners. Of them all, those set up by Breton
were, not surprisingly, the ones which most revealed the combative

mentality of the movement. What then were these trials? Who condemned whom? Why, and in the name of what? When looked at in detail, there are four different headings under which charges were made.

1. The dogmatic errors are, on the whole, the most easily understood. For example, Breton believed in the unconscious and in automatic writing. He believed the novel was a minor genre and that patriotism, in all its forms, was infamous. It is thus conceivable in these circumstances – I say conceivable, which in no way signifies excusable or justifiable – that one might punish, or threaten to punish, those who in the course of their work questioned the validity of these dogmas. That is what happened to Soupault, who was excluded in 1926 for "incompatibility of aims" – what a splendid turn of phrase! The same thing might have happened to Aragon if he had persisted with the writing of *Défense de l'infini*, which was to all intents and purposes forbidden and very close to being fiction.

2. Violation of the code which established what one could or couldn't read was a slightly stranger, not to say more disturbing, category. Breton went so far as to establish an index – he called it an index as the Inquisitors of the Middle Ages had done! – drawing up a long list of forbidden books. Here, chosen at random, are some of the fifty-nine authors listed: Montaigne and Molière, Madame de Staël and Lamartine, Bergson, Claudel and Paul Valéry, François Mauriac, Kipling and Malraux, Balzac and Maurras; not to mention his pet hates – the chief of which was Cocteau. If a surrealist were found to be in possession of a book by one of these authors, or if he were suspected of having any kind of contact with one of them, he would have been expelled from the group without further ado.

3. There was also the crime of having a profession, alongside one's involvement with the surrealists, which was incompatible with the doctrine of the movement. Selling pictures was a compatible activity, working for a newspaper was not. Publishing a book which brought in a little money was again compatible; doing so with a publisher whose moral guarantees were inadequate was incompatible. Having a personal fortune like Leiris or Tual was compatible; being associated

with the theatre and the people in it, as Vitrac and Artaud were, was not. How then was the dividing line drawn? It was drawn according to a certain notion of surrealism, of its ethics and aesthetics, neither of which could be treated lightly.

4. In addition, there were errors of style or, if you prefer, of lifestyle, which related to what one did, who one met, how one spent one's time, and what one's leisure activities were, if one had any. This presented no problem for Breton, as he was always to be found in a café, where he drew up charges against others and laboured over his letters of insult. He didn't have a minute to himself, looking after the wretched Headquarters (yes, it was indeed referred to as the "Headquarters"). But what might others have been caught doing, what shameful activities were they involved in? Pierre Naville, for example, liked music: he was out! Jean Bernier liked sport: he too was out! A third, Bataille, who only went once to the Cyrano, behaved in such a way that it was easy to guess what his personal morality and dubious acquaintances were like: he was out! As for Crevel, a surrealist and a communist, but also a homosexual; how did he fail to realise that there were particular sexual crimes which Headquarters wouldn't tolerate? He realised in the end and didn't give anyone the chance to throw him out.

In other words, surrealism was a way of being, a way of life. One became a surrealist for life. For every action and every moment of one's experience there was a corresponding and appropriate surrealist attitude, thundered Breton. When the surrealists proclaimed: "We are not literary hacks," when they took up Vaché's remark that "art is nonsense" or Breton's that they had "no talent", they were seeking to make a point. When they kept trotting out the line that "Surrealism is not a poetic form" or claimed that one of their number was guilty of pursuing "an absurd literary adventure" they were in fact trying to say that surrealism was a full-time occupation. It was as all-embracing as having an identity – and should not simply be viewed as another literary school or cultural clique. There were surrealist women, surrealist love affairs. There was a surrealist way of dressing, doing one's hair, and expressing oneself. Not a single aspect of one's being could escape the all-seeing eye of surrealism.

Optimists might conclude that it had insanely immoderate

ambitions which went well beyond anything which literature had achieved in the past. And I confess it was difficult for adolescents of my generation not to be impressed by the scope of that overwhelming ambition. In 1966 when I entered "hypokhâgne"[2] at the Lycée Louis-le-Grand, I can remember being with Olivier Cohen on the Boulevard St-Michel or on the Métro, and interminably calling to mind Breton, Eluard, Nusch, Gala, Péret, and even Nadja, who, whether they were real or imaginary, were much more our contemporaries in spirit than Marx or Lenin. What was it we found in them and what overwhelmed us about them? It was precisely the demands they made, the intensity of their existence, the fact that they were fired by their own work. It was their madness too, their sickness, sometimes their death, their suicide, and the risks they had taken, which were so far removed from what subsequently happened in literature. There was also the fact that, in addition to their savoir-vivre, they had passed on to enthusiasts like us a proper way of reading with infallible rules. Though more prosaic, this was no less important for such eager readers as we were. Certain books were of course forbidden, but others had been rehabilitated. Others still were reinterpreted, reinvented almost, as a result of the way Breton made us look at them. It was like a great breath of fresh air sweeping through the library shelves and reclassifying the books in unexpected ways. Our "hypokhâgne" was in fact divided into two camps. On the one hand, there were the kids who read in a scholarly way, that's to say in a random manner. They admired Mauriac and Valéry, the poor fools, because the news hadn't reached them that Swift and Arthur Cravan could be considered fashionable writers. On the other hand there were the really sharp minds, those who read surrealistically, who followed as closely as possible the choices, the bias, and the reading methods of Breton. How we sang the praises of Petrus Borel! What subtlety we showed in suggesting that three pages of Rigaut[3] were worth more than the whole of Drieu La Rochelle! How disdainfully we shrugged our shoulders when people mentioned Cocteau! How self-assured we were in maintaining that only Baudelaire's translation of De Quincy was worth reading or that Lautréamont's *Poésies* were superior to the *Chants de Maldoror*! What I liked about Breton was the way he turned our literary gestures into truly important, almost sacred, acts.

Pessimists, on the contrary, would see in their intensity and in the demands they made a facet – and not the least significant – of that will to purity which, at a later stage, I will show to have been at the very heart of the totalitarian vision. They would take the view

that literature had never had aims like that before and had never set
its sights so high in terms of its ambitions. They would add it never
attempted to penetrate the writer's heart to such a degree, or the
reader's either if that were possible. For them, that represented the
unacceptable obverse of an attractive coin. What, for example, was
the formal difference between an inquisition conducted by Breton and
one conducted by "real" inquisitors, between the ritual trials held at
the Cyrano and other trials, the rumours of which were soon to
spread? Was there any difference, other than one of degree, between
the thought-police methods used on Artaud and Soupault and the
more sophisticated techniques used by large, modern police-states?
Why was it acceptable in one sphere that people should be subjected
to imposed uniformity and forced to believe the same things, whereas
it was considered intolerable if done by real despots? Did the alibi of
literature make it more acceptable to dream of changing man and the
world and in the meantime to keep a close watch on the way people
lived, their sexuality, and the company they kept, when this is precisely
what we condemn in the Khmer Rouge and in Pol Pot?

It will be clear, without my having to endorse all the prejudices
of the pessimist, that I tend to side with the view he takes. At the same
time, it should be remembered there is no justification for confusing
literary, and therefore symbolic, terror, with the effects of real terror,
and that when the Moscow trials occurred, Breton was one of the
very few who opposed the fellow-travellers and refused to accept the
crime being committed. It is not that I have renounced the enthusiasms of my youth. Nor, when I chance upon them in a library, have
I become insensitive to the delights of *Nadja* or to the even greater
charm of a certain poem, the title of which I forget, but which contains
the line "my wife with champagne shoulders". Whenever I say this
line or write it, as I have just done here, it reawakens something of
the emotion which stirred in me in the past when I spoke it at the
top of my voice, articulating its magic syllables, whether or not I was
accompanied by the one who was for me *the* model surrealist woman.
But more than twenty years have elapsed since that period, and there
are more important things than the lingering emotions of youth. One
of these, and of much greater importance, is the huge black cloud of
the totalitarian era which, as I've already said, is beginning to lift
before our very eyes. But, like all periods of absolute rule as they draw
to a close, it is in the process of delivering up its secrets somewhat
haphazardly. In so doing, it illuminates scenes from the past, as if
from behind, in the intense, almost harsh light which it produces. Are

the surrealists more excusable because they are totalitarians who have a certain charm? Is one inclined to be more indulgent towards them because they are, *on the evidence*, more seductive (notably from a literary point of view, which is not insignificant) than most of the "bourgeois writers" whom they intended, in Aragon's words, "to judge in the pure light of terror"? The answer is and *must* be no. One ought really to argue, with sound logic, that they should be even more roundly condemned because their role was the more gratifying. In any case, I cannot easily see how a democratic intellectual at the end of the twentieth century could conclude other than by saying: long live Breton, long live women with champagne shoulders, long live the sublime "peasant of Paris",[4] and long live the no less sublime "Nadja". But at the same time, he ought to say: down with surrealist doctrine and its system of thought – the nightmare of their letters of insult and their thought police.

FURTHER FINAL THOUGHTS ON SURREALISM

Five or six years ago, I returned from a trip to Asia during which I had visited Taipeh, Hong Kong, Seoul, Tokyo. In Peking, I had looked for the last vestiges of the Maoist adventure which had so marked my generation, but which were harder to find than those of the Manchu empire. As I had returned with a book,[5] it was suggested to me that I should do a "Grand Echiquier" programme.

The "Grand Echiquier" was a television programme – the best of its kind at the time – in which singers, musicians, stars of the cinema and show business were invited to appear. The aim was to choose, if possible, a person of some stature with a guaranteed BLC (built-in legend coefficient) proportional to the audience. Around this individual, Rostropovich, for example, or Nono, or Abbado, would be grouped a whole galaxy of people who were supposed to pay the star compliments, take great pleasure in honouring him, if their talent and their presence alone were insufficient. They were the undisputed cream of show business. It was altogether the kind of programme for which I knew in advance I would earn the reproach of that invaluable band of friends of mine who "wished me well".

To appear or not to appear? I thought about it a bit and hesitated. But having weighed things up, I decided to accept. If I did so, it was not, as one might think, as a result of consuming narcissism or because of any liking for the show, the producer of which, Jacques Chancel, was incidentally one of the masters of his craft. Still less did I accept because I was flattered to follow the likes of Nono and Abbado, whom I admit to my considerable shame came a long way behind many, many writers in my personal pantheon, who in most people's eyes would be classified as minor figures. Moreover, following them was not the least of my problems with the programme. No, what decided me was really the underlying principle of the programme; the thought of having a free hand in bringing together in one place and for two whole hours the men and women of my choice, who would in themselves represent every facet of my taste, my style, and my vision of the world.

On the day I accepted the idea and began – with great joy and pleasure – to work out who would be on stage with me, I now realise I fell into the totalitarian – or totalising – trap which I was talking about a moment ago in relation to the surrealists. Why? Because it involved musicians (it was *the* constraint of the programme), painters, writers, designers, actors, sculptors. I remember I arranged for models of the Japanese fashion designer Yamamoto to parade live, as he was supposed to incarnate the "fashion" aspect of my view of the world. Also, because I felt it was necessary to think in terms of creating something totally coherent, rather than allow links to be created between the people involved and the different sequences as a result of inspiration and chance, which is what normally happened. No one expected total coherence, but I constantly reminded people of it.

The idea I had was of a certain "sensibility" which obeyed the same rules, whatever it was focused on; or of a certain "awareness", of which neither the form nor the precepts changed, even though it might shift from Joyce to Yamamoto, from Martinez to Victor Segalen. Crazier still was my idea that ethical and political choices (amongst those whom I had really wanted to have on stage was Harlem Désir and some of his "mates" from SOS Racism)[6] should be dictated by the same principles as the most apparently frivolous aesthetic choices. So I arrived on stage, not like previous guests with the intention of presenting a show (even of my own arrogance, my alleged qualities, or of my friends) but to offer proof of the profound harmony (albeit secret and impossible to explain) which underpinned all the choices an intellectual such as myself could ever be induced to make.

It's what I called a "Weltanschauung", or in less pedantic terms a "wavelength". In my view a good intellectual was someone who didn't change "frequencies" when he moved from fashion to philosophy, from literature to journalism. My dream was to talk about the most serious and the lightest subjects, the most tragic and the most abstract, in the same "voice". The actual programme was merely an initial approximation to that dream. My principal point of reference was the passage in *La Prisonnière* where Proust says of Vinteuil that he "was in touch with his own essence at a level of his being where, whatever question one asked, he would answer in the same tone, namely his own." In the same passage, he also attributed to Vinteuil the merit of intoning "whatever subject he was talking about in the same unusual song, the monotony of which was proof of the unchanging nature of the constituent parts of his soul, because, whatever the subject, he remained essentially the same."

Yet, though my chosen references were sophisticated, the fantasy I had was, at bottom, no different from that of my friends the surrealists who believed that their "total" understanding was advancing at the same speed in all branches of knowledge, politics and taste, however different they might have been. I didn't mention them at the time, perhaps because I didn't think of them. But it was their example which I had in mind, whether consciously or not, when I described the literary eye as being like the beam of a lighthouse sweeping with controlled precision over every sphere of knowledge and of life. I can still hear myself making one extremely stupid observation which strikes me today as typical of a simplistic kind of surrealism. What I suggested was that, just as my artistic and decorative tastes were inevitably homogeneous with my political options or choices (though the homogeneity could neither be fathomed nor demonstrated), so someone who voted for Le Pen could not, in my view, buy their furniture from Stark or their clothes from Yamamoto. I did indeed say that! And no one on stage or in the press the next day challenged it.

If I were invited to appear on the same programme today, I would, I think, still do it. But I would avoid idiotic statements of that kind and abandon once and for all the idea that the least important acts and gestures in the lives not only of writers but of ordinary people as well belonged on the same "wavelength". Indeed, I would return to the stage of the "Grand Echiquier", prepared on this occasion to confess that my tastes were disparate and having the courage to admit that a writer is not always, in all areas, totally modern. I would be prepared to say that I never listen to music and that I don't like simple songs; that my passion for detective films and westerns doesn't "fit" very well with my liking for Kafka, Broch, Proust or Malraux; that even my tastes in painting are varied and sometimes incompatible; that I like Giotto and Mondrian, Piero della Francesca and Matisse. And I would admit that there is no profound and ultimate harmony, inscribed God knows where, between my anti-racist choices and the style of my everyday life.

I would admit to my ambiguities instead of putting on the clever air of someone seeking to imply there is a "certain point" – still that "certain point" referred to by Breton – where my enjoyment of good literature and my persistent attachment to a particular kind of bad detective novel would cease to appear contradictory. I would confess, proclaim, my right – your right – to have different kinds of ideas. Better still, I would proclaim my right – your right – not to have the ideas which suit my life nor the life which suits my ideas. In short, I would counter the preconceived notion which has so poisoned the lives of "progressive" intellectuals and which they got in fact from surrealist terrorism: the notion that one should live in accordance with the way one thinks, speaks and writes.

My message would be: long live nonconformity and the idea of being at odds with oneself. I would do everything I could to break free of my own image and to contradict my self-definition. I would do everything I could to escape that state of watchfulness to which I have condemned myself: by hiding, assuming disguises, not allowing myself to say this or think that, to smile over photos, to share my enjoyment of women and luxury, by not letting anyone suspect I might have a slight weakness for *Gilles* or Cocteau's *Journal*, by appearing solemn on television, a grumbler on platforms, by being all of a piece, wholly consistent; in a nutshell, by not revealing anything which might suggest I had the slightest flutter or wavering of conscience.

That's what I would say, and in so doing make myself the advocate of complexity. I would praise duality, duplicity, multiplicity. I would say that the only writers' lives worth anything, the only ones which seem to me to have been successful and to be envied, are the rich, many-sided, slightly absurd, chaotic and contradictory ones. It isn't obligatory to make a success of your life. You can choose to ruin or sacrifice it. Like Flaubert, you can decide not to have a life at all. But even if you do, even if you choose a real life that isn't eclipsed by your writings (and such a choice is, to say the least, anything but obvious; witness Blanchot and Beckett, Michaux and Cioran), you might as well do it straightforwardly. In that way, your life will not be a substitute or a pale reflection of your work. What use is a life if it merely duplicates your books? What's the point of being full of life, pretending you are alive, if you are doing nothing more than acting out an inferior version of your work?

I would say all that because it's true. Doubtless, I would also say it because I'm the sort of person for whom life would otherwise be suffocating. I would propose several new rights, including the right to a double or schizophrenic existence, in addition to those which Baudelaire wanted to add to the rights of man (the right to contradict oneself, the right to die). But at the very moment I made them, a subtle but insistent feeling of nostalgia would, I know, overtake me. It would be nostalgia for the time when writers (the surrealists) could aspire to a straightforward identity, without flaw or fault, when they imagined they could move forward at the same pace etc. etc.

Is this another contradiction?

Is it my own major contradiction?

FINAL THOUGHTS ON SURREALISM, CONCLUDED

What was equally intolerable about the surrealists, yet which might at the same time constitute one of their original contributions to this whole adventure was their sectarian mentality.

But what is a sectarian mentality. What do I *mean* by a sectarian mentality?

It is not the feeling one has of belonging to a clan, a family, a school of thought, or a style. What could be more commonplace, more traditional than that? Is there any period in our history which has escaped that temptation? Is there anything one could object to in it?

It isn't either the "whiff of the secret society" which Ribemont-Dessaignes detected around Breton-as-Leader. That was indeed absurd, slightly inane, but it gave one no cause to get worked up. Moreover, it wasn't very different from the obsession with conspiracies which one comes across throughout the nineteenth century and which many writers fell victim to long before the surrealists.

It is not even the inclination to rigidity and orthodoxy which generally go hand in hand with sectarianism. For this can be looked at in two ways. Either that rigidity leads to terror and the desire to annihilate one's opponents – and I've already expressed my views on that – or it suggests something quite different, namely that everything is neither equal nor bound up with everything else. In which case, one defends the principle that a clear distinction exists between what is just and what is unjust, between good and evil, between the will to truth and the desire to lie. In other words, it's a question of attempting to cut or separate ("secare" in Latin, which is the proper etymological origin of the word sectarianism) values and attitudes which are deemed to conflict with each other. Not only do I have nothing against such a nostalgic concern, I am more strongly in favour of it than most people.

No, when I talk about the sectarian mentality of Breton and his friends and when I say they invented that mentality, I am thinking of something much more odious. What I am referring to (and I shall return to it when I discuss the twenties, the "Collège de Sociologie", and my meeting with Michel Leiris) is the idea that literature itself is a sectarian activity; the idea that it is the fruit, the pure product, of a sect. It is the idea that the works themselves (books or paintings which "authors" pretend to put their names to) are not personal and unique creations, that they are not the result of an encounter, a struggle, between an individual and the forces which inspire him. It is the view that works do not have authors, that no one creates them or can claim responsibility for them, other than falsely, because they have only one author worthy of the name: the group as a whole.

Commenting on automatic writing, Breton said: "I believe I can say, without any kind of reservation on my part, that we practised the collectivisation of ideas." No I'm not dreaming, and nor are you! He did say "collectivisation" and "without any kind of reservation on my part". A writer, a great writer, is telling us that literature must be the product of a shared creative process.

When Artaud and Soupault were expelled, Breton again, but on this occasion with Unik, Péret, Aragon and Eluard, punished them for what in surrealist eyes was the most criminal offence against their principles: "The pursuit in isolation of that most absurd activity called literature." The important words here are "in isolation". One couldn't have a better example of the "Headquarters" at work. Rather than suggesting a coming together of authors, each of whom would preserve his own originality and identity, it was in essence, and in almost organic fashion, the one and only creator of the works of surrealism.

Furthermore, when Breton pondered on the mystery of poetic inspiration, the images that came most readily to him were those such as "hidden fountainhead", "sea", "inner ocean", "age-old depths", "innermost secret darkness", all of them metaphors the distinctive feature of which was to refer yet again to realities shared by very different people (a fact he was always ready to remind us of). What could be less private than a "sea", what less personal than a "fountainhead"? And what better way of saying that the poet was a diviner of springs – Breton sometimes used the word medium – whose talent lay in bringing forth water, which was the property of all and in no way his own?

The surrealists claimed Freud as a source of inspiration. They were considered – and still are – as the first intellectuals to have taken psychoanalysis seriously. What a joke! What a lie! As if it were not perfectly obvious that the governing idea of Freudianism – the individual, personal nature of the unconscious – was fundamentally contradicted by this whole network of metaphors. As if it were not equally obvious, if one is talking of psychoanalysis, that the only version which fitted the idea of a group of writers drawing collectively on a common stock of dreams and images, or, if you prefer, the only one compatible with the practice of hypnosis and with automatic writing, was not Freudian but Jungian psychoanalysis.

The surrealists claimed the Romantic notions of creativity and of genius as sources of inspiration. They were thought of – and still are – as men who had a heroic conception of literature and who rejoiced in the writer as a born adventurer, at odds with the world at large in his arrogant and splendid isolation. What an error! What a mistaken view that is too! It is the opposite of what they said and represents the counter-image of what they prided themselves on. In their eyes, the writer was merely a medium, an interpreter, a mouthpiece, an ear. He was no more than the humble instrument through which the voices of darkness and of the fountainhead could be heard. Was he not then an arrogant adventurer? That too is a joke. He was, on the contrary, humble and attentive, listening for the sounds of the original voice, the mutterings of the cosmos. In comparison, he was so small, so insignificant. He no longer had any stature, a face even, and it is not clear that he retained an identity. When he truly fulfilled his function, acting as a channel of communication, an interpreter, he abolished what remained of his individuality in order to merge with the group and, through it, the cosmos in those well-publicised dream sessions.

It is clear, however, that the major works of surrealism were not written in this way, and when Breton wrote *Nadja* he was the first to disparage the theory. Yet it is no less clear that a certain conception of literature was elaborated, became established, and was trumpeted by them. What's more, it has to some extent reached us via numerous mediations and subtle distortions. That idea which emanated from the surrealists is stupid, dangerous and unproductive. Furthermore, as an idea, it patently runs counter to everything which modern literary experience teaches us. Surrealism is at odds with modernity.

I believe that writers are unique individuals. I also believe that their inner world is similarly unique, that their inspiration, their phantoms and their fantasies are properly their own. When they speak, they do so, I believe, in the name of no one else and maybe not even for the benefit of anyone else either. Lastly, I believe that the belief itself is utterly banal since it has been accepted for many centuries by most of those, whether great and small, who write or at least reflect upon literature. For all of them and for those who have memories of how utterly unique literary experience can be, it is one more reason, and by no means the least important, for forgetting all about surrealism.

NOTES

1. Lamartine became a Deputy in 1833, was an ardent Republican during the Revolution of 1848, and served briefly as Foreign Minister in the provisional government. Hugo at first supported Napoleon III, then turned against him and went into exile, producing the lampoon *Napoleon le Petit* in 1852.

2. First-year class for those preparing to take the entrance exam to the Ecole normale supérieure.

3. Cravan was the anarchic editor of a review and often seen as a precursor of the Dadaists. Rigaut, a cynical and disillusioned writer, was associated with Dadaism and, to a lesser extent, surrealism. Petrus Borel was a nineteenth-century poet and novelist who sought to scandalise his readers.

4. A reference to *Le Paysan de Paris* (1926) in which Aragon celebrates the marvellous in everyday life.

5. A reference to Bernard-Henri Lévy's book *Impressions d'Asie*, published in 1985.

6. A powerful anti-racist movement of young people which came to prominence in the early to mid-eighties and was led by Harlem Désir. The slogan on their badge was "Touche pas à mon pote" ("Don't you touch my mate").

15

"A group of young philosophers"

A CONVERSATION WITH HENRI LEFEBVRE

Why did Henri Lefebvre agree to meet me? Why did he bother to welcome someone so much younger than himself and to talk about numerous figures from the past such as Nizan and Politzer, Morhange, Barbusse and Kojève? It was all the more surprising since he was so weary, so worn down by life and old age, and had little time left to live. When the conversation began, I couldn't help imagining myself in his place – at the age of ninety – recalling for someone I didn't give two hoots about the ins and outs of a period of history which now seemed remote, time having moved on. Would I have welcomed it, found it interesting or enjoyable? Would it have been a chance – the last chance – to remind the world of my existence? Would I have done it out of duty or altruism, like opening a museum, saving a threatened library or a book of magic spells?

At all events, he was tired that afternoon. His face was pallid, his eyes bloodshot. I felt he was overwhelmed from the start and clearly bored at having to answer my questions. He spoke with difficulty, and when the memories were painful, it was sometimes hard for him to mention certain people I got him to recall. He told me several times he would rather talk about the present and the future, about things going on around him in the world. He simply wanted to behave like an intellectual who was still full of life. Indeed quite recently, 1968 in fact, he'd been one of the intellectual mentors of those like Cohn-Bendit who sought neither gods nor masters. He prided himself, per-haps rightly, on being the author of a body of work which had introduced Marxism into France. Most of all he would have enjoyed talking about his next book or about current ideological issues. But that wasn't what I'd come for. What I really wanted him to talk about was Nizan and Politzer. The astonishing thing is he understood what I wanted and went along with it. We exchanged questions and answers, arguments and clarifications. I'd come hoping he would play a certain role, and this he did with a show of goodwill I hadn't expected. I have to admit he also did it with skill and with style.

You were one of the first French intellectuals to be drawn to Marxism and to join the Communist Party. What significance did that have for a young man of twenty during the period 1920–25? Tell me about Marxism and the Communist Party at that time.

I was born at the beginning of the century which, as you know, was a time of promises; promises of permanent peace, promises of prosperity. And what did we get? Wars. First, there was the war of 1914 which gathered around us like storm clouds. I tell you, we didn't expect it at all as we were counting on peace and prosperity. I remember very well the upheaval, the fear, the break-up of families as people left, the hardships. The general suffering was borne lightheartedly and concealed in all sorts of ways, such as dancing, music, and going to plays. Beneath that there was a deeper suffering on account of the dead and the wounded. It's strange remembering that war and the one which followed, how injuries and deaths were masked by a superficial ideology and a certain gaiety beneath which suffering persisted. Those are terrible memories. For me, the Second World War wasn't greatly different except that I was older and had a clearer understanding of things. I would want to stress that the wars were the major events of the twentieth century.

They were indeed, with the revolutionary events which accompanied them. Because, from 1918, one felt a deep-seated revolt, one felt . . .

1925 was the crucial date. I would want to emphasise that, because it is passed over rather lightly in history books. My memories of it are very precise. A room was hired in the Rue Jacques-Callot, near the Ecole des Beaux Arts, for a meeting between the surrealist group – with André Breton and Aragon – the "Philosophes" group,[1] and various other avant-garde groups like "Clarté". The modern revolutionary movement was created at that point. We imagined a different economic system, a different social base, and a different State superstructure. What we had was a revolutionary plan in place of the vague aspirations of the '14–'18 War and of the immediate post-war period.

All the same, there was 1917 . . .

Certainly. There was the Russian or Soviet influence and that of Lenin, who was beginning to be read at the time. Marx was already being read a bit, but it was around 1925 that Lenin began to be translated. I remember it was in 1925 that I was asked my opinion on the French translation of *Materialism and Empirio-criticism*. It probably came out in '26 or '27. I don't remember the exact date as the translation took a long time. The reason I was consulted was not because of my knowledge of Russian, which was slight, but because of my knowledge of French philosophy. Lenin's thought had to be made intelligible in French vocabulary. So 1925 was a crucial date for me. For others it was 1929, I know, the crisis etc.

1925 was also the date of the Rif War.[2]

That's right. One had to take a stand. One was either for it or against it.

Can you say a little bit about the "Philosophes" group. Besides you there was Guterman, Morhange and . . .

Politzer.

That's right, Politzer. What exactly was this group?

I was attending courses at the Sorbonne in '22 or '23 and I noticed a young chap who wasn't quite like the rest of us on account of his boldness and his cheek, his considerable cheek. He'd begin to speak in lectures and interrupt the professors. I got to know him: it was Pierre Morhange. He was a major personality, a key figure during that period. Not that he'd written a great deal, but he had a whole group of people around him, as Barbusse and others did. I joined them and became something of a theoretician. The whole group (Morhange, Norbert Guterman, Politzer, etc.) has been somewhat forgotten, hasn't it? For example, does anyone today talk about Benvéniste who became a professor at the Collège de France at the age of twenty-eight or thirty? Almost no one.

You mean the linguist?

Yes, the linguist. He was a very important figure for us at the time. We were seeking to promote an idea which was part of the French tradition. Like the surrealists, we wanted to maintain a certain nationalist line rather than a patriotic one. It's perhaps difficult today to represent the discussions we had at the time. But the left, to which I belonged, maintained it was more nationalist than the right. Hence Benvéniste. Hence Descartes and Diderot . . . Our France.

Did the surrealists go along with that?

Their views weren't very different, because we amalgamated almost totally in 1925 at the meeting in the Rue Jacques-Callot.

What were your relations with Breton?

Good on the whole. I went to see him one day, near the Place Pigalle, and I noticed Hegel's *Logic* on the table. Breton said to me: "Read that first and then come and see me!" He gave me a brilliant exposé of the Hegelian doctrine of surrealism and of the relationship between the real and the surreal, which was a dialectical one.

I'd like to talk a little about Georges Politzer.

I knew Politzer well. I got to know him as soon as he came to

Paris. I met him at the Sorbonne. He spoke almost no French, having come from Hungary. He spoke German fluently, which enabled him subsequently to insult the Nazis in their own language when they tortured him.

You met him then almost at the same time as you met Morhange.

Yes. We formed a group straightaway. We were a rather strange combination, since I had a Christian background (my first piece of unpublished work was a critique of Christianity), and Politzer, Morhange and Norbert Guterman were Jewish. It's funny. It forged a link between us. Instead of creating disagreement, it created a link. We shared almost the same critical position vis-à-vis the Christian tradition. It was extremely strong at the time even in the university. They did so in the name of certain Jewish values which they retained and I did so in the name of something different.

So you formed a group which : . . .

We used to meet at Pierre Morhange's place, near the Place Pigalle. There were a whole lot of girls, almost all of whom became well-known later, who were interested in our ideas. The group broke up subsequently. But for several years it was very homogeneous. We were something of a rival group to the surrealists. We used to say that the surrealists spoke on behalf of poetry and that we spoke on behalf of philosophy.

What was strange about the reviews of the time, including the Revue marxiste, *was that the truly Marxist imprint was rather slight.*

We argued a lot about the nature of the *Revue*. Pierre Morhange wanted it to be a general, all-embracing review, welcoming almost everybody, including people like Cocteau, Albert Cohen and Drieu La Rochelle. I was against this eclecticism. I wanted its orientation to be more defined. For example, I was furious when we met Cocteau. I couldn't help feeling a sort of juvenile disdain for the man. Perhaps wrongly, but that's how it was.

What about Guterman and Politzer?

Norbert was always hesitant. Politzer was very aggressive. I was more cautious than him, but I felt the same way about things.

What sort of a man was Politzer?

He was a Central European Jew. That is how one should perhaps describe him. His knowledge of civilisations and languages was universal. At the same time, his critical thinking was extremely well-developed and vehement. He was a violent, fearsome individual. I recall a discussion we had in a little port on the Atlantic coast. I don't remember very well how or why we had met up. There was a low wall running along by the sea, and we were arguing quite violently. The tide was coming in and crashing against the wall. In his anger, he pushed me and I almost fell into the sea, into the waves. He was very violent, implacable, and with a toughness of character and mind which served him well, moreover. Imagine this tough, stubborn character facing his Nazi torturers. I've been told, and I've no reason to doubt it, that he went on insulting them until he died, calling them everything under the sun. In German too, in German, which astounded the Nazis. There was something tough and heroic about him, but for me very attractive as well. He was a man who refused to accept things, in the fullest sense of that phrase. He joined the Communist Party, which was rather sectarian and hard-line at the time, and quite quickly became a figure of importance within it. It suited him. And then he was arrested, brutally tortured, and executed at Mont Valérien. His was a hero's life.

Albert Cohen was also around.

Yes, he came to the "Philosophes" group. He attended our little meetings, but not very often; two or three times. I don't know what happened. He went off to Egypt. He had links, especially in English-speaking circles, which we rejected completely. For us, they were colonialist, imperialist circles. He had links in Egypt, but I'm not sure what they were. He did go to Egypt, didn't he? Anyway, we liked him and he liked us.

Then, of course, there was Nizan who arrived in 1928 . . .

Yes, Nizan arrived one day, I don't know how. And something very strange happened. I've already told you I was attracted to Judaism; especially as Morhange, Politzer and Guterman were of Jewish extraction. Something very funny happened; I thought Nizan was Jewish, only to discover after a while that he was from Brittany like me! We had an odd relationship, a mixture of suspicion and liking. What I reproached him for was his ambition, which he made no secret of. I totally lacked ambition. I aspired to the role of originator of theory, but in no way did I wish to ascend the Party hierarchy. Nizan, on the other hand, wanted to be on the Central Committee, the Politbureau, and to have a political career. What's more, he started out on that path. It cost him dear, poor fellow. I became friendly with his wife, Henriette Nizan. I remember conversations we had in the Luxembourg Gardens (I won't go into details) during which she disclosed her husband's innermost thoughts and ambitions. He wanted to make his way. He wanted to become a political leader. His ideas were very precise. He set out on this career too: writing for L'Humanité and producing other articles as well; then he became chief editor or deputy, I don't remember, and moved in the upper echelons of the Party.

Were there also political and ideological disagreements?

On the question of Nazism, yes. I remember Nizan saying to me: "It will last for twenty years and then Nazi Germany will swing to socialism and to communism!" I didn't agree with him. I said: "I've been to Germany. I've written about Germany; it goes much deeper. Nazism isn't a superficial phenomenon. It has taken root much more deeply in the country. At first, it was perhaps simply an ideology, but that ideology has become established and Germany is more Nazi than you think. It won't just go away. There will be some disasters." And disasters there were. I foresaw them.

After Nizan's death, when the Party initiated a whole campaign against him, what did you do?

I said nothing because I had little respect for Nizan. But when he died, there was a great deal more respect for him.

All the same, didn't he have a certain charm about him? When one reads Sartre's description, for example, the way Sartre described him . . .

Perhaps each of those judgments should be used to qualify the other. I saw Nizan as a fiercely determined careerist who would stop at nothing.

A dandy as well.

What?

A dandy . . .

He hesitated for a while between Christianity and Marxism. Then came the moment when he had to choose. So he chose. Because when I knew him, he was still quite close to a form of social Christianity. After that he became a Marxist. It happened at the time. There were people who got involved in the revolutionary movement and the Communist Party without much conviction and then acquired it. It happened to others. Perhaps Nizan came into that category too. I saw very little of him after a while. I began to see him again when he joined *L'Humanité*. He asked me for articles, which I didn't do. When? As war was drawing near.

There's a character we haven't spoken of at all and whom I've thought about because of Nizan, that's Henri Barbusse. He was very important at the time, during the thirties, wasn't he?

In my opinion, he was completely forgotten by 1930. On the other hand, when the "Philosophes" group first came together, we went to see him at Chantilly, or near Creil, somewhere in that area. We were made to feel welcome by him. He was a distinguished writer and lived in quite a nice house. It must have been Morhange, Norbert Guterman and myself who went. I don't think Benvéniste ... or perhaps he did go. However, Nizan wasn't there. He hadn't yet appeared on the scene. Barbusse received us very well. We dined with him. But it didn't work out. As we were leaving, Pierre Morhange said something to me like: "He's not on the same wavelength as us." That wasn't exactly the vocabulary of the time, but it's more or less what he was trying to say. For him, we represented youth, youth in revolt if not revolutionary youth, and that's how he received us. What he said to us seemed a bit remote, a bit out of tune with our concerns. I have to admit, we had lots of illusions. We really believed that the '14–'18 War would be the final war. It had caused so many massacres, so many deaths, so much bereavement that we couldn't believe it would possibly start again. But it was Barbusse who was right. I seem to remember him saying – but memories are vague: "Look out, the danger still exists."

Today, one has the impression that Barbusse was the whipping boy for the younger generation. For example, when Nizan tried to exclude him from Monde *on the orders of the Party* ...

There's something in that. Yet at the same time there was deep admiration for him. The one doesn't exclude the other. When one is dealing with a celebrity – because at that time he was an extraordinary celebrity – one can simultaneously want to free oneself from him, be rid of him and also feel admiration for him. That's rather how we felt during that period and on the particular day we talked to him. Anyway, he did most of the talking.

Did you know Rappoport[3] and Souvarine at that time?

Yes, but not very well. We were suspicious of them, more of Rappoport than Souvarine. Souvarine seemed to us more forceful, more lucid than Rappoport, who seemed like a historical phenomenon.

All the same, he was the first French Marxist.

Yes, but I felt he was behind the times. I can't really remember. I know we spent several hours having a discussion with him. I wasn't the only one. Pierre Morhange and perhaps Norbert were also there, but I don't remember. His ideas seemed to date from the pre-war critique of capitalism. Whereas we were post-war people. It's all a little confusing. But I remember feeling a slight disdain, that there was a generation gap. There wasn't a gap of any kind with Souvarine. It's curious. I don't know why.

Could you say a word or two about Kojève to finish with? You said that you went to his lectures.

I had a few conversations with Kojève. He made a great impression on me because of his knowledge of Hegel. He knew Hegel and German philosophy better than I did. But he drew no practical or political consequences from them. It was enough for him to know what Hegel thought. So that created a gulf between us. Because, for me, Hegel's propositions about contradictions seemed interesting only if they were applied to the present, to current events, to the real society of the day and not to that of the nineteenth century. Having said that, Kojève was a major figure. Just think, only half a century ago Hegel was not only unknown but proscribed in France. People often used to say (I heard it said): "A Boche . . . he's a filthy Boche!" German philosophy was ignored on account of Bergson and a certain conception of the French philosophical tradition. Kant was just about acceptable. But Hegel was unknown territory, the unknown monster. Kojève put an end to that situation. He introduced Hegel into French thought.

NOTES

1. A group of young philosophers who challenged orthodox Kantian philosophy as taught in universities. Though many of their ideas were ill-defined, they wanted thought to be more closely allied to revolutionary action, hence their interest in Marxism.

2. A war between Spain and the Rif and Tibala tribes which lasted from 1919 to 1926. The French joined in on the Spanish side in 1925.

3. Of Russian-Jewish origin, he was one of the group of militant socialists who wanted the Socialist Party to affiliate to the Third International in 1920. A member of the Directing Committee of the original French Communist Party.

16

". . . not to judge the past in terms of current prejudices"

A QUESTION OF METHOD

Clausewitz said somewhere: "The essential thing in any analysis of strategy is to put oneself in the position of the protagonists." He went on: "The essential thing is to discover the circumstances, all the circumstances, in which they then found themselves." As a principle it seems sensible enough, yet if it were applied to the letter it would go against all I have written and said so far. It would run counter to that tendency, which certain people sometimes rightly claim I have, of behaving like Fouquier-Tinville,[1] a sort of public prosecutor of literature. Take communism, for example. It has turned out to be the maddest and most enigmatic of political adventures, and most of the thinkers I'm concerned with here lost their way as a result of their involvement. One can offer a judgment on the nature of that adventure and even condemn it. One can list the grievances and pile up all the charges imaginable against those who calmly covered up for a criminal regime, and I need hardly remind people that I've not exactly refrained from doing just that. It shouldn't be forgotten, for example, that the horrors and the cover-up began as early as 1918 with the very first Moscow trials against the "Mensheviks" and the "revolutionary social-ists". Having said that, what still needs to be explained is why they did so and how it happened. It was in fact "circumstances" which led Barbusse and Rolland, Gide and André Malraux to accept the unacceptable. Therefore, what I still have to do – what I've never done or attempted to do – is to penetrate the skulls of those concerned, to get inside the minds of the protagonists. The real voyage of dis-covery would be to explore the innermost being of these unusual and sometimes inspired figures who nevertheless mysteriously went astray. It is quite possible that an undertaking of this kind will give offence. And if people were not so stupid at the present time and had better memories, some smart individual would come forward and produce previous texts of mine as evidence of my having defended an alterna-tive point of view. Because it was in those texts that I flayed over-subtle scholars who made Drieu's delusions seem ordinary, on the pretext of "understanding" him and getting to the heart of a fascist's "real motives". To an impossible antagonist such as this, I would simply reply that times have changed; that, as communism is dead and communist man is quietly expiring before our very eyes, the time has come to deal with him in the same way as one deals with a defunct species.

NOTES

1. Public Prosecutor attached to the Revolutionary Tribunal during the Terror.

17

"The new religion"

It is, I think, quite clear that communism can be likened to a civilisation. Admittedly, it is a miserable civilisation without glitter and dazzling deeds, and it may well leave behind it none of those glorious or infamous "traces" which every other civilisation has prided itself on since the world began. Yet nonetheless it is a civilisation, a true cultural entity with, most notably, its celebrated "new man", heralded by the Stalinists and whom Zinoviev claimed partly to embody. What has to be stressed, on the other hand, is that it was also a religion, and the consequences of that need to be argued and proved, as does the fact that, by rallying to Stalin, the Party and its Word, one was embracing a faith in the true sense of that term.

For the moment, let us consider a few texts which give one the feeling that the excessively political image usually conveyed of communism was somewhat wide of the mark. Those texts are based on images of the destruction of churches and the repression of priests (or on "messianic" shots by Eisenstein and Dziga Vertov, which amount to the same thing). They will also convey the impression that communism was the latest – perhaps the last – of Western Europe's great wars of religion.

Take the case of Rolland, whose eulogies of the "new man", hymns to Stalin and even to Robespierre, bear witness at every stage to a kind of vitalism. This, together with the pagan and orgiastic tone of his writing, which was obsessive in its promotion of youth, can only be understood against the background of an age-old and intimate quarrel with the God of the Jews and of the Christians and their descendants.

Then there was Gide who, in his *Nouvelles Nourritures*,[1] addressed as "comrade" the character whom he had formerly addressed with the "too doleful name Nathanaël", and announced (this was in 1935) that "no rational argument" would stop him from following "the road to communism". "I have wiped the slate clean and broken with the past," he said. "I stand naked on virgin soil ready to invent new gods!" He went on: "Who said that the great god Pan was dead? I have seen him in the very breath I breathe; I press my lips towards him; did I not hear him murmuring this morning 'what are you waiting for'?"

Then again, as if to affirm more powerfully his hysterical and insane naturalism, he wrote: "You whose heads are bowed, raise them! You whose eyes are downcast, lift them from the tombs and look towards earthly horizons rather than empty skies."

Still on the subject of Gide, there is an astonishing "Letter", signed by Ramon Fernandez, who was still a prominent anti-fascist at that time. I have to admit I didn't know of its existence, but I found in it the confirmation, and more, of my argument. Adopting the tone of an abbot giving instruction to a novice, Fernandez wrote that Gide's communism was the choice made by a *protestant* seeking in Moscow "the only effective refuge in the face of the Roman Church" and by a *Christian* who saw socialism as "Christianity taken literally". Finally, he saw it as the choice of a *pagan* who discovered in the new Russia a powerful echo of "his pleasure in living, his Prometheanism, his defiance of God, his idea of natural humanity".

There is yet another text, this one by the gentle Guéhenno, a sober humanist, whom I imagined, doubtless wrongly, to be untroubled by such concerns. When he recalled in his *Journal d'un homme de quarante ans* his very first reaction to the birth of the communist order, he too was not inclined to tone down either his emotions or his language. What he wrote was this: "I admit I was wild with hope at the time; I truly believed a new man had been born who had new senses – a sense of the people, a sense of the world, a sense of the future; I was close to thinking that we had witnessed the Passion of humanity which, *like that of Christ* (my italics), would open a new era; I was making a prophecy; you may laugh if you wish."

Then the other evening, when I was at Marianne and Pierre Nahon's, Klossowski let drop a secret when I was asking him about the period of the "Collège de Sociologie" and quoted to him Bataille's mysterious phrase concerning the emergence of communism: "God divided himself in two, then three." Standing in the middle of the room, Klossowski swayed from one foot to the other, as if beating time. He was terribly thin, emaciated almost, his face seemingly chis-elled by some perverse sculptor so as to make his gaze all the more striking. With his up-turned nose pointing at something far behind me, he answered in his high-pitched, nasal voice (I quote from memory): "Stalin was indeed an anti-Pope. He was the first anti-Pope in the history of Christianity; Louis XIV wasn't one, whereas Barbarossa was, but he yielded and laid down his arms before the real Pope. Stalin was the first anti-Pope whose schism was successful."

In two sentences he'd said it all – and Stalinism was reinstated in the sphere where it properly belongs, namely that of religious wars and the history of those wars. Consequently, to write that history and produce the secular account of a venture which, to all appearances, was essentially secular, what is really needed is theologians.

NOTES

1. The original *Nourritures terrestres* (1897) encouraged the youth Nathanaël to follow his impulses and live for the moment. In the *Nouvelles Nourritures* (1935), Gide addressed Nathanaël as "Comrade" and revealed his new-found faith in communism.

18

"Then there was the horror"

MY HOLY FAMILY

It's strange really that I should take such an interest in communists. Equally strange are the questions I keep asking and the explanations I produce. It is strange how I look for – and discover – so many circumstances and alibis which can only mitigate their wrongdoing, whether I mean to or not. Would I do the same thing if they were fascists? Would my analysis – of their motives, excuses, misunderstandings and blunders – be as detailed in the case of Brasillach or Drieu? To be frank, I think not. Yet when I try to explain why; when for example I attempt to offer an explanation to my son Antonin, I find it extremely difficult to say anything coherent.

If the appropriate criterion was in fact the scale of the crime, if what mattered – what discredited an intellectual – was the enormity of the massacre he witnessed or allowed to happen, there would in that case be no grounds for the slightest indulgence or sympathy. Haven't the communists committed at least as many crimes as the other side? Don't they have an even larger number of corpses on their conscience – if indeed it is a question of numbers? I am not saying it is the main criterion, but one has to admit its relevance. From this point of view, it's not clear why one should engage in special pleading on behalf of the more favoured faction.

If what mattered was the way the crime was packaged and presented, the way words, ideas, and ideology were used to cloak infamy, if, moreover, one decides to forgive those who, so to speak, "started out" with good intentions but "ended up" going down the wrong path, then the argument holds good for the Stalinists. What's more it's the argument that is constantly advanced. But can one be sure it isn't equally valid for the others? Didn't they also talk of "liberation", of "revolution", of "the new man", etc.? What justification would there be for giving credence to one side and not the other? On what basis can it be said that the brown revolution was less authentic than its red counterpart? I myself have never done this. I have also taken seriously Nazism's claim to "change" man and the world. There again, I would conclude that no grounds exist for favouring one camp rather than the other. If the will to purity, the desire to break the mould of history, even a love of mankind excuse anything, they excuse the young SA as much as the young communist.

It's also said that there was at least one crime which discredited Nazism and which made it not only inexcusable but absolutely incomparable. That crime was the Final Solution, the extermination of the Jews; and it didn't have its equivalent in kind on the other side. But how do you deal with those, precisely on the fascist side, who didn't go that far? How do you deal with those, and there were some, whose anti-semitism stopped short of the gas-chambers? What do you do about the Pétainists, who were moderate fascists and moderately anti-semitic, who in some cases revolted against the most glaring "excesses" of barbarity? How come that I'm not prepared to offer on their behalf the same kind of explanations or to favour them with the interest I've shown in the communists in the first part of the book, though it will seem unjust? Yet again it's not the right criterion, and I can't explain the reasons for my bias.

The truth, I know full well, is that there isn't a reason. What I'm trying to say is that there is no reasonable reason why a writer such as I should suddenly find himself strangely siding with the one and hostile to the other. I have, after all, devoted whole books – starting of course with *La Barbarie à visage humain* – to the business of establishing the equivalence of the two systems. If, however, I'm now to explain candidly and honestly why I'm inclined to confront the delusions of communism with some understanding and therefore a certain indulgence, having spent half my life dispelling the remnants of its prestige, I would have to say this: Communists have been swine, criminals, and sometimes monsters. Their infamy has been all the more inexcusable because it has usually been dressed up in the fine-sounding name of liberty. Yet however removed from these people I may be, however alien their lies and values, there remains a link between us which, were I not a writer, I would describe as a physical bond. But since I *am* a writer, I prefer to call it a bond of language.

Their language is my language. Their memory my memory. My history, my genealogy can be traced back to these misguided and unworthy people, whether I like it or not. So that when I try to recognise my "true lineage", as Baudelaire put it, when I endeavour to identify my intellectual elders, I find myself inevitably drawn back to these same people. They are, I have to agree, unworthy elders, elders I could do without. Be that as it may, they are still my elders, and we keep up one of those family discussions which everyone knows are absurd, incoherent, and often endless. There again, one cannot choose one's family.

II

DAYS OF CONTEMPT
(The 1920s to 1945)

I

"One of those disappointed followers of Maurras"

CLAVEL, BOUTANG[1] AND THE ROLE OF L'ACTION FRANÇAISE

The events I'm about to describe took place in Paris in 1979. I was on the point of publishing *Le Testament de Dieu*, which was meant to be a defence and an illustration of Judaism and of its essential characteristics. Thus, I found myself in the large room used by authors to sign press copies of their books at the publishing house of Grasset. Seated a few feet from me at another table was a man who was well past sixty, tall, and strongly built. He looked like an elderly giant, with large hands, big arms, and enormous shoulders, slightly rounded with age. As I remember it, he had a quiff of white hair and the slightly reddish complexion of someone who had had a stroke. The skin on the nape of his neck and perhaps on his hands too was wrinkled and worn – a scaly skin, I said to myself, like that of a fish or a tortoise. He had clear blue eyes. He was wearing a woollen shirt with a large check pattern that accentuated still further the "physical" side of his character, as if to say: "I did my body-building in bust-ups on the 'Boul' Mich' in the Latin Quarter." What was most striking about him was the way he read and, in these circumstances, wrote; for like me he was signing one book after another, his body hunched forward, his eyes an inch or two from the page. He had a disgruntled, almost vicious air about him, and lifted his head abruptly when he'd finished one book to consider what he would write in the next one. His name was Pierre Boutang. He had been the secretary and companion of Charles Maurras and was his spiritual heir. In my eyes he was the incarnation of the extreme right, and I don't have to describe the feelings he aroused in me. The work of philosophy he had just completed was called *L'Apocalypse du désir* and was intended to be a denunciation of "the deadly effects of the idealism of the Age of Enlightenment and of psychoanalysis".

We kept up our little game for more than half the day, with him at one end of the room signing *L'Apocalypse* and me at the other signing my *Testament*. He received his visitors, and I welcomed my friends. It was the usual circus one gets on the day a book is published. The people who came (his and mine) eyed each other up and down as they met, immediately recognised one another, then adopted a cold, fixed stare, as if word had been passed from one to the other or we'd told them to behave like this. They were ostentatiously indifferent, wearing a fixed look on their faces. Sensing the tension that had built up in a situation where people were usually much more convivial, the press attachés made it their business, having stopped at one table, to go directly to the other. Sometimes a journalist phoned and it was necessary to get up to go and answer the call. Did this mean that one of us passed in front of the other, that we exchanged glances or a vague nod? By no means! To me this fellow was the devil incarnate, as doubtless I was to him in some respects. Had it not been for the classic ploy we adopted of turning our back on each other, deeming each other nosey, and talking in an undertone and yet occasionally raising our voices so that the other would hear, you might genuinely have believed that we spent over half the day in each other's company behaving as though the other person didn't exist. It had almost reached the point of absurdity, when someone else arrived on the scene who happened to be his friend and mine. This was Maurice Clavel.

Clavel too was a huge, strongly built man. But his gestures and the way he walked were clumsy, and this made him appear paradoxically hesitant and vulnerable. He had, I think, just arrived from Vézelay. He used to talk about having been "in the wilderness". He'd spent a week there turning over various thoughts in his mind, the visions he had, his intuitions, the things that made him angry. Immediately he arrived at Grasset, he had to tell his friends all about them. He was particularly agitated that day. He was wearing the suit he always wore for special occasions, the one he'd worn the previous year when he lunched with Giscard and which made him look rather fat. His hair was all over the place and his glasses were askew. He must have shaved too quickly because there were great long grazes on his cheeks where the blood had dried. His whole appearance conveyed the sense of excitement which came over him whenever he felt he was in touch with the forces of the Mind, of Revolution, of Life, which he was dying to tell us about. He moved from one to the other, greeting Boutang first and then me. He was in turn fervent, confused, and inspired as he poured out his latest fulminations in a booming voice. He addressed the two of us together, without going into details and without noticing at first the atmosphere into which he had stepped. "What, you don't know each other? Both of you were here together and you didn't know each other? It's unbelievable, impossible! Come along, my friends, we must join forces at once and work together! After all, we aren't so numerous that we can afford to ignore each other or be divided." There we were, the two of us, each considering the other to be the devil incarnate, suddenly thrown together by Clavel's frenzied excitement.

He didn't stay long at Grasset's that afternoon. Obviously, we didn't know at the time that it was to be his last trip to Paris. He died a few days later, alone in his book-lined room in Vézelay. But perhaps, on the other hand, he knew; perhaps the premonition of his death made him more agitated and impatient than usual. He talked about Boutang's book, having just read the proofs, and he was going to review it or get it reviewed in the *Observateur*. He urged me to read it and, in his time-honoured phrase, "to get those around me to read it". As always when he liked a book, it became *the* book, which turned all the issues of the day upside down and threatened to shake the ground beneath our feet. Looking hard at his old friend, he referred to the imminent coming-together of the last of the royalists and the first of the leftists. He confided to us, with the air of someone hatching a plot, that he would take the initiative if necessary and bring together representatives of the two groups at his house in Vézelay. He talked about himself and the book he had published the previous year. He talked also of the "major philosophical treatise" he was working on night and day. According to him, it would "destroy utterly the enemy's position and resistance." He told us about what had angered him most recently and about his next article. "Let's talk a bit about you! What did you think of my last television appearance?" He talked about Heidegger, in his opinion, an idol who should be discredited as a matter of urgency. In this respect, one had to acknowledge that he was, as always, a few years ahead of his time. "Heidegger is the real danger, the next bastion to be attacked, the last pocket of resistance. Forward lads! We have to storm the headquarters of this last great thinker. It's the final push! The Patton breakthrough!" Poor Clavel, poor dear Clavel. He was in such a hurry that day, so agitated as he reviewed for the last time the troops in his own great army. He left us quite quickly, and we were alone again, stunned and astonished, but, thanks to him, ready to have a conversation.

First of all, and inevitably, we discussed anti-semitism. It was of course impossible for me to overlook the fact I was looking not just at Maurras's former secretary, but also at the author of *La République de Joanovici*, which had been published for some time and was reputed to be quite a lively book of its kind. Boutang explained himself, solemnly declared his point of view, listened to me and asked me questions as well. He was suddenly courteous and pleasant, almost too pleasant. Whether he was sincere or not, I don't know, but he made out those aspects of his life and thought were over and done with. He had the look of someone who wanted to be understood at all costs, to dispel all misunderstanding, but perhaps also at the same time the real causes of discord. He gave way on Dreyfus, the forgery by Henry,[2] on Vichy and L'Hôtel du Parc.[3] He also abandoned – seemingly? – the distinction, central to Maurras's thought, between "racial anti-semitism" (unacceptable) and "social anti-semitism" (excusable, on the other hand, indispensable even). We finally agreed that the god of the Jews and the Christians was "clearly the same". At one point, he seemed to check himself. He got up and sat down again. The disagreeable, querulous expression he'd had at the beginning returned. He picked up a book in front of him and looked as if he might have thrown it at my head, but he didn't. Instead of throwing it, he put it down again and opened it. With an increasingly angry look on his face and with his nose an inch from the paper, he started to scribble such a passionate dedication that there remains to this day the great blot he made on the page in closing the book. He performed this act as if to conclude the first part of our conversation. He was a strange fellow! I have his dedication in front of me now, with the great ink blot and his spiky, almost illegible writing. "We surely have the same God, and no other comes between us. Pierre Boutang."

We went on to talk about Maurras himself, his life and works and the countless misunderstandings which had built up around the man, according to his champion. "You've read him at least? You haven't? Then what are you talking about? You're talking of something you know nothing about. I'll tell you, explain to you. Oh, how wearisome it is being right." This time, Boutang argued, pleaded his case. He became Boutang the man of reason, the quibbler, the dialectician. He was Maurras's champion and the dispenser of justice. Fearless, beyond reproach, alone in the face of the whole world, which for the moment included me, he was intent on demonstrating the superiority of the monarchy, the excellent notion of the "primacy of politics", and the similar fate of Socrates drinking hemlock and the old prisoner of Clairvaux;[4] the formal beauty of *Anthinéa* and *L'Avenir de l'intelligence* and the prescience of *Kiehl et Tanger*, and lastly the extreme modernity of his critique of Romanticism. "I thought I understood a moment ago when you were talking to Maurice that you were writing against the Romantics? No? Yes? Well, read Maurras! Roam through his landscapes. They have such purity and such a contrast of light and shade. His is a real critique of Romanticism!" Boutang had evidently refound his vigour. There were moments when he seemed to adopt the tone, the look and the passion of his friend Clavel. It was I, on the other hand, in the face of such fervour and conviction, such knowledge and erudition, who was obliged not to back down but rather to admit my lack of knowledge. "Maurras was perhaps as you say he was. But allow me to reiterate my non-acceptance, my feeling of nausea, and my permanent dislike of him."

The third and most important part of our conversation concerned the role of "L'Action française", as he saw and outlined it. This is the substance of what he said: "'L'Action française' was not a fascist party. You understand nothing of what it meant and of the function it fulfilled if you say it was fascist. Fascism did exist, but 'L'Action française' was something else. Furthermore, it prevented a whole lot of young people from going over to fascism." Then, as I was, to say the least, looking somewhat sceptical, he went on: "I'll draw a comparison which will mean something to you. You know Maurice's view about the way leading intellectuals restrained the young leftists from going down the road of terrorism about ten years ago. Well it's the same thing! Relatively speaking it's the same thing. What Lacan and company did for the leftists, the followers of Maurras did for those other young people at the time. They too were potential terrorists and exasperated by what they referred to as 'l'inaction française'. They wanted to move towards a more radical form of commitment; they wanted to go right ahead in a totally Hitlerian direction. We restrained those young people, or did everything we could to restrain them. And as long as we were strong, we did restrain them. It was when 'L'Action française' collapsed, when exasperation swept it away, that fascism triumphed."

As I found his comparison with Lacan rather far-fetched and was obviously not prepared to shed the slightest tear over the fate of "L'Action française", he concluded by saying: "It's not a question of whether the parallel is extravagant, and your feelings in this instance are beside the point. One either engages in the history of ideas or one doesn't, and from the point of view of the pure history of ideas it is beyond question that Maurrassian ideas acted as a brake. Your psychoanalyst friends would refer to it as a super-ego. That brake or super-ego prevented excesses which, I assure you, were quite different from the brawls we were involved in when we were young. What's more, it's not finished yet; I'm not at all sure it's finished. I just hope the day won't come when you have to count the cost to the country of the demise of 'L'Action française'."

Since then, I've often thought about our conversation. I thought about it five or six years later when Boutang finally produced the monumental and very fine work on Maurras he'd promised for so long. It reminded of the remarks he made that day. I thought about our conversation again; I couldn't help thinking about it, when subsequently, in France but also in Europe, the ideology of communism was finally smashed. To us, it had been carved in granite. But it represented yet another criminal ideology, yet another living corpse, and there were very few who shed any tears over its ultimate fate – and I certainly wasn't one of them. Yet soon the view was expressed that this infamous system could at least be credited with having prevented an even more infamous one from coming into being. What is more, it might well do so now that the barrier to it had been breached. Personally, I don't believe that Maurras was the right-wing version of Lacan that Boutang talked about. On the other hand, after the Berlin Wall had come down, I kept coming across left-wing Boutangs who, whilst regretting that the ice floe had melted and that the muck it had held in check was now floating to the surface, expressed exactly the same views as he had done. Do these views have any value? In the history of ideas, the pure history of ideas, does the notion of a political super-ego preventing extreme upheavals in society have any meaning? It all seems very strange and very dubious to me. But let's be clear about one thing. It would truly represent a defeat for the idea of democracy and its powers. Let us wait and watch. One swallow doesn't make a summer, and History will have the last word.

NOTES

1. An "agrégé" in philosophy, he has taught in lycées and universities. As a journalist he worked on *L'Action française*.

2. Colonel Henry, of the Secret Service, claimed to have a letter from the Italian Military Attaché which proved Dreyfus's guilt. Henry subsequently admitted he had forged the letter.

3. The hotel in Vichy taken over by the government as its headquarters.

4. Maurras was arrested in September 1944, tried and condemned to penal servitude for life. He was released on health grounds in 1952.

2

"Pierre Drieu La Rochelle"

We come now to the case of Drieu. But there isn't really a case, or shouldn't be, if that implies that his commitment was half-hearted or equivocal. If one imagines his fascism was tempered by intelligence, elegance, or a touch of the dandy, if one pictures Drieu as a charming, nonchalant, even remote individual whose case was less straightforward and thus less blameworthy than that of a rank-and-file collaborator, then one should face the facts. Far from being lukewarm or ambiguous, he was frenzied, fanatical in his support of Nazism. The one thing that marked him out was that he succumbed more decisively to the lure of Nazism than anyone else in France.

There are pictures of him at Nuremberg, at the famous Nazi rallies of 1935, though it's Brasillach who is always talked of in that connection. He is the one who is usually quoted, and rightly so, since it was he who discovered the previous year "the poetry of the twentieth century" amidst the dancing, the dreams, and the flags. But what's to be said of someone who, confronted by the same spectacle the following year on the morning of the opening of the rally, talked of "greatness", of "fervour", of "strength", of "joy"? What do you say about someone who, that same evening, stood there enraptured, lost in the crowd that had come to acclaim Hitler? This is how he reacted to the scene in question: "There is a kind of virile and sensual pleasure in the air around me which isn't sexual, but which is extremely intoxicating." "My heart thrills, is wild with delight . . .", he went on, "Oh, I shall die, I shall die of passion tonight." How does one describe a writer who was capable of saying the next day, in a letter to his mistress, as he strove, quite properly, to express his emotion and sadness at having experienced the spectacle without her, that it: "surpassed all his expectations", that he had seen "nothing more beautiful since the Acropolis", that it was a form of "ancient tragedy", almost "overwhelming in its beauty", "with choirs and wonderful songs"? He suggested that being there without her, unable to "share" an "emotion" which was certainly "one of the greatest of his life" made "his heart burst." There is another picture of him with "five or six Frenchmen pressed together and consumed with anguish", which is undeniably a far cry from Drieu the dandy, the disdainful writer. As they witnessed the supreme moment of the Nazi parade, they asked themselves: "Who are we? What are we doing with our lives? What do we count for in the face of that? What meaning do we have?"

Two days later, on September 14th, there were further pictures of Drieu being taken by car to Dachau, having scarcely got over his emotion. Yes, that's right, he was visiting the concentration camp at Dachau. This was the focal point not of "aesthetic" Nazism but of its murderous counterpart and had been in operation for precisely two years. Was he moved? Did he feel indignant? Did the delightful Drieu begin to discover that the "ancient tragedy" was turning into a nightmare? No, he didn't, not in the least. "The visit to the camp was astonishing," he related, "I don't think they hid much from me." In the same text he went on: "The predominant atmosphere was one of splendid comfort and simple austerity. At the same time, certain elements showed a persistent and determined resistance." You might have thought you were dreaming, but that isn't so. He did indeed use the words "comfort" and "simple austerity". A distinguished French writer and Anglophile, who still has his devoted and nostalgic followers today, could visit a death camp in 1935 and, when confronted with grey barrack huts and the inmates they held, say that nothing was hidden from him and bring himself to comment only on "a persistent and determined resistance". Once he returned to Nuremberg after his pleasant trip and met up with the five or six Frenchmen whose hearts had burst with emotion at the dramatic art of the Nazis, he sighed contentedly, drank a lot, and had a good time. He cracked jokes with the journalists there, and then slept the sleep of the just.

He returned to Paris, and a year later this "man covered with women"[1] joined the PPF.[2] It was the main party in France hoping to meet the challenge of the revolution that had taken place in Germany. Yet again, one can't help feeling there was perhaps a gap, a certain irony. One imagines him in his well-cut suits and English-made shoes, with his long, podgy face looking down inevitably in a pseudo-aristocratic way on the frenzied activity of the crowd in the town hall at Saint-Denis – Doriot's stronghold – which witnessed gatherings such as this more and more frequently. But again exactly the opposite was true. The picture one gets of him – from Bertrand de Jouvenel, Emmanuel d'Astier de la Vigerie, and his friend Claudine Loste – on the contrary, is of a militant, or, better still, of a fanatic. His image was that of the intellectual who had found in Doriot the man of his dreams. Drieu was to be seen at meetings of the PPF, shoulder to shoulder with the providential leader, intoxicated by the man's braces, his black shirt, his corpulence, his sweatiness. Drieu was also seen in shirtsleeves, sweating, bawling his head off, and reminding the ecstatic crowd what cowards the communists were, and the liberals, and his friends at the NRF, without attempting to distinguish between them. "It would really make them choke to shout out Long live France!" But one thing he alone did at these High Masses, one liberty he took with party orders, was to utter whenever possible the word which the French "Führer" was loath to use, out of a mixture of prudence and cunning – or was it for reasons of patriotic reserve? – and that was the word "fascist". Drieu was the sole spokesman of the PPF openly to declare himself a fascist.

He was still in Paris a little later on when his "ideas" carried, or at least half-carried, the day. For though German rule prevailed in Europe, though that mixture of Greek and medieval "high-living" he witnessed in Pomerania had triumphed almost everywhere, though the magnificent display of youth, strength and health he admired at Nuremberg was gradually gaining ground all over the planet, and though in France itself we were, thank heavens, finally in good hands, there was still a great deal to be done to secure total victory. Drieu was one of those (and one has to admit they were numerous in the ranks of the collaborators) who found Pétain too old-fashioned – "much too old", he wrote, "and inspired by the archaic mentality of the old Centre-Right". More unusually, he carried his views to the point of suspecting Laval of being "a half-bred Jew cum gypsy", probably "conceived behind a caravan". His Nazism was so extreme, and he considered himself so pure and orthodox, that he even viewed the German Embassy in Paris as the haunt of liberals, bastards, traitors, and, yet again, half-Jews. The celebrated Lieutenant Heller, who presided over censorship and enjoyed the privilege of conversing with Parisian writers, came out of his first meeting with Drieu absolutely horrified. Confronted by such zeal and such determination to be vigilant over matters of doctrine, he, a German, found himself quivering and fearing (he wrote in his diary) that he might have appeared guilty and decadent in the eyes of this hard-liner.

Let's look again at what Drieu said, what he wrote in his private diary, as he recalled his allegiance to the sublime figure and leader of the Third Reich, Adolf Hitler. There are a thousand and one different ways of declaring one's allegiance. Publishers did so cynically, Cocteau did so unthinkingly, Montherlant wearily, and Gide almost did so from exhilaration. There was another style as well: "It's all very sad, but how can one do otherwise?" This was the tone adopted by a number of writers in the weeks following the defeat of France. There was the line adopted by those who wrote for *Esprit*. They had no sympathy for Nazism but were quite prepared (as we shall see) to take advantage of the collapse and the clean slate which it offered in order to construct a new France and to promote a national revolution. There are few examples, I think, of Drieu's chosen way, that of what I'd call the enthusiast who identified with and felt empathy for the cause. "I feel Hitler's impulses as if I were him. I share his sense of impetus. The masculine and positive part of my work is inspired by him and bears out his example. What a strange adventure it is to share these feelings." A little further on, he continued: "There is the same strength and the same weakness in Hitler (as in himself, he implies), but he has managed to overcome his weakness. He will only rediscover it when his strength is exhausted. My weakness surpassed my strength and I remained inactive and had little to say. In my early writings, when I was twenty-five to thirty, I expressed the main slogans of fascism." Could anyone have put it better? Was there a more emphatic way of declaring one's allegiance to Nazism?

To that must be added his equally incontestable anti-semitism (an issue frequently raised), his "I shall die an anti-semite", written in his pseudo-testament of 1939. Just after the armistice he had the nice idea of sending back "anyone who came from the countries of the Orient or from Africa" and of setting up a "Jewish colony in Madagascar". In case you think, as Berl did in his conversations with Modiano, that anti-semitism was something he contracted late "like a shameful disease or diabetes", just listen to the confession Drieu made at the time of his marriage to Colette Jeramec (the model for Myriam, a Jewess, who is obnoxiously caricatured in *Gilles*). He was, he said "incapable of feeling desire for a young woman and still less for a Jewess". It is possible to think, as I do, that *Gilles* is a fine novel and acknowledge the seductiveness of its author, which I shall come back to. What one cannot say is that he was only a half-hearted Nazi, or allow the idea to gain ground that his Nazism was tempered by his casual and arrogant manner. Drieu was an ultra, a bastard. If there is one "case" for which not the slightest excuse or the slightest extenuating circumstances could be adduced before a tribunal not of History but of conscience, it would surely be that of Drieu. That is my first point, the first item in my dossier on Drieu.

Let us turn now to the second point. Now and only now does it seem fitting to come to terms with the fact that such an ultra, such a bastard, must have had charm or moral qualities or an unquestionable capacity to impress, to fascinate, to inspire indulgence or fondness. What's more, it is verified by the fact that a great many different people – different also from him – remained attached to him from the beginning to the end, despite everything, despite Dachau and Nuremberg, despite his loathsome attitude, despite his Nazism, which could not have failed to strike his contemporaries as unequivocal and unforgivable. This poses a question and creates a certain mystery. But if there is a mystery about Drieu, it arises precisely from the position he occupied during this period, at a time when he ought to have been marginalised or banished because of the line he took.

As a young man, Drieu was of course not a fascist, since neither the phenomenon nor the word really existed. But he admired D'Annunzio and he wrote in praise of "things sacred to the nation" in the NRF. In his *Nouvelles littéraires*, he said that Maurras had been as important in his life as Rimbaud. Interviewed by another review about his intellectual mentors, he cited, as well as Maurras, the long line of "reactionary Frenchmen". And when at the beginning of 1923, the royalist leader, Marius Plateau, was assassinated by Germaine Breton, a militant anarchist whom the surrealists, for their part, referred to as "a wholly admirable woman", he, Drieu, was on Plateau's side and attended his funeral with Montherlant. So who were Drieu's friends at that time? Who were his closest companions during those years? Well, there was Aragon and Breton. The surrealist group as a whole either pretended not to understand what was happening (which would prove that it was in the interest of these young revolutionaries to remain close to Drieu) or they genuinely didn't understand (which poses another problem, namely that his contemporaries were blind to the fact that he was attracted to fascism and exhibiting more and more obvious signs of it). At any rate, the consequence was that this conservative nationalist and follower of Maurras was present at most of the group's activities – from the trial of Barrès (it was there that he spoke highly of D'Annunzio whom he called a "fine military man") to the "Cadavre" (the pamphlet against Anatole France which he might even have initiated) and including most of the meetings of the group "Littérature" (in which, it seems, his role was that of a simple observer).

The thirties was the period when Drieu was attracted and then converted to fascism. He was no longer subject to any doubts, nor did he waver or equivocate. But who do you think praised his play *Le Chef*, widely recognised as being fascist in inspiration, which was put on at the end of '34, just six months after his conversion? The communist novelist Dabit. When, in '35, he published *Socialisme fasciste*, a collection of essays the title of which makes clear his purpose, who responded to it, who hailed it, spoke of "nobility", and proclaimed his enthusiasm? Julien Benda in the NRF, who, six months later, was to be one of the leading figures of the great anti-fascist rally. Then Nizan, in *Monde*, even though he saw "in the bankruptcy of Drieu" a sign of "the general bankruptcy of bourgeois thought", could not help but admire the book's "authenticity", the author's "greatness", and his "style", which he described as the best "in French essay-writing today". When Drieu made his second trip to Germany and to the Nazi youth camps in Pomerania where he admired "the essential facets of Greek and medieval high-living", when he could not restrain his enthusiasm and was furious that "we French continue to remain in the wake and at the mercy of all the peoples who take risks and are creative," who was it who lent prestige to what he was saying, and where were these views expressed? In *Marianne*, which was Berl's paper and at the same time the official organ of the victorious Popular Front.

I have described his reactions, his boundless, sacred emotions, when he made his first trip to Germany in the thirties and went to Nuremberg, Dachau, etc. What I didn't mention – a fact which is truly staggering – is that once he had ended his trip to Nuremberg and Dachau, his travels didn't stop there, as he calmly boarded a train for the USSR. Another thing I didn't mention was that, before leaving Paris for this double expedition, he did what all travellers do when they are going to new countries: he took the precaution of arming himself with the names of contacts and their addresses. And who gave him contacts for the Russian part of his journey? Who did he go and see first and foremost in order to have recommendations once he arrived in Moscow? Malraux, of course, his friend Malraux, who gave him access to a whole range of his acquaintances and whom he saw on the morning of September 8th, the day of his departure, almost as he was about to board his train. He contacted Nizan too, Nizan the militant, who, despite the bankruptcy of the bourgeoisie, was sufficiently cooperative for Drieu to send him the most gracious note of thanks before he set off. Here, in substance, is what he wrote: "Forgive me for having put you to any trouble but Malraux has done what was necessary and I am about to leave." He then added with a casualness which in retrospect leaves one speechless, and which certainly tells us a lot about what the author of *Les Chiens de garde* was prepared to put up with before finally breaking with him: "In any case, I shall go via Nuremberg where I want to take part in the Nazi rally." Drieu. Nizan. As coolly as you like, Drieu announced to Nizan that he was going to acclaim Hitler.

During the war, he was a collaborator. Not content, as an infamous editorial writer, with rejoicing at the defeat of his country for, let us say, ideological reasons, he took advantage of his situation in order to gain control of the NRF, where before '40 he had found it increasingly hard to get his articles accepted. In a tone which from then on readers grew accustomed to, he angrily declared: "They will crawl at my feet. That load of Jews, pederasts, and surrealists can enjoy their miserable laughter. And Paulhan, deprived of Benda's support, will slink away with his tail between his legs." But what did Paulhan think or Benda say? Did they at least understand what Drieu had become? No, they still didn't understand. For example, in a letter Paulhan wrote to Jouhandeau, he said: "I am sure you are right to contribute to the new NRF. Drieu is totally loyal. It seems to him that he is doing a just, necessary, and, some might say, courageous job." Mauriac wrote to Drieu himself, saying he believed his decision had been wrong, and went on: "But what a pleasure it is to have the NRF again. Bless you for having made its resurrection, possible. French writers must come together, be united in affirming the permanence of our spiritual life." And if Eluard, Gide and even Malraux finally kept their distance, it didn't prevent the first of them from sending an article to the journal in 1941, nor did it prevent the second from having the most ardent correspondence with the director six months later or the third from inviting him to be his son's godfather. This was in September 1943 when yellow stars had been introduced, round-ups had taken place, camps were in existence, and there were rumours about extermination. No further proof was needed of Drieu's political commitment nor of the horrors to which it bore witness. Yet one has to recognise that, far from being shunned as a pariah, as one might have believed, he retained to the end the esteem and friendship of his peers.

But I was forgetting the very end of his life and the three famous scenes which occupy a key place in the golden legend of Pierre Drieu La Rochelle – and which might well trouble the historian of ideas. First, there was the apartment in the Rue Saint-Ferdinand where the fallen and hunted collaborator sought refuge with Colette, his first wife. It is referred to as the scene of "the Jewess", as she offered her ignominious ex-husband the only helping hand available to him, having forgiven him for his earlier offence. Then there was his final exchange with André Malraux (obviously conducted indirectly since it was done through Suzanne Tezenas – which made it all the more fantastic and likely to give his posthumous admirers something to think about). "Would you, in the name of friendship, accept me into the Alsace-Lorraine Brigade?" "Yes I will accept you, but I would ask you to change your name. My men wouldn't understand. On that condition I would welcome you." That was the extraordinary final offer or means of escape held out to this ultra-Nazi by a man who was soon to become one of the heroes of the Resistance. The fact that Drieu, having been reassured that Malraux still trusted him, ultimately turned down the offer and preferred to die doesn't in any way lessen the paradox of this final act of kindness. Finally, there was d'Astier de la Vigerie who, on arriving in Paris on September 1st, 1944, and moving into his ministerial office, learned that his old friend had tried to kill himself and so sent an emissary to see him: "Drieu must be got as quickly as possible into Switzerland. I can help by having the ambulance escorted by someone from the 'Sûreté'. But you must take up my offer as soon as possible. I shall only be a minister for three days." Yet again, Drieu did not respond. But the offer had been made.

There was the same eagerness to help him, the same activity on his behalf at the end of his life as there had been early on. Paradoxically, the same circle of friends and acquaintances remained faithful to him. Moreover, his work was treated with the same extraordinary indulgence as his life, though everyone at the time felt he had not fulfilled his earliest ambitions. Brasillach did not experience anything like it. He had not done anything worse than Drieu, and his literary work was, broadly speaking, as good as Drieu's. Yet he did not have the same circle of elegant women, communist marquises, and writers eager to take up his cause, which is the mark of those whose destiny is exceptional. Even if, in the end, there was a petition got up on Brasillach's behalf and the conscience of certain major figures led them to plead his cause, it was in fact the cause and not the man they were fighting for. There were none of the feelings which Drieu aroused and which explain why some people still find him an attractive figure today. That, I reiterate, is the enigma. It results from the gap which existed between his ultimately squalid life and personality, on the one hand, and his undeniably seductive power, on the other. It is that gap and the seductive power which need to be explained.

Why did he win favour and where did it come from? Why should he have been privileged? How could someone who was so unforgivable inspire such feelings? There are as many explanations of the source of his seductive power as there are commentators and witnesses.

For example, there is Borges who got to know him slightly in Buenos Aires in 1931, where Drieu went at the instigation of Victoria Ocampo to give a series of lectures on democracy and Europe. These two contemporaries talked a little and walked a great deal. At night for preference, they would endlessly pace those enormous, dead-straight avenues in that most European of American cities. When I happened to meet Borges almost fifty years later in Milan, I tried to get him to recall memories he had of that meeting and above all if he had any idea as to why Drieu could have exercised such an influence. "Drieu...", he told me, "oh, it's very simple ... Drieu was an aristocrat, or that's what he let you believe ... and you know how sensitive the French are about the aristocracy." It was, he admitted, a brief explanation; witty and provocative. But his interpretation was to be confirmed, though the other way round, by a story I came across a year later in Cocteau's Journal. Cocteau discovered there was a chemist "Drieu La Rochelle", run by an uncle of Drieu's in a suburb. The "prince of poets" decided to lead a whole band of jokers out there and kick up a great rumpus. Drieu was hopping mad – because he felt he'd been unmasked, that people would see right through him, having discovered the lie on which he was beginning to build his career.

There was also Bernard Frank, who didn't know him of course, but who devoted an extremely subtle critical essay to him in his *Panoplie littéraire*. According to Frank, the secret about Drieu was his weakness, his overwhelming weakness. What's more, his weakness was the key to his anti-semitism. (Frank comments that he termed his vulnerability a Jewish trait; so that his hatred of Jews and of Judaism can perhaps basically be seen as a way of hating and mortifying himself and of pursuing in himself the "old Adam", which cannot be rooted out and to which all totalitarians are hostile, as is generally acknowledged). It was also the principal reason why a fundamentally wounded man was able to stir the emotions of all sensitive souls. How could one fail to be moved by someone who, on all occasions, openly confessed his feelings. As a woman, how could you refuse the role he offered – at worst a nurse, at best someone who could redeem him? These are the twin characters of his novels, the two types of women he endlessly expected to give him back his strength. One can imagine the pitiful pleasure of Colette Jeramec, having been ridiculed and treated in his novels as the lowest of the low, when in that famous final scene he said to her: "I am weak! so weak! You realise all the wrongs I committed in the past simply reflected that weakness. Now

163

I have come back to you, helpless and in need, begging you to give me refuge and to show me pity."

On the other hand, he definitely had courage, of a certain kind. There was his suicide of course, though this cannot explain the indulgence he enjoyed during his life, to which I've referred. Also in the preceding months, he accepted the choices he'd made and took them to extremes, which one couldn't help but admire. He realised that everything was finished and that Hitler had virtually lost. This was just before the Allied landings in North Africa, which everyone was aware would be the turning-point in the war. Collaborators like him thought only of joining what was to become the largest army in the country; that of late converts to the Resistance. He did the opposite, the total opposite. In the well-known episode where he asked Malraux if he would accept him into his Brigade, he contented himself with a positive answer and did nothing further. In the meantime, as the landings were about to take place and everyone around him thought only of trying to appear virtuous again, he went off to the Gaumont Palace on the final day of the PPF congress, having left the party two years earlier. He no longer believed in it, and the file on him wasn't very considerable at that stage. Yet he took up his old place again alongside Victor Barthélemy and in a way signed his own death warrant. Needless to say, that act of bravado doesn't excuse anything as far as I'm concerned. But it explains a lot. I can also see that such a gesture might have helped to redeem him in the eyes of a Malraux or a d'Astier.

He was both courageous and weak, and his courage was achieved by overcoming his weakness. Drieu's secret was probably this: at the same time as he enjoyed displaying a certain cult of bravery, he never hid the wretched assortment of fears, doubts, and little cowardly deeds to which he was prey. His bravery was simply the product of having overcome those weaknesses. Take, for example, his stories about the First War or his *Comédie de Charleroi*. Montherlant would have chosen – did choose – that theme to present powerful, warlike scenes with faultless heroes showing total daring. Drieu did the same, in what one must term his slightly ridiculous, pre-fascist celebration of the glories of war. But he also wrote about his fears and his pitiful inner weakness. He spared us nothing of the terror he experienced at Verdun or of his feeling of helplessness after the death of Jeramec, the brother of his future wife, or even in "Prière d'Hargeville"[3] the way he had to exhort his "flesh", his "strength", his "soul" before every ordeal, so that they would not fail him. "You fear being afraid," the pacifist

Debrye says to the hero of *Gilles*, who makes no reply, knowing it to be true. Drieu was the opposite of Montherlant and had nothing of the false courage of those braggarts who like to think they are all of a piece. The consequence of this and the secret of his charm was that, whilst one didn't for a moment believe the braggart's boastings and secretly guessed that his wounds were merely scratches, and that he'd never been gored by a bull in Pamplona, Drieu's confessions rang true and showed the stuff of which real (and not just physical) courage was made.

There were, of course, the women, and the legend about the man covered with women which was obligingly perpetuated. There was the whole private side of his life involving passion, turmoil, and beautiful women seduced and abandoned, which rightly or wrongly Benda, Nizan and even Malraux probably believed he enjoyed. For myself, I've always thought the crucial factors affecting the influence a writer has over his contemporaries are the stories involving women – and seduction – together with his courage. Drieu perhaps proved this better than anyone. There was however the subtle but decisive twist he gave to the classic image of the seducer, which Bernard Frank was also aware of. Whilst such a figure is usually an "homme fatal", whilst he projects himself as an irresistible and arrogant man of iron, and derives all his charm from dominating weak women, Drieu would always confess that he was weak, that far from being the rake people imagined, experienced in the ploys and stratagems of love, he was unfortunately at the mercy of the passions he was supposed to unleash. Here again, he was the opposite of Montherlant and of Costals.[4] As a lover, he was more like Rodolphe in *Mme Bovary* than either Costals or Valmont.[5] It was as if Drieu (or his principal characters and especially Gilles, which amounts to the same thing) had realised from the start that there was an advantage to be gained from systematically transforming the recognised figure of the seducer. In this way, he was able to show that being fond of women not only had its hidden side, but also involved timidity, humility and pitiable indecision.

Lastly, there was his suicide, which left various questions unanswered: (What would have happened to Drieu if . . . what would he have been like as a member of the Academy . . . what aspects of his life would he have rejected . . . what books might he have written?). But even before the suicide itself, which inevitably cast a romantic aura over the life which preceded it, there was a fascination with suicide which ran right through his novels and which must again have made an impression on his detractors as well as his friends. There is the suicide of Blèche, of Alain in *Le Feu follet*, and of Hassib in *Beloukia*. In *Gilles* Paul Morel and M. Falkenberg senior commit suicide, as does Gilles himself in a way right at the end of the book. Then there are the suicides of Jaime in *L'Homme à cheval* and of Dirk Raspe. Does suicide occupy such a prominent place in any other body of contemporary writing? Is there a writer who has taken such pleasure in describing, in advance of his own death, the numerous reasons for putting an end to the difficult business of living? And is there a better way of allowing the painful ambiguity to emerge, which one begins to realise was the source of the fascination he aroused? In this case it doesn't much matter whether it reflected real unhappiness or represented, rather, an endless series of false trails, riddles and pretences into which he was finally absorbed. Yet again the crux of the matter is the image Drieu projected and the fact that everyone at the time believed, paradoxically, that he was the last of the line of young men who twenty years previously had emerged from the First World War deeply affected, and re-entered the world wearing their suicide in their button-hole, as one of them put it.

In short, there are numerous arguments, as well as plausible and sound explanations – numerous facets to the case, if you like – each of which sheds light on some aspect or other of our mystery. However, it is clear that no single one explains it altogether, and that even after discussing Drieu and women, Drieu and courage, Drieu and suicide, one still has the inescapable feeling of only having touched on a truth which goes much deeper. My own personal conviction is that the truth lies elsewhere and that, in order to discover it, one has to explore another realm where writers bury their secrets, namely their writing. Drieu was, after all, a writer. I believe it is in his books, in their language and tone, and in the way he expressed his enthusiasm for Dachau, his love of Hitler, etc., that the key to the enigma of Drieu will be found.

Let us turn then to the texts. Though no one reads the ideological and politically committed ones, the novels and short stories are certainly read, as are biographies of Drieu, however minor, but strangely no one thinks of looking at *Socialisme fasciste* or *Avec Doriot*, those books in which he set down the whys and wherefores of his choices, or the collections of articles and pamphlets in which he explained and justified himself. I've looked at them and I must admit I've found them most instructive.

What exactly did Drieu say and how did he present the cause of fascism to which he rallied? The first striking thing is that he talked of it as a movement of the Left rather than of the Right, which I imagine would surprise many of today's readers. He expressly referred to it as being of the Left, without seeking to be provocative and without imagining his argument would either seem excessive or particularly scandalise people. Fascism was left-wing and that's all there was to it. He was a red, a socialist. He maintained that the second element of "national-socialism" was at least as important and as meaningful as the first. In this respect, the portrait he painted of Jacques Doriot, his own pet fascist, was most significant. What people usually quote are his slightly stupid remarks about "Doriot the fine athlete" who "embraces the enfeebled body" of the old, "sick Motherland", France, and "breathes new life into her which he has in abundance." But equally important in his choice of Doriot was the fact that he was a worker and an admirer of Lenin, who boasted he had been one of the key figures in the Komintern. There was also the fact that as late as 1934 Stalin had been on the point of choosing him rather than Thorez as leader of the French Communist Party. Furthermore, far from disowning his past, this worker and communist leader intended to bring about what he believed in by offering the common people an alternative, as he felt they had been disorientated by the Communist Party becoming middle-class. His was to be national socialism, a communism without Moscow, a sort of early version of French Titoism, with the worker from Saint-Denis as the Marshal. That was how Drieu envisaged Doriot's politics, what he understood them to be. And that is what his friends on the Left thought he understood them to be.

Even more disturbing was that he never missed the chance of saying how national socialism, in both its German form and the one it was soon to assume in France, was clearly a revolutionary movement. He said as much in 1934 in his article in *Marianne* entitled "Mesure de l'Allemagne" and in 1939 in *Le Figaro*, when he portrayed a young German entering the SA in order to "bring about the revolution". He said so again in 1940, after the defeat, when he went to see Abetz and warned him: "Make sure that the German army does not appear to be an occupying army! It's a revolutionary army, an army of liberation, and like the great army of Napoleon which spread the message of revolution throughout Europe!" These remarks may seem strange, wild even, but they were, yet again, precisely what he said. There were people at the time who saw fascism as a return to the past and to tradition. There were, especially at Vichy, those who dreamed of a conservative, reactionary State etc. Drieu was not one of them. He had absolutely nothing in common with that strand of intellectual opinion. What appealed to him in fascism was its disruptive nature, its violent, seismic, apocalyptic side. In his eyes, Hitler wasn't going to manage things but to change the world. Hitler the "civilising force", Hitler "the educator", Hitler as a kind of "Augustus" was going to lay the foundations of a future society in violence and bloodshed. Was he like Stalin? Yes, he was like Stalin. Was he like Lenin? Yes, he was like Lenin, and Lenin wasn't as bad as all that. There was something admirable about the side of Lenin's character which called to mind "an abbot of the Middle Ages entering a forest with his monks to create a clearing". He was indeed so admirable that Drieu very nearly became a Leninist and a Stalinist, as I've already suggested.

But he didn't, it must be said. However "admirable" Lenin might have been, Drieu ended up by going over to the other side. In doing so, was he conscious of the choice he was making? Yes and no. One should look at the *reasons* he gave to justify his choice, of which there were three. The first was that "things being as they were and European communist parties having become large, soft organisations which were destined to collapse, the fascists were more revolutionary than the communists, if one compared the two revolutions." That is literally what the young Storm Trooper said to him in the article in *Le Figaro*, and what he himself wrote in his article of '34. So, in going over to fascism, he was not renouncing revolution but remaining faithful to it. The second was that, from the point of view of his goals and the means of achieving them, from the point of view of the actual strategy that a responsible intellectual should help to fashion, fascism represented progress towards communism. In other words, Drieu remained a "communist", and continued to believe in something which, rightly or wrongly, he called communism. For example, in his diary (an extract dated April 19th, 1944 but which refers to the pre-war years), he talked quite naturally of fascism as "a step on the road to communism" – which were the very words used by his left-wing friends who saw socialism in exactly the same light. His third and final reason is illustrated by the following comment: "In 1918, I detected that Russian communism was a means of creating a new aristocracy, and I wasn't mistaken. I seek in fascism, the European form of socialism, this new aristocracy." Everything was contained and expressed in that phrase: the European form of socialism. Fascism was no longer a "step" but a "version", not a "moment" but a "variant". Berl commented that for Drieu "fascism is the only form of communism which the small, old-fashioned nations of the West can assimilate." At the same time, there were people who became fascist out of fear, hatred, or a refusal of communism. Yet again, this was not the case with Drieu. In this connection, there is a page in *Socialisme fasciste* which is quite surprising: "I'll leave it to pseudo-revolutionaries to humiliate themselves by calling me paradoxical. What I have to say is that my faith in the future of socialism comes from the spectacle of fascist countries as they are at present."

So why did he break with fascism, on what basis, and when precisely? There were numerous possible reasons for breaking with fascism. He could have done so because of the camps or because he thought Hitler was a monster and mad. He could have acquired information about the "final solution of the Jewish question". He might have thought of Colette, of Berl, of the Jewish friends he had in the thirties, as well as of the faceless people put on trains in the early hours of the morning for Drancy or Auschwitz. But that's not what Drieu did. That wasn't why he distanced himself. He couldn't have cared less about Jewish children and what was going to happen to them. He had a much more serious and interesting reason for making the break. His was an intellectual's reason, since he viewed things from a superior, historical perspective and juggled with big ideas. He made the break, he tells us, because he suddenly had the feeling people were having him on and that Hitler wasn't the revolutionary he'd believed him to be. Even during the war one incident had troubled him: the fact that the Nazis banished from their museums the tormented, distorted paintings of Vincent Van Gogh. In what way and for what reason was he concerned? Was it that the Germans wanted to "escape the very violence which had created them?" At the same time, something else happened. Hermann Rauschning's *The Revolution of Nihilism* was published in Geneva. Rauschning confirmed in this book – and at the same time deplored – what Drieu himself had sensed "for a long time" concerning the revolutionary upsurge which had shaken Hitler's Germany. He now learned that Hitler's supporters didn't like the book and refused to accept what it said. Then in 1945, what illusions our social fascist had left were destroyed, and he had to face facts and accept the awful truth that "the Germans were not in the least revolutionary!", that they had been "completely overtaken by events" and were no longer pursuing "any political aims in Europe, which I have known for a year and a half". He made this disenchanted remark in his diary on March 5th. Eight days later, he added: "I no longer believe in fascism as there is too little socialism in fascism." It proves again, this time from the opposite standpoint, that it was indeed "socialism" and "revolution" that he had in mind in his earlier, euphoric state.

The strange attitude he adopted after the rupture affords the final proof, again from the opposite standpoint. Everything was possible. He might have become a democrat or a liberal. He might have discovered, late in the day, the virtues of Gaullism. He could have done nothing at all, believed in nothing, and taken care not to get carried away in future by his own enthusiasms, having learned his lesson. He could have taken up philosophy, finished *Dirk Raspe*, become completely absorbed in Hinduism. There were numerous things he could have done to get over it and to occupy himself. But no, he plunged straight back in, reactivating all his beliefs. One finds him declaring, in a tone which suggested he would not change his mind again, that things were clear and that he really understood he would remain and die a communist! After Mussolini's dismissal, he had muttered: "So that's all fascism was. For a year now, all my hopes have rested on communism!" He then wrote in *La Révolution nationale*, the ultra-collaborationist paper run by his friend and junior, Lucien Combelle: "With the Continent in the grip of socialism, can one expect to see anything but the red flag covering its entire surface?" A few weeks later, in a conversation with Karl Epting, the Director of the Franco-German Institute, he commented: "If Combelle survives, what I really want is for him to become a communist, which would be the logical extension of all we have fought for. The communists will be the heirs of fascism in Europe." In his private diary of April '43 he wrote: "I am coming back to the point of view of Boutros in *Une femme à sa fenêtre*, one of my books forgotten by me and by everyone else, that communism is the end of everything, the final stage of European decadence." So Drieu was bitter, felt cheated, nevertheless he rediscovered hope and started to believe again. He had complete confidence in communist Russia and was hoping it would win. What if Hitler also understood, pulled himself together again, reversed his alliances and joined hands once more with his kindred spirit, as he'd done in 1939? Sadly, there was no point in dreaming. The Germans, he fumed, were too "damned stupid". Secretly, he was forced to admit that Stalin, and Stalin alone, was wearing his colours. According to the critic Frédéric Grover, he insistently put the same ludicrous question to one of his mistresses: "What would people think if I went over to the Russians?"

Now his communism was, of course, rather special. It contained a whole rag-bag of racist, anti-semitic, and youth-oriented ideas which were carried straight over from his abandoned beliefs. Doubtless they would not have been entirely acceptable to "true" communists. That's as may be. But what I'm trying to say is that, yet again, the words Drieu used were the same, as were the questions he asked. His language, his field of interest, the whole gamut of his concerns, concepts and dreams was the same. A modern epistemologist would refer to it as the same problematic. Indeed, what we need is an epistemology of political discourse. We need a Foucault who would be able to describe the distribution of political passions in a given period, using the same knowledge and methods as he did for the distribution of science and learning. If such an epistemology existed, it would, I believe, be possible to point up the extreme closeness I'm trying to bring out. It would be seen that Aragon and Drieu, each in his own sphere and style, drew on the same stock of images, obsessions and emotions. One might also have gone to Roquebrune in the summer of '43, to the villa Malraux was living in with Josette Clotis, and eavesdropped on an astounding discussion which the two men had, as to whether Doriot or De Gaulle was best placed – *sic* – to create a revolution. In the end it would be clear that in constantly trotting out his obsessions about the decadence of Europe and the irreversible decline of the notion of democracy, Drieu was exploring the same issues as his pro-Soviet friends. Moreover, when he chose to call the little review which he and Berl founded *Les Derniers Jours*, it could have been the title of one of Nizan's books.

What explanation is there for the indulgent attitude towards Drieu shown by the Left and the extraordinary liking people had for him throughout his life? We can now answer that question. Even when these people clashed and hurled abuse at each other, they had something fundamental in common. Fascism, which to us seems aberrant and monstrous, and Nazism, which was the incarnation of ultimate and absolute horror, seemed to them to be one *version* of a single phenomenon. Drieu and Malraux, for example, and Drieu and Aragon were like Borges's two theologians who spent their whole life expelling or excommunicating each other but who, at the moment of their death, suddenly became aware they were two bodies inhabited by the same soul. God had placed one soul in two bodies, Borges commented ironically. God showed more imagination over bodies than souls. The same thing was true of our intellectuals. The God of the history of ideas, represented by the "épistème"[6] of a particular moment, readily casts the same passions, the same fantasies, the same forms of blindness into different bodies of discourse. It will, I presume, be understood that what I've said in no way excuses Drieu, nor clearly does it alter the moral blame which the texts we've been looking at can and should invite. However, I leave open that other question as to what those affinities of language indicated about the real nature of a "Left", ignorant of the fact that it so resembled its counterpart.

NOTES

1. *L'Homme couvert de femmes* (1925) was the title of one of Drieu's novels which centred on a number of liaisons.

2. The Parti Populaire Français was founded in June 1936 by the ex-communist Jacques Doriot. It was probably the most important extreme right-wing organisation of the period.

3. A poem which Drieu probably wrote when he was with American troops near Verdun in 1918.

4. The central character of Monther-lant's four-part novel *Les Jeunes filles* (1936–39), described by the author as a "libertine" or "a bad lot".

5. A libertine character in *Les Liaisons dangereuses*, the celebrated eighteenth-century novel by Laclos.

6. A term used by Foucault to describe "the total set of relations that unite, at a given period, the discursive practices that give rise to epistemological figures, sciences, and possibly formalised systems" of knowledge.

3

"Berlin had come to Paris"

A CONVERSATION WITH MYSELF ON THE SUBJECT OF COCTEAU

— There's something strange about you. You talk about Drieu and Brasillach. When Paul Valéry spent too much time in a cemetery, you branded him a fascist desecrator of tombs. Yet there is one writer you won't speak about, namely Jean Cocteau who, in your eyes, enjoyed extraordinary impunity. Why is this? Wasn't he also around? Didn't he have his table at Maxim's, his German friends, his theatrical successes? Didn't he write in *La Gerbe*[1] and *Comoedia*?[2] Isn't there also the testimony of old José Corti who went to see him in May '44 in the restaurant Le Catalan, where he ate regularly, and put it to him: "You eat with Germans – couldn't you therefore at least help me to save my son who has been deported?" And isn't it an established fact that "the prince of poets", either out of thoughtlessness or indifference, didn't lift a finger to help? And didn't he also realise straight away that his "Salute to Breker"[3] would have been the most incriminating piece of evidence in his dossier, were the situation ever to have arisen where that mattered? He did all these things and yet you spare him.

— That's true. However, the main point is not to confuse things. In terms of infamy or indifference, Cocteau compromised himself somewhat less than the others you've been discussing. Certainly, there was his "Salute to Breker", but he didn't pen a hymn of praise to Hitler nor was he euphoric about the German victory. He didn't write any *Solstice de juin*[4] nor any *Chronique privée de l'an 40*.[5] He certainly didn't denounce anyone nor did he make any anti-semitic declarations, in public at least. If he failed to respect the rules of honour over Corti's son, there were a number of people on whose behalf he did intervene, beginning with Max Jacob, even though his attempt was sadly unsuccessful, however sincere. Added to which, there is a second factor. Cocteau had a totally different side to him which also has to be taken into account in discussing these matters. You may not know that before the war Cocteau was one of the star leader-writers on Aragon's paper *Ce Soir*.[6] There was, then, a left-wing, anti-fascist Cocteau who was not in the least bit inclined towards Pétainism.

— I know that full well. There was his article on Guernica in June 1936 and the "Songe et mensonge de Franco" the following month. In 1938, when the flood of persecuted people, principally Jews, fleeing Nazi Germany began to swell, he made an appeal for France to have an open-door policy and to "offer asylum to the exiles of the world". There were also, I agree, his attacks on Wagnerian anti-semitism and his praise for the Popular Front. It's perfectly clear that Cocteau in his early guise could not be suspected of having any sympathy for the Nazi regime. But so what? Does that prove anything? Since when does the position a person adopted before the war serve to excuse the one he adopted during it? Surely I don't have to tell you that Cocteau wasn't the first "progressive" and vaguely "left-wing" writer to have totally gone over to the other side?

— Of course not, but there's something else in his case which distinguishes him. Instead of behaving like a Jouhandeau or a Montherlant and saying, "Alright, I'm a left-wing writer who has become a Pétainist. There's nothing wrong in that, and I shall go on being one", he readopted his old stance after the war and became a fellow-traveller of the Communist Party. He attended Eluard's funeral, was in the front rank of those demonstrating and appealing on behalf of the Rosenbergs, supported Sartre over the Henri Martin affair.[7] Cocteau backed Aragon in most of the major political events of the period and was the only artist, along with Picasso and Aragon, to be photographed with Maurice Thorez. Don't you find that both strange and intriguing? What interests me is the determination and zeal shown by the author of the "Salute to Breker" in rejoining at that moment what he obviously considered to be his original family. As I'm writing a history of ideas, that's to say a history of families, I'm bound to make something of this unusual and compelling change of direction.

— You must be joking! You know perfectly well what things were like at that time between Cocteau and the communists, and Aragon in particular. Aragon couldn't stand him. Berl said he was too close, Elsa said he was too distant. But be that as it may, Aragon realised it could be a major coup for the Party. "You've had it," he told Cocteau, "You're in it up to your neck; there's a dossier that thick on you and you've no chance of getting off. The Party will help you; it will clear your name for what you've done in the past and will shield you in the future. But in exchange for this truce, it will want manifestos, photos, editorials from you and will expect you to be totally loyal and obedient." This was a classic example of the way the victorious Party behaved at the time. One can imagine the "fou d'Elsa"[8] talking like that, having been put in charge of literary matters. As Cocteau wasn't foolhardy, he accepted.

— I would accept that in part. Besides, I prefer on the whole the bastard who redeems himself, who feels it necessary to redeem himself, to the one who sinks complacently into shameful behaviour. I would remind you that deals of this kind are more widespread than you think. All intellectuals have been through the process. Every act of commitment is the same. What has always happened – and not just in '45 or with the Communist Party – is something like this: "You're guilty, you're wicked, and there's something about being involved in literature which sets you apart from other people. So if you wish to erase the past, if you want a quiet life so that you can continue with your dismal literary activities, there's a price to be paid, and the price is commitment." I've been saying these things for a long time, insisting that a politicised writer is always a dubious figure who suddenly feels the need to do something positive. Well his is a particularly striking example, I agree. But that's why it interests me.

— Why dubious, why not damnable whilst you are at it? Could there have been a better – or worse – society poet at the time than Cocteau, someone who felt at ease living through that period, having none of the characteristics of the unsociable and gloomy writer, at odds with the society in which he lived. People listened to what he said, fêted and admired him. He was surrounded by his court and had a crowd of flatterers hanging onto his coat tails. There's a famous picture of some of his young admirers who had climbed up lamp-posts at night opposite where he lived, in the hope of catching a glimpse of him at one of his windows. There was Cocteau's levee which the whole of Paris hurried to, though only the privileged few were permitted to watch him getting dressed. Countless Parisians holding parties and celebrations fought over him and obtained his glittering presence. Forgive me for insisting on it, but he was a long way from being the hated and accursed poet!

— Well, I'm not so sure about that. I sometimes wonder if Cocteau wasn't *the most hated* poet of his time and of ours too. That hatred has been forgotten, as has the unbelievable way in which the surrealists, for example, continued to persecute him. Breton described him as "the most hated person of his day". Péret remarked: "Cocteau? he's an angel's dropping." Eluard commented: "So let's mention the name of Cocteau without blushing, as we're going to destroy him like some foul-smelling animal!" Then there were the copies of *La Révolution surréaliste* in which his behaviour was discussed quite openly, the phone calls to his mother denouncing him, and the fact that he was chased in the streets. Did you know that Cocteau was beaten up, that his shows were systematically disrupted? Did you know that during that whole period he had to leave the cinema before the end of the film because he was aware René Char would be waiting for him at the exit? With a touching note of despondency, he wrote: "They're using magic and casting spells." To console him, Max Jacob said those people were "possessed of the devil!" For my part, I'm sure this will be enough to modify your view of him as a poet fêted and showered with flowers and honours. Secondly, a man who was hated to that extent, a writer who attracted such reprobation, couldn't have been as bad as you pretend to believe.

— But everything depends upon the nature of the hatred and the *reasons* people had for condemning a person. In Cocteau's case, it was quite clear. There was the ambiguity, the dubious side of his character, as well as the Breker affair with . . .

— No, it wasn't clear at all. Because all the incidents I've mentioned occurred before the war. In any case, don't deceive yourself. The Breker affair didn't immediately cause the fuss it should have done. In the end it passed and people didn't complain much about it. Then came the time, in the months and years after the war, when Cocteau's case was settled. He was absolved by the Communist Party, which is basically what he'd counted on and which paid off. Except that one has to find another explanation for the hatred.

— So?

— It's to do with style.

— Style?

— Yes, style. Cocteau had a certain style, a way of living and behaving which didn't fit in with the dull-wittedness of the surrealists. Don't forget that Breton never got over the fact that he was a policeman's son from Nantes. For him, there was something intolerable about Cocteau's easy and casual manner.

— Isn't there something equally intolerable about reducing a quarrel between intellectuals to a simple confrontation between the sons of two different kinds of people?

— Let's put it another way. Cocteau had fame and talent. There was his legendary "ability" (you've heard the stories about him writing a poem in an hour, a novel in a single night, and about him dashing off brilliant sketches on the back of a napkin). There was his homosexuality as well, which those people found intolerable. That was something Crevel discovered too.

—I must stop you again, because it's got nothing to do with Crevel. He was one of the group, of the family, as you'd put it. As such, he was answerable to the surrealist code of behaviour.

—Precisely; and Cocteau was also one of the group. Or at least, those outside it thought he was. That's what exasperated Breton in the end. Remember that when *Le Sang d'un poète* appeared, the press hailed it as a masterpiece of surrealist cinema!

—So there was a dispute about boundaries, a conflict over who could certify and authenticate things, who was in command on the battlements. There was a form of literary trade war.

—That was part of it, and it could be seen very clearly when they vied for the patronage of a certain backer or art-dealer whose services they both required. But I don't wish to put too much emphasis on it. Because, as I've said, in addition to all that, and the fact they clashed like shopkeepers and could have settled things amicably, there was the question of Cocteau's dandyism, his humour, and his ostentatious and carefree manner which André Breton found intolerable. I wouldn't say as Cocteau's friends did: "They hated him because he had more charm, talent, genius, etc." But it's true I'd almost be prepared to defend Cocteau's unbearable lightheartedness in the face of the surrealists' resort to terror and their dreary solemnity.

—But what exactly do you mean by Cocteau's lightheartedness? What is left of it if you ignore his talent and genius? I'm aware of his friends in high society, of course, the money, the luxuries, and an awful lot of frivolity. I'm aware of the photos with the Rochas and the Molyneux. I'm aware of the grotesque ambulance driver who, in 1914, had his uniform designed by Poiret. I'm aware of the ageing juvenile, going to lots of balls and parties, and ending up having to play at being a genius for all those society people. It truly was a matter of style. But the question one must ask is whether the style of life he adopted was compatible or not with his concern to produce a body of work.

—That's the real issue. Let's say it's what fascinates me about the fellow. I've always liked losers, has-beens. I've always had a weakness for those who hover on the brink of failure. Also, I like the idea of a writer organising his life in such a way that it becomes parasitical upon his work, sabotages it, and ends up by undermining it.

—To the point of designing dresses for Schiaparelli, sweaters for Coco Chanel, of allowing Jeanne Lanvin to name one of her dresses "Heurtebise" and nightclubs to call themselves "Les Enfants terribles" or the "Grand Ecart". No, that's not "arrogance" or "lightheartedness". It's a crime against literature. It shows an enormous lack of respect for oneself and for the dignity of one's own work. For a writer, that's the ultimate sacrilege. And it was all because he wanted to push his way into a few hotels on the Côte d'Azur. He did have talent, your man Cocteau, but what I find disturbing is that he wasted his talent, frittered it away because of his absurd life-style. It just shows what harm women with social pretensions can do for a writer's destiny.

— Everyone has his problems. I'm touched to hear him complaining about the "monstrous injustice" done to him and to see him making such a devil of a fuss, in the hope that those associated with the NRF will see him as one of them. I'm also so touched to know he was deeply distressed when people shunned him and so happy when they were welcoming, and to read phrases such as,"My name gets around faster than my books!" and, "People look up to Malraux, Montherlant, Sartre, Camus, Anouilh; they look down on me." I'm also moved by his self-loathing and by the insults he directed at himself. There's also the fact that he was a film-maker of genius and a first-rate prose-writer, yet he did everything to ensure he remained a minor figure of the time. I'm glad this man so obviously played his life off against his work, without wishing to or knowing he was doing it.

— I'm afraid you're going to consider me a terrible killjoy, but I have exactly the opposite feeling. I'm even prepared to argue that Cocteau was a cunning individual who knew what he was doing. Far from allowing his life to get in the way of his work, he discovered the best way of allowing each to support the other. As you know, he had extraordinary flair. There was no one who could match Cocteau's ability to detect talent or genius in others. He seemed to have his own radar, to be able to detect them almost infallibly. There was Genet and Radiguet and others as well. What I really wanted to say was that he was certainly as perceptive about himself as he was about others. I can see him clearly, at the time of his earliest success, dazzled but also overwhelmed because he had so many different talents, and thinking to himself; I'll never be another Gide, another Picasso. I'm probably not even cut out to be the leading light of some movement or other like Breton. I'm just Cocteau, an average writer who can draw fairly well; in other words I'm an artist torn between my many interests. The only thing I can do about it is to fill my life with paradoxes. As a bonus, I might be able to pose as a writer who lost his way and make people think that, had it not been for a Schiaparelli dress and the odd excess or discreet folly, I would have been a Gide or a Proust.

NOTES

1. A collaborationist newspaper.

2. A paper devoted to the arts which came under collaborationist control during the war.

3. Cocteau produced a publicity article in May 1943 for the Paris exhibition by Arno Breker, Hitler's favourite sculptor.

4. A work published by Montherlant in 1941 which exalted the swastika as a symbol of the masculine principle that would vanquish the feminine one. He was critical of French weakness and intoxicated by the strength of the virile and victorious Germans.

5. A book by Jacques Chardonne which put forward a philosophy of collaboration with the occupying authorities.

6. An evening paper founded by the Communist Party in March 1937 as a rival to *Paris Soir*.

7. Henri Martin was a French sailor who was arrested in 1950 and condemned for circulating leaflets denouncing the war in Indo-China.

8. The title of a collection of poems inspired by Aragon's lifelong companion, Elsa Triolet.

4

"Lynchings and the Kristallnacht"

Was it known? Did they know? Were those great intellectuals of ours told the actual, final destination of the famous death trains? When, for example, Brasillach – and sadly he's only one example – begged his German friends "not to forget the little ones", was he aware he was sending these little ones to the gas chambers and the ovens? Strange as it may seem, I don't really care. Whether or not they knew exactly what was happening isn't of great importance to me. In my view, even if they were ignorant and didn't know the full horror which awaited these people, there was something about the act of putting them on trains, about the very idea of deportation and the insane hatred it implied which should have sickened them.

Imagine you were living at that time. Try to envisage a friend of yours being forced to wear a star or your doctor forbidden to practise. Think of a teacher disappearing, a shopkeeper having to close down, street names being changed, and actors being forbidden to appear on the screen. Visualise a restaurant with a sign saying: "No Jews allowed", the underground trains with special compartments. Imagine being harassed and humiliated. Then imagine policemen arriving in their capes one morning and knocking on your neighbours' door. You've lived next door to them for years, so you know them. They have their own life with its set patterns, its funny little ways, their small pleasures and major sorrows. It all comes to an end in a flash, is totally shattered. They are given just a minute or two to fasten a suitcase, pull on a coat, and then they're off, on their way to Drancy.[1] Their small pleasures and major sorrows are finished, gone for ever. There was nothing special about the life they led, but it was theirs, and now it has come to an end. Isn't that enough? Wouldn't it have been enough for *you*? Would it have really taken more to rouse you to indignation, to fill you with horror? Do you need more than this today? Does one have to prove, on top of everything else, that Drieu, Brasillach and company knew where these unfortunate people were being taken, the fate that awaited them and the appalling conditions in which they were to die, to earn the right to call them total swine?

Alright, so one does; then let's try to prove it by putting the crucial question, since those who persist in defending collaborators, in the face of the evidence, of dignity and honour, seem obsessed by it. Did they know? Was it known? Could they possibly have had any idea of what was to happen so far away at the end of the mystery journey? Wasn't it precisely a stroke of Nazi genius to have kept it quiet and made sure the whole affair was surrounded by a wall of silence and the terrifying idea of "secrecy"? The answer is yes. It was a stroke of genius. They were careful not to shout it from the rooftops that the Final Solution was under way. They prevented photos from being taken, hunted down witnesses, and, in any case, censorship was such that very few of the popular papers, either in Paris or the free zone, took the decision to discuss it. Yet even so, despite this degree of caution, there were so many admissions, testimonies, inevitable lapses in the system of censorship, indeed more and more evidence as the war progressed. Though it doubtless didn't reach the depths of the country, it couldn't have escaped the attention of the French élite.

One example is a programme broadcast by the BBC on June 2nd, 1942, followed on the 29th by a press conference given in London by the British section of the World Jewish Congress, and immediately followed up by a series of articles in a serious newspaper, the *Daily Telegraph*. The BBC programme repeated information which had come from the Polish Federation and been transmitted via a tortuous but reliable "Swedish network". Various things were discussed including actual extermination, the systematic exclusion from towns and villages of Jewish people, lorries carrying gas, thousands of men, women and children, sent off to Lublin in cattle trucks, who then disappeared without trace. At the time, it was reckoned that 700,000 Polish Jews had already been liquidated. It was a huge and precise figure, published, I repeat, by a major British paper, and no one at the time challenged it.

Another example concerns two press conferences given in Washington and then New York on November 24th and 25th, 1942 by the American Stephen Wise, and subsequently taken up by papers all over the world. Who was Stephen Wise? He too was a leader of the World Jewish Congress. What he reported was that the Führer's extermination plans, so often announced, had been put into effect. That must have been so since the number of Jews massacred or gassed in Eastern Europe alone was put at the terrifying figure of two million. Where did he get his figures from and why was he so sure of them? They came from a series of testimonies that had at first to be treated with caution but which were unfortunately authenticated by an investigation conducted by the State Department. That, in turn, was corroborated by information received from the Vatican. I should perhaps make it clear that these two press conferences were taken up by papers all over the world, reported by all the radio stations, commented on and discussed. It is clearly unthinkable that some faint echo didn't reach the ears of those most highly informed and prominent French collaborators.

Was it merely propaganda? Did the collaborators tell themselves it was too exaggerated to be true, that the whole story had been manipulated by the media? Perhaps. Well, here's another example which can't be challenged: Hitler's own statements. Whether or not they were a terrifying secret and despite his wish always to do things covertly, they reveal his intentions. Even before the war began, in a major speech to the Reichstag on January 30th, 1939, he said: "If international Jewish finance both within and beyond Europe were to lead the peoples of the world into another world war, the outcome would not be the Bolshevisation of every country on earth and the victory of Judaism, but the extermination of the Jewish race in Europe." During the war, he kept calling for the Jews to be exterminated, as if it were an uncontrollable obsession with him which he had to reveal. This was reported in all the Parisian papers, as various articles bear out. The headline in *Le Matin* of January 2nd, 1942 read: "The Jew cannot destroy Europe, he will be destroyed." On February 26th, in the same paper, he was reported to have said: "A long period of understanding and true peace between the nations will begin when the Jews have been eliminated." "The Jews will be exterminated", proclaimed *Le Cri du peuple*, quoting the Führer, also on February 26th. Reporting the same speech in a more sibylline manner, *L'Oeuvre* commented: "Preparations are in hand for the final settling of scores." And when Hitler proclaimed on October 1st that "the Jewish people have unleashed an international world war in order to destroy the Aryan peoples of Europe" and that "it is Jews, not the Aryan peoples who will be destroyed", the same collaborationist press unanimously took up what he said, quoted it, and used it of course for their headlines.

Add to that the common declaration signed on December 17th, 1942, by the eleven Allied governments, which had considerable repercussions: "The German authorities are implementing the plan which Hitler has often referred to of exterminating the Jewish people in Europe. Jews are being transported from all the occupied countries to Eastern Europe in terrifying conditions of extreme horror and brutality." In addition, there were the testimonies collected by the Red Cross, and on July 1st, 1942, Jean Marin, the future head of the French Press Agency, spoke about the existence of gas chambers on the BBC. Another broadcast on July 8th, 1943, referred to whole groups of Jews being "gassed, scalded alive by steam, or electrocuted". The clandestine press – *Combat, Franc-Tireur, Le Populaire, Libération Sud, Libération Nord* – had no hesitation in passing on information which it received about Auschwitz and Buchenwald. One final point worth adding, if you consider – and rightly so – that the clandestine press was not the most reliable in the eyes of those we are talking about, is that their *own* press also passed on the horrifying reports. Certainly, they did so cautiously, often without spelling things out, but in terms which left no one in doubt that the authors of the articles knew what was happening. For example, on March 26th, 1942, Constantini wrote in *L'Appel*: "One of the immediate consequences of the war is already taking place, that's to say the progressive elimination of the Jews." Also, on the day after the round-up of the "Vélodrome d'hiver",[2] one could read in a paper like *Le Pilori* firm declarations such as: "We now know that Jewish rule is coming to an end" and "the decisions taken concerning the accursed race are inescapable and irrevocable", and again that the Jewish race "is about to disappear completely from Europe, Asia and Africa", that "Jewish status" is only an "initial measure", preparing the ground for broader and *definitive* measures which are to be applied (*Le Pilori*'s italics), and finally "our statement should not be treated lightly as we are not in the habit of talking rubbish."

Do I need to give further examples? Could anything be plainer or more clear-cut? How could one demonstrate more plainly that the Final Solution was common knowledge at the time in Paris and therefore equally so for the readers of *L'Appel*, *Le Pilori* and other such papers? Our writers knew. They had the information. At any rate, they knew as much as the journalists whom I have quoted and whose articles they read every day. It is, however, quite possible they had difficulty in understanding, imagining, believing what they knew. Indeed, I'm quite sure it wasn't easy, as it never is imagining the unimaginable (it makes me think especially of communists discovering or rediscovering the existence of the Gulag). We even have the testimony of Aron, confessing in his *Mémoires* that he found it difficult to conceive of "the mechanised slaughter of human beings", and because he couldn't conceive of it, he only half "knew" it. Nonetheless, it would be a mistake to muddle things, to confuse a metaphysical issue (how does one comprehend a reality which literally defies comprehension?) and a totally concrete issue (had those intellectuals who collaborated heard what was to happen to the children of Drancy when they arrived in Poland?). Though the former issue is problematic, the latter is clear-cut; and though the one deserves to be raised and reflected upon, the other requires only facts, evidence, texts or testimonies in place of reflection, and I've provided some examples. Yes, Drieu knew about the existence of the camps. And yes, every day Brasillach read the latest news about the Final Solution in his favourite papers and the way it was progressing. Only bad historians claim these things were carefully protected by a heavy wall of silence. Those of you who present fascists such as these as pure idealists, lost in their dream world and unaware to the end of its negative side, are liars.

NOTES

1. A Jewish transit camp in the suburbs of Paris which was administered by the French until July 1943.

2. The first round-up of Jews took place on July 16th, 1942. Over 4,000 Jewish children were packed into this sports stadium.

5

"The vital adventure which had been initiated by the Vichy regime"

FINAL REMARKS ABOUT MOUNIER

1. Whether we like it or not, Emmanuel Mounier was one of those intellectuals for whom the defeat of 1940 was not a tragedy but an opportunity and a liberation. Amongst various things he wrote there was a letter of September 6th, 1940, in which he declared to a woman friend: "There is much to be done and we have been spared many deaths. I am at one and the same time pessimistic, because I believe our ordeal is only just beginning and that worse is to come, and optimistic, because we are entering a period of fervour." A few weeks earlier, he had written to his wife about Hitler (whom he referred to discreetly as 'he' in this second letter), and just as "he" was in the process of winning the war: "For France's sake it is essential that the ordeal impinges upon the lowliest gardener and petit bourgeois. 'He' will get to Marseilles and Bordeaux, because he wants to violate the whole country. But it will be a healthy lesson for everyone." Yes, that was indeed what Emmanuel Mounier, the editor of *Esprit* wrote. It was 1940, and the war was still raging. But the editor of *Esprit* had the effrontery to see the defeat of his country and the victory of Nazism in terms of a "healthy" experience.

2. As early as the autumn of 1940, at the same time as he sought (and obtained) permission to publish his review again, he affirmed his loyalty to the regime which set itself up in Vichy. He spoke of the "blessing" of the French State, of a "harsh outlook" but one in which "political virtues abounded." He knew that censorship existed which would not always be lenient towards intellectuals such as himself, yet he accepted and rejoiced over that too! In a fit of remorse that captured the mood of the time, he went so far as to exclaim: "As we quietly go about our research, we, too, shall cry out *"felix culpa!"* if the thought of the blue pencil restrains us each time we allow our critical faculties to override our creativity, thought to give way to ill-humour, and negativity to replace being." What a thing to say and how perfectly it justified censorship and the new moral climate! One could not have

renounced more decisively the role, the prestige of an intellectual. The lines were taken from the first issue of the new-style *Esprit* – which the occupying authorities obligingly authorised in November.

3. Not content with approving the regime, he offered to become part of it. Thus in September, he drafted a long report on youth movements which he passed on to the relevant authorities. What did they make of it? His own notebooks testify: "My report on youth movements which I drafted in September and am thinking of publishing has come back from Vichy with a gracious note from the Minister saying that they think it needs revision before it's published, precisely because it's given them such a fund of ideas." What did the report itself contain? We know this from the January 1941 number of the review in which it did nonetheless appear. Our gallant reformer offered the youth of his country an endless catalogue of "themes about life" which, it has to be said, echoed the obsessions of the new regime. Here, for instance, are some from the end: "Ninth theme: we declare war on the world of money ... Tenth theme: we wish to awaken pleasure in a job well done ... Eleventh theme: we shall restore a sense of leadership and of collective discipline ... Twelfth theme: we are joyful lads ... We shall rediscover French songs, communal festivities, theatre which grows out of people's jobs and the villages in which they live, the joy of building, great merry-making. A healthy nation is one which hums with activity, but also one which is blessed with festivals, liturgies, and recreational activities."

4. Not content with commending and taking part in it, he hoped he would be recognised as a pioneer of the "revolution" that was on everyone's lips and that he would be considered one of its earliest and worthiest instigators. In the editorial of the same issue of *Esprit*, published in November 1940, he said, for example, the revolution "was not just one idea amongst others, it gave meaning and a sense of vocation to twenty-five years of my life. Youth in general has found its bearings with us. We have substantially broken with the past and our action affects, I believe, what is happening at present." A little further on in the same article, he added: "All the precepts expressed today are tokens of hope for the youth of France." He was referring, of course, to the "precepts" proposed and expressed by the Vichy regime. "For years, we have been exploring them in depth and seeking

to disseminate them." In conclusion, he wrote: "In the dust raised by the collapse of a certain world, in the inextricable confusion of things being born and others still disappearing, a few precepts for living stand out, in which we recognise the dominant characteristics of our heritage: the struggle against individualism, a sense of responsibility, a sense of community, the re-establishment of the role of leadership, a renewed sense of nationhood together with a realistic sense of international solidarity, the restoration of the State linked to the playing-down of the State, the sense of man as a whole, body and mind, individual and member of a living entity." In other words, Mounier claimed as his own most of the major themes of Pétainist ideology. They were his themes, he maintained; part of the stock of his own recollections. They represented what he had been saying and repeating for years. The Ministers of the Vichy Government were simply less distinguished inheritors of an older system of thought of which he had the honour to be the original author. Could one possibly claim more clearly and more openly one's Pétainist credentials?

5. If he had one regret, if there was just one thing he reproached himself with, it was with not having been more robust in earlier years in his criticism of democracy. "We believed", he recalled, "that it was a parasitic growth on the body of France, like a spore or a lichen; we didn't realise it was eating it away like vermin, and was doing so as surely as spiritual ills or social disorder."

6. What did he make of the Gaullists and Gaullist resistance? "Those who prepare to flee and thereby block the roads that remain open to those who would work to create something", he thundered, "will be counted among the dead" (*Esprit*, November 1940, "Les nouvelles conditions de la vie publique en France"). In the same article, but aiming his remarks at those headstrong people who might have been tempted to raise their voices against the regime, he went on: "By the grace of God, let us first learn the virtue of silence, the pure, profound innocence of silence . . . Does it occur often enough to each one who looks today to the man charged with the collective destiny of France that, in the face of certain and unspoken suffering, to speak can seem indecent?" Then in another article, "Le mangeur de nouvelles", which also appeared in *Esprit* in January 1941, directed at those around him whom he thought a little too interested in the broadcasts of the BBC,

he wrote: "My dear compatriots, it would be better to build living poems with our hands, with our courage, with our fidelity, with our creative imagination, with our presence of mind than to seek at the turn of a radio switch a miracle that only our own resolve will bring about. We know that information can be false. We are less mindful of the fact that the broadcasting of clandestine information can unconsciously prepare us to accept falsehood." He used flowery language and roundabout rhetoric, but the message was very clear, as it certainly must have been to those who derived courage and hope from the broadcasts from the unoccupied zone of France. In Emmanuel Mounier's eyes, such people had to be suffering from depression and naivety, if they were not troublemakers or traitors.

The fact that the editor of *Esprit* did subsequently change and rally to the cause of the Resistance, as a result of which he spent a few weeks in prison, in no way alters the fact that from June 1940 to the end of 1941 he was one of the most genuinely enthusiastic Pétainist intellectuals. Certainly this had nothing to do with morality and in no way reflected compromise or cowardice on his part. The fact was, though, that his own ideology was a mixture of traditionalism and mistrust of classic individualism, a hatred of money and parliamentary democracy, a sense that liberal democracy had run out of steam and had to be rethought and refashioned from top to bottom, and thus it coincided essentially with the ideology of the men of Vichy.

6

"Amongst writers of some reputation"

A WORD OR TWO ABOUT GIRAUDOUX

Consider the case of Giraudoux. He stood for goodness and poetry, harmony between people and things, sensitive intelligence, enchantment, modesty of feelings, effusiveness and evasion. He loved gardens with flowerbeds and well-ordered houses. He was a man who wrote things in one go and enjoyed Laforgue and Debussy. He was the author of *Ondine, Intermezzo, La Folle de Chaillot,* had his portrait painted by Jacques-Emile Blanche, and worked on the Quai d'Orsay. Life appeared young and beautiful and women were without guile. He displayed a discreet sense of wonder and kept his wounds secret. He wrote *La Guerre de Troie n'aura pas lieu* and suggested that there would be no world war either. And then, after all that, calmly and with a certain style he observed: "We are in full agreement with Hitler in proclaiming that politics only moves onto a higher plain if it becomes racial," adding, in the extremely mischievous tone which, I'm sure, made him such a success in salons: "Why do I write? – because I am neither a negro nor a Jew." People don't talk much about Giraudoux. That's a pity, because he's one of the best examples there is of mild-mannered fascism.

7

"Breton and Bataille"

It is strange how companions to literature bracket together the names of Bataille and André Breton like two branches of the same family and as if the author of *L'Histoire de l'oeil* represented some minor strand or sect of surrealism. The fact that the two of them sometimes made a pretence of believing it and thus lent credit to the story proves nothing. In reality, you have only to read their books to see that their two sensibilities, two systems of thought, two visions of the world and of man were opposed in almost every respect. They could not have been more different. Between Breton and Bataille, as between Voltaire and Rousseau, Stendhal and Balzac, Baudelaire and Hugo, or even the Orléans and the Bourbons there was an absolutely clear divide. It was one of those essential, innate almost ontological divides which separate men into two clans or two disparate tribes and force them to choose, to define themselves and exclude the rest.

For example, Breton was a moralist and Bataille was debauched; Breton believed in passion, Bataille in eroticism. Breton wanted to ban brothels, whereas Bataille spent most of his time in them. Breton was attracted by the fantastic, Bataille by the sordid. Breton's sensibility was surrealistic, ethereal, poetic, Bataille was fascinated by filth, corruption and excrement. Breton longed for his soul to inhabit "a pure, clear realm, hung with white drapes". Bataille knew he would always have one foot – in the famous article in *Documents* he spoke of a "big toe" – in things dirty and nauseous. The one believed only in good, the other only in evil. One read only Jung, the other only Freud. Breton emphasised the positive elements in his reading of Sade, to the consternation of true sadists, whereas Bataille stressed his diabolical, cruel and tragic side. When they turned to politics and tried to imagine their ideal city state, one had a vision of a body politic which would be happy, naturally joyful and utopian, whilst the other was truly pessimistic, believing it would always have its share of suffering and adversity.

Inevitably therefore, you have to choose between Breton and Bataille. In all seriousness, it might be said the choice is almost as clear-cut as that between Nature and Culture, Matter and the Ideal, Gaullism and Pétainism and so on. Would it surprise you if I said my own choice is quite unambiguous and that just as the philosopher in me feels sympathetic to the pessimism of *La Souveraineté* so he realises he is out of sympathy with the surrealist state of bliss?

8

"Acéphale"

BATAILLE AND FASCISM

We come back to Breton and Bataille, but this time to consider them
in relation to their period and background and to see how they looked
to their contemporaries – even though this may cause some confusion
and blur the distinctions which separate them. It was, as I've already
said, a time when sects and secret societies thrived. And if you wished
to oppose Hitler, you had a choice between large organisations such
as the AEAR[1] or the Amsterdam-Pleyel Committees[2] etc. – and quite
small, discreet, semi-clandestine groups, in which movements both
Breton and Bataille were symbolic figures. There was "Contre-
Attaque" which they founded jointly in 1934 and "Acéphale" with
which only Bataille was concerned. There was also "Le Collège de
Sociologie", one of the chief centres of opposition to the spirit of
Munich. How did these organisations operate and what did they really
do? Did they exist to generate ideas or as sources of intellectual inspiration and idealism? Did those who instigated them look upon them
as miniature societies in which cultural values would be secured in
the face of a totalitarianism already seen as triumphant? Conversely,
what is to be made of the idea put around that, by attempting to
outmanoeuvre fascism, and by challenging it on its own ground, as
Bataille sought to do, some of these organisations mirrored certain
attitudes belonging to fascism, whether they meant to or not? In other
words, was there a certain impulse in Bataille which drove him towards
fascism, as has sometimes been suggested? Did "the dark forces" hold
some perverse attraction for him? Was he inclined to be indulgent
towards things diabolical? And haven't I over-praised his thought and
exaggerated his role in anti-fascist circles? I have tried to look more
clearly at all these issues and in doing so to avoid the slightly absurd
tone often adopted by commentators when they refer to "the secrets
of 'Acéphale'", "the mysteries of 'Contre-Attaque'", or "the initiation
rites" to which future members of the "Collège" were subjected in
1937. To this end I went to talk to two witnesses who also happen
to be amongst the greatest artists of the century.

NOTES

1. The Association of Revolutionary Artists and Writers, set up by communist writers in 1932 but open to all.

2. Barbusse and Rolland helped to found the World Committee against Fascism and War. It organised two conferences, the first in Amsterdam in 1932 and the other in the Salle Pleyel, Paris, the following year.

9

"That strange secret society . . ."

My first witness is Pierre Klossowski, whom I met on November 10th, 1990, at his small flat on the first floor of a rather ordinary looking building in the Rue Vergnaud which also served as his studio. It was a little bare, with a camp bed in the middle of the room, a chair and a very small wooden table cluttered with brushes, pencils and sketches. I used a piece of plank to write on. There were pictures stacked up against the wall as well as a jumble of canvases and folders, but neither books nor knick-knacks. It would be hard to imagine anything more impermanent or austere. Luckily, it was a fine morning and the whole appearance of the room was redeemed by the clear winter light which flooded in through the single window. "You'll see him waiting for you at the window. He always watches for his visitors at the window," Pierre Nahon, his dealer, had informed me. And it was true. The first thing I saw when I reached the entrance to the building was the figure of Pierre Klossowski leaning against the railing of his balcony. He was motionless, looking expectant and strangely tense.

Can we talk about Bataille? You once said of him that he was "attracted by fascist cynicism".

I never said that. That remark comes from Surya's book in which he portrays me as a traitor – which isn't fair.

Even if you didn't make the remark, what about the idea itself? However one puts it, do you think Bataille was attracted by fascism?

No, not by fascism. Having said that, I remember when he returned from Italy for example he talked to me about a fascist officer he'd seen walking along with his cloak trailing in the wind. There was something radiant about him. "He had radiance" was what he said on his return which he contrasted with the fatal impotence of Marxism at the time.

It wasn't a question of fascism then. But his remarks were disconcerting?

Yes, they were. And I wasn't the only one who noted what he said.

Did he say anything else like that?

No. Well yes. He wasn't very good at minding what he said. I remember one day for example we were at the Café de la Régence, as we often were. It was at the time of "Contre-Attaque" and we were in charge of things. I can still hear him saying: " OK, alright! so the Nazis have beaten up a few Jews! a few Jews!" You should have seen him at the end of the war when various documents started to appear, when the Americans and the Russians revealed to the world the horror of the concentration camps.

All the same, there were several remarkable initiatives of his at the time.

During the Popular Front and the Spanish Civil War, there was "Acéphale". It published a number against the Nazi exploitation of Nietzsche, which you may remember.

And then there was the "Collège de Sociologie" which he founded with Caillois.

People haven't talked much about it, but he and Caillois hated each other. I witnessed a furious slanging-match between the two of them at the "Collége".

Nonetheless, it was a place where some very important things were said, especially about Munich . . .

Bataille was as intimidated by Caillois as he was by Breton. He always thought he was being outshone on all sides! And he was always wanting to heal the breach between people, to get them to agree. After the war, at the time of the Camus–Sartre quarrel, for example, he really wanted to bring them together. It was a disease with him.

He was basically a strategist.

That's right. But he always thought about strategy in a Parisian way, which was wrong. Luckily, he was a close friend of Blanchot, who cured him of his fear of always being outflanked by everyone and also of his tendency to proselytise.

How?

Blanchot convinced him that his authority derived from his own inner truth which was not communicable. In this respect he gave him great moral support.

Let's stay with the pre-war period. What was Bataille's goal at the time? What did he want?

What he wanted was to create a godless religion.

That didn't really fit in with your own concerns, did it?

No it didn't and, what's more, he didn't understand that too well. He used to say to me: "Why go back to the Catholic church? You've got the gnostics." It's true that I'd remained deeply Catholic, but equally true that I was engrossed with the gnostics I was reading.

195

What about Breton? Do you remember when Bataille broke with him?

Of course! There was something absurd about the whole business. One day Breton arrived in force, with about a hundred people. Bataille only had a handful on his side.

What were the two men like when they were together? Can you describe an encounter between Bataille and Breton?

It was a struggle for ascendancy. That's what you certainly felt when you saw them together.

Who carried the day when there was a confrontation?

Breton couldn't help being impressed by Bataille. On the other hand, I suspected that Bataille was always inclined to consider Breton a little bit stupid.

Can we talk about the authority Bataille had over other people?

I'll give you an example. You know I often used to go and see Gide to tell him what was happening and give him news about various people. One day – it must have been after he returned from the USSR – he said to me: "This chap Bataille and the people involved in 'Acéphale' . . . I'd like to get involved as well, to work with them and write some things . . ."

What happened then?

Well, when I reported back to Bataille he said to me: "If we take Gide on, we've had it! we'll be discredited!" As I've said, Gide had just come back from the USSR. He was a whipping boy for Breton, and Bataille obviously didn't want to compromise himself.

I'd like to talk about the history of "Acéphale". Whenever people mention "Acéphale", they make it sound very mysterious, as if all sorts of secret things took place including an initiation ceremony.

As far as initiation was concerned, I remember we had to meditate in front of a tree that had been struck by lightning in the Forest of Marly. We all went there for the meditation. Did you know Ambrosino? You didn't? That's a pity, because he would have told you more about it than anyone.

What was the ceremony like?

It was splendid. But you felt you were joining in something which had meaning in Bataille's private world, which existed in his head. We all felt a certain compassion, but not in the sense of pity! We shared . . . We joined in . . .

Was it as if you'd become characters for Bataille, characters in one of his works?

I don't know. That's perhaps going too far. About twenty of us went by train to . . . What was the station called, that very fine station?

Saint-Nom-la-Bretèche. We arrived there one evening and he made the following suggestion: "You're to meditate, but to do so in secret! You mustn't tell anyone else what you've felt or thought." Bataille himself never spoke about it to us again. He never gave us any idea what the significance of such a ceremony was. All I can tell you is that it was very beautiful. I remember there was torrential rain that evening. There was a Greek fire at the foot of the tree and the whole thing was stage-managed. Presumably the tree struck by lightning represented the divinity of "Acéphale", like the drawing done by Masson.

Was Masson there?

No. He was always rather reserved. He was an ardent Spinozist and had a totally different way of thinking. Nevertheless, he gave the drawing which was used as the emblem for the magazine, but didn't do anything else.

Michel Surya talks about the whole business of initiation. Is it true that there was some sort of initiation into "Acéphale"?

I think the idea of initiation existed only in the mind of M. Surya. The whole thing never took on masonic overtones, though the idea perhaps existed in the background. Perhaps Bataille did dream of setting up something like lodges, but it didn't come about.

Some people have even suggested that Bataille had the idea of a human sacrifice to create a bond between the members of the "lodge".

It's possible. But he never talked about it seriously to me, as he knew I wouldn't have agreed with that kind of nonsense.

"... *about which very little is known*"

A MEETING WITH MICHEL LEIRIS

I met Michel Leiris on September 18th, 1989. First of all, I'd tried, without too much hope, to persuade him to let us film him. He had refused, thus remaining faithful to a principle he shared with a few others, but which he scrupulously stuck to. I'd renewed the request a few months later, this time for a tape-recorded rather than a filmed interview, and told him it would be about a few things I wanted to clear up concerning the history of "Acéphale", "Contre-Attaque" and the "Collège de Sociologie". After some hesitation, he finally accepted. Our conversation took place in his splendid bourgeois apartment, filled with beautiful *objets d'art* and fine furniture, on the Quai des Grands-Augustins. He was already living there at the time of the surrealists and it certainly must have impressed them. He was as I'd imagined he'd be, small and stocky. And he still had that same look of a boxer he'd described in the pages of *L'Age d'homme* which I knew by heart. Had it not been for the illness that affected his voice, which I was partly prepared for though I hadn't expected it to sound so cracked and painful, I would have recognised him without ever having met him. He was extremely courteous and exceedingly patient, and he gave precise and detailed answers to the questions I put to him.

Various people, and Klossowski in particular, have suggested that Georges Bataille was "attracted by fascism". What do you think?

As people have said, that wasn't something invented by Klossowski. In my opinion, Bataille was profoundly anti-fascist. However, it is also true that he was impressed by fascist techniques of propaganda and by Hitler's charisma. But one couldn't say he was attracted by them. He dreamt of discovering propaganda techniques that could be used by the Left which would be as effective as those displayed by the extreme Right.

A great deal has been said about "Acéphale", which was two things:

a magazine and a secret society. What exactly was the secret society?

I didn't belong to it!

I knew that, but why?

It was something personal. A number of us so arranged things between ourselves that we were almost like a secret society and there was no point in institutionalising it. It was better that it remained a tacit understanding.

Do you think it was serious in Bataille's own mind?

I think it was serious. I'm convinced of that.

Even though strange things took place and there were absurd rites.

I know nothing about them! I hadn't been initiated and those who were in on it behaved quite properly and never revealed the secrets of "Acéphale".

So you think there was an initiation?

There was an initiation, that I do know. I don't know what form it took, but it did happen.

So the magazine was the outward side of the affair?

That's right.

People have talked especially about strange goings-on at Saint-Nom-la-Bretèche.

At Saint-Germain!

No, no, Saint-Nom-la-Bretèche.

At Saint-Nom-la-Bretèche as well? I didn't know about that. I know absolutely nothing, because, as I've said, I wasn't initiated. I had friends who were, in particular one who is now dead, Patrick Waldberg. But they never breathed a word about the initiation.

Did it all seem a bit childish to you?

Slightly childish, I'll grant you that. Though it wasn't exactly childish, it wasn't far off.

It was also the time when a lot of work was being done on Nietzsche; rescuing Nietzsche from the fascists, one might say . . .

That's right.

What was the purpose of rehabilitating Nietzsche?

That was it, to claim him back from the fascists. Bataille was sufficiently anti-fascist to lament the fact they had appropriated Nietzsche. You know how they'd managed to appropriate him, of course? It was thanks to the extremely tendentious edition of his works done by Nietzsche's sister, whose name escapes me.

Elizabeth Foerster-Nietzsche.

That's it. Bataille's idea was to rescue Nietzsche from the clutches of the Nazis.

I imagine an undertaking like that made you feel close to Georges Bataille.

Absolutely! He knew much more about Nietzsche than I did. I have to confess, I've had almost no philosophical training, but I totally approved of what he was doing. That wasn't the case with "Acéphale".

Then there was "Contre-Attaque".

I didn't take part in "Contre-Attaque" either, though I don't know why. Or rather, I think it seemed to me ... For example, Bataille talked about celebrating the guillotining of Louis XVI on the Place de la Concorde. In his view, it was a form of left-wing propaganda. But it seemed childish to me, and that's why I played no part in "Contre-Attaque". I agreed with its aims, but I thought the things they did were, how shall I put it? a bit frivolous ...

And yet "Contre-Attaque" brought about the reconciliation of Breton and Bataille.

Of course.

So it ought to have fired your enthusiasm ...

Perhaps.

Could we talk about this reconciliation? Which one of them made a move towards the other?

They just became closer. I don't think it can be said that either made concessions to the other. The threat of fascism and the common danger meant that old quarrels were forgotten for a time.

Had Breton forgiven Bataille and forgotten the second "Cadavre"?

That was past history.

But the recent past, all the same?

Certainly.

Soupault told me one day that, far from it, Breton had never forgiven him and that when Bataille's friends attacked him, he was terrified as though he feared he might find himself quite isolated ...

Indeed, my impression is that he took the whole business of the "Cadavre" very badly. As everyone knows, Breton was bad-tempered. He didn't like anyone treading on his toes. But I don't think he was that frightened by it.

Whose initiative was the "Cadavre"?

I think it was Bataille's own idea.

Because there are two versions: a Bataille version and a Desnos version.

Desnos? Well, I didn't know that. I wasn't aware of that version. Mind you, I'm not the best person to ask, as I was closer to Bataille and he told me about it. So I had the feeling it was Bataille's idea.

What exactly was the idea?

I've told you, it was a piece of propaganda . . .

No, I'm referring to the "Cadavre".

Oh! the "Cadavre" . . . That's another matter! The idea was to shoot Breton down in flames, to attack him on his own ground. There'd been "Un Cadavre" about Anatole France. They wanted to take the same title and the same approach and use it against him. Having said that, and being serious, I don't remember what I thought about it at the time. What I can say today is that it seemed to me to be all a bit of a joke.

There were two or three individuals who dominated that period. Bataille and Breton certainly did. I find it difficult to imagine them together. I believe it was you who introduced them to each other.

No, no, I didn't introduce them. Or did I? At any rate, it wasn't done in a very formal manner. What I did do was introduce Bataille to Aragon. I remember that. Aragon was somewhat scornful about Bataille. He considered him a belated Dadaist. He told me so. I don't know if he exactly used the term "belated Dadaist". At any rate, that was what he implied.

And was Bataille impressed by Aragon?

Hmm . . . Not exactly. Bataille was certainly impressed by Breton. He was hostile, but impressed. By Aragon, I think not.

All the same, if one is to accept Michel Surya's book in particular, it seems you arranged the first meeting between Breton and Bataille. It was to do with Bataille's translating Fatrasies *for* La Révolution Surréaliste.

Yes, that's right. I acted as intermediary. Or rather I passed on the text of *Fatrasies* to Breton for *La Révolution Surréaliste*. Perhaps I did introduce them to each other at the time and did once take Bataille to the Cyrano. But, I say again, there was nothing formal about it. The meeting hadn't been arranged. One thing is certain, however, Bataille absolutely refused to put his name to the manuscript copy of *Fatrasies*, not even his initials, despite my best efforts. He agreed to give us the text, certainly, but without his name appearing anywhere at all.

Why?

Because he was wary about surrealism. He agreed to give the text out of friendship for me, but he wanted it to remain incognito.

So, Bataille was never attracted by surrealism. Yet it was the great adventure for your whole generation. And he didn't succumb to its appeal?

He certainly didn't.

If what you say is true, he must have been the only intellectual of the period . . .

The fact is, Bataille was basically rather like Breton. He enjoyed creating magazines, being surrounded by people, having his own group. Well, the surrealist group was a rival to the one he wished to create.

And which he did create?

Yes, at the time of "Documents". It's also clear that Bataille thought of Breton as an idealist, which to him was a mortal sin.

What did he mean by that?

He meant that the materialism paraded by Breton was purely verbal – which is definitely true. I don't reproach Breton for having been an idealist, but that's what he was. Without doubt, Breton's view of the Revolution was that of an idealist.

Bataille wasn't impressed by Breton's charm, was he?

Latterly, perhaps. Because, as you know, relations between Breton and Bataille mellowed enormously a few years after the "Cadavre". He came to accept that there was something impressive about Breton, who was pretty well known, after all. But it happened rather late. It wasn't the case at all at the time. Breton's manner was bound to irritate Bataille who was – how shall I put it? – much more down to earth.

Today, with hindsight, which of them was right: Bataille or Breton?

Naturally, I feel much closer to Bataille. I had a close friendship with him which I never had with Breton. Furthermore, I shared his view, and still do, that surrealism remained too idealistic.

Can we talk for a moment about "Documents"?

"Documents" was something of a rag-bag. It was made up of a mixed bunch of people from very different backgrounds.

Did it represent in Bataille's mind an alternative to the surrealist group? Was it very much his group?

Oh yes! Certainly! There's not the slightest doubt about that. What's more, there were dissident surrealists who contributed to "Documents" – me for a start.

Was that the moment when you broke with Breton?

Of course. At the time of the "Cadavre".

Did a reconciliation ever take place?

Yes, rather late on; but again it wasn't at all formal. We met at a bus stop. We shook hands and travelled together on the same bus.

What year was that?

I can't remember. It was only a year or so before Breton died.

If I understand correctly, he didn't forgive you at the time, that's to say in the thirties, for having close links with Bataille?

Certainly not! When the "Cadavre" was, if I can put it this way, still fresh, the breach was total and real. But it softened a little.

What about Bataille's religious side and his wish to create a new religion or, at any rate, to interest himself closely in various issues to do with things sacred?

The discussion of that by his biographer, Michel Surya, was very well documented. The first thing Bataille wrote was a piece inveighing against the Germans for the sacrilege they committed when they bombed Rheims cathedral in 1914.

I was thinking about the "Collège de Sociologie" and everything that went on there.

It's true that a concern with the sacred was at the heart of it.

You were closely involved with the "Collège"? In fact, you were one of the founders, weren't you?

Yes, I was. I'd written one of the articles announcing it in the NRF, together with Caillois and Bataille. But I considered that Bataille was a little too free with the ideas of Mauss[1] and I expressed this in a letter.

What do you mean?

He over-exaggerated the Sacred, implying that Mauss considered it to be an explanation of every phenomenon. In fact, that contradicted the idea of the "total phenomenon" which Mauss put forward. When he referred to the "total phenomenon", he said that all phenomena have a religious, an economic and a moral aspect, etc. The Sacred wasn't necessarily dominant.

What was Bataille's answer to that?

He recognised there was a problem. But in the letter I referred to, I requested that a large meeting be held, a sort of congress, at which the matter could be discussed. It never took place. I should also say that I sent the letter only shortly before the war. It must have been because of the war that it wasn't followed up.

In Denis Hollier's book, it's clear that you were involved in the first year, but that subsequently you disappeared from the scene.

That's true. I thought that Bataille went a bit too far. He exaggerated. It mustn't be forgotten that I'd actually been a student of Mauss. I'd attended his lectures. I felt I would have in some way betrayed him if I hadn't formulated my objections, distanced myself.

Forgive me for returning to it one last time. But did the issue of his being fascinated by Nazism enter into your decision to distance yourself?

I never thought that. Never. Klossowski may have made some

such statement. He can take the responsibility for it. It was never my own view.

Yet there are some strange texts, about the war for example.

It is quite true that Bataille was fascinated by the war. He said that one had to be equal to the challenge of war. Moreover that's reflected in the declaration concerning Munich made by the "Collège de Sociologie".

Which you signed...

Which I signed, somewhat reluctantly. But I did sign it.

Why were you reluctant to sign it?

I'll tell you frankly, I was very pleased that the spectre of war had been averted. But I shared the view, perhaps a little hypocritically, that the democracies and certainly France had not provided the people with myths which would have enabled them to confront war.

Weren't you embarrassed by all that writing about war, the calls for widespread upheavals and destruction?

I told you I was reluctant. You can sign something enthusiastically or you sign it thinking to yourself you don't agree with certain aspects of it.

When it comes down to it, the "Collège" was really Bataille's affair.

Certainly.

Was Bataille as charismatic as Breton? Did he have the same authority?

I don't think so. The proof is, he never founded a movement which was the equal of surrealism. And without Breton, as you know, surrealism wouldn't have existed.

Bataille was more solitary.

It's not that. You referred a moment ago to Breton's charm. Bataille didn't have that kind of charm. He had his own kind of charm, of course, but he wasn't Breton. And it has to be said, his ideology was much tougher than Breton's.

You mean to say that it was easier to side with Breton?

Yes, it was. He was a very poetic poet. He wrote some nice things. I don't say that to belittle what he did, but to point out it had more appeal than what Bataille wrote.

Did Bataille alarm people?

Oh, a great deal!

He was known for that?

More than anything else, he was known to be extremely debauched.

There's one other thing. The project which you had much earlier, in about 1924 or 1925, for an organisation which was to be called "Oui"...

That was Bataille's idea.

I thought it was yours.

No, it was Bataille's. It was to have been a movement of assent, in the spirit of Zen. I don't know whether he was acquainted with Zen at that time. But it was in the spirit of Zen. The idea was to assent to everything and to show total non-resistance. He thought we ought to set up a "yes" movement in opposition to the "no" movement of Dadaism. It would have been a Dadaism of assent rather than of negation . . .

Why wasn't it set up then?

I don't know. It's just something we talked about.

At the time, he hadn't written or any rate published anything, had he? Yet the striking thing is the tremendous authority he enjoyed all the same. That's a real mystery for someone like me. What was his authority based on?

On his conversation, the remarks he made. He certainly enjoyed great prestige . . .

There again, he was the opposite of Breton whose reputation rested on an enormous literary output.

Of course.

Do you still respect Breton today?

A great deal. I certainly wouldn't wish to over-praise Breton, as he had major faults. But I still have a lot of respect for him. I know I owe him a great deal because I owe a great deal to surrealism and, as I said to you a few moments ago, without him I don't think surrealism would have existed.

I imagine you must have met Lacan during that period? Was he close to Bataille?

Yes, I did know Lacan. I knew him very well and saw him frequently. I never went to his seminars. But we were friends, especially because his wife, Sylvia, had been Bataille's first wife.

When did you meet him?

I must have met him, wait a minute . . .I met him at Marie Bonaparte's, when I returned from Africa. It must have been in 1934. Marie Bonaparte was very interested in the expedition to Djibouti I'd taken part in. So I used to visit her. On one occasion, she told me she knew a young psychoanalyst who very much wanted to meet me. It was Lacan.

Did you become friends straight away?

I must say I was immediately staggered by what I would call his hyper-intellectual approach. There is a whole area of his writing which, literally, goes right over my head. But that didn't prevent me having a certain liking for him.

Was he really close to the surrealists at that time?

Yes, he was quite close.

From a particular point of view?

From the point of view of what Dali called the "paranoiac-critical method". That was it, I think.

Did he have any contact with Breton, for example?

Of course. They respected each other.

Let's come back to you. When you moved closer to the surrealists, I presume it was Bataille who was then offended.

That's right. I wanted him to become a surrealist as well, but to no avail. It wasn't exactly that he thought I was going over to the enemy, but that I was slightly betraying his friendship, ceasing to be completely in his camp in order to join Breton.

And what did you say to him?

Things were implied rather than said . . .Though he did refer to it somewhere or other . . . In *Le Surréalisme au jour le jour*, I believe . . .

One's impression of Bataille is that he was a very gloomy person.

That's a superficial impression. The one criticism which I would make of Surya's book, which is very well written and documented, is, precisely, that he didn't know Bataille and paints too gloomy a picture of him. Bataille had his jovial side. One mustn't believe all the stories that the orgies etc. were like black masses. I didn't take part in them. But I don't think they were as gloomy as all that. It was he himself who depicted everything in terms of transgression, of sin (thereby revealing his ingrained Catholicism). But, having said that, he was a person who could be cheerful in the dealings one had with him. Not usually cheerful but often cheerful.

You knew Colette Peignot very well, who was Bataille's companion at the end of his life.

Very well. She was a really fascinating person. She was beautiful, intelligent, but she could be inflexible and wouldn't accept half-measures. She'd been Souvarine's friend for years, I believe. That's the reason for the enormous hostility between Bataille and Souvarine, which Souvarine expressed most unfairly in his preface to the new edition of *La Critique Sociale*, when he accused Bataille of anti-semitism. It was an absurd accusation and totally malicious. The fact is that Bataille couldn't bear Simone Weil,[2] but that had nothing to do with it.

Was Colette Peignot involved in La Critique Sociale?

She wrote for it. There are articles by her and book reviews, signed Claude Arax.

Didn't she also provide some of the money for it?

I believe she came from a family which was comfortably off even if it wasn't rich – which wasn't true in Souvarine's case. So she must have contributed to the finances of *La Critique Sociale*.

Was she interested in politics?

I don't know. She wasn't a person who was ready to compromise, and someone involved in politics necessarily has to accept certain compromises. In that sense she didn't have a political brain. On the other hand, she was a passionate revolutionary.

Someone else who was around at the time and who was also the lover of Colette Peignot was Jean Bernier. He was a rather strange person too.

I knew Bernier a little, but not very well. I knew him at the time of the collaboration between *Clarté* and *La Révolution Surréaliste*.

Because you were there in 1925 at the time of the great reunion?

Yes, indeed. With Morhange, Politzer, Guterman. I went along with the surrealists who were keen on the collaboration. It all happened such a long time ago!

Thank you for all the details you've given me. The important issue for me was whether Bataille might possibly have been attracted by fascism. I really wanted to know what you felt about this.

My feeling is that Bataille truly *never* was a fascist. He was, if you like, fascinated by the genius the Nazis displayed in their propaganda. His one wish was that the Left should counter their propaganda with equal genius. I don't know if he chose the name "Contre-Attaque", he may have done. Because that's exactly how Bataille saw things. It was a question of a counter-attack. There was the fascist attack with its massive propaganda machine. Equally powerful measures had to be adopted for the counter-attack.

Do you remember the demonstration of February 12th, 1934[3] in which you took part with him and Roland Tual?

Yes, I think so. My memory of that demonstration is somewhat vague. We were there with Bataille, but, I have to confess, it didn't leave a very lasting impression. Wait a minute, though. Wasn't that the famous demonstration which brought about the Popular Front in the streets? I remember. It was a rousing occasion.

Was the Popular Front important to you or didn't it matter much?

Yes, it was important to me. I was working at the Musée de l'Homme at the time, which was very involved in the Popular Front, because of Rivet.

Were you a member of the "Comité de Vigilance des Intellectuels Anti-fascistes"?[4]

Yes, I was.

I didn't know that.

I wasn't an official on the Committee, but I belonged. Breton had joined as well.

I didn't know the surrealists were involved.

I belonged more because of Rivet, than as a surrealist. I'd broken with them by then.

Thank you very much indeed. I must apologise for having gone on so much. I know that . . .

Not at all! I know I'm one of the few remaining people, perhaps the last. Apart from Klossowski, that is.

NOTES

1. Marcel Mauss was a celebrated anthropologist who lectured in Paris at the beginning of the century.

2. Simone Weil was a committed left-wing philosopher and sociologist. Much of her writing is an exploration of her religious insights.

3. On the evening of February 6th, 1934, supporters of the right-wing Leagues and others converged on the Chamber of Deputies in a show of strength, which some saw as a threat to parliamentary democracy. In response to this, the socialists called for a strike on February 12th and the communists for a general strike.

4. Formed in the wake of the February 6th riot by the philosopher Alain, the physicist Paul Langevin and the ethnologist Paul Rivet.

II

"The 'Collège de Sociologie'"

BATAILLE OR CAILLOIS?

It was February 1938. The setting was the back room of a bookshop specialising in religious literature in the Rue Gay-Lussac. There, on a regular basis, the members of that strange group, the "Collège de Sociologie" met in an atmosphere of conspiracy which was common at the time.

Why a "college" and why "sociology"? No one really knows. It was just one of the many small groups which sprang up over the years on the fringes of surrealism. Such groups discussed everything – religion, for example, politics, Hegel, the Marquis de Sade and the French Revolution, celebration, Kierkegaard, Hitler's success, ways of resisting him – except sociology itself.

In any case, the people there were a very mixed bunch. There was Paulhan and Kojève, Jean Wahl and Pierre Mabille. Drieu La Rochelle sometimes went, seemingly rather dreamy and strangely unsure of himself. He might have bumped into Benda or Walter Benjamin. Anatole Lewitzky, who set up the first Resistance network in free France in 1940, talked about Shamanism. Klossowski would have been there as well as Jules Monnerot, Adorno and Horkheimer. But if these people were there, whether as regulars or occasional visitors, it was because three individuals had taken the initiative to organise the whole thing. They were Bataille, Leiris and Caillois, and they would speak at almost every meeting.

On the evening in question – a Tuesday as usual, it must have been nine or ten o'clock and the small room was particularly crowded – Caillois was to have talked to them. And he was eagerly awaited. It had been announced for weeks that his lecture on the relationship between power and death, the sacred and tragedy would be particularly important, given the circumstances (it was February 1938, don't forget!). Unfortunately, Caillois wasn't there. He couldn't come, Bataille announced gloomily, because he was confined to bed with an illness he couldn't shake off. But it didn't matter, he added, since he had a few notes his sick friend had prepared for the meeting, and he, Bataille, would try to draw some inspiration from them in order to give the long-awaited lecture in his place.

Give it in his place? That's what Bataille said and what he intended to do. He was already on the tiny platform, from which he had given his own lecture a fortnight before. There he was, with his fine head of white hair, his falsely innocent blue eyes, and two or three meagre sheets of notes in Caillois's own hand. And in a soft, slightly hollow voice, which at first he couldn't seem to pitch quite right, he began: "I must apologise first of all on behalf of Caillois, who should have given the talk that I'm giving today in his place. The only thing I could do was to meet him and discuss with him what he would have said had he been here instead of me." Then, having finished his introduction, he warmed up and got going, glancing once or twice at his notes. He didn't really need them, as the words flowed effortlessly. After a while, having developed his argument on the way in which the king became sacred in primitive societies and how the awe he inspired could quickly be transformed into a murderous impulse (an argument which the regulars would have recognised as one of Caillois's favourite themes), he seemed to take off, move outside himself. Like a planet changing orbit, he gave the impression that the words he spoke were floating in the air alongside him and were no longer his own. He was no longer Bataille, Georges Bataille the oh-so-strange author of *Documents*, but the very ordinary intermediary of a voice which wasn't his own and which his spellbound audience easily recognised as that of his absent friend.

You might find it a rather splendid and moving scene. You might be fascinated by the extent to which two people could be so close, or such friends. But you might also see it as an illustration of that "collectivisation of thought" which, for ten years, the surrealists had felt obliged to pursue. Breton had recommended that each individual should dream for others. Bataille was now proposing that he should speak for others as well. The idea that it might even be possible, that individuals as remarkable as Bataille and Caillois should go along with it, that no one in the audience laughed, protested or found it strange, that a writer could, on the basis of a few notes, re-create the ideas of a fellow writer who wasn't there, and the idea that such a recreative process (or act of ventriloquism) could result in a text which was circulated at the time under the latter's name is surely the ultimate expression of that fascination with collective activities which was a distinctive feature of surrealism, but which on this occasion went beyond the group.

I 2

"This new breed of writers"

MALRAUX IN SPAIN

As is always the case with Malraux, there are two opposing arguments about his role in Spain.

On the one hand, there are the ironic, disparaging accounts which call into question the efficacy and sometimes the actual involvement of the author of *L'Espoir*. One should, however, be aware that such accounts always emanate from the same sources, that's to say from communists or communist sympathisers who didn't forgive him after the war when he distanced himself and then broke with them, though he had been quite a zealous fellow-traveller in his day. It was an act of spite or vengeance and showed a desire to sully the reputation of a person to whom they had been sufficiently close to feel betrayed when he moved away. Take Garaudy,[1] for example, and his revolting *Littérature de fossoyeurs* which he published in 1947 in which he has the nerve to write that Malraux arrived in Spain with a properly signed contract guaranteeing him "double pay in dollars in Paris and pesetas in Madrid". Another example is that of Hidalgo de Cisneros, commander in chief of the Republican airforce; his recollections should *a priori* have been more credible – except for the fact that they appeared very late, thirty-five years after the events, and were written by a man who remained right up until his death a hard-line communist. "I don't doubt", he wrote (and the tone and context make it clear that he was settling scores), "that Malraux was, in his own way, progressive and that it was in good faith that he sought to help us. He may even have aspired to a similar role to that played by Lord Byron in Greece, but what I can affirm is that, whilst the support of a celebrated writer might usefully have served our cause, his contribution as the leader of a squadron turned out to be totally negative. André Malraux," he went on, "hadn't got the slightest idea about planes and I don't think he realised that one couldn't become an airman overnight, especially during a war." I have recalled these views out of a concern for honesty and in order not to gloss over arguments which had their proponents. But I would emphasise that they are partial and even malicious. I would also emphasise the fact that the status of the writers makes them as suspect, if not more so, than the facts which they seek to challenge. Can one really give credence to the case they put forward, which was so obviously dictated by disappointment, resentment and bitterness?

On the other hand, there are direct and, above all, disinterested accounts, such as those given by fellow combatants and even war reporters who happened to see him in action and who had no more reason to denigrate him than to idolise him. For example, Louis Fischer, an American journalist who himself supplied the Republicans with arms, wrote: "The government planes were old crates; Malraux then arrived and played an invaluable and truly historic role." Herbert Matthews, the correspondent of the *New York Times* commented: "The Frenchman I liked best was André Malraux. He was a genuine idealist and a man of great courage who commanded a group of French airmen nearly all of whom were killed at the very beginning of the war." Pietro Nenni, the well-known Italian socialist who commanded a battalion of the International Brigade, and an anti-fascist if ever there was one, told how: "Malraux organised a makeshift airforce which gave enormous support." Tom Wintringham, who commanded the British battalion of the 11th Brigade, paid homage in glowing terms to the writer-adventurer and his small band of friends, though he himself was a communist. Let us congratulate this handful of men, he wrote, who were "heroic figures" heroically engaging in battle in conditions of extreme isolation and who, during the early months of the war, "attempted to secure the skies with only a few weapons." Ilya Ehrenburg wrote: "The French volunteers had old planes which were in poor condition but, until the Republicans received Soviet equipment, the squadron commanded by Malraux was of considerable help to them." One could also mention the award which Malraux the intellectual received for services rendered as "benefactor to the Spanish Republic" and of which he was enormously proud. It was presented to him by the communist deputy Dolorès Ibarruri, better known by the splendid name of "la Pasionaria".

The truth is, of course, that Malraux did fight, and honourably. And, as history shows, it is far from certain that his role was a negligible one. Moreover, one can give concrete examples and assess what he did. Between August 1st, 1936, the date when his first squadron was formed, and mid-February 1937, when the second squadron was disbanded, there were at least six missions which very directly affected the course and the nature of the war.

— In mid-August, a motorised column of Franco's troops took Merida, in the province of Bajadoz. There was a Republican counter-attack and fierce fighting occurred in the area around the town. All those who witnessed the confrontation noted – and appreciated – the support given by the "Potez" and the DC2s of Malraux's squadron.

— On September 1st, in a scene worthy of *L'Espoir*, a peasant from Olmedo, in the province of Valladolid, managed to cross the rebel lines to warn those loyal to the government of the existence of a clandestine airfield near his village. Action stations were sounded and the airfield was immediately neutralised. Once again, it was Malraux's squadron which undertook the bombing raid.

— On September 3rd, the columns led by Yagüe, a general in Franco's army, were advancing on Madrid and took the town of Tala-vera. Colonel Asencio Torrado launched a counter-attack and had to retreat almost immediately as his troops were on the point of being routed. On this occasion as well, it was the airforce, and in particular Malraux's planes, which had, *in extremis*, to retrieve the situation.

— At the end of September, instead of pushing on to Madrid, the rebel leaders decided to make a detour via Toledo, in order to liberate the Alcazar which was beginning to acquire symbolic value on their side. The loyalists resisted and fought every inch of the way. They also inflicted considerable damage on the opposing forces. Yet again, Malraux's squadron provided air support.

— In December, the 13th International Brigade launched an attack on Teruel. It did, of course, open a second front and was a diversionary tactic. But the main aim was to draw some of Franco's troops and thereby loosen their stranglehold on the capital. On this occasion, Jacques Delperrie de Bayac described how Malraux's squadron gave it support by bombing the town every day.

— Finally, in 1937, the nationalists took Malaga and immediately instituted a campaign of ruthless repression. This caused panic and an exodus of the civilian population. Thousands of fleeing people were strafed on the road to Almeria by low-flying Italian fighter planes. Malraux's squadron was then based at Tabernas, near Almeria. It was called on to protect the fugitives, and this was its last mission before being disbanded in mid-February.

What is one to think, having read this brief account? Was he as insignificant as Garaudy, Hidalgo de Cisneros and his former com-rades turned political adversaries made out? And when the facts are known, can one go on reciting the same old story about Malraux the myth-maker who only went to Spain to enhance his own legend? The facts and the dates are there. Details about battles have been duly recorded in the best historical accounts of the war in Spain. And even if the squadron didn't change the course of the war, even if it didn't prevent – what could have prevented? – the final rout and blood bath, it is perfectly clear that, on occasions, it played a crucial role in certain battles. All honour to Malraux the combatant. All honour to Malraux the *condottiere*. Can you think of another writer who dreamed of leading men in war – and then actually *did it*?

NOTES

1. A communist ideologist and leading Party intellectual. He subsequently turned to Islam.

13

"Paul Nothomb"

MALRAUX IN SPAIN, CONTINUED

Paul Nothomb was the only remaining survivor of André Malraux's squadron. He was a very thin, handsome, erect old man. He had white hair, a slightly military bearing, and pale blue eyes of extraordinary intensity which constantly sought to determine the effect on me of his various anecdotes. He was living in the Midi. One or two novels of his had been published by Gallimard under the pseudonym Julien Segnaire and, for a number of years, he had been interested in Jewish mysticism. He was for me, first and foremost, someone who had known Malraux, who had fought at his side and above all seen him fight. He was, in short, the only person still alive who could describe in detail a conversation he had had on the road to Teruel or a bombing raid on Malaga. And here he was, a living monument, with a host of images and memories. Take careful note of what he had to say.

Can we begin by talking about the circumstances in which you met Malraux?
    I met Malraux for the first time in my life in Brussels. It was in 1935, I think, or the beginning of 1936. He had come as the guest of honour to a sort of anti-fascist meeting and was about to go to Berlin to take a petition to Goebbels on behalf of Dimitrov. The meeting was held at a very popular venue in Brussels, packed with Belgian workers, but it was also attended by the cream of the Parisian intelligentsia – including Gide and Jean-Richard Bloch. Malraux was the major figure there and he talked about the Red Army, the October Revolution and the great mythology of revolution. I can still see him pacing to and fro on the platform looking like Napoleon on the Bridge of Arcole.[1]
    You said that Gide was present?
    Yes, Gide was there. But when the chairman asked him to come and sit on the platform, he replied: "No, no, I've come to listen to Malraux." I think he was very impressed by Malraux and felt – how shall I put it? – very "literary" when confronted by him.
    Whereas Malraux . . .
    You know what Malraux's view of Gide was. In his opinion only

the *Journal* was of any importance. Apart from the *Journal*, he considered Gide's work rather uninteresting.

So, you met Malraux in Brussels and the following year you joined him in Madrid.

Yes. Well no. When I left for Spain I didn't know that I would meet him again. I was, as I've told you, a member of the Party. At first, the Party didn't allow members to go to Spain (because of the political line adopted by Russia, which went along with the Non-intervention Pact), except in the case of technicians. Now it happened I had been an airman for a year or two, a navigator-observer, to be precise. And so at the beginning of September, I went to the headquarters of the Party in the Rue Lafayette. From there I was sent to a section of the Spanish Embassy, but I don't remember where that was. I was offered a fantastic contract, including a huge insurance policy in case I was killed, and a large salary. I left the same day and travelled to Barcelona and then on to Madrid, where I stayed at the Florida, a luxury hotel in the centre of town. It was there that I met Malraux again.

How did he seem at the time?

He still seemed as he had in Brussels, like Napoleon on the Bridge at Arcole. He had a tremendous air about him and gave the impression of having a more powerful intelligence than anyone I've ever met.

Alright. But what I meant was: did he seem like a writer, a soldier, someone who could lead in battle, or a dreamer?

One shouldn't try to categorise him in that way. In my view, Malraux was just Malraux; if he had the idea of founding the squadron, it's because he was all of those things. At the time of the Spanish Civil War, Malraux was clever enough to realise what needed to be done. One couldn't just go along to the Café de Flore and discuss things – one really had to do something.

What exactly did the squadron consist of? How many planes and how many pilots were there?

In practical terms, there were thirty personnel and never more than ten planes (and sometimes only two or three) in working order. That was the maximum. Yet the part the squadron played was out of all proportion to its size. Because, as I've already said, Malraux understood straight away that, if we were going to help Spain, it would be by sending planes rather than holding meetings and rallies. The planes had to be bought, and so he set about acquiring them in central Europe with the help of Clara,[2] perhaps via arms dealers, but I don't know. As you're aware, planes can't be bought in supermarkets. He then reasoned that these planes which cost an incredible amount needed pilots who wouldn't destroy them. They therefore had to be experienced pilots rather than individuals with a romantic idea about flying. But people like that aren't usually left-wing. So, he decided to recruit them, at vast expense if necessary, knowing that they would at least drop their bombs on the fascists, whereas pilots who were revolutionaries would destroy the planes and be of no use whatsoever. And that's what he did. As Spain had the money, they made some available to Malraux so that he could engage individuals on a contract, realising that the only way to get professionals was to pay them. After it was over, Malraux was inclined to keep quiet about this episode of his life, but he shouldn't have. Because it proved that he was serious and was concerned about being effective. You can't imagine what it was like. Right at the beginning, I remember there were two Spanish civil aircraft which people went up in; then they opened the doors and pushed the bombs out by hand, like that, as if they were sweeping them out. You can imagine what the precision was like! Absolutely zero! But it did represent the earliest resistance.

Did you have one of these contracts, for example?

Yes, I had a contract. Everyone had one. You couldn't get into Spain without a contract, plus a certain number of passes . . .

So, you were a "mercenary" . . .

I wasn't a mercenary because I'd gone as a volunteer. But I was told I had to sign a paper, as the Spanish Government required foreign nationals to have certain sureties, especially relating to insurance, in case they died or in the event of their government making a complaint. So there were very large life-assurance policies, which were dependent on one's salary. At any rate, I remember I had a colossal salary. I'd never had anything like it before. And I was classified as a navigator, and therefore getting much less than the pilots. The pilots earned extraordinary sums. Anyway, that's how a certain number of pilots were recruited, including some who had imported alcohol into the United States from Canada, at the time of the Prohibition. They were pure adventurers, doing it for money. Having said that, the majority of them wouldn't have done it for Franco, even for money.

None of that fits very well with the classic image one has of a squadron of revolutionaries . . .

It does. Because of Malraux himself, plus a few people like myself, as well as the mechanics who were often workers who came over from the civil air lines.

It is said that you were the "political commissar" of the Brigade.

No, not at that time. I wasn't yet a political commissar because the squadron didn't yet have a proper structure. It was a case of getting by as best we could. Some people disappeared after a mission, they just vanished. It was complete anarchy. It went on like that until November, when the International Brigades arrived, which was also the moment of crisis for the squadron. Malraux immediately seized the opportunity and did away with contracts. That was possible because of the arrival of the Brigades. We could then recruit. The Brigades were in Albacete, where we also had an office. Anyone who had been connected with aviation could apply, but they had to pass an exam. So, from that point on, the squadron had no mercenaries, other than the odd one or two. The majority were attached to the Spanish army, and from that point the squadron which had been called "España" became known as the "André Malraux Squadron".

Who decided that the name should be changed?

I did, because, in Malraux's absence, I was responsible for relations with the Spanish Air Ministry. I went to them and said we ought to mark the renewal of the squadron and that, for us, André Malraux himself was more important than anything else. I added that everyone would be galvanised into action if the squadron could be called the "André Malraux Squadron". It was on our notepaper and on the squadron bus. We were all very proud to serve under his name, even though the squadron was attached to the Spanish army.

Who paid the members of the squadron?

The Spanish army. We all had Spanish army uniforms. Malraux set an example. Because, at first, we had all worn different things. He wore civilian trousers and a military cap. I was one of the very few who had been in the army, so I was the most "military" looking of us all . . .

In photos, you looked like an officer who had graduated from Saumur![3]

It caused me a great deal of bother. For instance, when I was shot down at the end of February '37 and was on the Almeria-Malaga road, having landed in the sea with the plane and managed to get out, the refugees on the road fled when they saw me. They said I was a Nazi! It seems I had a Germanic look about me. I had to shout out: "Republica! Republica!"

Did Malraux also have a military bearing?

I have never known anyone less military and at the same time as clever as Malraux! When one thinks of the rather grandiloquent speeches he has made, the one for Jean Moulin,[4] for example, I have to say that no one else could make speeches like him. I remember on one occasion he had assembled the whole squadron. I can still picture the large dining-room with thirty to thirty-five of us gathered there, which was the maximum we ever reached. He explained to everyone that they would now have to wear a uniform and that they were no longer playing at being soldiers. He did it in an extremely humorous way, by introducing himself as Colonel Blimp who was there to give us our instructions. Everyone had a good laugh and immediately agreed to wear their uniform.

The issue of the squadron's effectiveness is often raised.

I've said on a number of occasions that what I found interesting in the Spanish Civil War was not only meeting Malraux but the unique experience of belonging to a military unit which was totally effective. And it functioned without discipline and without constraint. If anyone in the squadron said: "I don't want to go on", the reply would have been: "Alright, you can take the plane back to France tomorrow." That was the only sanction. If anyone wanted to stop fighting, within half an hour he was on his way back to France. I've never known a fighting unit in which the combatants could decide whether or not they wished to take part in the next mission! And it worked! Compare that with the tribunals in operation in Albacete, with sanctions etc. We were a living testimony to freedom. And of course it all hinged essentially on the prestige of Malraux.

Did Malraux participate in operations?

Yes, on several occasions. He had no training as a pilot, but on two or three occasions he acted as front gunner in "Potez 42s" where there were seven of us! There were three gunners, a bomb-aimer, in this case me, two pilots and an engineer. There were three gun positions and Malraux often took one of them.

Do you have any precise images of Malraux in combat?

I remember extremely well a raid on Teruel. Anti-aircraft fire was making the plane shudder rather dramatically. And I can still see Malraux in the middle of the gangway which went from the cockpit to the rear-gunner's position. He didn't have anything to do, but he simply wanted to be with us. Even though he wasn't manning a position, he wished to show that he was part of the team. That's why the squadron functioned, because he was there. We knew quite well he didn't just want to be in charge and sit in his office.

So, he had real physical courage.

Great physical courage, and, as I've already said, a great sense of humour as well. There was never any ostentation. When comrades were killed, Malraux gave, what might be called a "funeral oration".

He was magnificent, saying just a few words, without any pomp. He was very restrained.

Did you lose many people in the squadron?

Almost everyone, as all the planes were destroyed. That's how the squadron and most of the people were lost. It was a fine way to go. There were a few who had a miraculous escape, such as me. There were two planes on the last mission I took part in, and both of them were shot down. In mine, only one person was killed, but four were injured. But we were very vulnerable, as there were no fighters covering us. That's why we flew our missions at night. On the opposing side they had German and Italian planes.

Didn't you have Russian planes at that time?

Yes, a few Russians came over with fighter planes. I personally spent the evening of November 7th, 1936, celebrating the anniversary of the Russian Revolution with some Soviet airmen on the airfield at Alcala. They were all in civvies, and kept themselves very much to themselves. They didn't have much to do with us, but on this occasion we did eat together. What's more, I remember to my great shame that I proposed the toast to Stalin. The Soviets were somewhat flabbergasted that a non-Russian should mention the name of their leader (though at the time Stalin was the revolution, wasn't he?). To us, he was Lenin's successor. The trials in Moscow had just about begun, and in our eyes they were all guilty. That tells you how we thought at the time.

For Malraux, Stalin represented above all the most effective means of combating the fascists.

Absolutely.

What I'm trying to say is it wasn't a question of "conviction" but of pure "Real-Revolution" . . .

Malraux wasn't a communist. He approved of the communists in Spain because they were the only ones who wanted to create an effective army. He was constantly saying that, in order to defeat an army, one had to have an army to oppose it. At heart, Malraux's sympathies lay with the anarcho-syndicalists, that's certain.

Did you discuss those things?

I'll tell you something. Malraux was one of the first to point out to me, with my stupid Stalinist beliefs, that the Soviet Union was much more interested in the Straits of Gibraltar than in world revolution. I accepted it from Malraux. It was one of the first cracks in my communist beliefs.

So, effectiveness came first!

That's right. That's what I said when I was talking about the business with the mercenaries. The same thing was true in the case of the Russians. He knew that only the Russians could wage war, as the French and the English had decided to opt out. It was the Russians alone who could give Spain arms. So, it was necessary to join forces with them. Although he was very sympathetic towards Trotsky, he considered that Stalin was right at that juncture.

Clara was in Madrid with the anarcho-syndicalists . . .

Yes I saw Clara drive up to the Florida Hotel in a car covered with POUM flags and hoot her horn in order to irritate André. She was a Trotskyist sympathiser. And although Malraux was an admirer of Trotsky, he realised at that point he couldn't go along with him. For the time being, he had to accept Russia and the Communist Party. But I'm absolutely certain he was never a communist. He often told me what he thought about the communists while we were in Spain.

What was a conversation with Malraux like during that period? Did you discuss politics, the war, other things?

We ate together almost every day, either in a restaurant or at the hotel. I can still picture us in Albacete, with all the people from the squadron. We usually had little tables, and I often sat with Malraux. What did we talk about? Women, France . . . On one occasion, I don't remember which member of the squadron said: " We're being conned, taken for a ride." Malraux got angry and retorted: "Don't be French moaners, we're here to fight for the revolution" . . .

Fight for the revolution or halt fascism?

Precisely. I myself don't think that Malraux went there for the sake of democracy. One has to be honest and say that we were all there to further the cause of revolution. We wanted to do it by stages, not like the anarcho-syndicalists who wanted revolution straight away. But we wanted it, all the same. We didn't at all subscribe to the line put forward in speeches on behalf of the Popular Front, claiming it was defending liberty, defending democracy, and so on . . .

Did Malraux remain a writer? Did he talk about literature, for example, or philosophy? Or was he completely absorbed by what was going on?

I know now that he was writing *L'Espoir*. But we didn't talk about it, of course. He was rather secretive about what he was doing. I discovered things afterwards that I didn't know at the time.

Yes, but did you talk to each other, and, if so, about what?

Yes we did; what sparked it off was when Malraux and I were in a car one day on the road from Valencia to the airfield. We were both in the back seat and all of a sudden, I don't remember why, I quoted Nietzsche to him. Malraux gave a start and said: "What? you know Nietzsche, you've read him?" I told him that Nietzsche was extremely important to me. Malraux told me later that discovering someone who could talk about Nietzsche, amongst all the engineers and mechanics, was somewhat unexpected.

And you feature in L'Espoir *as . . .*

Yes, he describes me, more or less. I'm depicted as the son of an extreme right-wing militant etc., etc.

You said a moment ago that you often talked about women. At the time, he was between Clara and Josette Clotis . . .

Yes, there was Josette. But he never talked about her. I found out afterwards that she'd come to Spain.

You never saw her?

No, never. I heard about it afterwards. Things like that, I heard about afterwards. He kept them from us, I think. I told you Clara had appeared, but solely to irritate him. You wouldn't catch Malraux talking about his personal relationships with women!

What was life like at the Florida Hotel?

We didn't live like proletarians, that's for sure. We stayed in luxury hotel rooms. And the hotel porter was always around, with his gold braid and so on. The proprietors weren't there. They'd disappeared. But the staff were.

And what was your role? You didn't answer my question about whether you were a "political commissar".

Lacouture has suggested that Malraux took precautions, as far as the Communist Party was concerned, by naming a political commissar who was a communist. That's ridiculous! I was just twenty-two years old. Malraux was someone with an international reputation, who had already been to Moscow several times and who was in contact with the Soviet Ambassador in Spain. He didn't need any guarantees as far as the Communist Party was concerned. That's just a joke.

Where did this idea come from then?

What happened was that, when the squadron was formed, each individual had to be given a rank. For example, Malraux was a colonel. I was a lieutenant. And each of us had to be given a function. There was the chief mechanic, the chief pilot, the chief . . . I don't remember any more. Since he had to give me a title, he said: "You can be the political commissar." That's how it was done. Each unit had a political commissar. But the image we have today of the political commissar is of a brutal type who was at the rear, raising the morale of his troops and eliminating any opposition. You realise it wasn't like that in Malraux's squadron! Basically, I think he gave me this title because I went to the Air Ministry in Valencia every morning and therefore had good relations with them.

The strategic command was in the hands of the Spanish, of course?

Yes, indeed. We had no autonomy as far as strategy was concerned. The missions were decided by the Spanish. I have to say that they often told us: "We're sending you out, and we're glad you're here because we wouldn't want to bomb one of our own towns."

How was Malraux treated by the Spanish? Did they see him as a military leader, or were they aware that they had a great writer on their side?

No. I don't think so at all. The Spanish military leaders were, if anything, against him. Malraux was a friend of the government leaders and of politicians. He'd been imposed on the heads of the army.

That's not what I meant. What I asked was whether they knew *who Malraux was . . .*

No. not really. They knew he was a writer, but that didn't mean much to them. Actually, I think the Spanish military people were pleased we were there to do their job, full stop. Don't forget that most of the airforce had gone over to Franco. There were only a few mechanics left. There was no Republican airforce. What's more, when we recruited Spaniards, they served as second pilots in our planes. We wouldn't let them be chief pilots, because it would have been very easy to go over to the enemy side with a plane.

When you look back on all this today, how effective do you think you were? Did you influence the course of the war?

I think we did and that we could have had an even greater influence. For example, it was thanks to Malraux and those patched-up planes that the fascist advance was halted at Talavera for several weeks, a hundred kilometres from Madrid. They only reached Madrid in November, and the revolt had begun in July. For two months, they remained at the same spot on the road to Madrid. The squadron certainly had something to do with that. And then later, there was the battle of Teruel. We were at Valencia at the time and we flew a number of missions to Teruel. It was almost exclusively the squadron which was involved. Subsequently, after Malaga had been taken by the fascists, we played a part in the defence of Almeria, and I was personally involved in that. We bombed the road, and, as a result, the front remained in the same place for a long time. There again, we halted or slowed the fascist advance.

Bernanos was also in Spain during that period. I believe you knew him. Did you meet?

Bernanos was in Majorca. He was extremely right-wing at the time, belonged to "Action française", and had written a book on Drumont. And then we heard that he'd broken with Franco! Malraux had a great admiration for Bernanos. He considered him to be the only real novelist of his day – much more so than Mauriac. For him, Bernanos was *the* novelist. I confess that I didn't entirely agree with him, but that doesn't matter. When he discovered that I knew Bernanos, he said: "I'd like to meet him." That was in 1937, the middle of '37. The squadron no longer existed, and we all met at the "Roi Gourmet", on the Place des Victoires, a restaurant that Malraux frequented a lot. Three of us were there, Bernanos, Malraux and myself. Bernanos described this meeting in *Le Chemin de la croix des âmes*. He attributed to Malraux something he didn't say. According to him, Malraux said: "I shall never attack the Communist Party." That's untrue! It's inconceivable! I took part in this conversation, and I can confirm that Malraux said nothing of the kind. The truth is that Bernanos said to him: "Malraux, how can you put up with the lies in *l'Humanité* and go along with *a paper that only tells lies?*" Malraux replied: "Listen; I will always be less embarrassed by the lies of *l'Humanité*, than you should be by those in *L'Echo de Paris* (or it may have been *L'Ami du peuple* or some other such paper of the time), because at least behind *l'Humanité* stand the poor and the oppressed, whereas behind *L'Echo de Paris* there are only the exploiters and the rich."

Did you see him again? Did you remain friends?

Yes, we kept up our friendship. There was a little-known episode which occurred in about 1938 which people perhaps don't remember. It concerned a Popular Front in Chile. Malraux longed to establish in Chile a successor to the old squadron. So there were one or two reunions of former members of that squadron. We no longer had any planes in Spain, but we thought we might perhaps find some in Chile. It remained at the planning stage [he laughed] . . . Apart from that, we saw each other regularly until the war, then after the war, when he published his first books on art with Gallimard. I did a certain amount of bibliographical research for him at the Bibliothèque Nationale.

NOTES

1. Napoleon led his troops into battle to capture this bridge in Northern Italy on November 17th, 1796.

2. Malraux's first wife.

3. A training school for cavalry officers.

4. Malraux gave the funeral oration when the ashes of the Resistance leader Jean Moulin were removed to the Panthéon.

14

"This crime which cast its shadow across events"

MALRAUX AGAIN

Thousands of Catalan anarchists were assassinated in July and August 1937. The revolutionary socialist party, POUM, was suppressed. The Soviet security organisation, the GPU, extended its control over the whole of the Republican side. And, despite his prestige, Malraux chose to remain silent and to accept the unacceptable. Does one conclude, as Trotsky did, that he went to Spain "to defend Stalin's judicial processes"? And is one also led to think that, in Spain, this anti-fascist writer became a jackbooted intellectual? No, of course not. But one thing disturbs me and, like it or not, it serves to condemn André Malraux. It is the fact that other writers took the opposite point of view and thereby proved that it is *always* possible to denounce what is unacceptable, even though they found themselves in exactly the same situation, had the same information and were as justified as he was in claiming that their involvement was both serious and effective. These other intellectuals – Bertrand Russell, George Orwell and John Dos Passos – were less heroic but more lucid.

". . . to New York, like the surrealists"

A CONVERSATION WITH CLAUDE LÉVI-STRAUSS

I wanted to see Claude Lévi-Strauss to get him to talk about "structuralism", of which he was one of the last practitioners, since Barthes, Foucault and Lacan were already dead, and Althusser died not long after. The fact that he was clearly irritated at the mere mention of the word structuralism led me to broach other subjects. I started with his stay in New York between 1940 and 1944, at a time when the cultural capital of the United States was also that of Europe. I discovered a Lévi-Strauss I didn't know about, someone who was closer to André Breton and Max Ernst than to Althusser or Derrida. What follows is a portrait of an ethnologist who was at the same time a good-tempered anti-fascist.

So you arrived in New York at the end of 1940 . . .
    I arrived in New York in 1941, as I was dismissed from my post as professor at the end of 1940, because of the laws of the Vichy government. I arrived in 1941 and returned immediately after the Liberation of Paris, having been called back by the Ministry of Foreign Affairs. And then six months later, less than six months I think, I was sent back to New York to be Cultural Attaché at the French Embassy, where I stayed until '47.
    What was New York like during the period 1941–44? What was the intellectual and political climate? And what were relations like between different groups?
    At that time New York was at its most cosmopolitan. There were refugees from every corner of the globe. There were Germans, Italians, French . . . So, it was an extraordinary place to experience different aspects of European thought, even though one wasn't in Europe. On the political front, I will limit what I have to say to the French community. It was divided into several cliques or factions, whichever you prefer, and some were politically committed, whilst others remained aloof from politics. The major division was between,

on the one hand, those who were supporters of Vichy or were playing it safe (basically that included the established French institutions in New York like the "Alliance française"), and, on the other hand, the Gaullist camp which itself comprised various factions. Apart from them, there were people who had little to do with politics, such as painters and writers – and notably the surrealists. And between all these groups there was either a certain amount of overlap or else very little contact at all. I found myself, as it were, with a foot in three camps, namely the Free-French group together with the "Ecole libre des Hautes Etudes de New York", which we had just founded, the group of surrealist painters and writers, and lastly the psychoanalysts, the majority of whom were foreign.

What exactly was the "Ecole libre des Hautes Etudes de New York"?

It was an institution created on the initiative of Maritain, Focillon, Francis Perrin (as well as his father Jean Perrin, who was also there), and a few other major French figures who had wanted to bear witness to the presence of French culture and thought in the United States, by gathering together not only French exiles but also French speakers. We ran courses and also exams which were looked upon favourably by the authorities of the State of New York and recognised by the Government of Free France.

At the same time, you were working for the radio.

In actual fact, I taught at the New School for Social Research for a very modest salary. The Rockefeller Foundation had undertaken to come to the aid of as many intellectuals as possible who were under threat and they provided us with enough to live on under the auspices of the New School. I was also an announcer on an American radio station called OWI – the Office of War Information.

Like André Breton.

Yes, that's right. As well as him, there was Robert Lebel and Georges Duthuit. We were a team of four and our mission was to send programmes to London, in dialogue form, which were relayed and retransmitted to France.

Programmes which you scripted and which . . .

Certainly not . . .

So, you were only announcers?

We were given scripts, and it was our job to read them as eloquently and as carefully as possible.

It's rather strange that people like you and Breton were used simply to broadcast texts written by others. Was there no thought of extending your duties?

The service which produced broadcasts in French was run by Lazareff,[1] and he was infinitely more competent than any of us to do this kind of thing. We were much happier that it should be like that. After all, we wouldn't have been very good at producing propaganda.

Who were the scripts written by?

By a team led by Lazareff.

You mean a team of journalists.

Yes, a team of journalists.

Were you ever tempted during that period to leave New York for London? Was there ever a question of it happening?

Yes, it was a possibility. Soustelle[2] was trying to regroup the French West Indies at the time, and I'd met him several months earlier in Puerto Rico. I was in a rather difficult situation and he'd helped me out by assuring the Americans that I was neither a spy nor a Vichy agent. Then when he passed through New York he was kind enough to try to persuade me to accompany him to London. But I preferred to stay in New York. The point was, I had an official position connected with Free France, as I'd signed a voluntary agreement and was a member of what was called the Scientific Office of Free France in New York. I also have to admit that I was terribly impressed with American libraries and with the first American colleagues I'd met. Until then, they'd always seemed to have a very unreal existence. They inhabited a superior realm, a sort of pantheon. Now I could get to know them and learn from them. I couldn't resist such an opportunity.

Though I can easily imagine you with Merleau-Ponty or Lacan, I have difficulty in picturing you with Breton. Given the circumstances, you must have seen him every day.

Every day is perhaps something of an exaggeration, except for the three-week period we spent on the boat crossing from Marseilles to Fort-de-France, when we did see each other every day. Breton enjoyed exchanging ideas and discussing things, which he did extremely politely, until he reached a point when he would explode. But for long periods things would proceed as if we were having an academic discussion. Breton would have made a marvellous professor. So, our relations were good. Then, in the United States, we remained close essentially because we shared an interest in so-called primitive art. That was a subject which enabled us to get along very well together. It's true that Breton didn't much care for ethnography, because he didn't like scientific methods being applied to the study of objects he considered magic or sacred. He didn't care for that.

You, on the other hand, must sometimes have been very irritated precisely by all the talk of things being magic and sacred etc.

Yes, except that Breton was never wrong about the quality of an object. He had an astonishing gift. Everyone knows the famous story of the forged Rimbaud poem.[3] But even with the most exotic object or one of unknown origin, Breton could immediately tell you whether it was a fine object or not and whether it was genuine. That earned him a great deal of respect in my eyes; after all, I had worked in museums.

NOTES

1. Pierre Lazareff was a journalist and had been editor of *Paris-Soir*.

2. He had been the Secretary-General of the Vigilance Committee of Anti-fascist Intellectuals in 1938 and joined De Gaulle in London in 1940. He subsequently became the Free French Commissioner of Information and directed intelligence operations in Algiers in 1943–44.

3. A long poem, "La Chasse spirituelle", was published in 1949 as a lost work of the poet Rimbaud. The day after publication, the real authors came forward.

16

"Once he was freed from captivity"

NEW THOUGHTS ABOUT SARTRE

How did Sartre behave from 1940 to 1944? Badly, rumour had it; very badly, according to the legend that lived on. One of the puzzles of the story I am telling is how such a rumour – such a legend – was started, how it developed, lodged in people's minds and memories, was passed on, distorted, gradually grew on the basis of unsubstantiated evidence, and then became accepted as authentic. From that point on, however much one pleaded or tried to correct things, whatever one attempted to do, was to no avail. However many times one drew people's attention to the things he'd done or the initiatives he'd taken, it was always too late. And yet he had behaved no worse than those holier-than-thou individuals who had initiated the case against him. But the die had inexorably been cast and his image and fate determined for all time. And even though you might object, there was always some clever Dick who would go on repeating, without checking his facts and as if it were self-evidently true: "Sartre behaved badly! Sartre behaved badly." Moreover, as a supreme mark of derision, he was held up as the perfect example of those intellectuals who, at best, had understood nothing and, at worst, brought disgrace upon themselves. I know what I'm talking about, since I myself was one of those clever Dicks. And I still recall rehearsing the well-known argument, which I repeated without the slightest scruple, that Sartre would not have put so much into his theory of commitment, had he not felt remorse at being ineffectual in the Resistance.

That is why I have decided to return to the question, even though it will serve no purpose and the few lines I write will alter nothing. I have to do it as a matter of conscience. And instead of ascertaining how the rumour developed, which would require the expertise of a historian, I will at least attempt to retrace the actual events of the man's life during the period of the Occupation. We'll begin in 1941, in January '41, when the author of the *Carnets de la drôle de guerre* was liberated from Stalag XII D, as a result of eye trouble which was partly feigned. He had spent eight months there and, like everyone else, had suffered from hunger, cold, lice and promiscuity. But, like everyone else, he had got used to it. He did what he had to to survive, made friends and tried to amuse himself and the others. To this end, and in order to pass the time, he wrote and then put on a very bad play. When he got back, he openly admitted that he "experienced in the camp a form of communal life" he hadn't "known since his days at the Ecole normale" and that in some ways he had been "happy". But that is not what we are concerned with at present. For he was now free, and living a normal life. He had returned to Paris and met up again with Simone de Beauvoir. He gently rebuked her for having bought tea on the black market, during his absence, and especially for having signed the shameful document in which teachers had to declare that they were neither Jews nor freemasons. He then took a number of initiatives, and continued to do so over the next few months, of which the least that can be said is that they do not square with the conventional image of a Pétainist and a shit.

1. At the beginning of April, that's to say six weeks after his return, he summoned his closest friends to a small hotel behind Montparnasse station. Then, a few days later, in another hotel in the middle of the Latin quarter, he got them together with the friends and pupils of Maurice Merleau-Ponty, who had created the group "Under the Jackboot" in the autumn of 1940 and in the somewhat confused excitement which immediately followed the armistice. Those who were present at these two meetings remember them more with amusement than emotion. It seems that the mood was one of happy confusion, which was perhaps not wholly appropriate for those who were about to embark on clandestine activities. But these young people were at least there, gathered around Sartre. And, in a clear and decisive manner, he outlined the course of action they were to stick to: "If we accept the Vichy regime, we shall be less than human; there can be no compromise with collaboration. From now on, it is a question of building a society in which the demand for liberty will not be fruitless." Whether or not there was a mood of happy confusion, it was certainly during those few days and in those wretched hotel rooms, which in retrospect seem a rather unlikely setting, that these two small groups decided to combine forces and establish a new group, to be called "Socialism and Liberty" which would absorb "Under the Jackboot". What was already known in Parisian Resistance circles as the "Sartre group" called for violent action, justified sabotage and terrorism, and distributed texts and tracts which invited people to engage in armed struggle. Some of its members were to be arrested. Others,

such as Georges Chazelas (who was caught sticking notices on the walls of the Faculty of Medicine which were alleged to inform students how to handle bombs and grenades), spent many months in prison. The Gestapo did all it could – which is itself indicative – to break up a network that had begun to grow by the early summer. This was 1941, don't forget; when the Communist Party, which would later become known as the "parti des fusillés",[1] had to justify the Nazi-Soviet pact in which it was enmeshed. It therefore condemned the "adventurism" of people like Chazelas and called upon the French working-class to "fraternise" with their "brothers" who were soldiers in the "Wehrmacht". So, one is forced to admit that, at this really crucial moment when resisters, either serious or otherwise, were few in number, Jean-Paul Sartre was clear-sighted enough to set up one of the first movements in the anti-Nazi struggle.

2. Then summer arrived. And Sartre simply couldn't help being Sartre. To be truthful, he wasn't yet the important figure who achieved recognition with L'Etre et le Néant, his plays, not to mention the war itself and the post-war reassessment of people. And so our teacher-writer, who as yet had very little to his name apart from one novel (La Nausée) and one short story ("Le Mur"), felt he had to rally a few major intellectuals to his cause, who would win over more people than he could. Because it was summer and the weather was fine, and because most of the intellectuals in question were killing time very agreeably in the sunshine on the Côte d'Azur, he and Simone de Beauvoir bought tickets for Montceau-les-Mines, put their luggage and bicycles on the train, and then rode all around the Southern Zone trying to find his illustrious elders, whom he so wanted to persuade to join him in his struggle. He visited Gide, in Cabris, with little success. (In the summer of '41, Gide was something of a supporter of the Maréchal and was only mildly curious to meet the excited couple who had called on him). The visit to Malraux was more interesting, as he welcomed the young novelist, listened to him, and doubtless studied him. According to Simone de Beauvoir, he also laid on a grand lunch at his villa in Roquebrune. But he cut Sartre short all the same, saying: "No, my young friend, this just isn't serious; we'll talk about it another time, shall we, when the American planes have arrived." Again, we may find Sartre naive, a bit of a boy-scout. We may consider the whole venture somewhat ludicrous and the situation pathetic and absurd. It may even look as if the representative of "Socialism and Liberty" was

treated like a travelling salesman who, having been shown the door, sets off back home a little crestfallen. He might also seem like a young upstart for having disturbed the great Malraux, who magnanimously treated him to lunch before sending him packing on his bicycle with a few well-chosen words: "Here, take this, young man, something to eat on the journey. Have a good trip and say hello from me when you get back home." Even so, no one has the right just to say what they like or ignore the simple truth for that matter. However ludicrous it might seem, Sartre was the Resister and Malraux the one who was indecisive. Upstart or not, he had travelled right across the country to try to win over a great writer, and it was that writer who, rightly or wrongly, decided the time wasn't ripe. We can reproach the author of *La Nausée* as much as we like, consider him naive, tactless, amateurish, even accuse him of being inclined to treat resistance as something of a picnic and armed struggle as fun and games, but the one thing we cannot say is that he hesitated, delayed or had doubts before joining the Resistance.

3. What should he have done at that point? What could he have done? After all, he wasn't yet well-known and had failed in his attempt to rally to the cause any of the great minds he had sought out on the Côte d'Azur. At the same time, the Gestapo had dismantled his organisation and the communists wouldn't forgive him for having been a friend of Nizan's (because the communists had finally woken up and were making up for lost time by extending their influence over a whole section of the Resistance). They wouldn't forgive him either for being a disciple of Heidegger or for the ultimate crime of having been an anti-fascist from the start and therefore in a state of revolt long before them. So, he adopted a low profile, became rather restless and spent most of his time – the year of 1942, to be precise – refining his doctrine of freedom which he elaborated in that enormous work *L'Etre et le Néant*; this, though it appeared difficult from the outside, turned out to be a political bombshell. But when circumstances altered and the communists, as a result of a change of tactics, came to him, offering explanations, excuses almost, and suggested they form an alliance, he immediately accepted! He did so with the same ardour, the same lively enthusiasm he had shown when he first returned to Paris from the camp. He accepted the hand they held out to him, even though just previously they had been calling him a German agent! Sartre still wasn't a hero. He wasn't and never would be one

of those who had to suffer torture, imprisonment, the firing-squad – which isn't something one should complain about. He joined the CNE,[2] published articles in *Lettres françaises*, demolished Drieu and condemned Céline and Rebatet. He was always in the forefront of any attack on these infamous people, whose voices, he said, "quavered in the silence". And he was also went to the meetings of anti-fascist intellectuals, at Edith Thomas's house in the Rue Pierre-Nicole, where they began to lay the basis of the France they hoped would emerge in the future. One can say that he was there where he should have been. At a time, it must also be said, when many future supporters of the Resistance were still hesitating about declaring their support, he joined those who were actively anti-Nazi, without any sense of pride or drama, but simply because he knew that was where he belonged. It seems to me, therefore, that one must have a very strange conception of commitment if one thinks of this man as a half-hearted individual who was sympathetic or indulgent towards the regime in power.

4. Then there was the fuss over *Les Mouches*. It was an error, a foolish mistake, which, it's said, provided those who wished to make a case against him with real ammunition. It supposedly proved that Sartre was first and foremost a careerist, who, when his self-interest clashed with his convictions, didn't hesitate a moment over associating with the enemy. Let's consider, then, the affair of *Les Mouches*. I wouldn't want to argue that the Occupation was necessarily the best time to put on this play, especially since it was staged at the Sarah-Bernhardt Theatre, which had been "Aryanised" and renamed the "Theatre of the City" on the orders of the Gestapo. But having said that, I would wish to clarify a number of issues. Firstly, it suggests considerable ill-will not to accept that the text itself reveals a certain spirit of revolt in the characters of Orestes and Electra – as well as a thinly veiled attack on regimes, like that of Argos, which make penitence a principle of government. The Sartre who wrote this was the same anti-Pétainist and anti-fascist who made his views known in "Socialism and Liberty". Secondly, those whose opinion mattered clearly had no difficulty in understanding the hidden meaning of the play – starting with Michel Leiris who, in his review for *Lettres françaises*, drew attention to the "great moral lesson" which could be drawn from it. Similarly, in the other camp, collaborators such as Alain Laubraux railed against: "This Cubist, Dadaist mish-mash which they've dared to put on for the

public to see". *Les Mouches* was, if you like, the subject of a heated debate, the outcome of which was uncertain, but no one could have been in any doubt as to the side the author was on. Thirdly and lastly, even if the play could only have been put on with the agreement of the occupying army, which necessitated seeking and obtaining the approval of the German censors, it equally sought and obtained the approval of the CNE, which, with all due respect to those latter-day censors, found nothing wrong with it. Why did they allow it? For what reason? One might well ask. But that's not the real question. Nor does one need to know what calculation or assessment of the situation Abetz and Heller made, which led them to agree to a play being put on that challenged their authority. The truth is each side did, in fact, make its own assessment and, as one would expect, interpreted it in its own way. Equally, as one would expect, both sides expected to gain something from it. The Germans hoped, of course, that they would be thought of as tolerant, and those in the Resistance saw it as a chance to make known their beliefs. For this reason, at least, the staging of *Les Mouches* can in no way be compared with that of *La Reine de Césarée*.[3]

5. All the more so, as, at the same time, the writer whom Alain Laubraux chose to denounce as "degenerate" re-established contact with Pierre Kaan, a former fellow-student of the Rue d'Ulm, who, since those days, had begun to work with Jean Moulin. Kaan was in Paris, charged by the CNR[4] with the task of establishing "technical support groups" specialising in intelligence but also in sabotage and the protection of individuals who were under threat. It was in the context of this mission that he met and consulted, on several occasions, the man whom certain people would have us believe was almost a collaborator. Annie Cohen-Solal has described these meetings. She recalls how Sartre considered "it was time for action" and that "it was good that a writer should be able to use a gun as well." She quotes him saying to a third party, who was also one of Kaan's contacts: "We have arms, we have hiding-places, and, as soon as we have the means, we shall be able to launch other terrorist activities and blow up railway trucks." It is true that, in the end, he did none of these things and that all the splendid plans came to nothing. The reason was that Kaan was arrested, that the students belonging to the irregular "Freedom" forces, of whom a great deal was expected, were arrested and executed; and so the whole network collapsed before it had achieved anything.

To insinuate that it was *bound* to fail and to proclaim that our philosopher friend was intrinsically incapable of carrying out what he intended, whatever happened, suggests one has perhaps crossed the threshold of hostility and prejudice. I would simply add that, knowing something of Sartre's hatred of bad faith and self-important stances and remembering what he said (in *Saint Genet*, I believe) about "comedies which clutter our minds and offer us a sense of nobility on the cheap", I would be doubly hesitant before suggesting that his reference to having arms and hiding-places was mere boasting or the result of a gratuitous sense of excitement. What is beyond dispute, in this case, is that a genuine activist – Pierre Kaan – considered it useful to make contact with him, and that he, for his part, clearly felt it was appropriate to answer that appeal. Thus, if words have any meaning, he was, at the end of 1943, a supporter of all-out armed struggle against Hitler's troops (and for an intellectual to be a supporter was surely sufficient).

I would reiterate one last time that it is not a matter of making him out to be either a saint or a martyr. And I also want it to be clear I am in no way an admirer of this man's philosophy or novels. Nonetheless, whether one is a Sartrian or not, I don't really see how anyone can suggest his attitudes were those of even a lukewarm Pétainist, given that he never ceased to express his hostility, his revolt and his hatred. It is incomprehensible to me that he has been branded a dubious type who had dealings with the enemy and missed a historical opportunity. It is one of those enormous and basically incomprehensible misunderstandings which have punctuated the history of ideas, cluttered and obscured it and thus prevented it from being taken seriously. Sartre made enough mistakes in his life for one not to attribute to him those he didn't make. He has said, and done, enough stupid things for one not to misrepresent the side of him which was revealed during the war and which, for the most part, was truly honourable. It's a matter of justice; for a historian, a matter of truth.

NOTES

1. The "party of the executed", so called because of the heavy losses they sustained during the Resistance.

2. The "Comité national des écrivains" was an underground organisation

of writers under communist control.

3. A play written by Brasillach whilst he was a prisoner of war in 1940. It was published in 1944 but only staged in the fifties. Demonstrations occurred

because of the author's collaborationist past and it was taken off.

4. The "Conseil national de la Résistance" in which Jean Moulin brought together representatives of the various Resistance groups in the two zones of France as well as those of clandestine political parties.

17

"A latecomer to the Resistance"

MALRAUX AND JOSETTE CLOTIS

Among the possible reasons for the strange delay in Malraux's decision to enter the Resistance, there is one which is scarcely ever mentioned and which should be. It is the considerable role played by his companion at the time, Josette Clotis. She was certainly a delightful creature, pretty and lively. There was a mercurial and even scatterbrained side to her nature which he must have found attractive and would have been a change from Clara. But she could be very silly as well and was terribly snobbish and opinionated. For years, she had longed to keep him away from conflict and from certain friends of whom she disapproved wholeheartedly. This we know from her confidante and biographer, Suzanne Chantal. She found fault with the English, the beastly Spanish, the warmongering Jews who wanted to take her André from her, as well as with Clara of course, who really wasn't "quite right" for him, she said graciously. Of all his close friends, Drieu was the only one she deigned to consider acceptable and handsome!

We have to think of her, tart that she was, sniggering at the idea of the Occupation providing the ideal atmosphere for illicit affairs. We must think of the two lovers, in that luxurious villa at Roquebrune, overlooking the Bay of Monte Carlo, lent them by Gide's friend, Dorothy Bussy. We can imagine them enjoying their huge, rather grand lunches, the butler wearing white gloves, the luxury and sensual delight. Then we think of her again, a minor novelist and the ex-society columnist of *Marianne*, simpering and saying she wasn't having in her house that "terrible crowd of outsider intellectuals, pederasts and madmen who feel the need to get drunk, take drugs, sleep around and have themselves psychoanalysed". What did the pro-communist colonel and ex-leader of the "España" squadron think about all this? What did the fighter and orator make of it, having spent the previous years sharing a platform at huge anti-fascist rallies with those very "outsider intellectuals"? All one can say is that amongst the bores who visited them, despite her strictures, were Sartre and Sperber, Bourdet and Roger Stéphane – all of whom, as well as having a natural weakness for drink and drugs, came to plead the cause of the Resistance. And each of them, as long as Josette Clotis held sway, were discouraged, albeit in a friendly manner.

Jean Lacouture has remarked that Malraux rallied to de Gaulle and to Gaullism in 1945, just a short while before the death of Bernard Groethuysen, mentor and professor of Marxism. Until then, his presence, albeit silent, had been enough to prevent Malraux from taking this step. Josette Clotis also disappeared from the scene a few months after her lover decided to take to the Maquis. Thus there is, relatively speaking, something strangely similar about the two situations. Furthermore, there is sufficient evidence of this young woman's temper and ill-humour – to say nothing of her claim, those last few wretched months, that she was a "hostage of the Maquis" – to fuel the suspicion that if Malraux re-established links with his past, in March 1944, it was in order to oppose her. I know something of this myself, if only because of what Madeleine Malraux, the wife of his younger brother Roland, has said. The hypothesis is certainly as valid as any other. Moreover, its great merit is that it has the plausibility of fiction.

18

". . . whether a writer was responsible for crimes which he had not committed"

ROBERT BRASILLACH

What is the responsibility of the intellectual? The case of Brasillach was, of course, particularly dramatic. But there was also Drieu's well-known reply to the question as to whether he would have the courage to kill Malraux, were he to come face to face with him in a civil war. The substance of his reply was: "Yes, certainly, I would kill him, because if I didn't, I wouldn't be taking him seriously." Then there was the case of the young Aragon, who had just rejoined the Communist Party, and, having produced the famous poem "Front rouge", found himself charged, on January 16th, 1932, with "inciting soldiers to disobedience and calling on them to commit murder in the name of anarchist propaganda". This aroused great emotion, and provoked protests and petitions of all kinds. The whole of the intelligentsia weighed in on behalf of freedom and against censorship. Breton produced a tract, other surrealists made numerous declarations, and the whole band of them actively set about establishing and proclaiming that the writer was not responsible for what he wrote. Aragon's superb reply to that was: "I would willingly sign a petition which asserted the writer's full responsibility and full rights – including that of going to prison."

III

LOST ILLUSIONS
(1945 to the 1960s)

"Colette Peignot, the legendary beauty"

SOME BRIEF REMARKS ON THE ROLE, IN LITERATURE, OF WOMEN WHO WEREN'T WRITERS

Since beginning work on this survey, I have kept coming across Colette Peignot, though the part she played was discreet, almost always behind the scenes, as if she were a shadow. Hers was a secondary role, but a genuine one all the same. Every time she made an appearance and especially when those who knew her referred to her, they did so in hints and whispers. It makes one think the woman was shrouded in mystery, that simply by calling her to mind, and mentioning her name, one entered the social circle of which she was the idol. Indeed, some of those who outlived her appeared still to keep alive its passwords and its secrets.

As the mistress of Jean Bernier, she was on the fringes of surrealism. It was he, you may remember, who undertook the difficult task of bringing Breton and the communists together. A little later on, she was at the centre of left-wing opposition to Stalinism, as Boris Souvarine had by then become her lover. She even helped to create (and no doubt also to finance) Souvarine's well-known magazine, *La Critique sociale*, in which most of the major figures who had been expelled from the Bolshevik International expressed their views. Later still, she was to be found in the company of her last lover, Georges Bataille, in whose arms, legend has it, she died, still young and pretty and with that fine yet weary expression already visible in photos of her with Jean Bernier.

When you didn't actually come across her directly, someone would mention her; and even if no one mentioned her, you felt her presence. In one way or another, the events of the day contrived her involvement in almost every situation. This was not surprising given who she was. She financed *La Critique sociale*, played a part in *Documents*, and acted as a mediator in the discussions between the surrealists and *Clarté*. She then became Bataille's partner in one of the blackest but, at the same time, one of the most unusual adventures ever undertaken by a writer in the history of literature. But she herself did not write many books. She was the author of just one, the famous *Ecrits* published after her death under the pseudonym of Laure, which was not important enough in my view to account for her prestige. What made her special was the series of passionate relationships she had. Though seemingly quite ordinary, they represented an extraordinary three-dimensional erotic experience with some of the most "magnetic" personalities of the day.

She was, then, a sort of Milena, an Anaïs Nin without the diaries, a Lou Salomé whose love affairs involved her in the most political of debates. In other words, she was one of those women who put more into her life than into her work, as is often the case, and who was clever enough to seek out the symbolic figures of the day, to latch onto them and play their game by entering into their life and work. And talking about the surrealist sphere of influence, the names Nusch, Gala[1] and Simone Breton could be added to the list. As I've said, Colette Peignot wrote one book, yet, according to certain people, had plans and ideas for others. But something, some sure sense of what she was doing, dissuaded her from following them up. It was as if an insistent, mysterious voice dictated her curious behaviour, as it did that of Nusch, Gala, Lou Salomé and others: "Forget about your books, forget all that. If you are to achieve the immortality so dear to your heart, you would gain more if you became the object of a myth rather than the author of some minor work or other."

One day, the story of these women must be told, the choices they made, the things they gave up, and the life they led. Some way must be found of expressing what each of them only thought or murmured about their pact with immortality. The facts must be established and a judgment made as to whether theirs was the right choice from the viewpoint of immortality, in heeding their inner voice. Was it better to be Gala rather than Elsa Triolet, Colette Peignot rather than Clara Malraux? Was it preferable to be a legendary woman who did not write than a woman who wrote books of little significance? Their role and contribution must be assessed, as must the extent to which they silently enriched the stock of images which sometimes passes for literary history. The precise nature of what they added must be uncovered and then weighed. Though they themselves decided not to write, someone will have to pick out carefully those features of which literature would have been deprived had they simply not existed. I have a vision of a historian, working like a geographer to produce a map, every version of which would certainly be different and distorted because it would be projected from a precise position on the globe. I have a vision of a geographer of ideas who would have the taste and time to rewrite the history of literature from the perspective of those women and the thousand and one ways they contributed to it.

In the first place, there were those who merely acted as a mediator or go-between. Then came those who happily collected literary scalps and, whether deliberately or not, established between them a whole network of relations, which would simply not have existed had they not performed their role. It is fun to speculate what Peignot might have remarked to Souvarine about Bernier and to Georges Bataille about Souvarine; fun also to speculate what Lou Salomé conveyed to Rilke about Nietzsche and to Freud about them both. People speculate too – or I do at least – about the four Maklès sisters (Sylvia, Rose, Bianca and Simone), who, in marrying Bataille, Masson, Fraenkel and Piel, created the strangest family and sexual OPA[2] in the history of modern literature. They also helped unify one of the most prominent "sub-groups" within the surrealist sphere of influence. Then there is the case of Alma Mahler, whose image as a seer came to overshadow her role as a genuine intermediary between the different worlds of art and culture, which, in my view, was more crucial. Think for a moment of the enormous gulf she bridged between those worlds and of all that she perhaps conveyed between Klimt, Mahler, Gropius, Kokoschka and Werfel. These were not ordinary women, they were channels of communication, live transmitters, early satellites complete with channels and stations which received and sent out vast quantities of information. They were like telephone operators whose sole plea-sure was in linking people, helping them make contact and keeping information flowing. That was their primary role.

As a variant on the part played by this first group of women, there was what might be called the "Jules and Jim" syndrome, namely two men but still only one woman. In this case, however, the two men were rivals and confronted each other through the woman in question; and within their triangle desire mimicked itself, was mediated, but at the same time remained in conflict. Though the structure and mech-anics of desire are well known, and its effects in this particular case were as might have been expected, they have never been analysed. The case in question is, of course, that of Eluard and Dali in conflict over Gala, and through her over whole areas of surrealism. The case of Drieu, Aragon and the enigmatic "lady of the Buttes-Chaumont" also comes to mind. She clearly had something to do with their quarrel in 1925 and played a part in the gestation of *Gilles* and subsequently of *Aurélien*. What Aragon's biographers have refrained from tell-ing us, however, is that the Bérénice of the novel was in fact called Denise and was none other than that most coveted companion of the surrealist-Trotskyist, Pierre Naville. Yet again, a legendary woman who aroused great desire and played a part in the political history of surrealism with its reversals, paradoxes, secrets and dark corners. Then there was Roland Tual, a marginal surrealist, who must have known when he married Colette Jeramec that the mythical figure he had fallen for was Drieu's first wife. We surely cannot ignore in this case the link between the future Nazi, who, it must be remembered, committed suicide in Colette's flat, and a representative of that same group he had felt some affinity for as a young man but then drifted away from. And I nearly forgot Lacan, who was, as you know, almost a contemporary of his true mentor, Georges Bataille, with whom he shared certain interests. Their closeness might have been better appreciated, had we called to mind the extraordinary coincidence of Lacan's marriage just before the war to Sylvia, née Maklès, and ex-Bataille.

Then there was a whole series of women – sometimes the same ones – who crossed more sharply defined boundaries. Their power and charm derived from the fact that they brought together not just different men but different worlds. Elsa was a Russian and Nancy Cunard had lived in wealthy high society. Florence Gould, Anna de Noailles and Louise de Vilmorin[3] also inhabited other worlds or rather a zone between two worlds, a sort of no-man's-land in which men suddenly had the feeling they were moving between different galaxies. These women were like stars, were even interstellar. They were truly and profoundly cosmopolitan, not because they moved from place to place but because being cosmopolitan was part of their soul and style. They resembled Germaine de Staël, whose reign would surely not have been so brilliant had she held court in Paris rather than Geneva, which seemed to incarnate the European mind. One might almost include those famous Americans in Paris, Sylvia Beach and Adrienne Monnier, who brought Joyce, Pound, Fitzgerald and Hemingway into contact with Gide, Paulhan, Larbaud, Breton and Valéry. It might be thought that anyone who kept open house, such as Halévy or Du Bos, could have done the same thing, though it isn't certain. The truth is, whenever intellectuals had a vision of worlds being brought together, it was a woman's face they saw.

What reinforces this view of women was their other function, which neither Halévy nor Du Bos could have performed: that of the silent figure to whom books were addressed and dedicated. A question professional writers are regularly asked is: "Why do you write?" What really should be asked is: "For whom do you write?" And in spite of the fact that Flaubert wrote, or claimed to write, out of hatred for the human race and for women in particular, and that Balzac expressed his views on this question in the very misogynist *Physiologie du mariage*, the history of literature is full of individuals who have made it clear they were inspired to write by women, and wrote therefore because of them and for them. One could cite again the case of Aragon, or that of the surrealists, even remind the reader that, in his *Carnets de la drôle de guerre*, Sartre explained how he became a writer to compensate for his ugliness and to seduce pretty girls. Bernard Frank has amusingly suggested that all Drieu's books were like huge personal advertisements of his own moral, physical and amorous qualities, addressed to women. Others unflaggingly paraded their personal details like sandwich-board men. My favourite story of this kind is the one told by Borges about Dante, in which he claims that he wrote the whole of *The Divine Comedy*, one of the greatest and richest monuments to the power of language, with the sole aim of conjuring up and representing, one last time, images of Beatrice. Whether it is true or false, the moral of the story is quite clear. Even though it may tell us almost nothing about Dante, it says a lot about Borges and of the conviction he shared with Drieu, Sartre and others, that the desire to write can be largely explained by the magnetic attraction of women.

If a woman is a source of inspiration of a specific work and therefore not just in some vague and abstract sense, her role is similar to the one previously discussed, but her status is enhanced. The first person who comes to mind is Hemingway who crudely confessed – to Fitzgerald I think – that he changed women for each novel he wrote. And Fitzgerald himself marvelled at having met – in Zelda, of course – the woman he dreamed of in his stories. She was his ideal incarnate and he wrote for her *Tender is the Night*. Turning to the surrealists again, one recalls Breton's emotion on seeing at the Cyrano, and then at the swimming pool at the Colisée where she worked, a woman called Jacqueline Lamba whom he immediately knew he would be able to use. There was also Nora, the little serving girl at Finn's Hotel, whom Joyce spied on, studied and plundered, before turning her into Molly Bloom, almost certainly unknown to her. But in transformations of this kind, those concerned have to remain ignorant and unconcerned. Malraux confided almost nothing to us of his practices in these matters, but it is worth noting that he stopped writing novels at the precise moment when Clara disappeared from his life. It may have been mere chance or a coincidence, and there were perhaps other, more "serious", reasons for what may seem like a conscious and calculated conversion to different forms of intervention. But I have listened to Clara's accounts of her own contributions. I have heard her describe how she, rather than her husband, sometimes saw, heard and felt things; how when they lived in the Rue du Bac, he would spend whole evenings appropriating the stock of stories, anecdotes and images she had gleaned during the day. I have listened to these things too often not to recognise some connection between cause and effect. When he broke with her, he accepted that the fountain would dry up.

But in the long history of women and their association with literature, everything is not as rosy or as splendid as you may think. It would be possible to approach the question from the opposite point of view and tell of the wretchedness of women, of their defeat and the price they paid in their lives when they chose to get caught up in the great maelstrom of literature. Women have been courted and abandoned, abused, sucked dry and left worn out. They have been shrivelled by the works they have inspired and the inspiration which they gave has then been mockingly rejected as of no importance. You only have to look at Hemingway for confirmation of what I have described. Women have been caricatured to the point where they could no longer bear the distortions of themselves. When they saw or heard how they had been depicted, they recoiled in horror or revolt, as Zelda must have done on reading *Tender is the Night*. Women have been driven crazy. They have been trapped and set like specimens or insects, but if they attempted to engage in some great ploy on discovering what had happened to them, or on realising they had been tricked into a pact, their action came too late. Zelda, for example, declared she would break the pact, ask him to return her money, and reclaim the very soul which he had stolen from her. Once the affair had finished and she was picking up the pieces, she wanted everything he had taken and which she had sometimes given. This was the famous episode of that wretched little novel, *Save Me the Waltz*, the subject, plot and characters of which she stole from him, without realising when it was finished that what she had written was sub-Fitzgerald. Other unfortunate women were totally vanquished, too, didn't have the strength to revolt, and came to resemble the heroine of Edgar Poe's "The Oval Portrait". This humble young girl faded away in silence, whilst her artist husband worked on her portrait in the gloomy half-light of a tower which had been turned into a studio. When he finished putting the last touch of varnish on her painted cheeks, finally put down his palette and his brush and exclaimed with almost ecstatic delight: "This is indeed *Life* itself," her heart fluttered one last time, like the flame of a lamp, and, as if she had been shrivelled or absorbed by the painting which replaced her, she quietly died.

This story could, and doubtless should, be told, since it would provide a useful counterpoint to everything I've said about women who became involved in literature without writing anything themselves. But, whether rightly or wrongly, it doesn't appeal to me. What's more, from the standpoint I've adopted in my survey of intellectuals, and concerned as I am with things that went on behind the scenes, with what remained unsaid or was quietly hidden, the drama of these women is unfortunately of little significance, however moving it may have been. So, I hope I shall be forgiven for saying that Colette Peignot's premature death, her attempts at suicide, or even her talent are of considerably less interest to me than what I have discovered about her in the books and memories of others. To look at it from a slightly different angle, let me turn to that incredible document which, for a century now, has unleashed, not surprisingly, the ire of musicologists who consider themselves feminists. I refer, of course, to Gustav Mahler's famous letter to Alma, in which, without a hint of embarrassment, the great artist begged his future wife to give up music, as it would create a strange situation of rivalry between them and, to quote his own words, would be "ridiculous" and "degrading". Yet I have to admit I am not filled with indignation at what he wrote, but fascinated rather by Alma's reasons for giving in and yielding to his request. In thus choosing to become a myth rather than to leave behind a body of work, she acted to her own detriment but in the service of art.

Notes

1. Gala was Eluard's first wife, whom he married in 1917. She subsequently left him and married the painter Dali. Eluard married Nusch in 1934.

2. "Offre public d'achat" which means a take-over bid.

3. All three were wealthy society hostesses who entertained writers. Anna de Noailles and Louise de Vilmorin also wrote poetry.

"Bukharin"

André Gide's failed meeting

Pierre Herbart told this terrible story about Gide's trip to the USSR.

Gide was in his room in the Metropole Hotel in Moscow, being helped by his friend Herbart. They were working on the speech he was going to give the next day at the funeral of Gorky, which was to take place in the presence of Stalin on Red Square. Suddenly, as he was putting the finishing touches to his peroration, there was a knock at the door which Herbart answered. When he opened it, he was surprised to find Bukharin standing there, who simply said: "I would like to speak to Gide."

"Really?" Gide replied, without looking up from his papers, when his friend quickly told him who was there and how important he was. He went on: " I'll be with you in a moment. I've nearly finished what I'm writing. Pierre tells me you were a friend of Lenin. If so, you can be a great help to me . . . !" The conversation that followed between the writer and the Bolshevik leader, who was already being harried, was an extraordinary dialogue of the deaf. It would have been hilarious had the circumstances, not to mention subsequent events and the imminent arrest of this "former friend of Lenin", not made it terrifying and tragic in retrospect.

Raising his voice in an absurdly exaggerated way, Gide tried out the speech on his visitor, who took advantage of pauses in the reading to try in desperation to get across that he had something important to tell him. Gide seemed not to hear and wouldn't be distracted from the task of trying to round off his speech. Addressing him as Bunin rather than Bukharin, he kept saying over and over: "You can tell me in confidence, Mr Bunin" or "Comrade Bunin understands," and wouldn't let him get a word in edgeways. In the end "Comrade Bunin" got the message only too well and left without saying a word. As he went, he looked at the two Frenchmen in what I imagine must have been an ironic, disdainful or decidedly disappointed manner.

No one will ever know exactly what he had come to say, since it was only a few months after the meeting took place that he was arrested, expelled from the Party, condemned to death and finally executed. "The Poles can perish as long as *Finnegans Wake* survives,"

Joyce is alleged to have said, though no one has ever testified to it. "Hang Mr Bunin, as long as *Retour de L'URSS* is finished," must have been the thought in Gide's mind that July day in 1936, when he could have listened to and perhaps even saved one of the most prominent targets of the regime he was in the process of denouncing. It was a question of a book versus a life, whether a life was worth more than a book. But what use are books if they don't save lives? This really was an outrageous piece of behaviour. But life – or was it the book? – took its revenge. For, on this occasion, Gide (like his readers) was deprived of the portrait of Bukharin, which, one imagines, would have been more successful than the one he did of Gorky.

3

"A strange regression"

THE COST OF POLITICS TO WRITERS

One question that isn't raised often enough concerns writers' involvement in the events of the day and the price they have to pay for it. For if their actions are to have any consequence, a ransom, whether symbolic or real, must be paid.

In strictly political terms, what happens is well known. Let us take the example of the post-war years and the way in which, in films, the "Stalingrad phenomenon", the Party's renewed prestige, the myth of the "executed", the prestige of Stalin himself and of his "glorious Red Army", spearhead of the Allied victory, erased almost miraculously the Nazi-Soviet pact, the Gulag, and the earliest details of the critique of Stalinism which had begun in the thirties. But we could have chosen the thirties themselves and the fact that large numbers of people knew about the camps and were fully aware of the perverse nature not just of Stalinism but of Leninism as well; but, because the anti-fascist cause demanded it, they thought they were behaving reasonably and responsibly in forgetting what they knew in order to make common cause with the USSR. This was true both of Aragon and Rolland, who, in a polemic with Barbusse that deserves to be more widely known, had already rehearsed all the arguments for unflinching anti-totalitarianism in 1921. But subsequently, in 1933, he dismissed them all from his mind as he threw in his lot with the Stalinists on the pretext of being more effective. It is above all true of the great man himself, André Malraux, who had nurtured a dream of revolution as far removed as possible from the reality of the Soviet model ever since his return from China. When, in 1935 or 1936, he sensed that fascism was spreading "its great black wings" across Europe, he made repeated gestures of allegiance to the Kremlin which, rightly or wrongly, he considered to be the likely epicentre of any riposte. This is the same Malraux who chose to remain silent, as an expression of "anti-fascist discipline", when Andres Nin was assassinated and when the anarchists of Barcelona were liquidated almost before his very eyes, at the same moment as the trials of Zinoviev, Kamenev, Bukharin and the rest were opening in Red Square. Certainly, Malraux was a dedicated anti-fascist, but his anti-fascism immediately resulted in an unprecedented impoverishment of his own political thinking. As an admirer of the author of *La Condition humaine*, how could one not feel uncomfortable listening to his wholehearted declaration of support for the soldiers of the Red Army, complete with clenched-fist salute, in a speech he gave in New York in the middle of the Spanish Civil War? We have all found ourselves in similar situations, relatively speaking. We have all experienced moments such as this when the heat of battle, the need to isolate or marginalise an opponent has forced us to accept alliances which, only the day before, might have seemed immoral or unnatural. Politics is a wretched business in the terrible simplicity it imposes on us. Whilst wishing to keep things in perspective, I can myself recall how, in some anti-racist meeting, I defended the exact opposite of my real thoughts about the extremely complex connections between racism, anti-semitism and xenophobia, which are so difficult to express. It was the same struggle. I insisted all three were equally vile. I would have been right, of course, had I meant that the struggle should be conducted with equal vigour on all three fronts. But I knew I was wrong in arguing that these three profoundly different forms of madness were in fact identical. Yet, not only is that what I said, it is what I allowed others to say too. I told myself it was the only message the public were prepared to accept at the time. That was the first price or ransom I paid.

The same thing happens on the aesthetic front as well. It is, after all, inconceivable that writers should go in for such approximations yet their work remain unaffected. Take, for example, the case of Gide: when he was a fellow-traveller, he wanted to use his talents in the service of his new-found faith and so produced *Les Nouvelles Nourritures* as a remake of *Les Nourritures terrestres*. Berl amusingly described this book not only as the worst thing Gide ever wrote but as the worst work of twentieth-century literature, and he was right. Malraux offers an even more clear-cut example, given that he had portrayed subtle and complex characters in both *Les Conquérants* and *La Condition humaine* and depicted their struggle against the absurd as well as against capitalism and oppression. At the same time, he retained a pessimistic and romantic tonality in his representation of their revolt which conformed to the conventions of fiction. There were certainly unpleasant characters in these novels, such as Borodine, Vologuine and Nicolaëff. There were also clockwork communists, who were all of a piece, but whose "Bolshevik mentality" was challenged within the novel by Garine. The fact is that they were criticised, judged, represented in relative terms, since there were figures like Garine and Kyo who prevented them from becoming privileged spokesmen within the narrative. But then, in 1936, at the point when Malraux accepted the scandal of the show trials and the murder of Andres Nin, he published *Le Temps du mépris* followed by *L'Espoir*. The main thrust of these two novels was to put forward and defend an argument and to plead a cause. Literature was truly being used for political ends which had suddenly become the only thing that mattered to him. And so, all his principles went out of the window, including his artistic ones. The subtlety and problematic nature of his previous books, their ambiguity and complexity, and the fact that they were concerned with metaphysical uncertainty were abandoned in the face of the need he felt to prove a point. Kassner replaced Borodine and there was Enrique in *L'Espoir*. In the eyes of both the readers and the other characters, such figures remained narrow-minded, simplistic, militant and stupidly calculating, but there was something new about them. The author now showed them in a favourable light but provided no kind of counterbalance. The ultimate absurdity was that they were approved of by Aragon, who, in the slightly mocking tone he was later to adopt in praising Fougeron,[1] hailed Kassner as a model of "verisimilitude", a "son of the people" turned communist. Is *Le Temps du mépris* a third-rate novel? That is Malraux's own judgment not my own. But after the emotional impact of the most powerful scenes in *La Voie royale*, after identifying with the mythical but authentic heroes of *La Condition humaine* or *Les Conquérants*, I cannot imagine anyone entertaining such feelings on being confronted by the huge, dis-embodied and over-talkative individuals who clutter the pages of this particular propaganda novel. Once he began writing as a militant, Malraux displayed less talent. And though due allowances should be made (one can't really compare what isn't comparable), devotees of Malraux who have read *Le Temps du mépris* are likely to have experi-enced the same embarrassment that admirers of Céline felt when they discovered for the first time his three notorious pamphlets.[2] It was the same author, the same trade mark, but the voice and the rhythm were different, and the charm of the earlier works was missing. You realise that when a great writer becomes a militant, defends certain ideas, transforms his viewpoints into hard and fast positions and hypothesis into thesis, and when the book he is writing has a purely political purpose, he is likely to become a mere shadow of the great writer he was and produce nothing more than pastiches in his own name.

There is a third aspect to this issue. The writer will doubtless no longer have the time he devoted to the books that made his name. One day someone should tell us how much time has been lost to politics by writers in general; time wasted which can sadly never be regained. Yet writers who know what is likely to happen nonetheless continue for some strange reason to sit on platforms at meetings and devote their time to endless petitions. Doubtless, there are examples of the opposite being true. Take the case of Barrès, who maintained one couldn't spend the whole day writing and that was why he spent his afternoons in the National Assembly. But did anyone believe him? Aragon claimed that he joined the Communist Party to have the right and the time to produce real novels, but one mustn't forget he had been a member of the "inner circle" of that super-party: the surrealists. Yet for each exception to the rule there are infinitely more examples which confirm the implacable impoverishment of a writer's work. And even if Aragon felt a wonderful sense of freedom on joining the Party, having previously been forced by Breton to burn his *Défense de l'infini*, considerably more lives have been wasted on partisan concerns. It makes me angry that so many writers have spent so much time often on futile tasks which they should have devoted to their books, sometimes as their lives were drawing to a close. Gide published nothing whilst he was committed, except for *Les Nouvelles Nourritures*, and Malraux turned out a third-rate work. It was only with great difficulty that Sartre completed his book on Flaubert by distancing himself from the mad militancy of his Maoist friends. And during the most political period of his life, Camus produced his poorest work. Klossowski also told me that Bataille only re-established his true mastery when he gave up politics. Other names could, of course, be added to the list, as if to confirm the law that when politics takes over, literature goes into decline. There is even the possibility that writers will dry up altogether if they feel impelled or choose to "value something more highly than literature", to quote Bernard Lazare. I would, however, like to make it clear I do not consider involvement in politics either pointless, illegitimate or questionable. I could hardly take that line, having felt some sense of obligation towards commitment for fifteen years or more, as I still do whatever the cost and the risks. There is a price to be paid, I know, and I shall have to pay it. My secret hope is that knowing and saying it aloud will help reduce that cost.

NOTES

1. A socialist-realist painter much praised by Aragon.

2. Céline's "pamphlets" are in fact three violent, hate-filled, anti-semitic works which he published between 1937 and 1941. They are *Bagatelles pour un massacre* (1937), *Ecole des Cadavres* (1938) and *Les Beaux draps* (1941).

4

"At the same time Aragon reigned supreme"

THE ADVANTAGE FOR A GREAT WRITER IN BEING A COMMUNIST

The great issue in any discussion of Aragon is of course communism, though not its theory or its politics. Nor are the reasons he may have given for his involvement of any interest either, even if he believed in them. Similarly, other reasons *we* might have put forward and just as easily dismissed (the new man, a fascination with the idea of the leader, a desire for purity, etc., etc.) are not worth bothering with. No, the real, existential question, which is almost a physical thing, is the fact that he actually belonged to a party like the French Communist Party for fifty years. What one wants to know is what he did, what he thought. How did someone as prominent as Louis Aragon live with himself and at the same time remain, for half a century, at the heart of the most stupid and reactionary party in the world?

What did Aragon think or say about Hungary and Czechoslovakia? How could he accept that certain things were both said and done? What made such a born rebel capitulate? How could this former surrealist and friend of Artaud and Jacques Vaché have accepted without demur such an appalling "Biafra of the mind"? After all, this was the individual who, at the age of twenty, provocatively stated that the October Revolution was nothing more than a vague ministerial crisis. How could he have written for them, glorified them? How did the author of *Aurélien* come to produce *Hourra l'Oural*[1] as well as various odes to the OGPU and at the same time accept the rubbish put out daily by the Party? Sartre was applauded by the students of the Sorbonne, whereas Aragon was insulted by Cohn-Bendit. Sartre tried to discover the secret of eternal youth, whilst Aragon assumed the mask of a cynical high-priest. How absurd!

Aragon was on the Central Committee, attended the festivals organised by *L'Humanité*, and was charged with the task of revealing the genius of Maurice Thorez. He would accept a minor role in any celebration organised by the Party and was called on – who else could they have called on? – when they needed a conscience to justify things that couldn't really be justified. When the pressure was really intense,

Elsa would regularly say: "Louis will commit suicide." But Louis never did commit suicide. On the contrary, he accepted the Party line and came back for more. He was in fact the only major twentieth-century writer who gave the impression of truly being established within the Party.

All the major writers of the twentieth century have at some time belonged to one organisation or another, tried out this or that and then, one fine day, discovered something that suited them. Like divas who practised their scales and did their exercises to find the sound they wanted, once they'd got it they decided to stick with it. This is what Malraux did, once he'd discovered Gaullism, just as Gide returned to immoralism. Camus clung on to a sense of what was just as Sartre did to his conscience, and Mauriac played at being the unruly child. Aragon, for his part, having changed direction, hesitated a great deal, tried out Dadaism and then surrealism and anarchism, finished by settling most improbably for communism.

And again, the question to ask is why? What was he looking for in the Communist Party? Did he have some reason or was there some advantage to him in throwing in his lot with them? The first reason, of course, is books. It must not be forgotten that Aragon had "returned" from surrealism. I say "returned from surrealism" as one says that someone has "returned from the front" or "returned from the dead". Because nothing could be more deadly for a writer – and especially for a novelist – than the climate of terror, of mental civil war that Breton fostered and which no one could escape, not even him. Down with books! Down with literature! Let's destroy the past! Those were the orders of the day. And as novels were fit only for the bonfire, they made him destroy his, the bastards. They also made him ashamed of his talent, which was too classical they told him. He still had that oaf Péret's jibes ringing in his ears after he'd read them some of his *Défense de l'infini*.

Now the Party had nothing against novels. On the contrary, they wanted more of them. They didn't turn up their noses. They respected writers and praised them. Comrade Maurice[2] might have been a bit simple, not understood very much, but Péret hadn't been any better either. At least Maurice believed in him and treated him as if he were someone really important. There was no organisation in the world in which writers received such warm and sincere encouragement as long as they toed the line. And the leaders of no other party in France would have treated him with the sort of respect you would get only from a servant or a chauffeur, just because he was Aragon. So, it's very simple. Breton prevented him from writing, whereas the Party encouraged him. That's the first reason.

The second reason has to do with a writer's life. What sort of life could a great writer such as Aragon have dreamt of? All writers have asked themselves this question and usually come up with the same answer. The life they dreamed of was one which afforded some protection, where they couldn't be got at. To put it another way, though the terms are slightly contradictory, it would be like having the life of a Brahmin in a democratic society. But in order to live like a Brahmin and to put as much distance as possible between oneself and the outside world, one had to have the support of a large institution. And in France there aren't that many institutions. There was the French Academy, which wasn't really his scene; a ministry, which was more in Malraux's line; or Parliament, where Barrès was already installed. So that left the Party which with the NRF and the Bank of France was, according to Abetz, one of the three real strongholds in the capital.

The Party was an admirable institution. It had power, it had its own mafia, and it gave support as well as an alibi. It also kept the riffraff at bay. Furthermore, whatever he did – the books he wrote, the practical jokes he played, the provocative remarks he made, the unseemly poses he adopted, indeed the whole extravagant pantomime in which this unrepentant Dadaist indulged – could henceforth be dedicated to the greater glory of the People and of Justice! Aragon joined the Party as Malraux did the Gaullists, because he knew he would gain maximum licence and protection. Money, merry-making and mischief – all his little weaknesses which had cost him so dear when he was with Breton were now exonerated, sanctioned, and even given the blessing of the Party! No one now dared cross swords with the aristocrat turned communist. Nor could he be hounded or insulted. They hadn't been able to touch Voltaire, and still less were they now able to touch a friend of the Thorez's. Aragon became a communist because it was the best way he knew of continuing to play surrealist pranks, without it being too obvious.

I met Aragon one evening in 1976 outside the bar in the Rue des Saints-Pères where I used to have a late cup of tea before going home to bed. He was wearing a large white woollen overcoat and a wide-brimmed felt hat. He walked briskly, his shoulders hunched forward and his eyes fixed on the ground. I was surprised to see that he had a limp. As chance would have it, I was at the time preparing to play the role of Paul Denis in a television version of his novel

Aurélien, which had been adapted by Françoise Verny. So I stopped him and said: "Excuse me, I happen to be about to . . ." He looked at me in astonishment, then rather hard and then suddenly more sympathetically when I said it was about Paul Denis. We talked about the film and about Françoise Verny who had mentioned me to him. The conversation lasted ten minutes, perhaps only five, but it was long enough for me to study the face of one of the writers I then admired the most.

There was no doubt it was him, the great poet, whom time seemed not to have altered. There were so many stories about him, so many legends about the mad nocturnal escapades of the phantom-clown, the inconsolable widower seeking, it was said, some ultimate transformation. But no, he was still the same as ever, in revolt, facetious, crazy about Elsa, or just simply crazy. He had the same bright look in his eye and the same proud bearing, but he still had the hair of an anarchist and the general appearance of an ageing dandy. Despite the lines on his face, his blotchy hands and his slightly shrunken appearance, he was still the same person he must have been forty years previously, when he used to visit the bars of Montparnasse with Sadoul and would be escorted out by gendarmes after creating a rumpus. He was unchanged, except that the shadow of the Party, like some final joke, hovered over him, giving him protection. And this he knew.

A CONVERSATION WITH EDMONDE CHARLES-ROUX

From 1956 until Aragon's death, Edmonde Charles-Roux was probably one of his closest and most constant companions. She accepted with pleasure the chance to talk about him, since there were so many misunderstandings to be dispelled and so many "infamous accusations" to be dealt with. In the bar of the Raphaël Hotel in Paris where I met her, I was struck by her beauty and by her determination to defend faithfully the memory and reputation of a mistreated hero. She spoke in a clear, slightly harsh voice, though at times with a studied softness. As will become apparent, her hypotheses were not always the same as mine, and she seemed concerned to give a favourable interpretation to things which I found enigmatic, cynical and mischievous.

When did you get to know Aragon?

I met Aragon the day after the Soviet troops entered Budapest. I went to visit him at the mill in Saint-Arnoult-en-Yvelines, the country house he'd owned for five or six years. The reason I went was because I thought he must have been feeling strangely isolated, given what was going on. So I spent the evening with him and Elsa. I already knew them a little, probably by sight, but I'd never had a private conversation with them. It was a long evening. We didn't part until five in the morning.

What sort of state was Aragon in? What was he saying and doing?

Aragon was deeply disturbed, wondering what he should and shouldn't believe, and already fully aware that the official statements put out by the Communist Party wouldn't be convincing. You know what they were like. They talked about provocation, about the involvement of the CIA, and more or less said that the Americans were responsible for the Soviet intervention. Of course Aragon didn't go along with that. He was too European, too civilised (and curiously civilised if you bear in mind that during his earliest years his horizons were limited to Paris and even certain districts of Paris), his whole background was too European for him not to sense some other terribly serious underlying reason. It was a turning-point, I believe, which didn't undermine his belief, didn't make him less of a communist, but which created doubts for the first time about the USSR.

Is that precisely what he said that evening?

Yes. There was no way he could accept a blood bath. It just wasn't on. I say again, he was too European, too middle-European to accept any idea of the kind. Even though, it must be stressed, it didn't lead him to break with the Party.

In your view then, Aragon felt that the '56 uprising represented a return to the European fold or a nostalgic concern with Europe?

Absolutely. At the same time, of course, he felt it was a crime on the part of the USSR. Something in the system wasn't working. One mustn't forget Aragon's cosmopolitanism was both natural and spontaneous. He was after all the lover of Nancy Cunard and the husband of Elsa. Remember too the verses he wrote: "I already loved foreign women/when I was a small child."

What were his views on nationalism? It was certainly quite strident in the fifties.

That was understandable. It was in the tradition of Barrès, whom he admired greatly.

So, on that day in 1956 his immediate reaction was that of a central European?

Wait a moment. I wouldn't want to attribute to him my own views. I'd spent seven years of my life in central Europe, and Hungary bordered on the country where I spent my childhood. Perhaps it wasn't entirely what Aragon thought. But he was at least raising certain questions, as was Elsa, even though they hadn't come to any conclusions.

Why hadn't they come to any conclusions?

I think they were living in hope. They had invested a lot of hope in the system and in the idea of communism. It was their pride and glory.

I have a more cynical view of Aragon.

Well, you're wrong. The way the French press has caricatured Aragon and Elsa is disgraceful. They were totally good and generous people. They were very concerned for others and did all they could to help young writers especially, but not just them, people they didn't know, as well. That was the situation. They lived with this great hope and then the bloody uprising occurred in Hungary. Though I have no wish to criticise them, one might be inclined to say: "Well it took a long time for the scales to fall from their eyes." Yes it did. That can't be denied. They didn't change their views until the events in Czechoslovakia.

Can we pause a minute and talk about that first day or evening. Do you remember the scene? Where and how did it take place? Where were Aragon and Elsa?

Aragon was in the living-room at the mill. It had a wheel in working order, so the water ran underneath and one could hear it as it fell. It was very cold. They were completely alone and the phone didn't ring once. I think they were very pleased I'd visited them. There was a samovar for the tea and Elsa was wonderfully hospitable. Time didn't seem to matter for the Aragons. That was something he got from Elsa, that Russian sense of time, as if it didn't exist. At any rate, it was completely different from our sense of time. Elsa was very sensitive and she had a better understanding of the truth that evening than any of us. People made her out to be a virago, but she wasn't like that at all.

Do you know André Thirion's book, Révolutionnaires sans révolution?

Yes

He paints a frightful picture of Elsa.

264

I know. I read it when it came out. I think he's responsible for the image people have of her. What could one reproach her for? Perhaps a woman can't be forgiven for the fact that she's loved by a handsome man. Perhaps a lot of people couldn't accept either that he was faithful and worshipped her.

My own theory is that Aragon was an aristocrat, a Brahmin and not really a communist.

That's your view. However, I think he was a communist and that one ought to try to understand why.

Absolutely.

In my view, he never got over his childhood. I don't think he could bear having a false name and being obliged to treat his mother in public as if she were his sister etc.[3] He was terribly marked by that experience and by the fact that he was brought up in a punctilious, narrow and rather fusty *petit bourgeois* milieu, which wasn't in the least bit aristocratic. That was what he wanted to get away from, when he made his big gesture and joined the Communist Party. He also retained something of the spirit of surrealism and Dadaism: "I'll show you what I can do, how far I can go . . ." It was bravado, if you like. He was full of bravado and bravura. But early on, in his childhood, he'd been terribly scarred. The Party enabled him to rediscover his identity. It was a sanctuary for illegitimate children and for women who had suffered ridicule. It was also the Party in which a woman bringing up a child was visited each month by a man wanting to know what they'd been doing.

So the break with the surrealists, his "betrayal" at Kharkov,[4] all the business with Breton was . . .

A hyper-surrealistic gesture, yes. In part it was a desire to outdo the man who dominated him, namely Breton. But that wasn't all. He'd thought it out politically and it was also, as I've said, a form of faith. Aragon was a creature of faith. I agree there was something aristocratic about him, as you've suggested. That was part of his provocative nature. For example, he readily admitted that those with whom he felt he had something in common were either working men or princes. He was a bundle of contradictions as you can see, but they hung together.

Another aspect of his decision to join the Party had to do with literature. Basically, Breton prevented him from writing novels.

First of all, it was a question of the sense of belonging to a "family". There was no sense of belonging as far as Breton was concerned, and he'd had enough of his authoritarian attitude. So, where could he go? He couldn't become a papist, so he joined the Marxists. But you're right in saying literature lay behind his decision. He realised he would be supported, respected and that he would have a genuine public. There are, of course, political explanations as well, but we never discussed politics.

That's very interesting indeed, the idea that he joined the CP because they treated writers well.

I remember the first time he took me to the 'Cité du Livre'. He said to me: "You see, people are ennobled when they buy a book. That's our true family."

Did he ever talk to you about Breton?

All the time.

So long after they parted company? It must have been twenty-five or thirty years after it happened.

It was. But he never accepted the breach. It was like a wound. He couldn't understand it. Friendship was important to Aragon, and he was loyal. I think he was knocked sideways by their quarrel; deeply wounded by it. He was always trying to get back on good terms with Breton and making excuses for him. He tried to play down their breach, but it was always there. It was probably the major event in his life.

Do you have precise memories? Do you remember conversations etc.?

Yes, of course. He would get out a drawing, quote something Breton said. He worried about who he was seeing and what he was doing. And then there were the letters. When he received a letter from Breton, it was an affair of State. He would re-read it five or ten times and talk of nothing else. It reached the point where we didn't want to discuss it, because we felt it wasn't doing him any good.

What sort of letters did Breton write him?

For example, he might write Aragon a letter after he'd published an article in *Les Lettres françaises*,[5] saying: "Come on, we're not on such bad terms as all that!"

And if Breton had said: "Alright, let's be friends again!"

Aragon would have opened his door to him and invited him in. But Breton was very tough. He would never have committed such an "error".

Did you sense something of the former surrealist in Aragon when he was older? Was it still part of him or had he totally changed?

It's difficult to know. So many things had changed. In the first place, he'd become the "husband" of Elsa, and people assumed he'd changed. Perhaps he had, but only in appearance. When you talked to him, you sensed he was still a surrealist, in the choices he made, in his freedom of spirit, in his desire not to get stuck in a rut or become trapped. But what I'm about to say may seem contradictory. He was, after all, trapped by the fact that he belonged to a party and also by his love for Elsa. But those who knew him intimately and spent a lot of time with him, whole Sundays in his company, knew that he was a man who remained incredibly *free*.

You mentioned his love for Elsa and his love for the Party. Were the two things linked, were they the same?

Through Elsa he got to know Russia. And he'd learnt Russian out of jealousy, because he wanted to be able to understand what was being said to Elsa. He learned it in less than two months as he couldn't bear the idea of people talking to his wife in a language he couldn't understand. That shows you to what extent Elsa and Russia coexisted in his own mind. But that wasn't the only reason. There was Mayakovsky and also Pushkin, who was his god at that time. You could spend hours discussing the impossibility of translating Pushkin. So, it was through a woman that he had an extraordinary grasp of Russian thought and of the Russian way of life. Conversely, it could be said his view of the USSR was shaped by a woman and his view of that woman by the USSR. A debatable point, maybe, but that's how it was.

Agreed. But, as you've said, there was also the "hold" the USSR had over literature itself and which didn't always have very happy consequences.

What do you mean? Are you saying that some of his poetry was uneven and that on occasions he was merely facile? I would agree. But he showed such courage in wanting everything to be published. To my knowledge, there were no deletions in his complete works, which he supervised whilst he was still alive. He didn't even omit the odes to Stalin. He had the courage to stand by what he'd done, which I find really tremendous. I don't think Claudel would have done the same thing. I never thought you could eliminate Aragon's past with one stroke of the pen just because he was a communist. Nor could the fact he was a surrealist be denied simply because he later became a communist. For me, everything was connected and as a character he was, how shall I put it? unblemished.

Did Aragon have charm?

I'm not very keen on the word "charm". Certainly, he was a charmer, but there was more to it than that. He had genius. I sincerely believe that anyone capable of writing *La Semaine sainte* was a genius. His genius was essentially French, revealing itself in his feeling for language, as was his ability to cock a snook at things. You were asking me a moment ago if he remained a surrealist. Well, he was totally disrespectful, which you didn't expect from someone of his age. He liked to cock a snook and he passed the habit on to others. That was good and quite unusual. He certainly wasn't a writer with whom one got bored.

You rightly challenge those who want to erase Aragon's communist and surrealist past. But wasn't he the first to do just that by blotting out part of his own past? I'm thinking of the Kharkov affair and what he wrote at the time to justify his break with the surrealists. It's something that doesn't happen very often. One thinks of Malraux after the war, Barrès perhaps, writers who, as far as the public were concerned, blocked out part of their own past.

As I've already said, we talked of nothing else in private. They were the most treasured moments of his whole life. But you're certainly right. He did obscure all that so that he could get on with the business of living a different life. He's one of those writers who had several lives. And, in any case, didn't the surrealists contribute to what happened by kicking him out? After all, he was excluded. They said to him: "That's it, you're no longer acceptable." And his response was to become even more deeply involved with communism. I say again, his break with Breton was the most painful experience of his life. That's what emerged from my conversations with him, and I believe it.

We agree then. Privately he was obsessed with it, but in public he blotted it out.

Yes, that's right. But he was also desperately keen to entrust some of his experiences to those he liked. He knew I'd arrived from another planet. Italy was, after all, another planet. He very much wanted me to know about surrealism, and so that's what he talked to me about.

Forgive me for insisting on it again, but can you give me specific cases or examples?

We talked a lot about Eluard and Nusch, for example, and about his love for her. We discussed surrealist films as well as the role played by society women in fostering surrealism. We talked about Marie-Laure de Noailles,[6] her judgments and all the things that went on around her. There was also the question which obsessed him as to whether as surrealists they had been right to mix in those circles. We spoke about Buñuel. But once we'd started on that subject, we quickly moved on to the much more important subject of the revolution in Spain and then on to other Spaniards who had been connected with the surrealist movement, including Dali of course. You see, it's impossible for me or anyone else to dissociate him from surrealism. It would be a wicked lie. When you got to know Aragon well, you realised that you were dealing with a surrealist, even though he no longer lived according to surrealist principles.

Then came '68 and the Prague spring. And he suddenly saw what he hadn't seen in '56.

Yes. It was absolutely terrible. Both he and Elsa broke with the USSR over that, she more than him. They wouldn't allow personnel from the Soviet Embassy to visit them any longer. I witnessed that and could give you names. They asked me to answer the door to some of their best friends and tell them they weren't at home. They were there, of course, just behind me. It was a very tense period. But let's not make out they were acting heroically. There were no risks in what they were doing, but they did do something.

What was their relationship with the French Party?

That's another matter. They neither of them broke with the French Communist Party.

What about communism itself, the idea of communism? You spoke a moment ago about their faith.

I don't wish to say anything about that, as I don't know. I think he'd seen and understood what was happening. The day he knew that the coup had taken place in Prague, he realised that *Les Lettres françaises* were finished and that one thing would lead to another. Don't forget, he'd supported all the Czech writers in *Les Lettres françaises*. He was expelled from *Les Lettres françaises*. That was his second expulsion.

Did you see him during that period?

Yes, I did. Elsa and I waited for him together, whilst he was at the offices of *Les Lettres françaises*. Aragon was a fragile individual who took things to extremes. He was capable of doing something very silly. There was something crazy about him. He proved that after Elsa's death. He was a crazy man. It just happens that other people called it something else.

Yet despite that, there was no break, barely a split or a rift.

That's how he was. They'd been his comrades in the struggle, and he simply couldn't do it, that's all. He was loyal, just loyal. Anyway, it all hung together. He was loving and loyal. He had a very loving and sensual approach to politics and history.

NOTES

1. A song of praise describing the rise of socialism in Russia and dedicated to the anti-fascist militants killed in February 1934.

2. Maurice Thorez, the Communist Party leader.

3. Aragon was illegitimate and his mother tried to hide the fact by presenting him as her little brother rather than her son.

4. In November 1930, Aragon went to the second International Writers' Conference at Kharkov. He signed a letter denouncing his former errors and subsequently adopted a stance in favour of dialectical materialism and distanced himself from certain surrealist positions.

5. Aragon was the editor of this left-wing literary journal after the war.

6. A wealthy society lady who entertained and supported artists and writers.

5

"The aesthetic obscurantism of the Party"

WHAT IF PICASSO DIDN'T ALWAYS SHOW GENIUS?

Stalin had just died and the Party was in mourning. Everyone paid their respects, made some complimentary remarks, and shed a few tears. Aragon, who was the editor of *Les Lettres françaises*, certainly didn't want to appear reluctant to make his contribution and so he asked the greatest communist painter, Pablo Picasso, to do a drawing for him, which he could put on the cover of the following week's issue. What he got was the famous "portrait" of Stalin, which was half moonlike and half cubist. His mouth was too pronounced, his cheeks too full, his eyes so large that they dominated the rest of his face, and his fringe of black hair had been hastily scratched in with poor quality charcoal. He looked more like a figure from *Les Demoiselles d'Avignon* than the great and glorious leader of the communists, who, from the highest to the most humble, were expected to sing his praises.

The affair then erupted into a scandal. Party militants exploded with anger, describing it as a disgrace and an act of desecration. In what was to become a major crisis which shook the Party apparatus to its foundations, both Aragon and Picasso were denounced as filthy intellectuals who had dared to attack the idol of the masses. Aragon's willingness to cock a snook proved, however, just how deep-seated the Party's cultural obscurantism really was. There is, however, another less serious and less "correct" explanation, which is also less flattering, one must admit, to an artist persecuted by fools who understood nothing about art. It was the explanation given by Cocteau, and I can't resist mentioning it briefly. What he said was that Picasso had taken about five minutes to do the portrait. He had done it too quickly, without due consideration, and, as sometimes happens, it simply turned out to be a failure.

6

"Billancourt shouldn't be driven to despair"

ANOTHER LEGEND

Jean-Paul Sartre once said: "We mustn't drive Billancourt to despair." It was one of those simple and powerful remarks, conjuring up an image of a vast working-class (Billancourt), ground down by insults and poverty, persecuted by the bosses and the State, who couldn't bear to have their illusions shattered on top of everything else. Because, in their eyes, the Soviet Union did represent a sort of paradise. It was a remark, too, which seemed to illustrate Sartre's political creed and views for a good number of years. I myself have quoted this remark when I wanted to get something across quickly and forcefully, as, for example, when I sought to condemn the objectionable practice of saying nothing about Hungary for fear of upsetting those Frenchmen who consider themselves revolutionaries. I have relied on it in fact to make my point.

So, when did Sartre first make this remark and in what context? The answer is, he didn't make it at all. You won't find it in any of his books, essays or articles. Indeed, you could scour them from end to end, but you wouldn't come across those words written down anywhere. Yet for some people they sum up Sartre's whole vision of the world. One should perhaps qualify this by saying that in *Nekrassov* – which, though committed and even Manichaean, is nonetheless a play and therefore a work of fiction – there is a phrase something like it which says exactly the opposite of what it is usually taken to mean. What the character, Georges de Valera says is: "Let's drive Billancourt to despair." So here we have a remark which is closely identified with a writer and his work and which has become a commonplace, passed on from one to the other, without being checked or verified. Yet it simply doesn't exist in the one place which should really count (until something else replaces it): the writer's own body of work.

What is undeniable is that the oft-quoted remark does represent Sartre's true thinking. It is equally undeniable that Georges de Valera, in suggesting they drive Billancourt to despair, comes over as a bastard. Sartre did genuinely believe deep down that it wasn't always a good idea to reveal the truth everywhere and on all occasions. That, amongst other things, was one of the basic reasons for his disagreement with Maurice Merleau-Ponty, then with Albert Camus and ultimately with the "new philosophers",[1] whom he suspected, as late as 1977, of condemning the Gulag only because they were (sic) in the service of the CIA. He made this comment in an article published by the extreme left-wing Italian paper *Lotta continua*. Yet despite all these things, the basic facts are rather strange, as is the flimsiness of what passes for the history of ideas.

NOTES

1. A heterogeneous group led by Bernard-Henri Lévy and André Glucksmann. From the mid-seventies they began to express their loss of faith in Marx, Lenin, etc.

7

"André Malraux, who appeared to turn his back on the ideals of his youth"

This was the man who had been a "colonel" and a communist sympathiser in the Spanish Civil War. As an orator, he'd spoken at meetings on behalf of the imprisoned communists Thaelmann and Dimitrov,[1] his fist raised in salute. He had been a fighter in the Resistance and was a revolutionary *par excellence*. He was also a rebel and a fellow-traveller. He might be considered, then, the very incarnation of the extreme left-wing intellectual thrown up by the thirties who triumphed after the war. Furthermore, left-wingers were indeed eager for him to speak at the time of the Liberation, during the early days of semi-victory. They expected him to give them hope, as he'd always done. And there he was in the Mutualité, just as he'd been in the past, wearing a khaki tunic with his pips on, his face constantly twitching and partially covered by a lock of black hair. He spoke excitedly with an incisive tone, and resorted to his usual stock phrases. His voice occasionally trembled, and you imagine he might have sounded like Hoche or Saint-Just. He was holding forth again, but instead of reaffirming his faith in world revolution, as might have been expected, instead of calling on the Red Army and its destructive hordes, instead of being the eternal rebel for whom friend and foe alike felt a certain nostalgia, he let it be known for the first time he was no longer one of them. Even when crudely summarised, what he said on that occasion still seems outrageous even today. He made it clear he was no longer a communist sympathiser or a revolutionary and that in the Maquis, then in Paris during the heady days of the Liberation, he had met General de Gaulle and the Gaullists and discovered Gaullism. What's more, he felt they would be criminally insane not to honour all the expectations fostered by the Liberation.

He was the novelist of his day, the greatest and the most celebrated, even if he was on the Left. No one else enjoyed such prestige and his talent was matched only by his courage and brave deeds. He was a unique writer who, as legend had it, felt equally at home in command of a tank, of a Potez 54 or a Latécoère or sitting in front of a blank page working on his latest novel. Malraux was an example, a model of the writer who was free. Young people – and not just young people! – dreamed of identifying with him, and no other writer would have thought of challenging him or even have dared to. Gide no longer counted and Camus was as yet a rising star. As for the great Sartre, had Malraux chosen to play the role of leading rebel intellectual which was his by right, he, Sartre, would simply have remained an Aron of the Left or a more appealing Merleau-Ponty. Even Aragon, prince of the post-war years and absolute monarch in the realm of literature, realised that had Malraux reappeared on the scene he could have reclaimed the position he occupied during the incident-packed period of anti-fascism, the importance of which had been magnified by his absence. In these circumstances, Aragon would have been relegated to the position of a superior Vercors or a more ambitious Eluard. Malraux did indeed appear, causing quite a stir as had been expected. But instead of adopting the role of honour, which would have allowed him to define the new landscape, and which no one would have disputed, he shattered the expectations of the Left and his own image; at the same time he changed his destiny. To everyone's surprise, he chose to become a minister and to join the RPF.[2]

My reason for emphasising this is that we have become accustomed to thinking of Malraux only as the latter-day and ageing figure with a slightly wild and haggard look. This is the image you get, for example, from the well-known photo of the old minister walking arm in arm with Michel Debré and Maurice Schumann at the head of the counter-demonstration of May 30th, 1968. As a result, we find it extremely difficult to imagine what impact his sudden metamorphosis must have had on his contemporaries, coming as it did out of the blue. At a completely different level, it was a bit like Kojève abandoning philosophy, or Rimbaud giving up poetry. It was as if Rimbaud, instead of going to Harrar (too chic and too poetic), had returned to Charleville to teach Latin and French; or as if Byron had returned from Missolonghi and quietly ended his days in the splendid surroundings of the House of Lords. Or to choose contemporary examples, it would have been like Drieu becoming a member of the Académie française, as many others did, rather than committing suicide; or the heroic figure of Lawrence having a long career as a journalist, lecturer and teacher rather than dying in a motorcycle accident. It was as if Sartre (who enjoyed nothing like Malraux's glorious past either before or during the war), with his parka, his packet of Boyard cigarettes, his pockets stuffed with copies of La Cause du peuple, making him look like an ageing and gawky anarchist, had announced after May '68 that he was becoming a minister in Pompidou's government. That's how shocking Malraux's decision was. And no retrospective sense of illusion or adjustment of the eye and the memory can alter the fact that his repudiation of what he stood for in his youth, together with his adoption of a new life, remain one of the most powerful enigmas of contemporary literary history.

The strange thing is, however, that his immediate contemporaries, those who were present when he announced his conversion, who had known the earlier Malraux and been with him until just before the announcement, could offer no analysis which measured up to the enormity of the event. It was inevitable they would be shocked by the suddenness of his change of heart, yet not one of them, either at the time or with hindsight, had an adequate explanation. First of all, I talked to his former friends on the left, those who felt betrayed. I went through copies of various papers and magazines, including *Combat*, *L'Humanité*, *Les Temps modernes*, and *Esprit* and came upon expressions of anger and disappointment. Malraux was a bastard ... a turncoat ... He was known to be a fascist ... one suspected as much ... one could sense it ... now the mask had fallen and his true identity had been revealed. The articles were full of insults and opprobrium, as might have been expected, but scarcely any reflection or analysis of his "betrayal". I then went to talk to people on the other side, his new friends in the RPF. I questioned some of those who had been leading lights in the Gaullist party at the time, thinking their astonishment or at least the memory of his past would have made them more talkative. I tried to get them to say what effect it had upon a teacher, a subprefect, a Christian-Democrat deputy, a *petit bourgeois* who belonged to the Centre-Right when the supreme veteran of the Spanish Civil War suddenly stood up on the platform at the congress and joined in the singing of the "Marseillaise" quite unaffectedly; a congress which will go down in history as the one marking the break with the communists and what they stood for. I got nothing from them either. They remembered nothing, felt nothing, and, though I laboured the point that they must have found it "fascinating", they had the cheek to take the line: "Do you mind? Do you really think so? Who do you take us for? Why the devil do you imagine Malraux's arrival should have astounded us to that extent? He was there, where he belonged, with us, that's all. We were a fine bunch of friends." That was no explanation, nor was their memory genuine. They were merely pretending to be blasé, to consider it natural that the greatest French writer, at the height of his fame and his powers, should have become a colleague of Jacques Baumel.[3] They, too, left us without an answer to our enigma.

So I've tried to arrive at my own understanding of what it was all about. For years now, with various means at my disposal – a situation, a sign, a half-confidence, an image, and when neither image nor confidence were available to me I relied on my imagination as an unrepentant admirer of Malraux – I've attempted to re-create what was really going on in his mind during those weeks. Firstly, he made a pure, cold calculation. Of necessity, he also assessed, weighed up the situation he was leaving behind in a totally methodical way, the risks involved, as well as the gains he might nonetheless make. Baudelaire made the same calculation, according to Sainte-Beuve and Valéry at least, in his celebrated phrase: "Lamartine has appropriated the heavens, Victor Hugo the earth and more, Laprade the forests and Musset passion and debauchery." It seems to me equally easy to imagine Malraux doing a similar thing at forty, considering every possible position, conjuring up every conceivable image of his own destiny, and finally choosing to become a convert, fully aware of what he was doing. "Right," he must have said to himself. "I'm a communist sympathiser and a rebel, which gives me a role for life. What's more, I won't live long enough to exhaust its full potential. But is it really the life I want. Wouldn't it be totally banal? I've fought in Spain, been in the Alsace-Lorraine Brigade, I've known Stalin and defended Thaelmann and Dimitrov, wouldn't it now be absurd, having risen so high in left-wing circles and mythology, to devote the rest of my days to presiding over purges and lunching with Vercors?" Malraux was a wily and cynical individual. He was also wild, capricious and a gambler, and, as one realises full well, wholly incapable of living indefinitely on his laurels. He was a past master at playing different roles and assuming different identities. Moreover, he hadn't died at Missolonghi or taken an overdose at Colette Jeramec's, and he understood at once he had to find a solution, invent some sort of way forward. He had to discover an idea which would enable him to relaunch his own legend rather than manage what remained of the old one. Given the situation in which he found himself at the time and bearing in mind his objectives, I am totally convinced in my own mind that he reckoned the disconcerting image of a revolutionary turned minister, though initially somewhat unsatisfactory, would suit his purposes quite well and further his legendary aims.

Then there was his realisation of the importance of the nation state. Malraux had always known that the history of the twentieth century represented a confrontation between the nation and the forces of internationalism, of whom Trotsky, Stalin, the Spanish Republicans, and Thaelmann were on the whole the most notable figureheads. Until that point he had backed the latter, unreservedly and unquestioningly. But, all of a sudden, he had the feeling it was a gigantic confidence trick, coupled with the sense, on his own part, that he had made an enormous error of judgment. "The most important phenomenon of the last twenty years has been the primacy of the nation," he admitted at the time. He then added: "In this particular sphere (which involves a true appreciation of the forces controlling the world and the crucial passions determining human behaviour) it is not Marx but Nietzsche who is the prophet." He even came to the conclusion that communism was a more potent force when it was linked to nationalistic fervour: "Russian communism", he said (I'm summarising the main points), "is more Russian than communist. And that is why, when we talk about nations and acknowledge that conflict between nations dictates world events, we French must be on our guard where they are concerned." Did Malraux recall at that moment reading Barrès at the age of fifteen and admiring d'Annunzio at eighteen? Was he revealing a hidden part of himself, opening up an area of his memory? There is one certain fact: the man who fought at Teruel had become an ardent nationalist by the summer of 1944. He was trumpeting it sufficiently for there to be no doubt about it. Though the two situations were neither comparable nor on the same scale, it might have seemed as if Malraux's experience was similar to the one Drieu had thirty years earlier. He too, having just come back from war, had become a convert to the idea of the nation as the ultimate reason for the way things were.

Communism, having been revealed to the world in the curious guise of nationalism, was seen in its true colours. To put it bluntly, it was nothing more than a powerful machine in the service of the Russian empire. Malraux understood communism, having both witnessed it in action and, on occasions, been actively involved in its furtherance. He therefore knew what it was like in practice, as we understand a machine we have seen working or an animal whose muzzle we have touched and whose breath we have felt. He knew it intimately, from within, as an initiate. In my view, knowing the devil's secret as he did, probably gave him an advantage over the General. Not having witnessed any of these things for himself, the General must have asked his new friend to talk to him about what he'd seen.

Malraux doubtless obliged with an account of his journey to the end of the night[4] and his memories of the house of the dead. He must have spoken of his involvement and of the fact he'd given it up and also mentioned to him what the communists were like and how far they might go. He could do this because he'd been involved at the highest level and therefore understood that they had to fight communism with the same passion and energy they'd shown in the successful fight against the horrors of Nazism. Why did he understand at that point, given that he'd witnessed the liquidation of anarchists and members of POUM at the hands of the GPU in Spain and had neither said nor done anything? It was the war itself and the nationalistic side of communism which opened his eyes and ears and drove him to proclaim what he'd seen and heard. As Jean Lacouture has pointed out, something else helped reinforce his conviction at that time: the death of Bernard Groethuysen. For it was Groethuysen, we must remember, who taught him his communism and helped him swallow Stalinism. When Grout, the teacher, died, Malraux, the disciple, realised the truth and began to think for himself. This hypothesis appeals to me since it has the plausibility of fiction.

Lastly there was Gaullism itself and the fact that it was a powerfully attractive force for men such as Malraux. It has to be borne in mind he was not an ordinary individual, as he had no family and no ties. From the earliest days he had constantly attempted to deceive people about his origins and to falsify his own biography. He was like those individuals, with an anonymous and deliberately obfuscated past having no clear reference points, whom the General described with some amusement as being amongst the first to join him in London in 1940. To men such as this Gaullism seemed to offer what they most lacked, a sheet-anchor and an alternative genealogy. Judge for yourself! It offered a father-figure, a family, friends who were like brothers, a legend, unlimited heroism and bravery, memories which were truly French – Joan of Arc and Valmy, the Kings and the Revolution! Was there a better alternative? Communism certainly might have been, which is one of the more reasonable explanations for Malraux's allegiance pre-1940. But communism was by definition no longer a meaningful proposition. It might still work for the Russians, but unfortunately they weren't Russian. It would have worked had the communists won, had France fallen (and I don't mean to insult Malraux by saying that, if the revolution had been successful, he might not have abandoned it). But France stood firm, communism was unsuccessful, and Malraux's conversion occurred the day after de

Gaulle's meeting with Stalin and the disarming of the communist militias (which again was indicative). Thus communism no longer provided him with a replacement family structure, but the birth of Gaullism offered an alternative. That was certainly another key to his decision, another possible interpretation, even if it doesn't yet add up to a full explanation, since the crucial factor hasn't yet been mentioned. Not surprisingly, that crucial factor was the personal encounter between the writer and de Gaulle – which was straight out of some extraordinary work of fiction.

Almost everything has been said about the relationship between de Gaulle and Malraux, the prince and his poet, the lord and his loyal servant. It was a meeting between two exceptional individuals, linked by their solitude and their shared disdain for ordinary mortals. Both felt the need for greatness and both, inevitably, enjoyed grandiloquence (viz the loyal servant comparing his prince to the lay equivalent of Saint Bernard de Clairvaux). There were misunderstandings as well (it is a well-known fact that, other than Maurras and Chardonne,[5] de Gaulle only really enjoyed Mauriac and had a very sketchy idea at the time of *La Condition humaine* and *L'Espoir*). Cynicism came into it too, as when Malraux said of the man who made history on June 18th[6] that he had "cleansed the concept of nationalism." He doubtless wished to praise de Gaulle, but coming from the lips of an anti-fascist who was in the process of rallying to his cause, there was an element or a hint of calculation in the remark. The circumstances of their meeting are known, indeed we have been almost overwhelmed by the numerous versions, each of which seems more hackneyed than its predecessor. As with all legendary events, it could be said that the episode has given rise to a welter of far-fetched and unverifiable accounts. Did the meeting in fact take place in the autumn of '44 in snow-bound Alsace, when Malraux's brigade was camped just outside Strasbourg, or six months later in the Hôtel de Brienne in Paris, where the first group of Gaullists set up their headquarters and which resembled a beleaguered fortress? Did de Gaulle really murmur: "I've met a man" and Malraux "I have married France?" The consequences, however, are known. Each person has in his mind's eye an image of this somewhat unusual minister seated at the President's right hand for a good many years. Yet the interesting thing is that no event, incident or chance occurrence disturbed the harmonious relationship between these two individuals who were so dissimilar. The final scene which took place one winter at Colombey has become even more famous. As he had done in the past with Borodin, Sun Yat-sen and Andres

Nin, the old writer transformed his suzerain into the hero of a new book, *Les Chênes qu'on abat*, and reaffirmed with considerable flamboyance his loyalty of twenty-five years' standing. All these things are known and have been talked about on many occasions. Except that if they were to be discussed properly, these various images, with their somewhat facile glamour and built-in emotion, would have to be viewed in relation to what I would describe as the pact of immortality which the great man and the writer entered into. In referring to it in this way, I have in mind what I said earlier about the covert relationship between women and literature.

It was Cocteau, I believe, who said that France was a country in which most writers were failed politicians and most politicians failed writers. I myself would say that the best of our statesmen have always taken the view that true excellence existed in the realm of books and the written word – in the same way that everyone who has had a literary career, and certainly a successful one, has secretly thought that nothing could match the value of action and combat. Furthermore, I have observed that for these two men, the writer who sought action and the man of action who couldn't console himself that he didn't write, everything was the result of shared understanding and dialogue. Each expected the other to give him access to a realm he longed to enter, but each finally came to realise that the command he exercised in his own sphere prevented him from ever having equal authority in another sphere. This occurred over a period of time and with a growing sense of resignation. It was the story of Chateaubriand's dealings with Napoleon and vice-versa, of Voltaire and Catherine II, and Descartes and Queen Christina. It resembled the strange relationship, of which we know almost nothing (except that it was based on a similar "exchange"), between Plato and the tyrant Dionysius. One could also mention Auguste Comte and Napoleon III, Marxist intellectuals and Stalin, Lenin and Mao, and even perhaps the fact that a certain Rector of the University of Heidelberg, Martin Heidegger, rallied to Hitler. One thinks too of Barrès, won over to the Boulangist cause, who, on the night of his election in Nancy, "seized his moment of political glory, which alone was to give him satisfaction", as Mauriac so rightly put it. In short, it illustrates the never-ending attempt of those intellectuals who, drawn by history but despairing of ever playing a significant role, seek an interlocutor, an intercessor or a correspondent – perhaps the most appropriate word – who is drawn in his turn by literature and despairs of ever winning fame in that sphere. The details of the pact vary according to the individuals involved. The first model would be that of the intellectual as adviser to the prince, offering: "advice in exchange for power". The second is that of the intellectual as courtier, providing: "panegyrics in exchange for friendship and favours". The third type, in existence since the time of Plato, is that of the king-philosopher and the philosopher-king: "No friendship or favours – but the feeling on my part that I am enacting laws through you and that you, on your part, are philosophising through me." The extreme case, which oughtn't to be forgotten; that of Chateaubriand and Napoleon, might be expressed in these terms: "I hate you and you hate me, but there is in our hatred a form of recognition which is as valid as any other." The principle underlying the relationship is always the same, namely that you have identified in the other camp your chosen figure, who has also chosen you. Through that person the failed politician or writer has the sense that he can satisfy his frustrated desires, even though it may be only an illusion.

In most cases, of course, it doesn't work. The pact may be fine on paper, but in reality it involves people, their character and their passions. There are also the circumstances in which they find themselves, the other roles they have to fulfil. The fact is, dialogue is never truly engaged, or, if it is, it breaks down. Not that a complete breach ever occurs, and if it does, it can be overcome and even turned to advantage. For instance, think of Chateaubriand and Napoleon (or, nearer to home, Maurice Clavel whose righteous anger, reprobation, invective and curses were directed at the man who still remained "his" General). These cases remind us that great quarrels should still be seen as versions of the pact or understanding. But no, misunderstanding and disappointment always set in at an early stage. There always comes a moment when the writers mutter to themselves: "No, this isn't what I wanted; I don't recognise myself in this despot, this traitor, this petty individual." One of the partners always reckons or worries that his aspirations aren't working out as expected or don't coincide with those of his co-partner. It is always a disturbing experience for an intellectual – and also of course for a man of action – to discover that his chosen partner and ideal correspondent, the figure who was to have magically stood in for him in his fantasy world, someone he considered to be his twin or double, whom he expected not only to wear his colours but to fulfil the destiny denied him, turns out to be incapable of doing so, or, worse still, insufficiently concerned to carry out this proud and awesome task. Those were Barrès's sentiments when the Boulangist movement, in which he'd had such faith, ended in farce and derision. It was also the experience of Martin Heidegger.

At the end of the war, he had to open his eyes to the truth about Adolf Hitler, when confronted with the horrors of the camps that had excited neither his revulsion nor his condemnation. Plato too must have felt something similar, to judge from his melancholic Letter VII. Aron was disappointed by Giscard, Kissinger by Nixon, and Debray discovered he'd been mistaken, or felt he had, about Mitterrand, having chosen him as his correspondent in the world of politics. Then there's my friend Jean-Marie Benoist, who seemed so bitter the day – if indeed it happened on a single day – when he finally realised that the man he thought of as Tocqueville, Churchill and John Locke rolled into one was merely Jacques Chirac. In this long, sad history of repeated disillusion and sometimes tragic misunderstanding, there was perhaps a single exception – which is what I wanted to come to – that of "Colonel Berger",[7] who recognised in the author of *Le Fil de l'épée* his ideal double.

Indeed, theirs was an exceptional partnership. They were two outstanding men of destiny, equally talented in their own sphere. But before they met, each had made a brief foray into the other's territory – Malraux as the leader of a squadron and de Gaulle as a stylist of great ability. As a consequence, each had the same regrets, the same slight sense of bitterness, and the same feeling that, because he excelled in one sphere, he couldn't persist with something else. They also felt that resounding success prevented them from fulfilling their destiny in another sphere. But, without any misunderstanding and with an amazing sense of fellow-feeling, they shared the same deep desire to meet a kindred soul who might, at least in part, be the incarnation of their aspirations. Try to imagine, one last time, Charles de Gaulle and André Malraux on the day they met. Imagine each discovering in the other gestures and words which might have been his own. Think especially of Malraux who had spent so much time – he was then forty-four – hoping but failing to find an intermediary. Think then of Borodin and Trotsky, Saint-Just and Hoche, and all the men of action, in China, Russia as well as in France and Spain, who had been conjured up in turn by his fertile imagination. He had devoted his life and work to this, and each had been inextricably bound up in the pursuit of a double, whom he had never found, and which had caused such tribulation. At last, however, he had found that double. He would have picked him out from all the others, if only because he possessed that mixture of lucidity, culture and aptitude for action, which were the attributes of the hero described in the postscript to *Les Conquérants* – or even on account of the rare gift he had for being guided by his own invisible star (a great Idea or Myth), represented as the attribute of the saint in *La Tentation de l'Occcident* and so clearly visible in the founder of Free France. There was no doubt he had found his true double, having so often projected the role onto others only to take it back again. He had been forced to make them his intermediaries even though they weren't worthy of it, but the right man had now appeared and the pact was formalised.

Malraux also thought about Drieu that day and many others as well. He thought of those poor unfortunates who, like him, had sought their double but, unlike him, had not had the good fortune to find one. But his thoughts turned especially to his poor old friend Drieu who had spent his whole life wondering about a double. He thought about *Gilles* and *L'Homme à cheval*, books he loved and which, like his own, reflected their writer's obsession with the possibility of ever finding men of History, in other words men of vision and action, with whom they might have something in common. And he inevitably thought again of their last real conversation, one warm night in the summer of 1943, on the terrace of the villa at Roquebrune where he was then living with Josette Clotis. The two friends spent the evening wondering if a double existed and where he might be found or come from. Who would be the ideal figure with whom one might establish a pact and bid for immortality? De Gaulle? Pétain? Mussolini? Hitler? Doriot perhaps? Malraux had no ideas at all, though he knew who it wouldn't be. Drieu, on the other hand, knew or believed he did. The poor chap had decided it was Doriot. Throughout his life, poor, naive Drieu had dreamed of someone who would wield a sword as he did his pen and he ended up choosing the most wretched duellist imaginable. He staked everything when he made that abortive choice. The mistake the author of *L'Homme à cheval* made by backing the worst possible horse was a crucial decision that was to cause his downfall. Choosing a double is no trifling matter and it mustn't be treated lightly. An error of judgment, a false step, a tragic miscalculation, such as that which made him think Doriot was a great man and the PPF an answer to his problems, and you are in trouble. You end up with your head in the basin with the gas taps turned on. He thought of Drieu alright, and merely thinking of him and recalling the face of his wayward friend who had damned himself by not choosing the right double, or was unlucky enough not to have recognised it in time – which came to the same thing – caused him to act without delay. So it was farewell Spain! farewell *L'Espoir*! farewell to the intellectuals with whom he'd belonged and who were to make him pay dearly for his desertion! farewell to fiction! farewell to the Nobel prize! When destiny calls and reveals so clearly another side of yourself, which until then had seemed to be blocked, you do not question it, you heed that call. The answer to the mystery of Malraux's decision to become a Gaullist is to be found in Drieu.

NOTES

1. Ernest Thaelmann was a German communist leader and Georgy Dimitrov the Bulgarian communist leader.

2. "Rassemblement du Peuple français" ("Rallying of the French People") was the political movement founded by De Gaulle in April 1947.

3. A veteran Gaullist who was active in the Resistance and later became a propagandist for Gaullism.

4. An allusion to Céline's nihilistic novel *Voyage au bout de la nuit* (1932).

5. As well as his *Chronique privée de l'an 40* he wrote novels about his native Charente.

6. June 18th, 1940, the date of De Gaulle's broadcast from London in which he appealed to the French forces to join him.

7. One of the protagonists in Malraux's novel *Les Noyers de l'Altenburg* and the name he took when he entered the Maquis.

8

"All Saints' Night"

I read in a history of the Algerian War that the first victim of the
uprising – and thus the first death in a war which was to claim so
many more – was a twenty-three-year-old primary-school teacher
called Guy Monneret. He had gone to Algeria full of enthusiasm
to spread knowledge and culture in those distant "departments" of
France. The event itself was of little significance, certainly when
measured against the immense horror of what was to follow. The
reason I have recalled the incident and find it interesting is that it
had a symbolic value, which must have struck those who read of it at
the time. Just consider what he stood for. He was a primary school
teacher – a legionary of the Republic! – one of the mythical heroes
of liberal, humanist and democratic France, a sacred figure so long
extolled by Ferry,[1] Péguy and others. It is only a short step from that
point of view to the idea that knowledge, democracy and culture were
being opposed by a dubious mixture of obscurantism, fanaticism and
tribalism, and it was a step that, sadly, a number of intellectuals were
quick to take. The "Algérie française" movement is always represented
as a bunch of fascists, Pétainists and assorted scum. But that is to
ignore another issue and to fail to recognise what was a reflex action
on the part of a section of the French intelligentsia – and not necessarily the worst elements at that. It also fails to recognise that a whole
range of other people had the feeling that, in taking a stance against
independence, they were defending universal values of democracy,
however strange that may seem.

One could cite as examples, Albert Bayet, an old anticlerical
teacher, who was president of the Confederacy of Teachers, and Paul
Rivet, a former member of the Committee of Vigilance of Anti-Fascist
Intellectuals, who in 1957 published a long article on what he saw as
the risk of decline for the Algerian people were they to become separated from Europe. There was also Jacques Soustelle, himself a former
member of the CVAI, and a Gaullist who had belonged to the Resistance, who reasoned as follows: "We would be arrant swine were we
to abandon to their own destiny people who count on us to liberate

them from their ancestral and religious dependency; they are half-way there by their own efforts and are on the road to democracy. Can we now, have we the right to abandon them in that half-way state?" Georges Bidault, whose image latterly was that of a seditious character, had all the same founded in the summer of 1940 the movement Combat, had become president of the CNR, the National Council of the Resistance, on the death of Jean Moulin and been a minister in de Gaulle's first government after the Liberation. His argument again was: "A choice has to be made; either we believe in the inequality of the races, we consider that democracy, the Rights of Man and parliamentary government are acceptable on one side of the Mediterranean but not on the other – and I would then understand if we decided to abandon the Algerians; or we are humanists, universalists to the end, and we consider that parliamentary democracy, the generalised right of habeas corpus, and the rule of law are preferable for the Algerians as well. In those circumstances, our sole duty and Republican obligation is to treat the Algerian people as the people and language of Brittany were treated a century ago." Lastly, one could cite the case of Robert Delavignette, a former governor-general in the colonies whose attitudes were highly typical of a certain colonial humanism which might be thought of as stupid, absurd, or reprehensible, and which had already been condemned by history, but which couldn't be described as totally infamous. When, in May 1957, a decision was taken to hold an enquiry into torture in Algeria and to set up a "permanent commission to safeguard individual rights and freedoms", he was one of twelve chosen as a representative for his "unquestionable moral authority". Subsequently, he was one of three on the commission who, given the inadequate means of enquiry granted them and the little notice taken by the authorities of their initial and appalling conclusions, chose to resign rather than lend their name to what seemed like an odious masquerade.

We should turn next to the case of the OAS, that hated and criminal organisation and army of killers who can in no way be excused for what they did. Yet, they *too*, it should be remembered, adopted a strange tone in certain of their tracts. The senior officers claimed they had something in common with the Resistance and at the same time adopted, imitated and misused its slogans. They even went so far as to name their supreme organisation, which on May 30th, 1962 was charged with the task of overseeing all their operations, the CNR. So much so that when certain people declared in the press or elsewhere that it was a scandal, and tried to protest over the OAS's falsification of the meaning and ideals associated with these words, they took a malicious pleasure in recalling the past of Bidault (the successor, as I've said, to Jean Moulin in the original CNR), of Château-Jobert (who went to London in July 1940), of Pierre Sergent (a member of the Maquis at seventeen), of André Jouhaud (head of the French Forces of the Interior for the Bordeaux region), of Colonel Godard (who had been on the Plateau de Glières in the Vercors) and of Roger Degueldre. This latter had belonged to the FTP[2] in his youth and was remembered in the Northern region for his bravery; twenty years later, however, he headed the sinister Delta Commandos and was guilty of committing abominable and bloody crimes which the Organisation referred to innocently in their jargon as "limited operations", but which resulted in his being executed at the Fortress of Ivry in 1962.

It was a strange episode in the history of France and, when one goes into it a little, considerably more complex than the usual stories and images suggest. It should be clearly understood, however, that I am not in the process of minimising in any way the responsibility of the murderers and those who inspired them. In addition. I would doubtless have been on the *other* side (that of radical anti-colonialism, to summarise it rather hastily) had I been old enough. All I'm trying to say is that the story is vague and confused, and that the dividing lines between people were considerably more problematic than they appear to have been with hindsight. What I really mean is that it wasn't a question of their being divided into the "good" and the "bad", the "pure" and the "damned". Any such distinction which appears clear-cut in the light of historical judgment, or any extreme behaviour which I would be embarrassed even to countenance today, were at the time infinitely more blurred. In moral terms, a person could be in favour of a French Algeria without automatically being a monster. In terms of their ideological lineage, there existed between one group and another, between the Good and the Bad, between anti-fascists who had joined the OAS and those who carried bombs in bags for the FLN, many more connections than those who are wise after the event would have us believe. In the collective imagination, the war in Algeria was an event of major importance. At the same time it was seen as a very straightforward issue which could be reduced to an opposition of Manichaean simplicity. In reality (the reality which confronted those who were part of that history in the making), it was an ambiguous and dangerous experience, the chance occurrences of which it should be possible to reconstruct. I am in favour of history which respects chance occurrences and ambiguity. When you are confronted by an event the essential nature of which muddies your terms of reference and shakes your certainties, only one type of discourse is possible. It is one which, far from reducing complexity, is dedicated to preserving it.

NOTES

1. He became Minister of Education in 1879 and introduced free, and subsequently compulsory, education in public primary schools. A champion of secular education.

2. The "Francs-Tireurs et Partisans" ("Irregular Forces and Partisans") were the communist Maquis groups.

9

"Aron declared himself"

RAYMOND ARON AND ALGERIA

The other important example who came to mind, when I thought about such casual interpretations of events and the misunderstandings to which they gave rise, was Raymond Aron. He adopted various positions in relation to the Algerian affair. His texts are still referred to as models of commitment yet without any partisan nods or winks; their clear-sightedness, boldness and courage spoken highly of. This man of the Right who belied his origins and disowned those with whom he naturally belonged earns our admiration. At the same time, there's no denying the embarrassing predicament in which he found himself as well as the heroic position he took. It should be remembered, too, that he was not so much forced to leave the paper for which he wrote (in this instance *Le Figaro*) as to seek a kind of political refuge in *Preuves* because of what he had to say about Algeria. As a result, people have gradually got the idea that on this subject Aron was "in agreement" with his fiercest enemies – beginning with his "old friend" Jean-Paul Sartre – despite the fact that there existed an unbridgeable gulf between his view of the world and theirs.

What in fact did he say in those texts? He certainly stated clearly and unambiguously that France should leave Algeria. What's more, he did so quite early on, as the first part of *La Tragédie* comprises a memoir which he addressed in April 1956 to the prime minister at the time, Guy Mollet. But when you read them a little more closely and look at the reasons which our friend suggests made withdrawal necessary, it was not a matter of revolt (he opposed the manifesto of the 121 when it was drafted); nor, it goes without saying, was it a question of counting on an Algerian form of socialism (nothing was more alien to him than the tactics of the Left for whom independence was only a first step); still less was it the prospect of the revolutionary virus spreading to metropolitan France (though that also provided the motivation for a section of the Left); it becomes clear that it wasn't torture either (in the long chapter in his memoirs which he devotes to the Algerian affair, there is not the slightest allusion to the "gangrene" which, according to some, threatened the Republic itself); nor was it fear of the OAS (again, in his memoirs he is very clear on that subject:

"I didn't make a tragedy out of the OAS, which was disowned by the majority of French people"); Aron's motivation turns out in fact to be only incidentally moral. What it hinged on was revealed in the message he addressed to his contemporaries, which I've again taken from the version he gave in his memoirs, the gist of which was – the Algeria you love and whose independence would cause you an irreparable sense of loss is a burden rather than the blessing you think it is.

Clearly, Aron's stance stemmed from a theoretical analysis of the issues. Colonialism, contrary to what Marxists had always said, was not the correlative of capitalism on the defensive. One could be in favour of capitalism, fear that it might be on the defensive (which was precisely what he thought), yet consider it by no means inevitable that a colonial empire had to be clung to regardless. Economic calculations came into it as well, since he thought that an empire could be a source of prosperity (as had been true for France in the recent past), but it could also become a source of crisis and perhaps even of impoverishment (which, according to Aron, was exactly what was happening). Thirdly, there were historical considerations to be taken into account; they might have been referred to as "historicist" were it not for the fact that the author of L'Introduction à la philosophie de l'Histoire disliked that word intensely. What he said (with the aggrieved tone of a visionary who could see what was going to happen and couldn't prevent it) was: "The era of European domination is over", adding that in the new era France would no longer have "the means" to maintain the luxury of an empire ("means" is the word he used and he reminded people he'd already made this clear in his conversations with the Gaullists in London in 1943). So what he said reflected a mixture of foresight and reasoned analysis, of anticipation and detachment. In addition (and it was clear the idea was similarly inspired) he was convinced that "integration wasn't practicable, however one interpreted it" and that "the rate of growth of the population on the two sides of the Mediterranean was not sufficiently matched for peoples of different race and religion to be part of the same community." Furthermore, he considered that "Algerian representation in the National Assembly" if by any chance it were granted "in proportion to population" would be the surest means of "bringing about the destruction of the regime". It was that combination of convictions and reasoned arguments (in which ethical concerns could not be said to have been to the fore) which meant that Raymond Aron understood straight away that France had to give up Algeria.

One thing should be made clear; I'm not saying Aron was either right or wrong. Nor am I saying his attitude "lacked" this or that attribute – whether feeling, generosity or warmth. Moreover, in thinking of the "generosity" of others and calculating the price that ultimately had to be paid in the end for the extremely "sentimental" socialism which so-called left-wing consciences wanted to impose on the Algerians, and remembering Fanon's calls to murder, Sartre's third-world lunacy, and Francis Jeanson's notion of "democracy", it is possible to point to an element of humanity and of unmatched goodwill in Aron's cold analysis. The argument I am putting forward is basically that the positions of the one were homonymous rather than synonymous with the other, and that when they uttered the simple phrase "Algeria will be independent," the words were the same, their resonance was the same, but what lay behind them was absolutely different. There existed the same fundamental difference between their states of mind as that which existed, according to Spinoza, between a person of sound and another of unsound mind. Though each might claim "it was daylight" at midday, the one did so by chance, but the other was aware of what he was saying. What I am suggesting, in other words, is that if you want to write a history of ideas, if you are interested in the origins and true bases of people's thoughts, if you study what texts really say – as well as what they imply or infer – and not what they appear to say on the surface which gives rise to misunderstanding, then you must stop mindlessly repeating, as people have been doing for thirty years, that on-this-subject-at-least Aron was on-the-same-side-as-Sartre.

Which side was Aron really on? As far as the history of ideas is concerned, bearing in mind the relationship and genuine similarity between what different people thought (which was more a question of sharing the same basic ideas and principles, even if this wasn't immediately obvious, rather than having said the same thing), I would place him with those who were simultaneously saying that colonialisation was costly, that it swallowed up huge amounts of resources, and that the money squandered on the distant Kabyles would have been much better spent developing French territory. The fact that these people – who were called "Cartierists" after their leader, Raymond Cartier[1] – were a rather unsavoury bunch alters nothing. It doesn't matter either that certain positions they adopted in relation to Algeria were fundamentally at odds with the radical support for independence put forward by the leader-writer of *Le Figaro*. What I'm talking about is underlying attitudes rather than positions, principles rather than their consequences. Indeed, I'm concerned more with cultures than principles, and in fact less with cultures than with what underpins and programmes discourse, even though the discourse itself may differ fundamentally from that. From this standpoint (which alone is of interest to the historian of ideas), Aron was closer to Cartier than to Sartre and Jeanson, and his true kinship, his ideological and moral affinity was essentially with the former rather than the latter. He might have used the same arguments as Sartre and his followers, but there was something much more important he shared with the Cartierists, namely the origin or source of those arguments.

My reasons for setting the record straight had to do with a desire for historical veracity and my irritation that certain stupid myths had gained ground over the years. Fortunately, these didn't stand up to serious scrutiny of the texts in question. Even more decisive was my conviction that if the art of "debating" or "disputing" an issue, if the enjoyment of "democratic argument" were to be rekindled, the first thing to do was relearn to recognise them where they still existed. Some of us had indeed deplored their decline and Aron told me, in a conversation we had in the past, that, if the enjoyment of democratic argument disappeared, it was, in Montesquieu's opinion, a sure sign that a society was sliding towards tyranny. It was time to call a halt to consensus at any price as well as to end the mania of always choosing the lowest common denominator, whether in the realm of ideas or of politics. This is what I myself have called for in one book after another over a number of years. Perhaps I might add that History itself is the original and archetypal creator of consensus which, by eliminating differences of opinion concerning past events, not only stops us from recognising them but also from anticipating them in contemporary affairs. Thus, if consensus is to be done away with and the pleasure of debating and disputing issues rediscovered, if, in other words, it is acknowledged that a democratic mentality and culture will not exist unless an arena is re-created in which opposing views can be hammered out, it is through this kind of historical account that a start will have to be made.

According to the rules of logic, it should be the second guiding principle of an historical account of intellectuals. First you describe the situation, then the differences of opinion to which it gave rise. At the same time you seek to do justice to the silent truth "of the moment" and the "constraints" it placed upon the participants, you also seek to bring out the tumult of contention and conflict they provoked. For History, aware of the ultimate compromise towards which tumult secretly leads and knowing that those who had been at odds would themselves, in the end when it was all over, be heard murmuring, wearily: "What a lot of fuss about nothing! how stupid the quarrels were and vain the conflict," might infer that, even in the heat of battle, tumult was nothing more than meaningless froth on the surface of events. So, instead of giving a happy, soothing historical account of this kind, instead of a cosmetic exercise involving the revision of events that would merely satisfy our desire for consensus, you would instead produce a polemical and bruising account which would restore to the debate all its forgotten virulence. The second principle then is that meaning needs restoring where it no longer exists, and, as with an old landscape that has become shapeless and featureless with time, an attempt should be made to rediscover the original, seething and cataclysmic chaos, of which it is no more than a still and silent reminder.

A PORTRAIT OF RAYMOND ARON

Raymond Aron belonged to that fearful section of the Jewish community which appeared ashamed of its Jewishness and did nothing to draw attention to itself. He was one of them in every fibre of his body, whereas I belonged to the opposing camp. Which of us was right or which of us in the long run would be proved right? Was it Aron, who knew I was not mistaken in detecting virulent anti-semitism across the spectrum from Thorez to Vichy, but, even though he knew it, thought I should have kept quiet about it? Or was I right, even though I knew his fear was justified over a book like mine[2] and that it might irritate a few idiots and thereby stir up old hatreds? But I made the additional point at the time that, if it were true, they obviously had to be confronted and their every statement answered. It was necessary to have faith in the power and virtue of language and above all not commit the error of allowing oneself to be intimidated and silenced. Future events will settle the argument, and perhaps sooner than we might think. What I'm certain about is that these were not only two conceptions of Judaism but of the nature of discourse itself (to him it was something dangerous and intrinsically bad, whereas for me it was positive and capable of exorcising evil). As a consequence a controversy was inevitable.

In raising this affair, at the same time as trying to resurrect the other Aron, the one I used to meet in the Restaurant Tiburce or in his office at the Ecole des Hautes Etudes and whom I questioned tirelessly about Berlin in 1933, about his perception of Nazism, or the way in which Nizan decided to set off for Aden eight years before that, I have a mixed collection of images in my mind. On the whole, however, these images are engaging and agreeable. Aron was an eminently "virtuous" man and that quality was revealed, despite himself, in the slightest remark he made. He was indeed virtue incarnate, bearing witness to it in his life and thought. He was virtuous as Malraux was heroic and Mauriac Catholic. Just to hear him talk about his relations with de Gaulle, his break with Hersant,[3] his fight against the Union of the Left,[4] or his failed meetings with Giscard constantly made you want to cry out: "Oh! what a splendid individual . . . what an exemplary character . . ." Then there was that special lucidity he claimed for himself which you were sometimes prepared to concede he possessed. Aron was infallible, his judgment faultless. And in all circumstances his vision of things was desperately accurate. It was annoying, as far as friendship was concerned, as it made complicity difficult. On countless occasions I've come away, having had lunch with him, telling myself I'd just spent two hours with a man who could be summed up as a combination of intelligence and conscience! One day I made him laugh. It was in 1978, just before the legislative elections which the socialists might have won in alliance with the communists. He had patiently demonstrated to me (and as usual he was right!) that the "lingering sympathy" I told him I still felt for Mitterrand was an "absurdity". As I was leaving, I'd remarked to him: "How wearisome it is lunching with a superego!"

In a similar vein, his conversation was always slightly disappointing; not that it was boring or lacked brilliance. There was, however, even in his way of speaking – and even though his remarks were overwhelmingly correct – something which made you lose interest and therefore, not unexpectedly, your enthusiasm. He never repeated himself, and his voice was too perfect, too perfectly controlled. It lacked any hint of agitation or emotion, was remorseless. When he talked, he gave the impression his utterances emerged from the hidden depths of his consciousness where they had long resided and been purged of any trace of feeling or passion. It was a brilliant but neutral voice; one of those voices with perfect resonance and rhythm which lead people to say a person speaks as he writes (in his case you would have to say the opposite, that he wrote as he spoke – which was *the* great disappointment of his memoirs). Durkheim or Brunschwig must have spoken like that. I'm certain all those great professors of the pre-1914 period had the same voice and used it simultaneously in the service of Ideas and of France. In Aron's case, it had been purified still further (perhaps made more sophisticated), as he had eliminated all those modulations in tone which indicated he was addressing another person and trying to attract his attention. I suppose he considered them of no purpose, degrading, even as devices of satanic manipulation. He was exemplary in that respect too, in the very nature of his voice. Everything had to reflect the truth, be reduced to its essence; even though his interlocutor sometimes had the impression that no exchange of views was possible and that he wasn't really being addressed.

On the other hand, he had a wonderful face which radiated goodness, and this made up for what might have seemed like inhumanity or coldness on his part. I have a photo in front of me which dates from the beginning of the forties, when Aron was in London in charge of the review *France Libre*. He was young, and life had not yet left its mark on him. But already around his eyes, at the corners of his mouth, and on his cheekbones there was a network of lines which deepened with the years. Even at the time, they gave the lie to the message conveyed by his voice. His was a kindly, gentle look, and his air of benevolence illuminated his appearance from within. What made things more fascinating was the fact that he also conveyed the impression of weariness, and perhaps of disappointment, which seemed to contradict, or at least to diminish, the slightly exaggerated promise of his goodness. He exhibited then a mixture of goodness and sadness, of comfort and bitterness, which seemed to imply at one and the same time: "I'm with you and I commiserate with you in your grief" and "don't expect too much from me by way of sympathy; don't imagine, dear friends, that pity can work miracles; humanity is such a disaster and history in such chaos; if you only knew all the reasons that exist to drive you to despair." I must have been twenty-five the first time I saw Aron. I was still something of a Marxist and vaguely leftist. I had no obvious reason for feeling despair about anything. But confronted by his strangely composed face and the combination of promise and disappointment, of extreme gentleness and no less extreme melancholy which it conveyed, I remember how, for the first time in my life, I found myself thinking without the least sarcasm or disparagement: "This is the face of a liberal pessimist."

What is also striking with hindsight and again makes him seem terribly attractive, was the way he had of pushing his "liberal pessimism" to the point of denying he had even an iota of talent. I remembered the conversation we had had in 1975 for *Le Nouvel Obser-vateur*, in which he made some very moving remarks about his work, the fact that it remained incomplete or was by nature circumstantial. He made similar statements in his memoirs, such as: "I am not totally satisfied with any of my books"; or "Having come into contact with philosophers of a high calibre, I realised that I would never be one of them"; or again "Admiration prevents me from aiming too high and, by the same token, from suffering on account of any gulf which might exist between my ambitions and my actual work." He revealed the same attitude every time he referred to the destiny of his illustrious contemporaries, whether in writing or in conversation. There was Sartre, of course, about whom he had very few complimentary remarks to make, especially at the end – but also Nizan and Malraux. And, as if to denigrate himself, he never missed an opportunity of recalling he had been a kind of principal private secretary to Malraux after the war. Was it their novels he admired, the artistic side of their character? Was he dazzled by the image of Sartre going behind the scenes in the theatre and mixing with the actresses, as he once led me to believe with an uncharacteristic little chuckle? Or was it something else – a wound he'd suffered or a secret? The facts are, however, clear. This man who was covered with glory and surrounded by disciples and sycophants, and who, during his own lifetime, could pride himself on his widespread influence and the fact he had affected the decisions of certain major historical figures, spent his life repeating: "No, no, you're mistaken . . . there's a misunderstanding . . . my work is of no value at all . . . it will be forgotten when I die."

Some will put these insistent remarks of his down to affectation and will see them as a marked form of self-esteem and pride. For there comes a time when this kind of tactic becomes part of a person and, as a result of repeating: "I'm unimportant, worthless, I've wasted my time and my energy getting involved in things that had no future," he ends up by convincing not only others but himself as well. Thinking about it, Aron was the only intellectual who presented his thesis three times. He submitted it officially as *L'Introduction à la philosophie de l'Histoire*. He reworked it unofficially on two other occasions, as if it were constantly a question of buying his entrance ticket to the holy of holies. Firstly, there was the enormous book entitled *Paix et guerre entre les nations* which he'd been "thinking about for fifteen years". Pierre Nora told him "as a friend" that it was like "submitting a second thesis". Then, when he was "nearly seventy" and "wouldn't have had the courage to write [these are still his own words] had it

not been for my desire to justify my place in that illustrious institution," the Collège de France,[5] he produced his immense work
Clausewitz. He was certainly the only one, as far as seeking "positions"
was concerned and looking after his own career, who systematically
shunned the top institutions which the principal intellectuals of the
day were expected to belong to: he was involved with *Le Figaro* instead
of *Le Monde*, *L'Express* rather than *L'Observateur*, and Julliard or
Calmann-Lévy instead of Gallimard which was the one that mattered
and with which he had only intermittent dealings. On every occasion
he picked the second best and chose a low profile, as if a mixture of
pride, certainly, but extreme humility as well had constantly dissuaded
him from meeting his peers on the same ground and measuring himself against them and thus confessing the sense of inferiority he certainly felt.

In conclusion, I would simply add that one of the more moving
aspects of this strange character, in spite of or perhaps because of, his
supposed inferiority, was the fact that he spent most of his life pursuing
a distant dialogue with his peers, who if they weren't already dead
had quarrelled with him. It's not clear what mattered more to him,
his desire to maintain some sort of contact or the will to justify himself
again and to be in the right. Literary history offers other examples of
such relationships. It is a fair assumption that, at the very end of his
life, Drieu was absorbed in a silent conversation with Malraux whom
he no longer saw. Twenty or thirty years after their quarrel, Aragon
was still haunted by the shadow of Breton, to the extent that he
appeared to write and do things only for him. There were also a
number of surrealists who continued to live their lives after the master
had died as if he were still watching them – "What would Breton
think of what I'm saying? What would he think of the way I think?"
But in Aron's case – and particularly in his relationship with Sartre –
there was something especially moving about the situation: the humility of the man, of course, but also his generosity and willingness to
express his admiration. Even more poignant was the fact that the
dialogue was a monologue, and that whilst Aron spent his life provok-
ing and challenging his "old friend" of the Rue d'Ulm so touchingly
and with such determination, his friend spent his time avoiding him
and ducking the debate, with no regard at all for the niceties. Even
if Breton would have nothing to do with Vitrac, he did respond to
Aragon. Indeed, one senses they had a similar desire not to cut all
lines of communication, and shared the feeling that when they shouted
things from the rooftops they were secretly addressing their estranged

or rejected friend. Whereas, right to the end, Aron's challenges were not taken up and therefore received no reply.

I can still see Aron as an old man, as he was on the day of our discussion for *L'Observateur*. He was so cold on that occasion, so self-important. I remember his mouth had a bitter look about it and his eyes appeared more pessimistic (less tolerant) than usual. I can still hear his clear voice and the peremptory and disagreeable tone he adopted when answering questions he found irritating, as if to say they weren't worth bothering with. Then when I referred not just to Sartre but to the Left in general which had repudiated him, and to which he thought he still belonged, and again when I quoted Jean Daniel's celebrated quip that: "It was easier being in the wrong in Sartre's eyes than right in Aron's," he seemed moved and shaken, almost overwhelmed. All of a sudden, Aron appeared melancholic, extremely gloomy and tired. He was capable of embracing the views and reasoning of his opponents to the point of madness. To that extent, he was complex, unsure, paradoxical. I too "retain a certain nostalgia" for the Aron who displayed those characteristics, and from this distance I simply wish to remember him for his "nobility of feeling".

NOTES

1. A correspondent of *Paris-Match* who, in a series of articles in 1963–64, attacked the French policy of giving so much aid to developing countries.

2. Bernard-Henry Lévy's book *L'Idéologie française*.

3. A powerful newspaper proprietor who took control of *Le Figaro* in 1975.

4. An electoral alliance of the Socialist Party with left Radicals which was formed in 1973.

5. An independent institution of higher studies, the foundation of which dates from 1530. It enjoys considerable prestige and autonomy.

"In this new crusade"

MAURIAC AND ALGERIA

It was in 1952 that the Academy of Stockholm awarded François Mauriac the Nobel Prize for Literature. When the writer declared he was going to "cast his Nobel Prize on the waters" and intended to dedicate it to the struggle for justice, dignity and freedom, he was thinking of Morocco – not about Algeria. Does that mean the author of *Bloc-Notes* was less committed and concerned when the Algerian affair began? Good gracious, no! Indeed, I would remind those in any doubt, and the few people here and there who have tried to cast doubt, of what he wrote in an article which appeared just after the riots took place on All Saints' Day 1954: "The police must be prevented from using torture, at all costs." He went on: "The immediate accountability of the fellaghas in no way lessens our responsibility, which has been bearing down ever more heavily on one generation after another for a hundred and twenty years."[1] In his closing speech to the week-long programme organised by Catholic intellectuals, he made the following declaration, which deserves to be quoted in full: "It is not so much the imitation of Christ as of Christ's executioners which has too often been the rule in the history of Western Christendom [. . .]. We have pretended to believe that Nazism poisoned the peoples it subjugated and that in practice torture re-established itself in our midst as a consequence of the Occupation [. . .] Flagellation and the crowning with thorns were unlikely to produce a confession, but doubtless, in Pilate's mind, they made [Christ] appear so wretched that even his enemies might take pity on him. Today, when we bind a man to a stake or tie him up in a police cell – I say 'we' because in a democracy we all share the responsibility for these things – we have no desire to arouse anyone's pity [. . .] After nineteen centuries of Christianity, torturers today never see Christ in their victims. His Holy Image never appears in the face of the Arab as he is punched by the police officer. Don't you find it strange that they never think of their Lord, tied to a cross, delivered up to the soldiers, especially when they look into one of those dark, semitic faces. Nor do they hear their Lord's voice above the cries and groans of their victims, saying: 'You do it unto me!'"

This was November 1954. There were relatively few intellectuals in November 1954 who were aware of the horror – and what was at stake – in the long battle just beginning.

NOTES

1. A successful expedition to Algiers in 1830 marked the beginning of France's North African Empire.

"Between justice and his mother"

FOR ALBERT CAMUS

It's a phrase, a simple phrase. He didn't write it or even really say it, if it comes to that. It was a tiny, insignificant remark he dropped in passing during some lecture or other he gave in Stockholm as part of the activities surrounding the Nobel circus. Camus was tired at the time and couldn't stand the speeches, banquets and festivities, and giving interviews from morning till night. In the lecture theatre where he was giving his talk, it so happened a man had been interrupting him for an hour and challenging him over Algeria. He was getting at Camus and doing everything he could to provoke him. What was it all about, and who was this idiot who seemed unaware of the writer's denunciations of squalor, of torture and of colonialism? Camus was exhausted and almost at the end of his tether. He had the same feeling he'd had in the past in Bab-el-Oued when a young lad picked a quarrel with him, and he would try to flatten him. Well, on this occasion he found a way of shutting the man up. What he said was, if he had to choose between justice and his mother, he'd always choose his mother. He hoped that was good enough and that he'd made himself clear. Camus was content. The public applauded. The chap involved sniggered, but remained silent. And Camus went on with his lecture.

Except that, the remark was now out; he'd said it. And he'd barely uttered it, before it was picked up by a journalist in the lecture hall. Then another, who hadn't been there, got hold of it, and a third and a fourth and so on, until all the journalists in Stockholm, in Europe, in the world, forming a diabolical chain, passed on to everyone far and wide the most recent Nobel prizewinner's famous remark. Albert Camus said: "In a choice between justice and my mother, I would choose my mother." The remark was taken up by people all round the world. It was now down on paper and fixed for all eternity. Camus wasn't aware of what was happening – as you never are in these situations – but the remark preceded or followed him everywhere he went. For hundreds and hundreds of people who barely knew his name, that remark summarised his position; but not just that, his philosophy and his life as well. And as his life was nearing its end (though he didn't know it, he had only two more years to live), for those who had only just discovered who he was, and sadly for many more besides, it was the last remark he made.

He made that inept remark and then died. Just as a government falls on some stupid vote or on account of a misunderstanding, he was brought down by an insignificant remark. You never know in advance what will bring you down, or what phrase will be used to sum up, fix or fossilise your whole destiny. Writers should be on their guard against using little phrases like that; they should try to avoid them, root them out before becoming ensnared in the lies they express. Their books contain so many of them. They have nurtured and mulled them over for so long! They have produced so many fine phrases assuming they wouldn't misrepresent their meaning! Basically, they should do what dandies do and live each minute as if it might be their last. They should act as if every little remark might be the one they are remembered by. But it isn't what Camus did that particular afternoon in Stockholm. He was tired but happy. That same evening, he put on his ceremonial jacket which, in the archive photographs, made him look like a socialite setting off for a dance or a gangster in his Sunday best. He didn't suspect that his remark had already become a sort of additional disguise, like a mask or a badly made-up face, which would be part of him for ever. Dear Camus . . .

I like Camus. In the first place, I find him admirable and courageous. What's more, you don't often come across an intellectual who shows courage or a writer who almost always displays nobility of spirit. I'm sure, too, he was funny, if a little pompous; he liked having a good time and would have been a good friend. I have the feeling he had the same sense of humour and liked the same kind of women as I do. I'm also certain that, had he still been alive, he would have been the intellectual – perhaps the only one – to whom I would have shown the proofs of my book *La Barbarie à visage humain*. He was born in 1913, and therefore when *La Barbarie* was published he would only have been sixty-four. You hardly think of Camus as your contemporary. I did once, in 1977, at the height of the controversy over the "new philosophers". A friend and I had just seen *Casablanca* on television and, almost simultaneously, we said how different the controversy and how much pleasanter the atmosphere would have been, had Camus been alive. I like Camus because, of all my precursors, he's one of the few to whom I feel really close, and I long to write a book one day which would do him justice. If you are going to say he was in favour of French Algeria, you might just as well say he supported the OAS or was a fascist. He's already been turned into a philosopher for sixth-formers. How idiotic!

The question of Camus's views about Algeria and colonialism should, of course, be dealt with, but properly and in depth. It is time to look again at the articles he wrote in 1937 and to re-read *Misère en Kabylie* which, with Gide's *Voyage au Congo*, is one of the classics of the anti-colonialist tradition. After all, he played a pioneering role in that field over a long period. His remark that the wretchedness of Tizi-Ouzou constituted a "denial of beauty in the world" should be quoted and commented on. Finally, people should be reminded of the tremendous outcry which his reports caused amongst those in the French community who read *L'Echo d'Alger*. There is also the issue of Camus's attitude towards torture. There again, he refused to accept that criminal acts and terror might be committed in the name of politics. It is true he refused to come down on one side or the other, that he wouldn't talk about independence and clung to the old idea of the French as an "indigenous" population in Algeria alongside the Moslems. Camus's position was complex; he had divided loyalties. He desperately struggled to find a solution which neither compromised the rights of one side nor humiliated the other. I don't say Camus was right in attempting to do this. At the time, I think, somewhat exceptionally, I would have been closer to the position of Jeanson and those who carried bombs in bags. Camus was, of course, to live for only another two years; two years for those who supported the idea of a French Algeria to come to terms with their impossible position – or to resign themselves to behaving dishonourably. What would Camus have done with these two years; which side would he have come down on? No one knows, of course, though I have my own ideas on that score. One thing is certain, during that period, neither the "positions" he adopted nor his "silences" were ever shameful.

Then there was the clash between Camus and Sartre, in which Camus got the better of Sartre. It cannot be repeated often enough that he got the better of Sartre and the whole *Temps modernes* group. Camus condemned the communist camps and refused to draw a distinction between deaths that could be justified and those which could not, between victims who were considered suspect and torturers who were seen in an acceptable light, as the Left were inviting him to do. Camus was a just and upright man, a philosopher of what was right, of the Rights of Man, and of democracy. Think of the way he reproached d'Astier: "I discovered poverty in the streets, not in books." There's another remark of his I repeat to myself in private when I'm feeling particularly isolated in the cut and thrust of intellectual debate: "Solitary, you say? You would be truly lonely without these solitary people." Camus showed nobility of thought and displayed a sure touch as a prose writer. He had the strength of character to resist to the end easy paradoxes. He was high-minded but never superficial; he made errors, of course, yet was scarcely ever cynical. I will stop there, as I've said enough for my present purpose. I shall need a lot more time for the book.

12

"As at the time of the anti-fascist movement"

Call to mind *L'Homme révolté* and the debate to which it gave rise in the pages of *Les Temps modernes*. Sartre had wanted to put an end to the nightmare associated with the name of Camus, ever since the beginning of the debate about existentialism, because his own life (and image) had been poisoned by this pseudo-philosopher who happened to be a good writer. This time they would settle things once and for all. The boil would be lanced and all misunderstanding dispelled. Of course, Sartre didn't carry out the operation himself, but, as in all good mafia families, he appointed the executioner. And there he was, in front of me. Believe me, it was a very strange feeling coming face to face with the man who began by giving Camus a philosophy lesson before shooting him down.

But that wasn't why I'd come to see him at his home near Bordeaux on this particular occasion. I knew we'd talk about Camus, certainly, because I couldn't resist the temptation of getting him to tell me the story of what had happened from *his* point of view. I wanted to know who had set the whole thing up and why, and whether he now regretted it or would have gone through it all again exactly as before. The real reason for my visit, however, was the *other* major affair in which he'd been involved and which, as it happens, did him great credit. His name was Francis Jeanson, and during the Algerian War he was one of those intellectuals who saved the honour of his country and his own as well.

What were you doing and what was your state of mind in 1954 when the war in Algeria began?

I was working for the Editions du Seuil not only as an author but also on their editorial staff. My state of mind was that of someone who had been to Algeria two or three times, met a number of nationalists, and returned feeling rather alarmed. All the more so, since I went back to the country a few months later, in very different circumstances, for a lecture tour. On that occasion I met people who were in the upper echelons of the colonial system. And I have to say that the things they told me so obviously confirmed what I'd gathered from the nationalists that I was quickly convinced. In particular, I shall always remember a sub-prefect taking me through his town and showing me a spot in a public square, a mound, where all the Algerians who had demonstrated at the time of the Armistice in May 1945 had been shot down. The chap said to me: "They gave us trouble, M. Jeanson, but we got our own back! a thousandfold!" When I got back to France, I wrote an article for the journal *Esprit* in which I made it clear that things couldn't go on as they were, and that some sort of explosion was likely to happen at any time. I pointed out there were two tendencies within the Algerian nationalist movement – the one moderate and the other rather "extremist" as it was put – but that there was no point in counting on disagreements between them, as they complemented each other and were leading the people towards total insurrection. That's exactly what took place four years later. And from the moment it began, my primary concern was to provide as much information as possible. That's the reason my wife and I began to write *L'Algérie hors la loi.*

You're apparently one of those people who are very quick on the uptake. What strikes me, on the other hand, is the incredible blindness of the politicians and especially left-wing politicians . . .

Yes. It seems that for many of them the myth about three departments of France was sufficient. But what is astonishing is that you would have expected people to react strongly to the fact that war had broken out between France and three of her departments. But not at all! It was referred to as a police operation. Subsequently, the term pacification was used. It was only conceded much later that a war was taking place.

What was your reaction to that collective blindness at the time?

At first, I was surprised, demoralised. But the urgent matter was to demonstrate to the Algerian people that France shouldn't simply be judged in terms of her official political policy. Then you had to try to show solidarity with the people. I didn't understand how they'd put up with the situation for so long without a violent uprising, especially as all means of expression were denied them.

How did you express that solidarity?

First of all, by just being with them. Then, it involved running back and forth across Paris, arranging meetings and places in which members of the federal committee of the French Federation of the

FLN could stay. Gradually, that led to organising the crossing of frontiers and obtaining false documents. It also involved the collecting of funds, such as subscriptions to the FLN, and the transfer of that money outside France, essentially to Switzerland, and various things like that.

So you were involved in clandestine activity straight away?

For the first year (and even up to July 1957), I was very pleased not to be acting clandestinely and to be able to give some lectures about Algeria in which I said what I thought. There were no problems as far as the police were concerned. As I had nothing else to do, I could express myself on the issues involved without alarming anyone. Then the head of the French federation of the FLN changed, and he thought I was being a little rash and asked me, at that point, to go underground, which I did.

That lasted . . .

Five years. My clandestine activity ended on July 5th, 1962, when Algeria became independent.

Where were you during those years?

I was in Paris almost the whole time, though in '60 and '61 I visited Switzerland, Germany and Belgium. But until February '60, when various arrests were made, I was constantly in Paris.

What did it mean and how did you live clandestinely, given that you spent most of those five years in Paris?

Personally, I have no unpleasant memories of that period, firstly because I was always made to feel most welcome by enormous numbers of people and could therefore move around without difficulty. The one worry I had during the whole time was that we might do something stupid which would endanger the security of those Algerian leaders for whom we were, theoretically, responsible. That was my great fear.

One basic and elementary question is why you did all that. What motivated you? Was it idealism?

Oh, I don't think it was anything to do with idealism.

What was it then?

Listen. These people had no right of speech and were kept in a state of permanent humiliation. They simply had to do something about it, and so they chose the path of violence. Personally, I hate violence; it's something deep-seated in me. But it was clear that in their case they had no other option. I couldn't stand the idea that France didn't give a damn about these people, was gagging them, and doing so in my name. It was self-evident that one had to show solidarity with them in their struggle to exist. That's all. It happened quite naturally, and I didn't have to go in for any soul searching.

So, when you heard your enemies talking about "the defence of France", "betrayal", "desertion", these were terms that had no meaning for you? You were convinced that what you were doing was right?

These terms did have a meaning for me, but it was the opposite of what was being said. I had the sense that France was betraying herself in Algeria; that official French policy was betraying French values.

You say that you had a physical horror of violence. What happened when the FLN decided to extend the war into France? Did you discuss it with them? What did you think about it?

I had two thoughts, which I expressed to the leaders at the time. Firstly, I thought it would be a catastrophe for the Algerians who were in France, because, though it might well achieve reasonably spectacular results for a few days, it would lead very quickly to them being hounded throughout the country. Secondly, I said it would put an end to any possibility of good relations in the long run between the French and the Algerians. At the same time, underlying these arguments was my horror of violence. That's why I requested that they didn't engage in systematic attacks on people. Attacks on places and equipment didn't bother me, but those against people did.

That's what was agreed in the end. Do you think that debating things openly with people like you played a part in the ultimately reasonable attitude adopted by the FLN?

I'm certain of it. Because in the end I had to say to them I didn't think it would be possible to maintain the support of a network of people for a French FLN federation, if it went onto the offensive in that way. The leaders sent an emissary to Tunis to emphasise the arguments I'd put forward, and they received the authorisation to stick to physical targets.

Were you informed, for example, about the attempt on the life of Soustelle?

No, we weren't informed. Even if we had been, it wouldn't have been a problem for us. Our conception of solidarity was global, and at the same time wholly relative. It was the opposite of being absolute, in the sense that, as far as our solidarity was concerned, there were things we approved of and others which were hard for us to accept. But we certainly didn't have to question ourselves about every detail, since we weren't the ones leading the struggle.

Alright. But a moment ago, you were saying you discussed things, that emissaries were sent to Tunis etc.

Yes . . .

Didn't the execution of a minister (or the plan to execute him) raise real questions? Didn't it also warrant the sending of emissaries to Tunis?

No. Because, for me, the message sent to Tunis related to a much more fundamental issue which risked putting a question mark against the whole future. An attempt on the life of a minister, on the other hand, raised no questions as to what might happen next. After all, it was their business if they considered it important from a strategic point of view. It would have been self-indulgent of us to pass judgment on their decision or their behaviour in general. It wasn't possible. Either we gave up supporting them altogether or we supported their actions, whatever we thought of the relative merits of those actions, and even if we sometimes found them disagreeable. That is genuine support. If they had done solely what we desired, it would have been our struggle and we would have been leading it.

So they conducted it in their own way?

It was, I repeat, *their* struggle. We thought that what we had to do was stand beside them. Thereafter, it was they who conducted it, though they acted within certain limits. There was a French network of support which couldn't possibly have accepted the elimination of ordinary French citizens, who had no particular responsibility in this affair. Whereas Soustelle, on the other hand . . .

There were intellectuals at the time who considered it their duty to express their reservations, or their disapproval, in the face of such things as the Mélouza massacre. I'm thinking of people like Jean Daniel and certain others . . .

I think it's always a good thing there are protests of that nature. It wasn't for us to make them, as, once again, we took the "overview". But we couldn't disagree with such protests. It was so much the better that someone made them!

The Algerians and the FLN were at war. Did you also feel that you were at war?

You couldn't really say you felt you were at war living in Paris, when the only risk you ran was that one day you might be put in prison. On the other hand, I did feel they were at war.

In the last two years, you ran real risks. After all, it was the period of . . .

The risk of being imprisoned . . .

Yes. And also physical risks. It was the period of the OAS and of various assassination attempts . . .

I have to tell you, I had a different view of things from the moment I first decided to support them. I'd thought to myself that one day I'd be shot by an Algerian who would see me as an enemy, given that we had to do some strange things on occasions and go to some strange places where they might wonder who we were. That's what I was expecting. But certainly the OAS . . . They were a risk as well, of course.

What exactly were the Jeanson networks during that period and how many people were involved? Was it an organisation, an infrastructure?

It was an organisation, certainly, with a number of sections. I couldn't know everyone who worked for it (nor was it right that I should). At first, I did most of the recruiting. Subsequently, the heads of the different sections had to do it. Even today, I meet people who say: you know, I was part of the network. As to how many there were. Overall, I think several hundred were actively involved, and there were a great many more who were sympathetic to the cause. I used to say at the time that, had we been able to use small ads in the press, there would never have been a shortage of people. We would have recruited as many as we needed, as there were a lot of people who were prepared to do something. I believe I only ever had a refusal on one occasion when I was recruiting, and that was a qualified refusal.

Even so, there wasn't particular enthusiasm in the population at large.

No, that's certainly true. I'm talking about a minority, of course, a small minority. But it wasn't as limited as you might think. Above all, I don't think it's right to talk exclusively of intellectuals. I would also like to point out that there were a number of militant communists who wanted to work with us and who had to give up the idea, because the federation learnt about it and compelled them to stop.

Because the Party . . .

. . . was to say the least cautious . . . ! It was obsessed with the idea it would be declared illegal.

Didn't the Communist Party, or its leaders at least, think the rank and file wouldn't follow, that the working class wasn't ready, etc. etc.?

That's what Casanova[2] told me when I met him on different occasions. He used to say: "The working class is racist, colonialist and imperialist." Alright, statistically speaking, there was an element of truth in that. My reply to him was that the Communist Party, which claimed to be in the vanguard as a party, didn't exist simply to be dragged along by the working class, but, on the contrary, to try to help it to evolve. All the more so, as there were signs of a possible evolution amongst the Party militants we met, who were prepared to help our cause.

Did you see Casanova on a number of occasions?

I'm not sure, I must have seen him six or seven times. The last meeting we were to have had – we met once a week – Waldeck Rochet[3] came in his place, and that was the end of it. I managed to discuss things with Casanova, even though it didn't serve much purpose, though on occasions I thought it might. The editorials in *L'Humanité* on the following days would be a little different. But when I met Waldeck Rochet, there was no dialogue at all. It came to nothing, and the series of meetings ended at that point.

What was the object of those meetings? Did you undertake them on behalf of the Algerians?

Actually, I undertook them partly on my own behalf. In addition, I think the leaders of the FLN were keen to know what the possibilities were of any developments in the attitude of the Communist Party.

When you discovered that nothing was possible, what conclusions did you draw?

You know, I'm not very good at accepting disappointment. I may have been irritated at the time, regretted what had happened. But, too bad, you had to move on to something else. Anyway, I'd already got used to the general attitude of the Left over a number of years. What did seem strange to me was that these people claimed to be part of the international proletariat and at the same time showed themselves incapable of affirming their solidarity with those who were struggling for their independence. That was annoying.

You say: "I'd already got used to the Left." I understand. But the Communist Party wasn't simply "the Left". It was, or claimed to be, the party of the working class, of intellectuals, etc. Wasn't there therefore a break at that point, a change of policy?

I don't know. For me, the break didn't occur as suddenly as that. My impression was that the Communist Party, which refused to fight for independence, was the same party that had been in existence for some time. And unless you were very optimistic, it was only with difficulty that you could envisage it changing its attitude. But it's always irritating to have to confirm that's how things are.

The one new feature was, however, that for the first time in twenty-five or thirty years, the extreme Left was organising itself on a different basis.

Certainly, that was new. Because up until that point, a number of people were already aware that the Communist Party had veered off course. Yet no one was very sure if there was an alternative, whether you might express your militancy in a different manner. That's certainly where it began.

At that point, most of the intelligentsia found themselves more or less outside the Party.

You could say that. Strangely, however, it was at the point when we experienced difficulties, when arrests were made, that this latent or hidden tendency began to crystallise. There were the 121 ... Sartre's testimony ... the trial ...

Sartre precisely ...

Well, my relationship with Sartre had been slightly distant between '56 and '59 as the result of a misunderstanding over our reaction to the entry of Soviet troops into Budapest. We saw each other every day, usually in the morning, but it so happened I met him one evening in the Rue Jacob and he asked me point-blank to sign a text. I looked at it, and as well as his own signature there were four others, those of the co-sponsors of the text. They were notorious anti-communists, former communists in fact who had gone over to anti-communism.

So?

Well, I didn't think much of it, because I felt they simply wanted to have the satisfaction of saying: "You see, we told you." So I asked Sartre to think about it. As a result, and rather stupidly, our relationship cooled. It was also the point at which I began to lead a semi-clandestine life. Shortly after, it became totally clandestine. Then, in 1959, or the beginning of '60, I said to myself: "This can't continue, it's absurd; I really ought to let Sartre know what's going on."

What was the attitude of Les Temps modernes *at the time?*

It was somewhat reserved. Sartre was very active over China and things like that. Before our relationship cooled, he always used to say to me: "Oh, your Algerians are violent people, they're violent!" And he explained that the Chinese weren't violent at all, that they were much more serene even during the revolution. Anyway, in the end, I said: "This is stupid, Sartre must be told." And so I sent word that someone he knew well wanted to meet him. He accepted straight away, absolutely immediately. As soon as he saw me he said: "I was sure it was you, and I wanted to say that I'm in total agreement with what you're doing. Everything I have is at your disposal." And he gave me an interview there and then for the clandestine bulletin *La Vérité pour.*

313

That was at the beginning of 1960. What is your interpretation of his relatively reserved attitude up until then. It was, after all, a period of six years?

I think that . . .

I said relatively because he did take a stand on torture.

Yes. But, the core of the problem was that he had no faith in the reality of the Algerian situation or of the Algerian people. As far as *Les Temps modernes* was concerned, it wasn't clear. And I think he may also have taken the view that one had to have a Marxist ideology to engage in a real liberation struggle. I think that was part of it. It was also a little too nationalistic. Then their views changed.

The case of Camus is even stranger than that of Sartre.

Oh yes . . .

I'm not going to question you about Camus. But . . .

Camus's case was stranger and, in certain respects, more understandable. He was, after all, a "pied-noir". Camus fought a great deal for very valid causes, and sometimes with considerable energy and effective use of his pen. But I believe the Algerian problem was a thorn in his side. It's difficult for me to judge. The fact is, however, I couldn't accept at all the phrase he used in Stockholm, when he solemnly declared that between justice and his mother, he would choose his mother. It seemed rather dangerous to me.

Wasn't it above all a sign of considerable confusion?

I never debated the question of Algeria with Camus in person. In fact, the only time I had anything to say about Camus's thought, in public, was in 1954, in connection with *L'Homme révolté*. At that point, the issue of Algeria hadn't arisen.

Indeed the whole business of L'Homme révolté *and your article in* Les Temps modernes *caused quite a stir . . .*

Yes. It was unfortunate. We hadn't in the least wanted it to end like that.

You said: "we hadn't wanted it." Who do you mean by "we"?

No one at *Les Temps modernes* wanted it to end like that. For months, we had been in a state of suspense. Not one of us wanted to write the article. In the end, Sartre said: "It can't go on like this. Silence is as hurtful as criticising the book." Then he added: "Perhaps Jeanson ought to do it, as he will at least do it politely." I don't know why, but I must have had the reputation of being polite. That's how it came about that I did what none of us wanted to do.

So, Sartre knew in advance the tone of the article and its content?

Of course! He read it . . .

No, no. Before you wrote it. At the point when he got you to do it, did he already know that you were going to slate it?

Oh he knew . . .

What did he know? What you thought of it?

Yes, he knew I had serious criticisms to make. But he couldn't have been expecting Camus's reaction. I must say I myself was surprised, especially by what happened subsequently. Camus tried to arrange for some of his friends to have a meeting with me – which I willingly accepted – but he always refused to see me. As a result, I had no contact with Camus.

If you were to re-read that article on L'Homme révolté *today, would you stand by what you said? Do you have any regrets?*

I haven't re-read it for a long time.

What about your memory of it then?

Perhaps it's something I should do. But I think if I were to re-read it in its entirety, I would regret having driven the point home in a second article. But it was Sartre who suggested I do that. He said: "I'm going to reply to what he said, but you answer him as well." I think that was unnecessary. But I don't see why I should have any regrets about the first article. What was wholly unacceptable in my eyes was the kind of arguments he used; the philosophical aspects, related to his second-hand reading of Marx and Nietzsche. I truly found it very, very trying. He also had a way of judging things with a certain Mediterranean indifference and of ignoring that there existed a French working class for whom belonging to the communist move-ment had some meaning, which he gently belittled by attacking the Soviet Union.

Why did Les Temps modernes *decide to slate the book? Why didn't Sartre decide to open a debate and discuss it, for example?*

I wonder if that would have been possible.

One final word about the Algerian war. During that period, when you lived a semi-clandestine and then a totally clandestine existence, how did you view other intellectuals? Did you still feel one of them? When you saw Mauriac, for example, or Malraux, taking up positions, what were your thoughts on all these antics?

I didn't take much notice of them. Occasionally, I felt slightly angry. I sent a letter to Jean Daniel. When people made pronounce-ments I found particularly unacceptable, I'd have a go at them. But it wasn't a permanent preoccupation of mine. We were doing what we could and that kept us sufficiently busy for us not to spend our time thinking to ourselves: so-and-so should be different, express himself differently, carry his opposition further, etc. Having said that, I must confess I was glad when that period came to an end.

What did you do in 1962 after the war?

People had predicted I would have great difficulty reintegrating myself. But I had no trouble at all. I started to write and to publish again. There was the radio, the press, people to see. Everything was quite straightforward. Having said that, I wouldn't want anyone to think that the Algerian war was the most important period in my life. I would even say my commitment became much stronger as a result of subsequent experiences, at least that's what I feel. I am, however, happy to have lived through that period. But what I did subsequently in two different contexts, in connection with culture in Chalon, and then in the psychiatric field, seemed to me in the end to be more real. It was the opposite of what I might call "the exoticism of politics".

NOTES

1. Disciple, confidant and biographer of Sartre.

2. Party intellectual and member of the Politburo.

3. The leader of the French Communist Party from 1964.

13

"*121 rebellious intellectuals*"

AFTER RECEIVING A LETTER FROM MAURICE BLANCHOT

What has always seemed to me one of the oddities of this study of mine has been the idea of Maurice Blanchot taking part with others in the drafting of the Manifesto of the 121 calling for insubordination during the Algerian war.

Just think! Here was the author of *Thomas l'obscur*, the apostle of a literature concerned with void, with absence and evanescence. You never saw or heard of him; he was in fact the only French intellectual who made sure his face never appeared in a paper or archive of any kind. He was truly the invisible man, who had disappeared completely. He was the first writer to have achieved what, as everyone knows, Proust called for in *Contre Sainte-Beuve*: the elimination of one's own biography, or what Valéry recommended, which amounted to the same thing: "to die without confessing anything". This man was behind the famous Manifesto, spent days and nights not only drafting it and then discussing it with Nadeau and Mascolo, but also telephoned people to get them to sign. On that occasion he came out of his lair, and was prepared to let himself be seen. The man whose face no one knew, whom it was difficult to imagine being alive, or going round chatting like ordinary mortals (let alone becoming militant, demonstrating, speaking at the Mutualité), suddenly decided to "play at being an intellectual" like Sartre or Zola. To me, there was something almost unbelievable about this situation and also about the gap between the man and his own being and ethics.

Moreover, the proof is that, thirty years on, no one seems to have any memory of the episode. I went to see people who witnessed it and questioned Nadeau, Claude Simon and others about it. I asked them the most straightforward questions, such as: what did he say? what did he do? what did he look like? how did he behave, enter a room, wear his jacket? How did he react on that famous afternoon at the Mutualité when the police charged at them and he suffered a broken rib or wrist? In short, what was it like seeing a phantom writer who had suddenly re-surfaced? Yet, however much I insisted, and however talkative they were throughout our conversation, I only had to touch on this subject for them to become mysteriously silent.

Blanchot had been there, beside them, and for a few weeks, he'd been a "normal" intellectual doing what intellectuals normally do. But they remembered nothing, not an incident or an anecdote. They suddenly became embarrassed, and their silence said a great deal. It was as if they were secretly privy to certain facts; or as if Blanchot-the-militant hadn't left any lasting impression, like colours which hadn't been captured on film.

So I wrote to Blanchot, and what I said to him in substance was: "I know you won't see me, that you never see or talk to anyone, but I would at least like to have in writing your version of that episode; how it came about, and why, and in what circumstances, at what level of horror or shame, someone who has disappeared from the scene is tempted to return to the land of the living. Why did you choose to do it over Algeria and on that particular day? If it is true, as you yourself have written in a celebrated article, that an intellectual is someone who interrupts now and again his absorption in his work to return to the upheavals of human life, why did you choose this particular upheaval and not, for example, the one which occurred five years previously when the Russian tanks crushed the Polish and Hungarian revolutions?" He replied courteously, and almost at once. Except that, instead of responding, even if only indirectly, to the things which preoccupied me, he took obvious delight in clouding the issue still further. His reply was literally "beside the point". I had asked him about Algeria, and, against all expectation, he answered me by talking about the Carmelite monastery at Auschwitz.

These are the main points of the letter which I received in my office at Grasset on September 15th, 1989. "Thank you for your letter. Please forgive me for not being able to reply as you wished. I no longer see even my closest friends, although our friendship has not diminished. Today my thoughts are only of Auschwitz. How is it that a place of extreme suffering can become the subject of controversy? You who are now dead, you who died for us and often because of us (because of our shortcomings), you must not be allowed to die a second time, and silence must not mean that you sink into oblivion. Please accept this expression of my sadness and regret. M.B."

When I read these lines, three thoughts came into my mind.

— Firstly, I felt a certain disappointment. The fact was, he simply hadn't deigned to answer my question, and I was no further forward with my attempt to explain how, in certain circumstances, a man who has been invisible re-enters the real world. It was a genuine role in my commedia dell'arte, and he understood it like no one else. I didn't know how you played the part.

— Then, of course, I felt real joy. I hardly have to say how deeply affected I was by the affair of the Carmelite monastery at Auschwitz. I was – and still am – one of those who consider that the cemetery at Auschwitz should remain a place of silence. I was – and still am – one of those for whom the idea of establishing something on that site, even if it were a place of prayer and contrition, was profoundly shocking. How satisfying it was, therefore, to know he was on the same side! What a sense of awareness on the part of a Christian! I would have liked to put his words into the mouths of the spokesmen of Judaism! Thank you, Maurice Blanchot.

— Thirdly and lastly, I reflected on the strange trait of character, and of destiny, revealed in what he wrote. Like everyone else, I knew all about his past as a supporter of Maurras, and indeed as an anti-semite, and that at the end of the thirties he had written articles in *Réaction*, which might have been penned by a talented disciple of Drumont. And I had – and still have – no intention of dwelling on a dossier which, rightly or wrongly, seemed to me to have been closed by the accurate and well-documented book, published ten years earlier by the American, Jeffrey Mehlman. What was disturbing, on the other hand, was to see how the same writer reacted, half a century later. I asked him about Algeria; he replied about Auschwitz. I referred to "commitment"; he replied about "extermination". I hadn't made the slightest allusion to the debate concerning the anti-semitism of his youth, which, I repeat, was over and done with, as far as I was concerned. It was as if he still felt the need to justify himself about that, when addressing me. I emphasise that the date was September 15th, 1989; the point at which, what is generally referred to as the "Heidegger Affair", reached its peak in France. What a difference! What a contrast between two ways of dealing with incalculable guilt! On the one hand, there was the national-socialist intellectual confronting his past, his half-confessions, his real errors – albeit somewhat late in the day. There he was, the great philosopher and author of *Sein und Zeit*, in a forced manner and after years of silence, evoking his "enormous stupidity" in joining and then remaining faithful to the Nazi party. On the other hand, there was the immeasurable remorse of Maurice Blanchot.

14

"In the promised land"

ISRAEL IN EUROPE

When Theodore Herzl had the idea of a Jewish state, when he evoked the principle and tried to formulate the imperatives which, in his view, should govern its creation, he obviously spoke of Palestine: a land and a history which were holy. And he couldn't help thinking, however confusedly, about the Holy Bible which, for centuries, had foretold the return to Zion of Jewish communities both within and beyond Europe. He said something else, too, which had nothing to do with that and which, in his eyes as in mine, was infinitely more important – even though his adversaries, and some of those who claim to support him as well incidentally, are inclined to ignore it today.

It was the height of the Dreyfus Affair. Herzl was a journalist "covering" Zola's trial. He was appalled, he said, at the excessive surge of feeling created by the Affair. The feeling expressed was anti-semitic, of course, but also nationalistic, chauvinistic and militaristic. He sensed that a form of communal and tribal regression which was disfiguring France at the time might gradually spread throughout Europe and deflect it from those humanistic values which remained at the core of its heritage, until a new order was established. If he wanted a Jewish state, it was in order to fight those feelings and to resist the current trend. It was also in order that one place at least would exist in which nationalistic and tribal regression would not hold sway. In other words, he had the idea of a State in which liberal and universal values might continue to be displayed, just as European, and for the moment French, culture were beginning to turn their back on them.

As a consequence, it was never primarily Herzl's intention that Israel should be a state which was a "refuge", a "home"; and still less a communal, tribal and nationalistic one. Rather, it was to be a state based on an idea or a concept. The idea from which it grew was that of re-creating, in another place and on a different basis, those values of tolerance, liberalism and secularism which belonged to Europe and which Europe was, seemingly, in the process of forgetting. Fifty years later, when the State of Israel was created, Herzl would have answered those who reproached Israel for being a European "bridgehead" in a non-European land by saying: "But of course! That was precisely the core or essence of my project." And to those who, today, would wish it to merge into the region and become one of a number of Middle-Eastern states, he would have retorted: "No, certainly not, you poor fools! The attempt to become part of the region would be a fundamental error which a Zionist ought not to commit." Those were truly the fundamental principles of his programme, even if his successors have tended to ignore the fact. What he wanted was certainly not a replica, a copy or something fixed, but a re-creation and a relaunching of the European ideal. He seemed to be saying: "It is important to remake that Europe of our dreams, a Europe which may soon, sadly, only be a subject for nostalgia, since its collapse is already only too obvious. That noble and historic task will, at the appointed time, fall to the Jews, its finest sons (and also, you may recall, its original founders)."

Let's put it another way. In considering ideas, everything depends on the idea you have of Europe. Either it's a geographical area, a collection of countries, the famous "promontory of Asia" which Valéry spoke of – but that's not what Theodore Herzl was thinking of; or it's an idea, a set of values. Europe as such is that set of ideas, that combination of spirit and mind; or rather the land, the continent of Europe are their cradle. Yet, it may not necessarily be so! It could be argued that, since the European idea is partly identified with the Judaeo-Christian values on which it is founded, its cradle was *already* those Middle-Eastern lands in which the prophets and Apostles of the Bible were born. I would say that, though the continent of Europe is the cradle of the idea, it can in no way be considered as the only sphere in which it is to be found. So, if we take as our definition that "Europe" refers not to a region of the world but rather a concept of humanity, then nothing prevents Israel from sharing that concept and being part of that Europe.

What conception of Zionism did Herzl and his earliest intellectual followers have? Given the nature of the man as well as his personal and national genealogy, it is not surprising that his thought was basically similar to that of the great central European writers, who were his near contemporaries and who also thought of Europe as an almost abstract mental space in which you were the offspring of an Idea rather than of a place or a tribe. It was a Lacanian or Middle-European notion; a notion which could only have been born in the mind of someone who was the pure product of that Austro-Hungarian monarchy which, by imposing itself on all the ethnic and distinctive groups which made up the Empire, obliged its citizens to identify themselves with a principle (a Central European one) rather than dwell on their actual identity as (Croats, Slovaks, Slovenes, Magyars, etc.). It was a notion which Broch or Musil might have had or which might have come from any of those writers – such as Werfel, Thomas Mann or Joseph Roth – who graced their civilisation and culture at the turn of the century. They made this culture and it was part of their lives. In order to enjoy it, it was sufficient for them to enter any café in Vienna, Prague or Budapest, where, according to the popular image, they would find a copy of every newspaper in the world and in every language. Herzl, on the other hand, had the feeling it was already at an end, that the apocalypse was imminent, and that the wonderful State in which would be preserved the meaning of secular and cosmopolitan values still remained something to be conceived and built. With this single reservation, his inspiration was the same as theirs. Moreover, we shall misunderstand Zionism if one loses sight of the fact that it was there, in that particular world of knowledge, sensibility and style, that it had its true epistemological and political origins.

I don't know if Herzl's successors would recognise themselves in this portrait. Putting it bluntly, I'm persuaded quite a number of them – a majority perhaps – would claim not to comprehend the logic of those origins. That can't be helped. It's their misfortune if they imagined that Israel was primarily a piece of land on which it was merely a question of setting up a state similar to every other state; they might just as well have looked upon it as nothing more than a homeland. But in so doing, they missed the essentials, and also glided over the radical universalism which Zionism inherited from its European connections and which supports and rejoins a similar universalism belonging to Jewish philosophy. It is a universalism which always set against the idea of particular characteristics, idioms and tribes the pure notion of the Law. It might be described, then, as a blend of the Bible and of Europe; a blend in which Biblical universality has been reinvigorated by Renaissance and Enlightenment universality. The order to destroy the accursed "sacred groves" was taken up again, even though Herzl was unaware of it in his ignorance of the relevant classic texts, living as he did in a Central European environment where a sense of belonging was only conceivable if transcended by means of an abstract identity without colour or smell. That is how Zionism was born and those are the details of its conception. It also explains why his was one of the finest and noblest contributions to ideology in modern times.

IV

THE DEMISE OF THE PROPHETS

(The 1960s to the 1990s)

I

"That same incurable fascination with youth"

FINAL THOUGHTS ON THE CULT OF YOUTH

What made Lenin and Stalin set up concentration camps? They did it, as I've already said, in the pursuit of purity; or perhaps to get rid of social parasites. That's as may be. But what inspired their undertaking was a dream they had proclaimed out loud. What they hoped their purges would achieve was the mirage of a new society, filled with new men and women, whose thoughts and aspirations, life and death would be equally extraordinary and unprecedented. Communism, they repeated, would rejuvenate the world.

What did Hitler say, a few years later, when he declared war on the Jews? What did he have in mind when he embarked on the strange project of destroying not just a people but their collective memory as well; a project, one has to keep repeating, which was so strange that it remains unique in the history of humanity? He said they were the remnants of a terrifyingly ancient people, whose history began way back in the mists of time. But he knew that sooner or later the fact they had existed from time immemorial would create an irreducible problem. Nazism's aim was similarly to "rejuvenate" the world. Hitler, too, dreamed of a new, regenerated man. How would he deal with that age-old language of the Jews?

What did the Cambodians say forty years later? What was it that drove them to sacrifice a third or a quarter of their people? I have described elsewhere how they set about their task and analysed the reasons for what they did. However, there was one word I didn't mention and which constantly recurred in everything they said. That word again was "youth". We want a youthful world. We long to have young men. We have the means of rejuvenating the old world, old men, and old beliefs. We also have a method of dealing with those who might resist or who have too many (old) ideas in their heads. It is quick and sure, and we acquired it from our patron saint, Nechayev, a total nihilist. It was he who, in his day, founded the famous Society of the Axe. What you do quite simply is to cut off the head of every rebel who has passed the age of fifteen. To be fair to Pol Pot, he did refine the method. He hesitated before he cut off heads, made speeches before he killed. There was a choice in Cambodia between the cult of youth (in re-education camps) or death (in extermination camps).

And what have *our* totalitarians said? What was it that excited them about the burgeoning totalitarian regimes they saw? You only have to re-read Brasillach, a former student of the Ecole normale supérieure, who knew his classical culture inside out and therefore loved the ancient world. When he discovered fascism in 1937, he was attracted and at the same time intensely fearful of what he saw; yet in the end he claimed that "for a long time" it had been "the poetry of the twentieth century". Brasillach got its message absolutely right. After all, it was in a *youth* camp that the revelation occurred. What aroused his enthusiasm was quite naturally "the friendship between the *young people* of those nations which had woken up". What moved him even more, what "filled him with wonder," he said, was the spectacle yet again of "the *young fascist*, drawing strength from his race and his nation, proud of his healthy body, his lucid mind, despising the crude materialism of the world; the young fascist in a camp together with his friends, the young fascist who marched, worked, had dreams" and who was "first and foremost a joyful individual".

Take the case of Drieu La Rochelle. He was a refined and elegant Anglophile who bought his clothes at Diltich and Key, wrote the preface to a novel of Hemingway, and remained to the end a friend of Malraux. In 1917, he became convinced that when "life" has "grown weary of producing too many ideas", it "demands that process of rejuvenation through blood and sweat", which is brought about by a fine and healthy war. What saddened him, when he returned to civilian life, was to discover that France was senile, that a "conspiracy of women and old men" were absolutely determined to reduce "the potent drive of animal forces". The position he adopted at the time resembled that of a character in one of his novels who, when asked about his political leanings, replied: "I'm not left-wing; are you right-wing? I'm not right-wing either; what are you? I'm against the old guard." The decisive factor which jolted him out of his pathetic state of indecision was, as we've already seen, the revelation at Nuremberg of "that magnificent display of youth, of strength, health and beauty, which now embraces the major part of the planet". Once again, the key word here is youth. Similarly, one of the most important experiences in this period of Drieu's life was his involvement with a small review, which has now been forgotten and was run by the young Bertrand de Jouvenel. It was called *La Lutte des Jeunes*, and its slogan was "for young people everywhere, and for them alone". Its programme was to unite youth in all countries in order to defeat, as it put it, "the national union of the elderly". What was particularly interesting about it for my purposes was that it was the vehicle chosen by Drieu on the eve of February 6th to make the first solemn declaration of his fascist faith. Everything else followed from that, beginning with his visit to Nuremberg and the impact on him of witnessing the "overwhelming beauty" of serried ranks of Nazis. As a simple Frenchman, he had feelings of melancholy when he realised that "the whole affair", the "vigour", the "handsome men", the "virile sensuality which filled the air", as well as a mood of "generosity" were "unknown in France". He was exalted, almost in a trance. And last but not least, there was his famous visit to Dachau, subsequently described by him in a stupefying commentary, which would, I believe, be incomprehensible if one failed to relate it to his fanatical desire for a programme of rejuvenation, even if it involved forced labour, re-education and correction! ("the visit to the camp was astonishing; I don't think they kept anything from me etc., etc.")

Take the case of Gide the fellow-traveller. Thirty years after he wrote the original work, the author of *Les Nouvelles Nourritures* seemed to have lost his inspiration as he reintroduced Nathanaël in the disguise of a communist proletarian. What also fascinated him was the "vitality" of his hero, his "vigour", and his "strength". What inspired his "love" for the young Spartan Republic, in which people were motivated by selflessness and fervour, was the feeling he had of dealing with a new, almost virgin, society, which had miraculously been reduced to a state of nature by the revolution. (In a famous passage of his *Journal* dated May 1st, 1933, he used the word "love" as he announced his recent conversion). Similarly, what caused him to break with communism, precipitated a crisis of conscience, and led him ultimately to renounce it altogether was not repression (which he had accepted in advance), or the suppression of freedom ("I have come to believe more and more that liberty is a snare," he wrote, also in his *Journal*). What settled matters was the shattering discovery of a world that had nothing in common with the community of young Titans he fondly imagined to have existed (and that, if one reads it attentively, is the true subject of *Retour de l'URSS*). He had been anticipating the City of Joy and had expected to meet enthusiastic people on every street corner. He had hoped to find them celebrating youth and beauty. What in fact he found, when he looked more closely, was a society which was as old and mediocre as the democratic world he wanted to escape.

Take the case of Rolland in his later years, when he wrote *Quinze ans de combat* or better still *L'Annonciatrice*, the final volume of *L'Ame enchantée*, which Radek referred to as "our greatest victory". He knew all about the reality of the Soviet system, having revealed the lies on which it was based in his polemic with Barbusse as early as 1921. (From that point, everything was out in the open, and people knew what was going on). Now, suddenly he felt old and inexplicably tired. It was as if he had been overcome by lassitude in the evening of his life, the same sense of lassitude which for some while had appeared to engulf the world around him. Yet, on the other side of Europe, there was a country which looked strong. It was the very incarnation of that blend of purity, angelic innocence, and strength which was the best remedy for the sickness from which he was suffering. In his novel we see Marc, "the young wolf", Assia "the young cat", and the "young people of the whole world" miraculously come to the aid of those whose virility has been enfeebled. He noted how "the Soviet Union, despite its faults, represents the richest and most vibrant possibilities for the future of Europe, not only in the field of social progress but for intellectual forces as well because of the prodigious vitality released by its rejuvenated people." In another passage he wrote: "In spite of the disgust one feels, despite the horrors, the errors, and the savage crimes, it is the new-born and the child to whom I'm drawn. They offer hope, pitiful hope for the future of mankind."

Some talk of the "new-born" or the "child", some of "young giants" conquering the skies. Others have a more sophisticated model which seemingly contradicts their phobia about things Ancient that they share with all the rest. They dream of a state in which youth will appear so perfect and childhood so radical and complete that it will be like returning to the dawn of civilisation. What they have in mind is not exactly that: "One day, in a new and future age, a man will emerge the like of which no one will have seen, heard, or conceived of before." Rather, they take the view that "once, long ago, in an almost forgotten age, a man existed whom no one now remembers. He is the embodiment of our lost innocence, and when he returns the world will be born again in all its innocence." In both cases, however, the end product is the same. The dominant idea is of youth which, whether forgotten or still to come, is the incarnation of what is Just and True. So much so that I sometimes wonder if the cult of youth rather than the "will to purity" was not ultimately the essential ingredient of what we in this century have referred to as "totalitarian" regimes. Might it simply have been a question of barbarity dressing itself up in the clothes of youth? That is what I suggested in my book *Le Testament de Dieu*, published at the end of the seventies. It was the most appealing aspect of the madness of totalitarianism and therefore the one to be most feared. It is also the one that might have the best chance of catching us off our guard today, though we live in times of great lucidity, believing we understand completely the fatal logic of events and therefore have nothing to fear. But we should always fear the cult of youth and fight against it more than ever. Otherwise, the ghost of the past may one day return to haunt us in this guise.

There still remain a few things to be said about the cult of youth and also about the issues which have no doubt been raised by my condemnation of it.

My first question is this: if totalitarian regimes have always initiated cults of youth, is the obverse true? Is the cult of youth a harbinger of totalitarianism? Or, more precisely, if there is a tendency towards the cult of youth, which is after all quite a common phenomenon, is there a threat of greater dangers and excesses? At the risk of shocking readers, I would answer, yes. What I mean is that the cult of youth, an obsession with immaturity exploited for demagogic ends and turned into an absolute value, is the surest sign that a writer or thinker is about to go off the rails. One example would be the case of Sartre. In my view, the charges laid against him have often been false. Despite the shortsighted and stupid things he has said, which everyone can recall, and despite the idiotic and sometimes irresponsible texts he has produced, overall he is more likeable than many intellectuals who have been "less mistaken", as it's usually put. I cannot say why I feel this way (though I *should* be able to). There was, however, one false notion which he clung to until the end of his life and never explained, which was that "young people" had a natural inclination towards what was True and Good. This explains why, early in his career when he was in Le Havre, his young friend Olga was the first person he asked to read *La Nausée* and why he let it be widely known that her judgment mattered more to him than that of any well-read critic. When I think of him trembling with delight at her verdict: "Well done! it's really quite good," I can't help thinking that, from the extreme third-world attitudes he adopted at the end of the Algerian War to his ultra-Maoism in the wake of the events of '68, many of his most misguided views and deeds were foreshadowed, if not directly inspired, by that most basic and banal assumption of his concerning youth.

Secondly, I would like to know what it is about the cult of youth which links it with the kinds of aberrations I've referred to. Why has it given rise to such insane and bloody deeds? More specifically, why didn't Sartre and others like him idolise youth in a harmless and peaceful fashion? The answer is that youth is synonymous with immaturity and that means doing things on the spur of the moment, in a hurry, without attempting to find a middle way. It involves acting impulsively, instinctively, and perhaps even violently. Whoever defends basic and primitive values of this kind will be less likely to resist other violent impulses either in himself or in others. A further point I might make is that young people lack knowledge and expertise. Therefore anyone who counts on them despite their shortcomings will be relying on their spontaneity and on the fact that the knowledge they have lacks depth. And even though that knowledge and the intuitions to which it gives rise may not be particularly good, they will be preferred to knowledge based on reason and culture. When you idolise youth, and therefore believe in the pre-eminence of innate as opposed to acquired knowledge, you are bound to disdain books and learning. A further point worth making is that to view youth and childhood as special and sacred is clearly to distance yourself from the theologians' view of childhood as a state in which one is "naturally vicious". It does not coincide either with Bossuet's view that it was an awkward and "bestial" age, or with what Bérulle said: "It is the vilest and most abject state of human nature apart from death." It is similarly at odds with Freud's idea that it was a period of "polymorphic perversity" from which we emerged as we learnt to be civilised. On the contrary, those who fall under the spell of the cult of youth see it as a time of initial happiness, a blessed and essential period, which Rousseau sought to safeguard and preserve in *Emile*. It was the Romantics' view of youth ("childhood is our future"), as well as that of Céline ("childhood is our only salvation"). It is to see childhood as something pure and spotless because it is close to nature and to the original state of man. What these paedophile-philosophers cherish above all is the happy notion that their might exist a period of our lives, and therefore a zone of our being, where the unbearable burden of sin does not exist. Thus their vision of the world coincides with that of totalitarianism. For it too shares the fantasy of a world (or, to begin with, a brief moment, a stage, a period) purged of the enigmatic and eternal reign of Evil. Finally, that is why it is wrong to suggest that fascism merely "adopted" the cult of youth. There was, in fact, between the smiling face of youth and the dark madness of the fascists an essential complicity. The cult of youth leads inevitably to barbarity.

Thirdly, I wish to consider how we should respond most appropriately to the cult of youth in order to counter its effects. What arguments might be used against it? The first line of argument, though inadequate, is the political and historical one. As I've already pointed out, totalitarianism was fascinated by the concept of youth. You only have to look at the films of Leni Riefenstahl or Soviet propaganda films of the twenties and thirties to see this. You cannot help being struck by the resemblances between their two world views and by the disturbing nature of their respective hymns to youth. The second line of argument is a Freudian, Catholic, or Biblical one, which was also developed by Philippe Muray in his book *Le XIXe siècle à travers les âges*. According to him, the fact that childhood and youth are taken to imply closeness to an original state would lead one to think of them not so much in terms of purity as of impurity and corruption. In the eyes of the theologian, such an argument is used to justify baptism (as the child is seen as sinful from birth, the sacrament of baptism is necessary as a deliberate act of symbolic and cultural assimilation which may at least counteract, even if it does not eradicate, the stain of sin). In literature, it was the position constantly adopted by Baudelaire (he recalled how the child – he might also have said "young person" – was closer to the state of original sin and as a consequence all the more "loathsome"). The view which underpins this argument is that time and patience are necessary, as well as education and some form of mediation, to turn a person into a civilised being. The third line of argument relates to art and to the genuinely concrete logic of creativity and was put forward by Dispot in his *Manifeste archaïque*. He argued that the question of age didn't enter into the argument concerning the finest works of art. If youth was an intrinsically fertile period associated with creative genius, then Rimbaud's Latin verses, which he wrote at the age of fourteen when he was in the lycée at Charleville, would be even better than his *Illuminations*. Similarly, the scales with which Mozart dazzled the Viennese court when he was just five years old would be superior to the works of his mature years and therefore, by definition, to his *Requiem*. This simply isn't the case. Indeed, the opposite is true. What is striking about both Mozart and Rimbaud is not just the obvious inferiority of what they achieved early on, but also that it appeared studied, diligent, and rather too grown-up, compared with the originality and the sublime brilliance and boldness of their later work. In the same way, what strikes us about Chagall or Cézanne, about the collages of Matisse or the last paintings done by Picasso is that they represented the late flowering of a body of work which was not only admirable in itself, but also

331

new, luminous, and brilliant, qualities which are normally associated with "youth".

Should we therefore forget about youth, never mention it again, even banish the word itself? Of course not. What I would say, on the contrary, is that it should only be used in a such a way as would enable us to include rather than exclude what Picasso did in his last years and Chagall in his nineties and to apply it to those pieces of work. Youthfulness would be used to describe a state of mind, having less to do with age than with one's inner Being. Eternal youth alone escapes the cult of youth. Moreover, it is the only concept of youth which I would defend to the end.

2

"Danton, what a claim!"

LETTERS TO RÉGIS DEBRAY[1]

August 14th, 1989

But of course I enjoy arousing antipathy! I get great pleasure out of
doing it with my books and with various other related activities. All
writers like stirring up feelings of disapproval, for want of a better
word. Flaubert said some splendid things about it, as did Kafka.
There's also a famous letter of Baudelaire in which he stated that his
aim was to "set the whole human race against him". Then there was
poor old Cocteau, who did everything he could to be judged in a
favourable light and as a right-thinking person. He became a friend
of Aragon's, wrote for *Ce Soir*, committed himself on various issues,
and even initiated a huge petition on behalf of the Rosenbergs (which
people have forgotten about). He did all sorts of things, only to discover in the end that it had been to no avail. He was still treated as
the pariah of the literary world, mocked by some and vilified by others.
In the thirties, he even had to leave the cinema before the film had
finished fearing otherwise that he'd be beaten up by the surrealists.

I'd have to agree, however, that Cocteau isn't perhaps the best
example I could have chosen. But his case is a useful illustration of
the fact that it isn't a good idea for writers to do everything they can
to win people over. It's a mistake for them to try to appear friendly
and approachable. They should perhaps engage a little less in politics.
(One day, someone should try to assess to what extent bad conscience,
a desire to compensate for that and to redeem oneself, played in the
whole business of "commitment" on the part of intellectuals). If they
are wrong to get too involved in political action, that's because there
is in their very existence, in the fact that they write and then publish
those writings – which goes to the very heart of the question – something which is bound to make them absolutely unbearable to other
people. Unless of course they are either no good, or phoneys, or make
a professional habit of sugaring the pill. I know certain writers who
get very upset about these things. With me, it's completely the opposite. To date, I've written two novels, and I'm not lying when I say

that what gratified me, gave me a sense of pleasure and pride in both cases was the feeling that my little stories had been received with mistrust and a sense of discomfort rather than approval and delight.

The same is true, and to an even greater extent perhaps, as far as philosophy is concerned. From the outset, I firmly resolved to take issue with the beliefs to which I thought my contemporaries were most attached. I wouldn't like to convey the impression I'm complaining, but I hope, my dear Régis, you are one day on the receiving end of the kind of insults I received from the Left for *La Barbarie à visage humain*, from the Right for *L'Idéologie française*, and from Jewish, Christian, Moslem, and secular ayatollahs for *Le Testament de Dieu*. I hope they treat you as a forger, a fixer, and a sectarian. I hope one of the major daily papers writes a headline about you, without bothering in the least to examine or check the evidence, which reads "the shame of Régis Debray"; all because some half-crazed woman has accused you of plagiarising a book you hadn't even read. I hope you are banished from all scholarly and intellectual circles, except for a little band of friends who continue to have confidence in you and to befriend you, though Heaven knows why. You may think I'm exaggerating, but I'm not really. That's what my life has been like for the past ten years. If things are now getting slightly better, if my ideological crimes seem less serious (though these things can't be ordered), it is with a certain nostalgia that I think back to the time when *a priori* I was considered guilty of holding every wrong opinion and when intellectuals *en masse* closed ranks and asked those who were "in charge of the media" to place me "in quarantine".

The funny thing about it is it wasn't a position I should have found myself in, as by temperament I'm rather orthodox and by nature conformist. In my everyday dealings with others, I'd normally behave in a civil and courteous manner, which is quite different from the angry and vituperative adversary you take me to be in your letter. And I can scarcely recall that much more remote period of my life, when, as the model student who had absorbed all the key ideas from the key books of the day, I went from Althusser to Foucault and from Foucault to Barthes and Derrida, giving each of them the idea that I was their most zealous admirer. Strangely, I made a clean break with all that. In attempting to answer the question why I did so, I expect you'll find all sorts of "cynical" explanations, such as that in strictly "media" terms I had much more to gain from the activities of the "nouveaux philosophes" than from remaining faithful to my former mentors. My own explanation shows me in both a more and a less favourable light. For the most part, I think, everything happened behind my back, and I didn't therefore have to, as you put it, "pray to God to give me the strength to become disagreeable". That's because, quite frankly, I found it impossible to start to think for myself without spontaneously and *systematically* challenging the orthodoxies of the day – beginning, by the way, with the one which you embodied.

This leads me to think there is a flaw in your current bearish declaration. Think for yourself, you proclaim. Resist all conformity. Disregard the pleasure principle. Set out to achieve as few plaudits and as little approval as possible. That's all very fine. But you'll have to explain to me how you got on when you were one of Mitterrand's advisers and had an office in the Elysée Palace. During that period, you spent your time explaining to people why they should maintain their hopes and beliefs. Last but not least, you'll also have to explain to me what you did when you still accepted the reassuring doctrines of Marxism. Let's be clear about one thing. I said a moment ago that there were two kinds of writers: those who disillusioned readers and those who sugared the pill. In the same way, there are two kinds of philosophers: the pessimists and the optimists; those who disturb and those who comfort; those who say: "No, no, everything's fine . . . things are moving in the right direction . . . have faith in progress and things will turn out alright." There are those, on the contrary, who explain that there's no such thing as History, that the general well-being doesn't exist, and that adversity, as the Bible says, will always be with us. Until recently, you belonged in that first category. Perhaps your views have subsequently changed. If that's the case, welcome to the club. But if that isn't the case (if, more precisely, you still retain the slightest philosophical illusions as to the validity of, say, "socialism"), I can't see how your "desire to arouse antipathy" can be anything other than a pose, a superficial attitude, or a pious wish.

What I for my part need to explain is the relationship I have with the media. Otherwise, I imagine, you'll take great delight in raising the issue of television and asking me why, if I'm so deeply pessimistic and enjoy being so disagreeable, I accept to play along with it. I'll give you three answers. The first is that I'm a writer, and every writer retains the hidden desire to seduce his readers, which is like a counterpoint to his wish to be repudiated. The second is that I've got a terrible reputation, and therefore, rightly or wrongly, I've long believed that resorting to the media was my only means not of convincing people (which is sadly impossible and anyway I'm not that naive), but simply

335

of surviving and not being completely suppressed. Thirdly, though it's too bad you probably won't believe it, I've always felt when I've been interviewed on television, not that I've set the record straight, improved my image, or gained some supporters, but rather that I've roused more antipathy. I had the idea for a book the other day which might be called *Lettre ouverte à ceux qui ne m'aiment pas*. I would have a field day, settling scores with all sorts of people, as you can imagine. I would end it with one addressed to the person I consider to be my worst enemy, namely myself; not the real me or the one who writes my books. The character I have in mind is that other version of myself who has been turned into a puppet by the media, who is unbearable, sometimes obnoxious, and whom I'm not always sure I'd want as a friend. It would, however, give me great pleasure to track him down in all his guises from one interview or programme to another in order to establish his biography.

But to be completely honest with you – and to tell you what my real "beliefs" are on this issue – I would have to say that there is *also* intrinsic pleasure for me in these antics involving the media. Yesterday evening, after I'd read your letter, I came upon a page of Heidegger with which, on this one occasion, I was in agreement. What is "fame"? he asked. Being in the "newspapers" certainly; on the "radio". It's a kind of "semblance" or "doxa", a "doubtful acquisition which is tossed or distributed here and there". To sum up, it's nothing but a bundle of vain promises, of illusions, and reflections which it's difficult not to view as "almost the opposite of being". Except, he adds almost immediately, doxa also signifies "revealing oneself in the light" and that by "bringing something into the light", by "showing esteem for someone and making it known", one is in a way "glorifying" them and thereby giving them "stability of being". There is a certain affinity between glorification and poetic activity; a correspondence between "fame" and truly authentic "creation". Allowing for differences in terminology, it's exactly my position as regards the television pro-grammes with which I'm preoccupied at the moment. You'll just have to wait and see whether they turn out to be investigative or a settling of scores. What you should realise is that, though I enjoy being repudi-ated and have a certain nostalgia for seducing the public, these feelings haven't overridden an equally tenacious desire of mine, which is that of deceiving people, in the strongest sense of that word. Please excuse my ramblings. That's all for now, with best wishes.

November 29th

I fully agree with you, my dear Régis, that we should attempt to "give a better definition" of what we mean by "imaginary" and "real", and distinguish between "political" and "fictional". I'm all the more ready to do so, because there is a current line of argument I find exasperating, and which was illustrated in part I'm afraid by your last letter.

For example, don't you think there's something false in this business of conducting "inquiries", and in the fetish you seem to have for "facts", for "details", and for "concrete evidence"? Can't you see that it's a bit stupid, something of a pose, and in the end rather *demagogic* to rid oneself, so to speak, of all one's own ideas and prejudices and allegedly to confront "things" in an unblinkered and unprejudiced manner? Writers have always done exactly the opposite, as you're well aware. Whenever they travel anywhere, their heads are full of preconceptions which they can't wait to test out on the facts. Like Roussel, they travel round the world without leaving their cabins. They talk about America (as Kafka did) or China (as Malraux did) without ever going there. When Claudel was in Tokyo and came across a detail which challenged his own ideas about Japanese theatre, he decided to ignore it, to preserve his own prestige, and to give precedence to his own imagined "bounraku" rather than the real one. At the same time, his interpretation of that theatre was richer in meaning and insight and more powerful than that of the specialists.

Claudel did, of course, have the advantage of being an immensely important writer. And I would hesitate to recommend his approach to the average theatre correspondent of our favourite papers. But it does suggest two things. Firstly, that literature itself provides us with very considerable insights (which are the equal of those achieved by erudition or by what you take to be so sacrosanct, namely observation). There are those who write novels for the simple pleasure of telling a good story and offering a means of escape. What interested me in writing *Le Diable en tête* was to try to understand the period in which I was living. What I tried to do in *Les Derniers Jours* was to generate knowledge – the word is rather ponderous but it's the word I want – on a number of issues (suffering and death, misunderstanding and fame, what happens to books which remain unfinished, criticism, creativity), which I could equally well have dealt with using the classic methods of the theoretician. Because of the technical resources available to me, because of the freedom I had to tackle problems from the inside rather than as I usually did from the outside, because of the fantastic powers of integration which the genre itself seemed to me

337

to allow, and lastly because of a narrative technique, involving multiple voices, which enabled me to offer different focuses, and to present numerous different angles and points of view, on account of all these things, therefore, I think the novel is able to "raise many more things to the level of consciousness" than a philosophical essay.

Secondly, whether or not one includes the novel, I believe we overestimate the role of "observation" in our general understanding of the world. You contrast it, I know, with my own "exalted" and "inflated" style, and you may have a point as far as the latter is concerned. The tone, enthusiasm, and somewhat conventional fervour of certain of my books – *La Barbarie à visage humain* at least – irritate me when I re-read them. But that is not the real issue. You've travelled as I have and knocked about all over Europe. With a gap of a few years, I must have seen the same people, been over the same ground, and made the same rough analyses as you have. Well, what I'm going to say may shock you. At any rate (knowing as you do that I'm right), it would shock those poor fools, were they to hear what I'm saying, who still want to retain their respectful belief in the fine idea of the naive writer who is open to the world and all its surprises and who with his blank gaze and impressionable mind is content to register "the angry configuration of facts" (to quote a phrase which Foucault used about one of Glucksmann's books). What struck me on each occasion, what I remembered of these journeys and of the reports I produced, was the extraordinarily slender additional knowledge I gained from the investigation itself. I spent days and days looking at things, sometimes weeks engaged in finding things out, and all in aid of a barely perceptible amount of extra knowledge, in relation to what had already been gathered and was available. Perhaps this extra bit of information does make all the difference and is the measure of the worth and reputation of the true journalist. But only if one is prepared to concede that what really matters goes on at another level, and that the best analyses are those which in the main verify what we already know. In other words, it's the mind's eye which does more work than the real eye. It would be totally absurd to allow the idea to gain ground of the wide-eyed journalist who puts his prejudices to one side in order to discover the world as if it were strange and new.

That of course explains my scepticism – to put it no more strongly – in the face of your tirades against abuses of the imagination and of fabrication etc. Certainly, it has an impact and reassures decent people. Basically, however, what you say doesn't hold up. It bears no relationship to the way in which ideas – whether political, scientific or any others – are conceived in reality. What's more, I'd be ready to prove it to you from an orthodox epistemological point of view, if the time and occasion presented themselves. Chance, or in reality my film about intellectuals, have caused me to re-read recently Canguilhem's[2] books. They are, as you know, detailed analyses based on extremely scrupulous investigations. Everything is studied in minute and meticulous detail, which would, I'm sure, give you great pleasure. So what does this meticulous man say when he reflects on the way in which a concept is created or a discovery crystallised? He talks about experimentation, about tools and technical procedures. He reminds us of the importance of microscopes, laboratories, theorems. He insists on the role of models and on the negative role of those celebrated "epistemological obstacles". He adds, however, – which is truly exciting – that nothing is created without the aid of another faculty; not logic, or the experimental method, or intuition, or deduction. What is necessary, quite simply, is the capacity to fabricate!

There's a splendid passage, for example, in which he describes how much Darwinism depended on a dreamlike meditation on the laws of Malthus. There's another passage in which he shows how much Oken's theory of cells owed to the political ideas of Novalis and German Romanticism. He wrote a whole book on Willis's incredible invention of the modern theory of the reflex arc. He suggests that Willis was a great thinker and an unrivalled experimental scientist. He understood that it was necessary to escape the limitations of Cartesian physics. But his real stroke of genius was to have had a mad vision concerning the circulation of animal spirits. Similarly, he worked out in his imagination that the reflex mechanism had something in common with the reflection of light and heat. He spent years and years thinking about a whole range of strange instruments, of which the least that can be said is that he didn't come across them in any scientific collections: a burning-mirror, an air-lighter, cannon powder and so on. As a consequence, more or less the whole of modern physiology is derived from "imaginative" processes rather than from "observation". It's the product of a scientist who was as much a poet as a physicist and mathematician. In his case as in that of all the others, it is clearly impossible to distinguish what was imagined from what was the product of rigorous thought. There is no point in separating them as you do between "mythos" on the one hand and "logos" on the other.

There is another form of complexity which concerns me, that of

339

ideas, or the *battle* of ideas which the "construction of Europe" gives rise to. It is with this in mind that I have tried: (1) To warn people of the naive assumption that the "liberated" countries of Central Europe would purely and simply become part of a great liberal utopia. I don't believe in this convergence of interests. I don't believe that the end of communism implies *ipso facto* a rallying to the cause of liberalism. That's why I've placed more emphasis on a political mix involving ecological forces, as well as organic community elements, and a renewed form of socialism as a possible replacement for a totalitarian ideology. (2) Not to fall into the trap of applauding, unreservedly and unthinkingly, everything which happens on the other side of the Iron Curtain. Our friends in the East have much to teach us – initially in terms of the way they envisage Europe from a cultural angle. But I would add that we not only have a message for them but also objections to make, and were we to refrain from offering them and merely to display open-mouthed admiration and have a silly emotional response, they would be justified in reproaching us for political paternalism which would do neither them nor us any credit. (3) Lastly, to draw attention to the fact that what is being argued over at present is to all intents and purposes what a handful of writers like Habermas on one side and Kis and Kundera on the other have thrashed out in detail. This isn't mere name-dropping on my part, but an attempt to save time by outlining a debate of which the stakes, the main lines, and the scope are, so to speak, known in advance. If you prefer, it's a way of recalling that there's a certain nostalgia surrounding the idea of Central Europe but also a possible nightmare as well. What remains to be seen in the coming years is which forces will win the day on the ground and also in people's minds. Will they be those which embody the finest qualities of a Europe which produced Freud, Musil and Mahler? Or will they be those which remind us that Central Europe has been a terrible battleground, the scene of various nationalistic, chauvinistic and irredentist quarrels, and the home of the wilder forms of Romanticism? To put it more plainly, you could say that what we are witnessing, as everyone knows, is an extremely exciting phenomenon and one which occurs rarely in the history of any society, namely the re-emergence of a civilisation which had been frozen for almost half a century. Its restoration has been perfect and the fact it has occurred in such a detailed way is astonishing. There is, however, one "detail" which alters the picture. Millions of Jews have disappeared from the scene without trace. The question I would therefore like to ask, without malice or any ulterior motive is: what is the likelihood of there being *no Jews in Central Europe* at the beginning of the twenty-first century?

We should spend some time discussing European affairs in greater detail one of these days. It's all very well to talk about a "consensus" and to say as you do that you foresaw the collapse of communism before most people – which is no doubt true – and that you anticipated the re-emergence of a "Europe" which you fear may become a "substitute myth". The one thing which isn't clear to me personally is whether we are talking about the same thing, though we are using the same words, and whether by some miracle we are on the same wavelength.

There is one question I'd like to ask you. If you really did predict all that has happened and even if you did travel the length and breadth of Europe carrying out your investigations and discover the exact number of prisoners held in Soviet concentration camps (and I don't dispute that you've been more farsighted than most people), might I ask why, my dear Régis, you've got bogged down with the minutiae of these figures? How is it that so little was been seen or heard of you when it came to getting these men out of prison though you knew all about them? (It doesn't matter whether there were thousands or millions of them.) Why, on the other hand, were you so bent on ridiculing the idea of the reinvention of democracy by an intelligentsia which had only just been de-Stalinised? In my view, it was very much to their credit. My suspicion, as you've guessed, is that this wasn't your struggle, and that you didn't give a fig for what seemed to me to be essentially important values. If today with hindsight we have the impression that we were both looking forward to the re-emergence of the same "European spirit", it's a misunderstanding which arose because we understood something different whilst using the same words.

Words, as you know, are for me not just words, but carry with them a whole range of implications and connotations which give them their importance. But there are other issues I want to settle before we establish whether we are both under the influence of the same "Eurocentric opiate". Is your attachment to Europe, which you refer to as "the rugged landscape which made you what you are", sufficiently strong for you to want to restore the values which it embodied? How positive is your message, and does it recognise the universality of the rights of man which have long been denied in a Third-World context? Do you wish them to expand and spread? Are you prepared to condemn dictatorial regimes in the Southern

Hemisphere without constantly going on about the responsibility of the West and the legacy of colonialism? I'd also like to know if you're ready to admit that a hatred of Europe which was for a long time one of the strangest attitudes exhibited by European people was both bad and stupid.

I will stop there, my dear Régis, as I feel you are about to accuse me again of being bombastic and over-emphatic. With best wishes.

NOTES

1. A former Marxist intellectual who had been with Che Guevara in Latin America. In June 1981, President Mitterrand appointed him adviser on Third World Affairs.

2. Professor of the History and Philosophy of Science at the Sorbonne. He supervised Foucault's doctoral thesis.

3

"The structural revolution"

IS IT POSSIBLE NOT TO BE A HEGELIAN WHEN ENGAGING IN
THE HISTORY OF IDEAS?

Luc Ferry was certainly right when he criticised the anti-humanism of the sixties from the lofty perspective of certain immutable principles. He was also right to point out that an anti-humanistic hatred of the "subject" and of all discourse relating to him condemns in some respects the eponymous figures associated with philosophy at that time. He expressed his regret that French thought became bogged down for so long in such barren and sterile territory, in which the concept of a free man as a subject under the law and a citizen of a secular and democratic society were, from a theoretical point of view, almost inconceivable; and I understand what he meant in pursuing his analysis and seeking to establish the common ground between all the different strands of thought which were current in '68. He wasn't totally wrong in believing he had identified a "French form of Nietzschism", the influence of which had been all the more secret and pernicious since it had not been openly expressed. I accept all that he said, particularly because I was aware of what happened subsequently. I witnessed the kinds of impasses in which people found themselves, and even experienced some of them myself. I saw Michel Foucault tie himself in all kinds of knots in a laudable but pathetic attempt to go on defending the rights of gays, prisoners, immigrants, and other oppressed minorities as human beings – having begun to question the very existence of human beings as such. I heard Clavel muttering that if man was dead, then the rights had no substance. I myself said that one couldn't perpetually contradict in practice a particular philosophy one claimed to believe in; nor, I insisted, could a philosopher put metaphysics to one side and live on his moral capital. I understand, therefore, the position of Ferry and Renaut and the thrust of their argument.[1] Though it may surprise them, I would suggest that their line of philosophical enquiry was one of the most interesting of the eighties.

Having said that, one question which remains to be answered – and which anti-structuralists refrain from asking – is why the substantial critique of totalitarian thought which had been anticipated for a long time finally emerged in the wake of the events of '68. Having dutifully noted that Foucault was "anti-man" and that Althusser was "pro-Stalin and Mao", it still has to be explained why it was from the ranks of their disciples or prodigal sons that the recruits came who were to storm the Marxist citadel five to ten years later. The story which Ferry and Renaut are unable to tell – and I refer to it in this way because the particular story of each individual's development is of the greatest significance when dealing with this kind of subject – is how it was that former disciples of Foucault, Lacan and Althusser came to welcome the dissidents, to become spokesmen for Alexander Solzhenitsyn. Why did they lead the anti-totalitarian campaign with such vigour, whilst liberal thinkers seemed resigned to coexistence, having grown weary of the fact that they were in the right and yet nothing had changed? It's a story I know well; it started with the "left-wing anti-communist" movement of May '68, which, under the banner of Maoism, attacked the French Communist Party – a Party that suddenly seemed reactionary, Poujadist, and sometimes racist. It's a story I was involved in, along with André Glucksmann, Jean-Marie Benoist, Christian Jambet, Guy Lardreau and Jean-Paul Dollé. It's also the story of "la nouvelle philosophie", which everyone I think now agrees played an important part in the history of French thought (whatever one's other criticisms of it). But people are inclined to forget that it wouldn't have played this role had it not had its roots in the events of '68.

This is obviously neither the time nor the place to set out the main lines of Lacan's system of thought. What I can bear witness to, however, is the impact of many of his ideas in France during the sixties and seventies: the law and castration; the unconscious structured like a language and language structured like the unconscious; the durability of the concept of the master; the resolute attempt to dispel semblance; the fact that there is no imaginary wholeness; no desire without pro-hibition; no liberated sexuality; no recovery of some "hidden state of innocence". There is a "censor" – but with no beginning and therefore without end. There is "repression" – but no initial freedom which has been stifled. Lacan could be seen as a pessimist who dispelled illusions and chided his students for "wanting a master". He certainly didn't sugar the pill and his system of thought quickly brought one back to reality. We had all cheerfully assumed that revolution was inevitable and believed in the messianic political message of a "new man", which would bring renewal. The concept had, of course, already been in existence a long time. But these aspirations and illusions were quickly dispelled. Like the Fathers of the Church before him, Lacan reminded us of the law of finitude. He brought us back down to earth and destroyed the wild schemes we had devised. The fact that some of us came to realise that radical evil was not something to be treated lightly and that a desire for purity was at the heart of all totalitarian discourse was due to the influence of Lacan.

This isn't the place either to reconsider the detailed argument of Althusser's works *Pour Marx* and *Lire le Capital*. But I do know he affected the way we thought with his unusual approach to the subject. He reinstated Marxism in all its purity and pleaded in public for the retention of the concept of the "dictatorship of the proletariat". But it soon ceased to carry any conviction. We knew full well that such ideas wouldn't last and that Althusser himself didn't really believe in them; yet his critique of the young Marx, his deconstruction of the concepts of "alienation" and of "human Nature", his view of history as "a process without a subject", of "over-determination", of "metonymic causality", the way he conceived of change from one "means of production" to another – which was so rigid, giving little place to the consequences of social constraint – all of these things combined with Lacan's ideas to contribute to the critique of philosophical naturalism, which we now know to have been at the heart of the totalitarian system. Althusser didn't convince me, for example, in his *Réponse à John Lewis*, that Stalinism was an "economic system" crossed with "humanism". It wasn't from him either that I learned of the "epistemological divergence" which, in 1856, divided the corpus of Marx's work in two. But it was from him I learned that history was endless because it was without a subject and that no ultimate upheaval would reveal the truth of human history or exorcise its evil aspects.

I won't discuss here what Foucault really meant when he claimed that "man" was not "the oldest problem" or even "the most persistent" in the history of mankind. But I do remember his critique of the concept of "power", his notion of "knowledge-as-power", and the fresh attention he paid to what he called "the infinitely small elements of political power". I also remember the way he elaborated the concept of the "physical nature of power" from book to book. I remember the picture he drew of the social body as a scattered constellation of forces which confronted each other and of monads which balanced each other. Today, I am aware there was no better or newer method of confounding and then eliminating the old Marxist notion of power viewed as a gigantic macro-structure with its intricacies and procedures. It isn't a question of determining whether Foucault's system stands up or whether his objection to Marxist politics was the "right" one. As you will recall, Foucault urged those who read his books to use them as if they were boxes of tools. That's what we did, and our reason for doing so was that they were the appropriate tools for dismantling a system we no longer needed. If you compare Aron's methodology with that of Foucault, you realise how old and worn out it is, having conveyed an overwhelming sense of rightness for several decades. You'll become aware that it doesn't work and never did. *Surveiller et punir* offered an alternative philosophy with which to demolish other systems. You didn't find this in *Dix-huit leçons* and *L'Opium de intellectuels*.

You can say what you like about the thinkers of the sixties and endlessly criticise Foucault and Lacan. It may also be a good thing that most of us are no longer influenced by structuralism, which in the end would have stopped us from thinking. Structuralism did, however, have an influence and was part of the intellectual climate and therefore affected the way individuals thought. It was a vehicle used by the history of ideas, which might be compared to a ship sailing under a flag of convenience. Ferry may have regretted what happened and felt that it was an inappropriate vehicle which deflected the history of ideas from its proper course. But there are no short cuts and such deflections inevitably occur. It's a wearisome kind of history which imposes its own rhythms and calculations. You are bound to make mistakes and lose your way. In any case, what was Ferry doing whilst I was wasting my time with Foucault and Althusser? Why didn't he publish his treatises on political philosophy at that point rather than later? No doubt his answer would be: "I was reading – and translating – those books which structuralism had banished from the library shelves." But he knew full well one only reads what one writes! Everyone knows that if an intellectual reads Schelling without making use of him he isn't really reading him properly. Whether he accepted it or not, Ferry was patiently biding his time. He allowed others to be deflected by structuralism on his behalf. The consequences of all this are clear. Given the state of French philosophy and the particularities of his own development and discourse, the various strands of thought which emerged around '68 were necessary for us to arrive in the end at the democratic consensus which we provisionally shared.

Some people will perhaps be surprised to hear me talking about these things in a strangely Hegelian tone. It's certainly true, but I don't think you can avoid being something of a Hegelian when dealing with this kind of history. You would, I believe, produce a naive version of the history of ideas, if you pretended that the concepts were always there, lurking in the shadows, waiting quietly for a more dynamic M. Loyal[2] to come along, who would be less patient with the slow progress of dialectics and speedily introduce them into the debate. Getting involved with the history of ideas is dreadful, like being in a quagmire. You can only make slow progress as you keep coming up against things or have to retrace your steps. It involves all kinds of tricks as well as feelings of remorse. You do not know where you are nor where you have come from, and you make progress by going backwards and vice versa. It's like watching the movements of an eel. It lunges forward, retracts, coils round on itself, stretches out, and then draws back again. No one will be surprised to learn that it was thinking about these movements which gave me the idea of calling both the book and the film *Les Aventures de la liberté*.

NOTES

1. Ferry and Renaut wrote a book together on French philosophy of the sixties which they subtitled "an essay on anti-humanism".

2. The bailiff in Molière's play *Tartuffe* who, in the nicest possible way, tells Orgon he must leave his house within twenty-four hours.

4

"Naked revolt in the lycées"

HOW HATRED AFFECTED PEOPLE'S THINKING

They were twenty years old and the latest bunch of deserving lads from the provinces to receive scholarships from the State. For a century, young men like them had set out to enter "khâgne"[1] at the Lycée Louis-le-Grand. They still wore a grey school overall and had an unhappy, old-fashioned look about them, reminding one of Alain-Fournier's characters. They went to classes in their slippers and kept their scarves around their necks. Even without these articles of clothing which distinguished them from the rest, their dishevelled hair, unwashed faces, and the sour smell of the dormitory which hung about them in the late morning revealed they were boarders. Another difference (which to me seemed like a privilege at the time) was that each of them had a locker at the back of the classroom in which, together with stocks of dried sausage sent by their families, they kept a few old books under lock and key. These they had inherited from some uncle or other who had been at the Ecole normale supérieure, and rumour had it they gave one a crucial advantage in the preparation for the entrance exam.

They weren't the best students, but they were the swots, the most openly hard-working. Of all of us, they were certainly the ones who showed the least spirit of revolt. Books in general (and not just the old ones which supposedly gave them special powers and which none of the rest of us could get hold of) were the most important things in their lives. They had books in Greek and Latin, books they read in the morning and others which they read at night. There were also books they read in their free time and between lunch and the beginning of afternoon classes. They weren't simply bookworms, they'd become living books. They were little old men at twenty, weighed down by all they'd read. There was no hour of the day or any circumstance in which they could imagine themselves being without a book. Like Balzac learning of his father's illness, they could almost have said: "Let's get back to reality and Eugénie Grandet's wedding;" or like Borges who replied on being asked about his life: "I don't think I've ever really escaped from my father's library."

Then came April '68. Strange rumblings from the streets, that had nothing to do with the world of books, were carried into the Lycée on a spring breeze which they were unaccustomed to in such surroundings. Our bookworms heard these rumblings from afar and were surprised and vaguely shocked. At first, they cursed the noise which distracted them from their books. But they started to listen and then to pay attention to what was going on. I watched them become restless and start to stir in their seats. I was surprised when they took off their school overalls and their slippers. For two, three and sometimes four years, without any apparent show of emotion, they had foregone the pleasures enjoyed by young people of their age in order to live the cloistered existence of those preparing "khâgne". Theirs had been a life of books and silence. Suddenly, they drew a line under all that and renounced their former selves. Without any feeling of anguish or regret or any sense they had wasted their time there, they joyfully went down into the streets as if they had been liberated. In their turn, they joined in a movement which took as one of its slogans the idea that you should give up books.

Books, they now proclaimed, were a kind of disease, the fruits and product of adversity. Just as the excess labour of the proletariat forms the basis of capital, so excess knowledge is stolen from simple souls and on the basis of this shameful theft books are produced. It was agreed therefore that books should not be burnt but ignored or erased. The destructive memory which they contained should be obliterated. The only thing of Borges worth remembering was the remark alleged to have been made by Caesar when someone came to tell him one day that the library in Alexandria was on fire and that the collective memory of mankind might be lost. "Let it burn", he said, "the memories it contains are infamous."

I know – already knew – that hatred of thought was an attitude widely shared by thinkers. I know – already knew – that from the Dadaists onwards the rejection of literature has been the main feature of what was taken to be true literature. What I hadn't been aware of was the nature of their passion. I hadn't realised that boys who had so valued books could take equal delight in claiming they knew nothing. I didn't know that even their faces and bodies could undergo such a dramatic transformation. All these boarders, with their overalls and their spots and their odour of the dormitory, changed their appearance once they stopped reading and suddenly eyed me with an air of authority and disdain, which the most imaginative novelist wouldn't have dreamt of. The fact that most of them got over it, once things calmed down again, and became journalists, writers, or just teachers, rather

than solicitors as Ionesco had predicted, in no way lessened the impact
of my initial impressions. During those weeks, I suddenly discovered
the perverse pleasure that intelligent and knowledgeable individuals
could take in denying their true nature in order to assume the role
of militants. More seriously, I also discovered that, far from demeaning
them or making them disagreeable, the denial of their nature gave
them a certain charm which I still find attractive today.

Not all of them did get over it; or if they did, it was in a more
unobtrusive, less obvious manner (which Borges would have described
as "infamous"). They resembled those who spoke with tongues during
the early years of Christianity, using languages which didn't exist and
which they forgot almost at once as they lapsed back into ordinary
speech. What happened to these friends of mine, not the ones who
entered leftist groups as if they were an alternative to the Ecole
Nationale d'Administration[2] and who engaged in revolt as if it were
a means of seizing power, but those who truly spoke with tongues?
What became of them? What did they do? They seemed inspired,
almost to have a touch of genius in my eyes, when they were haranguing people or discussing Lenin. They must have sunk into some sort
of state of social or mental non-existence.

Heaven knows, I don't like the word genius, and the romantic
aura which surrounds the idea of the precocious and precarious genius
has always seemed to me rather fuzzy. Still, I do have very clear
memories of particular moments, of faces, of names too sometimes,
and of the physical shape of certain individuals, though the fact that
in my mind's eye I superimpose the schoolboy's grey overall and the
parka of a Maoist leader means that I'm likely to confuse their identities. I remember Martin D., for example, who was thought to be a
bishop's son and who arrived in "hypokhâgne" wreathed in glory, so
to speak, at having obtained first prize for his Greek prose or translation in the "Concours général".[3] He was so ugly and dirty that year,
and so pleased at his own ugliness that it was almost obscene. The
following year, he'd become a rebel and looked handsome, having
forgotten his Greek and become one of the most brilliant commentators on the military strategy of General Giap. He too was swallowed
up in the black hole which claimed all those who had fallen silent,
having earlier spoken with tongues, and all leftists who had gone to
the dogs.

The last time I saw him he was mixed up in petty crime in London
with a certain Benjamin C. The last time I heard from him he was
serving a prison term in Pau, having gone on to more serious crime.

I don't know why, but I didn't answer his letter at the time. I wonder where he is now and what he's doing, and whether he remembers that strange, brief period when he seemed to come under the thrall of curious gods which were soon to abandon him. Well, I've answered him now. Poor Martin D.! You lost your head and ruined your life. But were you aware that for me you epitomised that whole period?

NOTES

1. See page 100, note 1.

2. The Ecole Nationale d'Administration is the postgraduate civil service college founded in 1946 which trains France's technocratic élite.

3. A competitive exam with prizes open to all secondary school children.

5

"Terrifying young men"

CONCERNING BENNY LÉVY

I have always enjoyed the misunderstandings which have occurred throughout literary history and sometimes made the relationships between writers so absurd. Flaubert had little regard for Stendhal, and Stendhal mocked Balzac. He, in his turn, seemed totally oblivious of Baudelaire. Lecomte de Lisle made fun of Mallarmé's "unintelligible poetry". Then there was Claudel's celebrated remark criticising Proust, who was already an established writer: "There are other things in life than idle people and their flunkeys." The case of the ageing Gide is less spectacular, though he did enjoy enormous renown and prestige at that stage in his life. Whether at home in his flat in the Rue Vaneau, on the platform at the earliest anti-fascist rallies, or in the Congo, he seems to have embodied the conflicting qualities of a "prince of youth" in the manner of Barrès and of an "intellectual supporter of Dreyfus" in the manner of Zola. Yet the mind boggles at the thought of him in his old age appearing so timid, so full of fears and misgivings when he found himself being judged by someone younger than himself in the person of Ramon Fernandez.[1] Though as Fernandez's son Dominique pointed out to me, his father could in no way have been considered a timid young disciple, having published *La Vie de Molière* and *Le Pari* and also founded the newspaper *Marianne* and the AEAR (this future supporter of Doriot had indeed founded the first anti-fascist movement!). Nonetheless, the idea of the elderly Gide writing to Dorothy Bussy that "he could hold his head up high again thanks to the encouragement of Fernandez" is both fascinating and moving. He wrote to Martin du Gard that it was due to Fernandez that he had "taken a stand" and "saved his honour"; and he noted in his own *Journal* that Fernandez had enabled him "to free himself from the pernicious influence of Mallarmé and of German philosophy". The idea of Gide as a disciple of Fernandez is hard to believe.

My own generation has witnessed a similarly strange and surprising example of this role reversal in the person of Sartre, who, in the sixties, became a follower of the young Maoist intellectuals.

(Concerning Benny Lévy; does one or doesn't one continue to give way over ideas?)

The dialogue between Sartre and Benny Lévy might be put under the heading: pathos. The Maoist began by saying: "What some of us find difficult to accept is your apparent inability to produce anything immediately useful to the movement which grew out of the May events and the fact that you simply continue writing your book on Flaubert instead. Wouldn't it be more useful to write a popular novel?" To which the philosopher sheepishly replied: "I've been studying Flaubert for a good number of years, using techniques and methods which I've tried to modify. I don't think the masses can immediately take me to task for that." After the Maoist had stressed again "the demands of the ideological revolution" which needed to be expressed in a popular novel, Sartre responded with a sigh, almost plaintively: "You think it's easy; that all you have to do is suggest I write a popular novel. I need to know what a popular novel is." Then, having run out of arguments, all he could do was to appeal to the better nature of his ruthless young opponent (a sceptical militant who wasn't going to let himself be taken in). And in a whining tone he said: "It's my age as well. I'm getting on now . . . I'll be lucky if I finish the Flaubert . . . Perhaps after that I could try a popular novel . . . but you're always asking me to do things, so I haven't got as much time for my own work . . . you expect a lot!"

As a conversation, it reveals a great deal. The youthful arrogance of the one contrasts with the pathetic humility of a poor old man who could be easily snubbed and who, like the character in Edgar Allan Poe's short story, apologised when someone bumped into him. I imagine the contemporary reader could react in two different ways. On the one hand, he might have the feeling it wasn't true, that it was a joke, and that the great Sartre wouldn't have allowed himself to be treated in such a manner. He would have reacted, taken back what he said, burst out laughing and made fun of this frightful young Maoist. At all events, he would have gone home, pleased to have escaped his clutches and to be able to get back to his book on Flaubert with a clear conscience. On the other hand, perhaps it did have the ring of truth about it; perhaps the author of *Les Mots* did genuinely believe that words were valueless and would have given up writing had he been able to. But he was too old, too addicted to his wretched words like someone corrupted by vice. Perhaps he really was a repentant man of letters who was about to be treated in the same way as the Red Guards in Peking treated their own professors. For someone like me, who remembers what Sartre was like towards the end of his life, the situation is plain. He was indeed contrite and was counting on the Maoists to help him purge some unspecified crime. He was an intellectual who felt his hands were too clean and who, unlike his Chinese counterparts, set in motion his own trial which was to confound and destroy him. He truly believed that writing the book on Flaubert was an error and that he would be purged by the Revolution. However much one might like him as a man and admire his work – especially the book on Flaubert which thankfully turned out to be a success – one has to admit he exhibited to an extraordinary degree that strange and passionate hatred of thought one finds amongst thinkers. That he did this towards the end of his life meant in principle that everything he had done previously would be viewed in the light of his ultimate gesture.

Writers are always classified according to the intensity of their commitment, or according to their courage, their lucidity, never without its imperfections, or the stand they have taken on specific moral issues which have usually been of major importance and captured the world's headlines. When confronted by a text such as the one we've just been looking at, I wonder if they shouldn't *also* be classified on the basis of an alternative morality, which for the sake of brevity I will call the morality of thought. On one side of this divide, therefore, would be put those like the late Sartre (on reflection, we might also have to look at the Sartre of the immediate post-war period) who considered that literature and thought were vaguely reprehensible activities which had to be expiated in some way. Worse still, they were thought of as less worthy activities, to be engaged in provisionally until Life, or the People, or the magical fervour of pure Revolutionary activity suddenly erupted and caused the individual to abandon them at once and without regret. Sartre would be included, then, but also Gide, Rolland in his Stalinist phase, and Aragon when, after Kharkov, he compared the free writer he had been to a "common criminal" re-educated in the "penal colony of Bielomorstroï". There was Brasillach too after he became a convert to fascism and Drieu who, having met Doriot, concluded somewhat glumly that the time for literature and thought had definitely passed. Whether pro-communist or pro-fascist, they were all intellectuals who considered the world of the intellect as a blind alley. It was something they accepted as part of daily life, but they hoped they could escape it for good, and in certain circumstances that seemed possible.

On the other side, there were writers who never yielded ground where thought was concerned, whatever the nature or extent of their commitment. That's true of Breton whose tracts were written as if they were poems. It was true also of his enemy-ally Bataille, a somewhat undecided and ambiguous anti-fascist, who nonetheless devoted time to his *Structure psychologique du fascisme*, which was the most complete analysis of its day. Because they were journalists, Camus and Mauriac needed less time, but whether they were writing about torture or purges, Stalinism or fascism, the Soviet camps in Camus's case or in Mauriac's case the Spanish Civil War, they could never be accused of simple-mindedness. Malraux was a committed intellectual, if ever there was one. You only have to think of him in Spain being chased in his Potez by a fascist Fiat, or in his old Latécoère where he had installed cameras in the place of machine-guns, or addressing his comrades from the Brigades in the Salamanca cinema in Madrid or bidding them farewell not long after in Barcelona. Nonetheless, he remained first and foremost a writer. They were an equally disparate group of intellectuals, but they had one thing in common. They didn't accept the strange notion that thought was something they should renounce or allow to become enslaved.

These intellectuals, I have to say, were neither better nor worse than the others. They too were capable of being small-minded and mean. Like Mauriac, they could be blinded by their allegiance to Gaullism, or like Camus they could remain deaf to the real significance of the Algerian revolt. And despite the quality and exacting nature of their analysis, they could, like Bataille, be less than wholehearted in their resistance to Nazism. Like Malraux they could assent to the liquidation of POUM and thereby accept for a while at least the fateful consequence of Stalinist control. There would even be an element of truth in suggesting that Malraux might not have gone to Moscow had he not had the idea of writing a major novel about oil; that he would not have been a fellow-traveller had he not had the ulterior motive of meeting Eisenstein and adapting *La Condition humaine* for him. He had also wanted to get scenes for his novel and images for his film in Spain and then to give them more weight and substance by adding high-flown thoughts, without which he always considered great art couldn't exist. All I'm trying to say is that this particular division between those who felt ashamed of what they were doing and those who persisted with it, between the contrite and the arrogant, is broadly speaking as valid as any other. Given that we're discussing intellectuals, that's to say men and women whose essential role is to write and reflect on things, it doesn't seem right that this particular issue is scarcely ever referred to. For myself, I am much happier about Malraux "using" Spain to enhance his book than I am about the ageing Sartre having his name "used" and his work decried.

Such a view is all the more justified since it's not unheard of for people to seek to adapt a political line to take account of or fit in with certain currents of thought. Take the case of Stalinism for example. One of the most telling remarks on the subject was made by Malraux at a Congress of Writers in Moscow in 1934. He was still quite young, having recently published *La Condition humaine*, and was proud to be taking part alongside writers such as Nizan, Pozner, Ehrenburg, Jean-Richard Bloch, Alexis Tolstoy, Aragon, Gorky, Zhdanov and Radek. They were gathered together in the imposing pillared auditorium, decorated in red and gold with huge portraits of Molière, Shakespeare, Cervantes and Balzac on the walls. Not long after, it was to be used for the terrible show trials. Aragon spoke about Courbet, Ehrenburg about literature, and Zhdanov reminded everyone of the official Stalinist line to the effect that an intellectual was an engineer of souls. Then Malraux, looking very pale, mounted the rostrum and dumbfounded his audience with his pithy remark that "if writers are engineers of souls, don't forget that the most important task of an engineer is to be inventive." Bearing in mind the date of this remark, no one could have challenged more effectively the idiocies of Zhdanov. What he said wasn't especially memorable or literary, nor was it daring or dangerous. It was purely and simply an intelligent observation, uttered by a man who was stubbornly defending his right to think and express his thoughts. A great intellectual is usually thought of as the opposite of someone who has quick reflexes and can improvise. A better definition would be that he's someone whose reflexes are all the more appropriate *because* they have been developed and mediatised.

NOTES

1. The author of various literary portraits and a friend of Gide.

6

"A desire for saintliness"

So far, each time I've spoken about the "religious dimension" of various forms of commitment in the twentieth century, I seem to have done so in the past tense, as if it were something only applicable to much earlier generations and we were set apart from the whole tradition. But that, I have to say, is a totally false impression, since those of my generation – the last communists – have had the dubious merit of carrying this form of madness to extremes. I can think of two examples, the first of whom, Daniel Rondeau, was a strange fellow. Seeing him today, it is hard to believe he was probably one of the first of those well-educated individuals who chose to become a factory worker. Thinking about it, I must have met him at the very end of that period, when he was still in Nancy and I used to go there to talk to the students. He seemed lost (and worse still: forgotten), living out his life as one of the remnants of that small, routed army of Maoists. He still retained the air of a dandy and had the same impatient tone of voice. Every time he walked back to the station with me, he had the curious habit of talking about Barrès (which should perhaps have puzzled me more than it did and which I put down to his desire to needle me). Individuals like him were neither Marxists nor socialists. They were "mystics", and what inspired them was the concept of "saintliness".

The other example is my friend Jambet. Of all the intellectuals of that period, he was the one who impressed me the most. He too was certain in his own mind that the vision shared by the extreme Left in France was absolutely pure. But the enthusiasm of these young people to work in factories, their keenness to engage in the slightly puerile "long marches" to Normandy and Brittany, not to mention the desire on the part of the more daring amongst them to get involved in dubious activities which drew them towards terrorism, had little in common with traditional militancy. In some respects, the fervour which inspired them was in fact more like that which drove mad virgins and honourable thieves out into the highways and byways of the Orient two thousand years earlier when Christianity was in its infancy.

Then there was the Foucault affair. I have in front of me the series of articles which the author of *Surveiller et punir* wrote in 1979 for *Corriere della sera* about what was happening in Iran. I won't dwell on them as they've already been discussed at length. Moreover, I'm especially tired of the way in which some people have treated such a major blunder as a cause for celebration. They seem to think it should have been registered for all time, in the annals of regained lucidity, as *the* last, appropriately huge, mistake of an intellectual class which thereafter was restored to its right mind. But whichever way you look at it, an error was made. A philosopher with a huge reputation was seen enthusiastically acclaiming as a new dawn the obscurantist movement emerging in Iran. What's more, he stuck to that view and never went back on it. It is difficult therefore to read his passionate praise for Khomeini himself and for his "political spirituality" without seeing it as further proof of the fact that, more than anything else, an obsession with religion has constantly blinded intellectuals who have been involved in politics. What we desperately need are theologians who can interpret this phenomenon.

7

"It's not altogether clear by what miracle France was spared"

LEADING INTELLECTUALS AGAINST TERRORISM

The question that was constantly asked in the immediate aftermath of the events of May '68 was why the French Maoists whose interest in terrorism was well known didn't in the end resort to it. What was it that held them back? Who curbed them? What halted the rising tide of violence one sensed in various places including the "popular courts" where the Maoists served as prosecutors? The same old answer trotted out until one was sick to death of it was: the intellectuals. Like benevolent elder statesmen, leading intellectuals from Sartre to Foucault to Clavel would, it was claimed, have used their influence to defend democracy which was seen as the lesser evil.

That may have been true for Clavel, but can the same thing be said of Sartre and Foucault? – especially when one thinks of Foucault's stance on Iran and Sartre's attitude towards his young Maoist friends. Sadly, he would have been more inclined to understand, to accept, and even to justify their wayward actions rather than curb them. We might also remember that Sartre applauded the despicable murders which were committed in 1973 in the Olympic Stadium in Munich. I've always thought that remarks such as – "leading intellectuals prevented the Maoists, etc." – were typical examples of the kind of cliché which I've already drawn attention to in this book and which don't stand up when one briefly examines them. How long do we have to wait for an honest appraisal of the non-role of our great thinkers in the history of the appeal of terrorism in France?

For the time being, we will have to make do with a hypothesis which I owe to my friend Marek Halter, who was a survivor of the Warsaw ghetto and a leading authority on Human Rights in France. His view was that the opposite might have been true, that it was the people rather than the intellectuals who restrained them. Something fundamental may have occurred in the confrontation between the Maoists who worked in the factories and the real workers with whom they came face to face. The Maoists venerated and engaged in a cult of the working class. They had made a conscious decision to accept every utterance of the working class as if it were holy law, but the message they received was clear. Real flesh and blood workers listened to what these visionaries had to say and couldn't help being sceptical about the claim that they would be liberated, though it might involve the death of their fellow-workers and perhaps their own as well. The Maoists were obliged to listen to them in their turn, as they had faith in everything the workers said. What they heard was good, sound sense from men who made it clear that the Maoists messianic and criminal vision had nothing whatsoever in common with the struggles and aspirations of their own ordinary lives. Sensible working people were against terror and shunned such madness.

Had the Maoists spent all their time during those years in the cellars of the Ecole normale, they might well have succumbed to the temptation of using terror. As it was, having abandoned their books in order to meet people, they came into contact with the working class. This was good for them, since it softened their attitudes and cured them of their folly. It was also their good fortune, and ours as well, that they found jobs, for in this way they met more moderate, more cautious people, who turned out to be more *petit bourgeois* than their bibles of terror had led them to believe. Baader didn't go and work in a factory and therefore didn't follow the same path as Daniel Rondeau. That was the distinguishing characteristic of ultra-leftism in France, and it also explains why in the end those involved in it were more restrained. Heaven knows, I'm usually loath to let sociologists have the last word! And yet . . .

8

"Revolution reduced to its purest state"

Whenever totalitarianism is discussed and people are asked about the essential characteristics of a phenomenon which, however moribund it may appear, has nevertheless dominated – and poisoned – this century, what they generally mention is the use of force, the State, or the total, collective appropriation of the means of production. Others mention the camps, the police, and torture. Conversely, if they are talking specifically about communism, they might refer to the fact that the people have power, that equality has become established, that the workers are in control. What we are beginning to understand today, and what the "nouvelle philosophie" in particular has taught us, is that behind the obvious and visible aspects of totalitarianism there lurks a more discreet, secret, yet decisive urge: the urge to purity.

Some talked of the purity of the race, others of the purity of the people. But the key word on the lips of the madmen who promised to regenerate mankind was purity. So that a true communist – or a true Nazi, come to that – was someone who, on coming across anything impure or second-rate, on feeling that things weren't quite right in the way men lived, suffered or died together, would exclaim: "Take heart, good people; we won't leave you in this mess or abandon you to a miserable fate." He would do anything, and I mean anything (including opening up concentration camps), to renew the community by giving it back its lost and longed for purity. I will take you as you are, he told us. I will accept you with all your defects and in all your filth. And you will see how I shall give you back that radiance you had at the first dawn, because the dark and evil side of your nature will have been purged.

Should we consider the communists or the fascists who behaved in this way as wicked people? It would in fact be wrong to consider them wicked or to suggest that they were out to mess up the human race. On the contrary, they loved the human race. They sought to flatter and cosset it, and were so concerned for its welfare that they wanted it to be more than human, superhuman. But in seeking to achieve their ends, they came across people who did abuse and insult the human race, people who believed that original sin could not be eradicated. They therefore had religious scores to settle, which explains why Stalinists were anti-semitic, why they declared war on Jews and on their Christian descendants, and therefore why they were like the Nazis. The simple fact was that a Jew, like a Christian, could in no way accept the systematic purging of people, because he knew that it would be a never-ending process, and the knowledge of that fact was unbearable. He knew that humanity's sinfulness and corruption existed from the beginning of time and would not be eradicated.

But all that is now behind us and, as if to prove the point, I need only cite the incredulity of my daughter Justine when I told her that during the troubles in Bangladesh I considered it quite natural that the local Maoists (known as Naxalites) sacrificed (in plain English killed) numbers of landowners around Calcutta. This was done in the desire to create a "new man" and to celebrate their refound purity. But to avoid such things ever happening again or similar aberrations recurring in a different guise, I propose two or three rules which might serve as a guide to future generations:

1. The "urge to purity" should be viewed wholly as a political concept alongside other concepts such as the "general will", the "social contract", and "dictatorship". It should also be seen as the essential motivating force of totalitarianism.

2. Have nothing to do with anyone who publicly calls into question, at least from a philosophical point of view, the notion of original sin. I would argue the case for the rudiments of theology to be introduced into civics lessons in secular State schools, which would at least underpin that point of doctrine. After all, it remains the best means of curbing the aspirations of those who defend the will to purity.

3. Avoid like the plague anyone who comes along and says that a society is "sick" – as has happened, for example, in the case of Eastern Europe which is now referred to as recovering – and that what is needed is some sort of "therapy" and a "therapist" or "healer" to put it into practice. Today, they talk about a healer, but tomorrow he will have become a purifier. Because anyone who talks about sickness is

talking about germs and therefore about prophylaxis. But underlying their well-meaning concern to cure their fellow-men, underlying the idea that mankind's sickness is curable, there still lurks that undying will to purity – which will inevitably be accompanied by camps, police, and violence.

9

"What if the revolutionary dream was an intrinsically barbaric one?"

MICHEL FOUCAULT

I can't remember when I first met Foucault. I remember him when he lectured at the Collège de France, of course, looking like a depraved Buddhist priest with his bald head, his slightly sonorous way of speaking, and his curiously contained laugh which gave him a fiendish air. When he laughed out loud in an unrestrained manner, one couldn't help thinking of Leiris's remark to the effect that Bataille had the "teeth of a wild animal". I remember meeting him for lunch at the Récamier and telling him stories which he enjoyed about the publishing world I was beginning to frequent. He also came to the offices of the review *L'Imprévu* one evening to bring an article, or perhaps for an interview for our first number. I met him at Jean Daniel's, one Sunday I think it was, and the conversation, which took a philosophical turn because of his presence, went on late into the afternoon. Unfortunately – or was it affectation? – he let it be known he was only interested in contemporary issues. So one of the guests, who was only too happy to take him at his word, filled him in on all the details of the rivalry between different groups in the Socialist Party. I remember him being absolutely fascinated, and his interest was in no way affected. He was like an entomologist who had just discovered a new species of insect; taking in all the details, asking questions. Now and then he would burst out laughing and slap his thighs with both hands. He was, I think, eager to feed his appetite for idiotic and absurd forms of classification. On other occasions, I have watched him being unbelievably patient as some arrogant individual or other, having read only the first chapter of one of his books, formulated objections which were dealt with in subsequent chapters. He would listen to what this bore had to say, nodding his head, and with exceeding politeness would attribute to him a "point of view" which thereby made his question meaningful and, at the same time, more interesting to himself. When the conversation ended, the other person would go away absolutely delighted having had, as he put it, a "discussion with Foucault".

The truth is, Foucault never discussed anything. It wasn't that he preferred, like Sartre, to talk about trifling things with his friends rather than philosophy with Derrida. What he thought – and said – was that if one adopted certain stances as embodying the "truth", they were ultimately identifiable with one's life and style. In his view, behind these "truths" there lay necessarily what Nietzsche referred to as "idiosyncrasies" or "viewpoints". Though he considered it possible to oppose a given viewpoint with another, and indeed desirable to "play off" one's own idiosyncrasy against that of a friend or adversary, the idea of "discussing" them was completely idiotic. Furthermore, it seems to me the distinctive nature of his thought was that he put everything into his books, and once they were finished there was nothing left to discuss. His thought was drained of its content. It was absorbed or swallowed up in the black hole of the finished work. There was no steam left in it for a subsequent debate. When I told him one day that in this respect he was quite unlike Deleuze,[1] he didn't deny it. You had the impression that discussion was always possible with Deleuze, since he seemed to have ideas in abundance.

As far as this book is concerned, my chief memory of Foucault relates necessarily to the conversation we had in his modern and strangely functional flat in the Rue de Vaugirard. There were no books (they had, I think, been collected together in his library which was in the next room), and the only literary touch was the presence of a cat. Why was he prepared to meet me, to show at least that degree of friendliness, given that I had, as he said, "played some dirty tricks on him"? Was I a form of distraction? Did he enjoy entertaining someone from time to time who talked about other things – women, for example? Was it that I made a change from the endless succession of militants who were doubtless closer to him, but who must have wearied him with their talk of nothing but prisons and what went on in the Rue de la Goutte d'Or[2] etc. Anyway, he agreed to meet me, and we talked about everything and nothing, including the arrogance of illiterate journalists. He had just published his *La Volonté de savoir*, and he told me he'd decided not to give any interviews, "because there's no reason at all to do what the papers should be doing for themselves." We spoke about the *Nouvel Observateur* which he half thought of as "his" magazine and to which he had granted this exclusive interview. We spoke about *La Volonté de savoir* and the whole business of power and resistance etc. We discussed what he meant when he said that the modern era was responsible not so much for censuring sexuality as for compelling it to express itself. We also talked about the extreme Left which was on the point of petering out, about Mitterrand, and about the Communist Party. Laughingly, he explained how, as time passed, he thought increasingly of leaving France in order to live in San Francisco. Then suddenly, whilst responding to a whole series of questions about "power", "resistance", the "pavement" and the "beach, "history" and "Nature", he came out with the following remark which stayed in my mind for a long time: "You know full well that the problem today is whether revolution is desirable." The reason this remark stayed in my mind was that he made it in March 1977. At a time when most French intellectuals were still absorbed by the interminable debate surrounding the demise of extreme left-wing politics, Michel Foucault was pointing up something enormously important which was as yet unnoticed. Ten years before the implosion of communism occurred in Berlin, he was alluding to the fact that the desire for revolution, which had so dominated our consciousness, was beginning to dissipate.

AN INTERVIEW WITH MICHEL FOUCAULT

In writing La Volonté de savoir, *you have embarked upon a history of sexuality which would appear to be a monumental task. What, in your view, justifies such an enormous undertaking at the present time?*

It isn't that enormous. Actually, it's quite a limited undertaking. I'm not attempting to offer an account of sexual behaviour covering all ages and civilisations. The thread which holds my book together is much more narrowly defined. What I'm trying to do is to consider the way in which sexuality and the quest for truth have been linked over a number of centuries in our societies.

In what sense precisely?

The problem is this. How is it that in a society such as ours sexuality is not simply something which permits the species, the family, individuals to reproduce themselves? Nor is it simply something which procures pleasure and enjoyment. How is it that it has come to be considered as the most privileged area of our experience, where we can discover the deepest "truth" about ourselves? The crucial fact is that, since the birth of Christianity, the West insisted on the fact that "in order to know who you are, find out about your sexuality". Thus, sexuality has constantly been the point at which our "truth" as individual human beings connects with the evolution of our species.

Confession, self-examination, an insistence upon the secrets as well as the importance of the flesh have not only been a means of denying sexuality or of eliminating it as far as possible from our conscious minds, they have also been a way of placing sexuality at the heart of our existence and of linking salvation to an ability to control these hidden impulses. In Christian societies, sexuality has been something which demanded vigilance and which had to be studied, confessed, and transformed into discourse.

This explains the paradoxical argument which underpins the first volume, that far from making it something which is forbidden or a major taboo, our societies have never stopped talking about sexuality and getting it talked about . . .

I wanted to underline two important things. Firstly, that sexuality has not simply been brought into the open, been "highlighted", in discourse, but in various institutions and practices. Secondly, that though there are numerous, powerful prohibitions, they form an integral part of a complex system in which arousal, display and the attribution of value also have their place. I want to change the perspectives a little by moving away from the constant emphasis on what is forbidden in order to look at all facets of sexuality. I'm always represented as a rather gloomy historian who dwells on the forbidden aspect of things and on the nature of repressive power and who describes everything in terms of two phases: madness and its containment, anomalies and their exclusion, criminality and its confinement. However, what I've always been concerned with is truth. How was it that the exercise of power in relation to madness produced the "true" discourse of psychiatry? I also want to re-examine the way in which power exerts itself in relation to sexuality. I don't wish to write a sociological account of what is forbidden from an historical perspective but rather a political history of the production of "truth".

In other words, power is not necessarily that which censures and confines?

In a general way, I would say that prohibition, refusal, forbidding something, far from being the most important forms of power, mark its limits; are in fact its crude and extreme forms.

That's a new idea compared with what you have said in previous books.

If I were to pretend for a moment that there was a certain coherence in my work, which isn't strictly true, I would say I've always been concerned with the effects of power and the production of "truth". I've always felt uneasy about the concept of ideology which has been so widely used in recent years. For example, people have used it to explain errors, illusions, in fact everything which prevents the production of true discourse. It's also been used to show how what goes on in people's heads is linked to their place within the sphere of production. What one might refer to, broadly speaking, as the economy of non-truth. What I'm interested in is the politics of truth. It took me a long time to realise that.

Why?

For several reasons. Firstly, because in the West power both reveals itself more and conceals itself better. What has been referred to as "political power" since the nineteenth century is the way in which power has displayed itself (somewhat like the Court at the time of the monarchy). But that is neither the way nor the place in which it functions. Power relationships are amongst the most secret aspects of the social body. Moreover, since the nineteenth century, every critique of society has essentially taken the economy as the fundamentally determining factor. That certainly reflects a healthy scaling-down of the importance of "politics", but it also reveals a tendency to neglect those basic power relationships which can be a constituent part of economic relationships. Thirdly, on account of a tendency which is common to institutions, to parties, to a whole current of revolutionary thought and action, which only sees power in the shape of the State and its apparatus. The consequence is that, when one then turns to individuals, power is seen to exist only in their minds (in terms of the way they see, accept, and interiorise it).

What is it that you have sought to do to counteract this?

Four things: I've tried to discover the most hidden aspects of power relationships; to uncover them in the economic infrastructure; to trace their various forms not only at the level of the State but also at lower and parallel levels as well; to determine their physical interaction.

When did you embark on that kind of analysis?

If you want the actual book, it was *Surveiller et punir*. In practice, it grew out of a series of events and experiences relating to psychiatry, criminality, and education, etc. which date from 1968. But I don't think the events themselves would have acquired such significance and intensity had it not been for the fact that behind them loomed the enormous twin shadows of fascism and Stalinism. If political thought in the nineteenth century centred on economic issues because of the poverty of the working-class, which was a kind of sub-existence, it was fascism and Stalinism – both overbearing powers – which created political anxiety in present-day society.

That raises two issues: firstly, how does power work? Does it actually function as a consequence of its capacity to impose severe restraints? Secondly, does it always operate from the top down and from the centre to the periphery?

I noticed the change of emphasis, the crucial shift in La Volonté de savoir. *That was when you clearly abandoned the diffuse naturalism which pervaded your previous books.*

What you refer to as "naturalism" suggests two things, I think. In the first place, there is a certain theory or idea that beneath the violence and artifice of power things must still exist in their original and vital state. It is assumed, for instance, that behind the walls of the asylum one might come face to face with the spontaneity of madness; that via the penal system one would discover a generous fervour at the heart of criminality; that beneath the repression of sexuality one would uncover desire in all its purity. Secondly, it implies a certain moral-aesthetic choice which designates power as evil, ugly, paltry, sterile, monotonous, dead, as opposed to that which is dominated by power which is seen as good and valuable.

Yes. In the end, that's what Marxists and neo-leftists have in common, the notion that the ideal exists just beyond the real.

That's one way of putting it. There are times when simplifications like that are necessary. A dualism of that kind can have a limited use when you want to move from one view of things to the opposite view.

Then comes the moment when you have to stop, reflect on things and fashion a new equilibrium.

On the contrary. You become aware that you have to move off in a new direction, because the process which involves shifting from one view of things to the opposite view goes nowhere and can only repeat itself. As soon as you start to repeat indefinitely the same anti-repressive refrain, things grind to a halt, and anyone can take it up without the slightest bit of notice being taken of them. The over-turning of values and truths, to which I referred a moment ago, was important to the extent to which it wasn't confined to mere sloganising (long live madness, long live criminality, long live sexuality) but allowed for new strategies to be adopted. What often bothers me today – what saddens me even – is that all the work I've done over fifteen years, often with difficulty and in isolation, is taken by some people as an indication that I adhere to this or that: that I'm on the "right side", that I'm on the side of madness, of children, of crimi-nality, of sexuality.

Isn't there a right side?

You have to get to the other side – to the "right side" – but so that you can then try to let go of those mechanisms which suggest that there are two sides, in order also to dissolve the false unity which exists and the illusory "nature" of that other side which you have moved to. That's where the real work of a historian of the present truly begins.

You've referred to yourself several times as a "historian". What does that mean and why do you use the word "historian" rather than "philosopher"?

Putting it in very simple terms like those of a child's story, I would say that for a long time philosophy concerned itself with the following issue: "In a world where everything perishes, what is it which remains? What are we as mortals in relation to that which remains?" Since the nineteenth century, it seems to me that philosophy has gradually shifted its ground towards the following question: "What is happening now, and what are we, who may be nothing more than what is happening now?" Philosophy is concerned with the present, that's to say with what we are, and that's why philosophy today is both totally political and totally historical. It is the inherent political aspect of History and the essential historical dimension of politics.

Hasn't there been a return to philosophy of the most classic, metaphysical kind?

I don't believe in any kind of return. What I would say, a little jokingly, is this. In the early years of Christianity, thinkers had to deal with the question: "What is happening now? What is this time in which we are living? How and when will God make his promised return? What should we do with what seems to be superfluous time? What are we other than a space between?"

One could say that at this historical time, in which revolution will of necessity return but has not yet done so, the question before us is this: "What do we superfluous beings represent at this time when what should be happening is not happening?" All modern thought, including all political thought, is dominated by the issue of revolution.

Do you still think about the question of revolution? Is it still in your eyes the key question?

Politics has existed since the nineteenth century because of revolution. Revolution isn't a form or a particular area of politics. Politics always has to be defined in terms of revolution. When Napoleon said, "the modern form of destiny is politics," he was merely drawing conclusions from this truth. He, after all, came after the Revolution and before the hypothetical recurrence of another.

The recurrence of revolution is what concerns us. Without it, the issue of Stalinism would be of no more than scholastic interest – relating to the way societies are organised and the validity of the Marxist project. Whereas Stalinism raises totally different issues. What concerns us today, as you know, is whether revolution is desirable.

Do you really want revolution? Are you looking for something which goes beyond the simple ethical duty of engaging here and now in a struggle on behalf of the mad, those in prison, the poor and the oppressed?

I haven't got an answer to that question. I do believe, however, that to engage in politics in such a way as to avoid mere politicking is to attempt as honestly as possible to discover whether revolution is desirable. It's to explore the way in which politics can so easily become terribly pettifogging.

If revolution were no longer desirable, would politics remain as you have described it?

No, I don't think so. One would have to invent another form or a substitute for it. We are perhaps witnessing the demise of politics. Because if it's true revolution opened up the whole field of politics and if revolution can no longer be discussed in these terms, then there is a risk that politics will disappear.

Let's come back to what you had to say about politics in La Volonté de savoir. *You said, for instance: "Where power exists, there will be resistance." Aren't you reintroducing that "nature" which a moment ago you said you wanted to get rid of?*

I don't think so, because the resistance I refer to isn't something which exists as such. It doesn't pre-exist the power it opposes. It is coextensive and totally contemporaneous with it.

Is it the reverse image of power then? It would amount to the same thing. The ideal existing just beyond the real, always . . .

No, that isn't the case. If it were nothing more than that, there would be no resistance. In order to resist, it has to be as inventive, as flexible and as productive as power. It must organise itself and achieve the same solidity and coherence as power. Like power it must also come from "below" and spread itself strategically.

To say that "where power exists, there will be resistance" is almost a tautology then.

Absolutely. I don't say that resistance exists in the face of power which also exists. There is simply a possibility of resistance. We are never trapped by power. We can always modify its hold over us in certain clearly defined ways and with a precise strategy.

Why do you use these metaphors of war, such as power and resistance, tactics and strategy? Do you think that from now on power should be thought of in terms of war?

I'm not totally sure for the moment. One thing is however certain. In order to analyse power relationships, we only have two models available to us: firstly, the model offered by the law (power as law, proscription, institution), secondly, the model based on war and strategy in terms of relationships of strength. The first of these has been used a great deal and has proved inadequate, since it's a well-known fact that law doesn't describe power. The second has also been talked of a good deal. But people have simply taken ready-made expressions or metaphors ("total war", "fighting for one's life") and not got beyond mere words, or they've adopted formal plans (strategies are very popular with certain sociologists and economists, especially American ones). I think an attempt should be made to tighten up the analysis of power relationships.

The model based on warfare was already used by the Marxists in their conception of power relationships, wasn't it?

What strikes me about Marxist analyses is that they always raise the issue of the "class struggle", but they pay very little attention to the word "struggle". There again, one has to draw distinctions. The greatest Marxists (beginning with Marx himself) always laid great stress on "military" matters (the army as an instrument of the State, armed uprising, revolutionary warfare). But when they talk about "class struggle" as the mainspring of history, they concern themselves above all with a definition of class, how the lines should be drawn, who should be included, and never with the concrete nature of the struggle. The one exception is Marx himself, whose historical rather than theoretical texts are particularly subtle.

Do you think your book will fill the gap?

I wouldn't make that claim for it. For the most part, I think that intellectuals have given up trying to be prophets – that's if intellectuals still exist as a category, or should still exist, which isn't certain or even perhaps desirable. In using the word prophets, I'm not simply referring to the claim they make to be able to say what's going to happen, but also to the function of legislators to which they have long aspired: "That's what you should do, that's right, follow me. You're all in a state of turmoil, but you can look to me as a fixed point of reference." Those who profess to speak or write today are still obsessed by three models, those of the Greek sage, the Jewish prophet, and the Roman legislator. What I long for is the intellectual who will destroy whatever is obvious and universal and who will seek out and reveal the weak spots, the openings, the lines of force which are there to be found amidst the inertia and constraints of the present day. I'm looking for someone who will be constantly on the move, not knowing where he will be or what his thoughts will be the next day because he will be too preoccupied with the present; someone who, wherever he finds himself, will pose the question as to whether revolution is worth the trouble, and if so which revolution and what trouble. And only those who are prepared to risk their lives bringing that revolution about will be allowed to answer. Questions such as: "Are you a Marxist?", "What would you do if you had power?", "Who are your allies and what are you a member of?", that's to say questions which seek to classify people or discover what their programme is, are of secondary importance compared with the question I've just referred to, which is *the* question of the day.

NOTES

1. A philosopher and literary critic.

2. In the basement of a building in this street in Paris Algerians were tortured during the Algerian War.

10

"In forcing people out of Phnom Penh"

PROOF IN CAMBODIA

Why is it that the revolution which took place in Cambodia was of such significance, though it wasn't immediately obvious? According to Christian Jambet, it's because every single revolution until that point had been aborted or left incomplete. In each case the attempt to change the world was abandoned halfway through, though for different reasons. Consequently, the disillusionment to which each has given rise (whether in the USSR, Cuba, Algeria, Vietnam or China) allowed some to say: "All right, it didn't work, despotism still exists, but it didn't go far or deep enough. People concerned themselves with the State, for example, or economic inequality, or the injustice of the relationships of production, but they forgot about sexuality, which subordinates women to men, and about the structure of language which is such a formidable weapon of power. They did nothing about libraries which, as Freud said, are repositories of human unhappiness. Books were protected and bourgeois memory respected. Out of naivety no one even gave a thought to the age-old distinction between producers and non-producers, thinkers and workers." In Cambodia, however, where the final revolution took place, and which, being the last, was able to draw lessons from those which had preceded it, people said: "Let's get on with it, and this time we'll leave nothing to chance. Did you mention sexuality? We'll control it. Language? We'll invent a new one. Libraries? Let's forget what they represent and burn them down! Memory itself is a sickness! As for distinguishing between intellectual and manual work, we'll speedily sort things out by sending the intellectuals off to work in the fields and the towns-people to the countryside."

So for the first time, there were a number of revolutionaries who were sufficiently serious to make sure everything was to their advantage and that there was no chance of the old order surviving. (I said *serious* enough, because their reasoning was beyond reproach, and looking at it in terms of ideas derived from Lacan or Foucault – even if the Cambodians themselves didn't give a damn about Lacan or Foucault – it is true that language, desire, etc. do give people powers of control). What was the outcome then of this chemically pure revolution? It was responsible at the very least for two million deaths, or, if you prefer, it achieved a world record in terms of the number of its own people which it destroyed. In other words, the perfect revolution actually produced a situation of pure barbarity.

As a consequence, the whole intellectual landscape was turned upside down and began to crumble. This was perhaps what Foucault had in mind when he talked about the desirability or otherwise of revolution. Berlin is rightly talked of a great deal as a symbolic moment in the death of the idea of communism. But we should *also* talk about Phnom Penh, because it was there that the idea of revolution, which was perhaps more deadly, was finally destroyed. What happened in Phnom Penh predated the events in Berlin. It's curious therefore that people don't think about it, aren't more aware of it; and though they are certainly moved by the Cambodian tragedy and deplore it in traditional humanist or human-rights terms, they accord it little metaphysical significance. What then is the "metaphysical" significance of Cambodia? It was a moment in the history of the Mind – as well as in Time – when it was clearly revealed that the more radical the revolution, the more bloody and barbaric it was likely to be. It was a moment too when the notion of "changing people's lives" and "transforming man so as to bring out the deepest aspects of his nature", when the idea of "wiping the slate clean" and "starting again from scratch" as far as human history was concerned revealed their fatally destructive and barbaric consequences. If the *true* history of French intellectuals is to be written, you have to forget your sense of horror, pity and revulsion in order to try and reconstruct such a decisive episode in the adventures of liberty. These events have to be commemorated in a fitting manner.

II

"The towering and exemplary figure of Alexander Solzhenitsyn"

I have to admit that Solzhenitsyn means a great deal to me. He is someone I have admired, indeed worshipped. Thanks to him and through him, I have developed certain ideas. I wrote my philosophical works in the shadow of his great shadow. Without him the whole "nouvelle philosophie" movement would very likely not have existed in the form that it did. On one occasion, I said he was something akin to the "Dante of our age", and I stand by that remark. My reason for saying it was that it seemed – and still does – that no one else could have described the hell of the Gulag as he did. So what exactly is happening today? Why do I, and others like me, have a certain feeling of uneasiness? Though he certainly hasn't changed, the mood of the times has. As a consequence, the same themes and the same source of inspiration which at one time suggested one thing have now assumed a different meaning.

The earlier period was one which witnessed the bitter struggle against the monstrousness of totalitarianism. Within the context of that struggle, it was legitimate to defend the Slav nation and homeland as well as its roots. It was also legitimate to hark back to these things – necessary too – in order to curb and undermine Stalinist "modernism". Even the most unpleasant themes in Solzhenitsyn's world view (a certain rejection of cosmopolitanism, for example, the defence of a Russian "nature" which could be seen in the faces and physical appearance of Russian men) took on a certain meaning and a positive function when set against an ideology which was a thousand times more pernicious. How could you reproach a man who was deprived of his roots for attempting to refashion an identity, albeit in a fantastical manner? How could you deny a former prisoner, almost broken by Marxism, the right to view the October revolution as the product of an "alien" discourse? How could you possibly deny that in the battle waged by heroic dissidents, for whom we acted as a mouthpiece in this country, the old words they used had a real force and played a major part in the final collapse of communism? (Those who take the line that one should be tolerant and indulgent because the poor devil didn't know what he was talking about always seem stupidly paternalistic, like those left-wing reviewers who adopted an orthodox line when dealing with such inspired works as *August 1914* and *The Gulag Archipelago*.)

The new epoch has been characterised by a fierce struggle between those who, as a result of the collapse of communism, sought a new identity in nationalist, populist and tribalist terms and those who supported a truly open democratic approach. In this context, it was no longer possible to defend the concept of one's roots, one's native soil. And unless one sought clearly to oppose democracy, one couldn't go on attacking the cosmopolitan intelligentsia, in however restrained a manner. Even the most innocuous aspects of Solzhenitsyn's vision (his praise for the "mother-forest", the nostalgia for "Zemstvo", his critique of western sub-culture and vulgarity) were likely to foster a Russian or Slavophile form of populism in opposition to other versions of populism which were re-emerging as a threat all over Europe. Though he used a similar language, the echoes were different; though the themes were identical, the backdrop was no longer the same, and as the rules of the game had changed those themes were differently orchestrated. It was quite likely that Solzhenitsyn wasn't in the least bit concerned about the backdrop, but there were no possible grounds for suggesting he should have changed to take account of the one or fit in with the other. However, the problem did undoubtedly exist and in a particularly acute form for those Russians who were engaged in the struggle in Moscow. Moreover, they clearly drew their own conclusions from the most recent stances adopted by their erstwhile mentor. And though they had fought against communism not only with him but thanks to him, their opposition to populism had to be undertaken without him – and perhaps even against him.

Let's look at it from another angle by going back a stage and isolating the assumptions on which the debate was based. One option was to bring Russia back inside Europe, though it should perhaps be viewed as more of a wager than an option. It was certainly a dubious option and difficult to argue. Thus, it's clear that *Rebuilding Russia*[1] was not only pointless but dangerous, despite the fact it was a fine book. The other possibility was for post-communist Russia to opt for a Slav destiny, without there being any more justification or certainty that it was the right choice, though it was said Russia was Slav by nature and culture. It was also argued that the country wasn't ready for democracy and that seventy years of terror had destroyed the basis for eventual westernisation, which was probably true. In other words, Dostoevsky and Tolstoy were played off against Pushkin, Herzen and Turgenev. In that context alone *Rebuilding Russia* can be seen as a sound, prophetic and important book. The two options therefore represented a genuine cultural division at the heart of what appeared to be a political quarrel, as is often the case.

NOTES

1. *Rebuilding Russia*, translated by Alexis Klimoff, (Harvill and Farrar, Straus and Giroux, 1991).

12

"*The wholesale demise of the intellectual*"

ROLAND BARTHES: FRAGMENTS OF A FRIENDLY CONVERSATION

Of all the great intellectuals of the sixties, of all the structuralists whose importance to me and my generation I've already alluded to, the one who taught me the most was Louis Althusser, and I shall come to him in a moment. Michel Foucault was another, but I had quarrelled with him and stopped seeing him several years before he died. Though I didn't know Jacques Lacan very well, I am indebted to him for several key concepts which appear in my philosophical essays. There is however someone else whose books are important to me but with whom I also enjoyed true moments of friendship and whom I've missed greatly since his death. That person is of course Roland Barthes. He was a charming, gentle, melancholic man, who feared solitude and had a phobia about being bored. He was also infinitely kind. We used to have lunch together at the Récamier and in our conversations neither of us attempted to score points. But we moved in separate circles and had different friends. I recall his review of my first book for *Les Nouvelles littéraires* in which he commented on "the texture of the writing". His favourable comments, with those of Sollers, were the ones I valued most at the time. I recall too that he lived in the Rue Servandoni and that his mother had the flat above his. I remember his reconciliation with Jean Daniel which, I believe, I helped to bring about. Then there were the short, subtle pieces of his which were published for a few weeks in *L'Observateur*. His one complaint about these was that he got no feedback. In 1977, *L'Observateur* also published a long conversation I had with him, the transcript of which I've recently found. Barthes comes over just as he was, or at least as I remember him, with his courteous, indirect and almost neutral way of speaking. It has often been said that there was a Proustian side to Barthes. There was something of Gide in him as well. But he had energy too and was resolute and determined in the choices he made and the stances he adopted. In the course of the conversation he answered the question which has preoccupied me throughout this book, and what he said could well serve as its conclusion. I asked him if he considered that the intellectual could be considered as "the salt of the earth". "What do you mean?" he said in reply. "The intellectual is a 'waste product', in the strict sense of the term." You are about to discover why.

Unlike so many others, you don't really have a "political past".

It's true that in my writing there's no political discourse in the thematic sense of the word. I don't deal directly with political themes or "stances". That's because I can't get excited about politics, and a discourse which doesn't excite its readers at the present time will simply be ignored. You have to exceed a certain level of decibels in order to be heard, and I don't reach that level.

You appear to regret the fact.

Politics isn't necessarily a matter of talking, it also involves listening. We perhaps lack that experience of listening in politics.

If one had to define where you stood, it would be quite reasonable to describe you as a "left-wing intellectual".

It would be up to the Left to say whether it saw me as one of them. I'm quite happy to accept that description as long as the Left is viewed not as a set of ideas but as the embodiment of an unyielding sensibility. In my case, it manifests itself as an unshakeable anarchist streak, in the strict etymological sense of the word.

So you reject the concept of power?

Let's just say I am extremely sensitive to the fact that it's all around us and seems to be permanent. It never weakens, but merely changes like a calendar. Power is a plural phenomenon. I feel that my own personal battle is not against power but against various powers wherever they exist. In that respect I'm more of a "leftist" than a straight "left-winger". What complicates things is that I lack the "style" of a leftist.

Do you think that having or refusing a "style" is all that is needed as a basis for one's politics?

As far as the individual is concerned, politics is a fundamentally existential choice. For example, power is not simply that which oppresses, it is also that which stifles. Wherever I am stifled, power exists.

Aren't you stifled at the moment?

I am, but I don't feel particularly indignant. Up until now, left-wing sensibility has been crystallised less by programmes than by major themes: anti-clericalism before 1914, pacifism between the wars, then by the Resistance, and finally by the war in Algeria. Now, for the first time, no such theme exists. On the one hand, you have Giscard, whose power to crystallise things is rather feeble, on the other, the "Common Programme",[1] which, however good it might be, doesn't strike me as a very powerful mobilising force. For me, that's what is new in the current situation. There doesn't appear to be a touchstone any more.

Is that why you accepted the invitation to have lunch with Giscard?

That's another matter. I accepted out of curiosity, because I wanted to listen to what he had to say. I was keen to pursue a few myths, and, as you know, in order to do that you have to be prepared to go anywhere.

What were your expectations of that lunch?

I wanted to see whether he spoke only the language of a statesman. Obviously, in order to do that I had to hear him talking in private. I got the impression that he did reflect on his own experience; that there was a secondary level of discourse. The interesting thing for me was to observe the "uncoupling" of various levels of language. Obviously, the content reflected a political philosophy based on an entirely different culture from that of a left-wing intellectual.

Did you take to him?

Yes, to the extent to which I was able to see how a very successful upper middle-class person functioned.

What did you talk about?

He did most of the talking. Perhaps he was disappointed – or happy on the other hand – at having to adjust his image slightly. We got him talking much more than we talked ourselves.

People on the Left haven't been very happy about this lunch.

I know. Even on the Left there are those for whom facile indignation is a substitute for the more difficult task of analysing a situation. For them it was shocking, not the right thing to do. You didn't have any contact with the enemy, didn't eat with him. You had to remain pure. As far as the Left was concerned, this was the "right way to behave".

Have you ever been tempted to go back to the "Mythologies" which you wrote twenty years ago so as to incorporate the Left; the new mythologies of the Left?

It's clear that things have changed over twenty years. There were the events of May '68 which liberated and opened up the language of the Left, even though they also gave it a somewhat arrogant tone. It would have been especially surprising if a certain shift or transformation hadn't occurred in the realm of social mythology. Myths go with majority opinion. So why have I put off describing this new mythology? I won't ever do it unless the whole thing is supported by the Left: *Le Nouvel Observateur*, for example.

Let me pick one myth from the many which exist. Is it obvious to you that Giscard is "the enemy"?

Those he represents, the men behind him who have pushed him to where he is, certainly are. But the dialectic of history may reveal one day that he was less our enemy than someone else . . .

Basically, your politics are permanently provisional, minimal and minimalist, rather like Descartes's provisional morality . . .

The concept of a minimal position interests me and often seems the least unfair. For me, fascism represents an issue in politics where it is possible to adopt a minimal position, since compromise is absolutely out of the question. I belong to a generation which experienced fascism and remembered that experience. My commitment would therefore be immediate and total.

Does that mean that, having set the limits of what is and is not acceptable fairly high, everything else is equally valid and that all other political choices are of little importance?

The limits I've set aren't that high. Firstly, fascism includes many things. More precisely, I'd want to say that from my point of view any regime which not only prevents things being said but also requires that certain things be said is fascist. Secondly, that's what power constantly and naturally tends towards. One tries to eliminate it, but it returns all too quickly, and the threshold is soon crossed . . .

Can someone who has a minimalist political position actively look forward to the possibility of revolution?

It's curious. Everyone sees revolution in a positive light and yet in reality it's undoubtedly a terrible thing. One can, of course, have a certain image of revolution, commit oneself to it as an idea and long for it in that form. But revolutions don't just exist as ideas in people's minds, they occur in the real world. And that's what complicates things. I would readily describe those societies in which revolutions have been successful as "disappointing". When we look at the places where they've occurred, many of us suffer a great sense of disappointment, because the State hasn't perished. In my own case, I feel it would be demagogic to talk of revolution, but I'm willing to use the word subversion. Its meaning is clearer to me. It implies undermining things in order to change them by trickery, to deflect them, to push them in unexpected directions.

Isn't "liberalism" also a minimal position which is ultimately quite convenient?

There are two sorts of liberalism. One is almost always underhandedly authoritarian and paternalistic; on the side of good conscience. The other is more ethical than political, which is why a new name needs to be found for it. It suggests a profound attempt to suspend judgment, and is like an all-embracing non-racist attitude which can be applied to everyone and everything. It's a form of non-racism which would move in the direction of Zen.

Is it an intellectual concept?

It certainly is.

There was a time when intellectuals considered themselves to be "the salt of the earth".

I would be more inclined to describe them as the "waste products" of society, in the strict sense of that term. That's to say they are of no use unless they are rehabilitated. There are regimes which do precisely attempt to rehabilitate us. But, fundamentally, waste products have no use, and in a certain sense neither do intellectuals.

What do you mean by "waste product"?

An organic waste product is the proof that matter has undergone a transformation. For example, human waste is the end-product of food which has been consumed. In a similar way, the intellectual is the waste product of a historical process. He embodies in the form of waste the drives, desires, complexities, and psychological blocks which are probably shared by the whole society. Optimists refer to the intellectual as a "witness". I prefer to see him as representing merely the "trace" of something.

So, in your view, he's totally useless.

Useless but dangerous. Every strong regime wants to get him to fall into line. The danger he represents is symbolic. He's like a disease which has to have an eye kept on it, an additional and rather tiresome thing which is preserved in order to stabilise within a defined space the fantasies and exuberance of language.

Of what particular process are you the waste product?

Let's just say I probably represent the trace of a historical interest in language as well as of numerous crazes which come into fashion as new expressions.

When you refer to fashion, are you talking about something up to the minute? In other words, do you read your contemporaries?

Generally speaking, I read very little. That's no secret. It's absolutely clear when you look at my books. I have three different ways of reading. The first consists of glancing through a book. Someone mentions a book or sends me one, and so I look at it. People hardly ever talk about this kind of reading, but it's very important. Like Jules Romains, who went in for wild imaginings about the panoptic vision of the blind, I would be prepared to argue that this first type of reading gives one para-acoustic knowledge, which, though imprecise and lacking in rigour, has its function all the same. My second kind of reading comes into play when I have a book or an article to write or a course to teach. Then I read books from cover to cover and take notes, but only for the work I have in hand. My third kind of reading is reserved for the evenings, when I get home, and then I usually read the classics.

You haven't answered my question.

My "contemporaries"? Almost all of them come into the first category. I glance at them. Why? It's difficult to say. It's probably because I'm afraid I might be seduced by something too close to me, so close that I couldn't refashion it. I don't see myself refashioning Foucault, Deleuze or Sollers. They're too close. The language they use is too immediately contemporary.

Are there any exceptions?

A few. The odd book has impressed me greatly, and I've absorbed it into my work. On the one hand, it's always slightly random and, on the other, when I genuinely read a contemporary work, I never do it immediately someone has mentioned it to me. I always leave a long gap. When something is being talked about, it gets in the way, and I have no desire to read it. For example, I read Deleuze's book on Nietzsche and his *Anti-Oedipe*, but only a long time after they came out.

All the same, you often refer to Lacan.

I wouldn't say it was that often. But I did, especially when I was working on *Le Discours amoureux*, because I needed a "psychology", and only psychoanalysis could provide it. That was when I had a lot of dealings with Lacan.

With Lacan's ideas or the Lacan "text"?

Both. The texts of Lacan interested me as texts, because they have such mobility.

Because of the plays on words he goes in for?

No, not at all. I don't really respond to them. I can see why he uses them, but I lose interest. The rest I like, often a great deal. Lacan represents that rare mixture of "priest" and "artist", to adopt a Nietzschean typology.

Is there any connection between the theme of the imaginary, which is central to your work, and Lacan's conception of the imaginary?

Yes, it's the same, though doubtless I distort it by isolating it. I have the impression that the imaginary is the poor relation of psycho-analysis. Caught between the real and the symbolic, its value is under-played, at least in the everyday language of psychoanalysis. My next book, on the other hand, is an affirmation of the imaginary.

Do you ever read, or rather re-read, your own books?

Never. I'm too afraid, either that I'll consider something good and never be able to match it, or I'll find it bad and wish I'd never written it.

Do you know, on the other hand, who does read you? Who do you write for?

I think you always know to and for whom you are talking. In the case of speech, you have a precise audience even if it is made up of a heterogeneous range of people. Whereas the totally distinctive thing about writing is that it represents the degree zero of communication. A space exists but it is empty. You never know who is going to fill it and for whom you are writing.

Do you sometimes have the feeling you are writing for posterity?

Frankly, no. I cannot imagine my works or an individual work of mine being read after I'm dead. I literally cannot imagine it.

You used the word "works". Are you conscious of creating what might be referred to as your "works"?

No. That's why I spontaneously corrected myself and talked of "a work" rather than "works". I'm not conscious of my works. I write each book as it comes, and each one reflects a certain continuity as well as tactical changes of direction together with various obsessions.

Can you think of any work which hasn't been produced in this way?

Perhaps not. I don't know.

NOTES

1. A programme agreed upon between the Communist and Socialist Parties in 1972. For the Communist Party it marked a significant step in the acceptance of pluralist politics.

13

"It was crumbling and would leave not a trace behind"

THE END OF COMMUNISM?

I was in Berlin in November '89 with Laurent Dispot at the beginning of a long journey which was to take me to most of the countries of Central Europe. The only thing on my mind was, of course, the unthinkable prospect of the "end of communism". I only half believed it, finding it difficult to conceive of it as being remotely possible. In spite of the wall and the ruins, the joyful crowds, and the countless signs of irreversible change, something in me rebelled and refused to accept the evidence which was before my eyes. I won't deny that I was one of those who, until the very eve of the events, went on saying that nothing would happen, that events had moved too quickly, that sadly there was an East German culture and identity, and that in the end a genuine nationalism had become established, albeit as a product of misfortune. It seemed to me therefore that though they had achieved their identity relatively recently (even if it was reinforced by forty years of history), it wouldn't be eradicated by some act of providence.

So there we were with our doubts (I should really refer to them as "my" doubts since Laurent appeared to see things a little more clearly) in a strangely different Berlin which I could not understand at all. We came. We went. And like the hundreds of journalists and assorted tourists who were there, we tried to share the feeling of exhilaration that was in the air. We saw a number of dissidents and celebrated with those who had survived. We tirelessly questioned artists, writers, ordinary men and women, who, some with their feet and others with their words, had destroyed the border which divided Europe in two, though their testimony was in the end very similar. In short, we paid tribute to the euphoria of the moment. When we had done fifteen or perhaps twenty interviews, we realised there was no point in doing any more because they were becoming tedious and that we should meet other people and try to get them to talk as it would be more interesting. The people we had in mind were the losers, the "has-beens", those who, until the day before, had enjoyed the most incredible power ever dreamt of by any despot. Then suddenly, overnight, they had gone from the limelight to oblivion, from palaces to bolt holes, in circumstances which historians would find difficult to unravel. It was obvious that these communists, whom no one came to talk to any more, would understand something of what had happened.

That's how we came to meet Stephan Hermlin. He was an old Stalinist writer, typical of the ousted intelligentsia, with white hair, pale blue eyes, an air of haughtiness about him, and the general bearing of a high priest of communism. He reminded me of Junger or of an old-fashioned Prussian Junker. There's no doubt he was surprised to see us, though he didn't say so of course. Circumstances had changed so fast and the telephone rang so rarely. But he had no intention of showing the least surprise or pleasure. On the contrary, he stood on his dignity and was rather disdainful. He had the cheek to tell me he had read *La Barbarie à visage humain* – in French, if you please! – and that he found it a "stupid" book. He spoke about the deposed President Honecker, whom he still respected, and about his colleague, Stefan Heym, whose attempt to play the hero he found less than amusing. He recalled the Spanish Civil War, the Resistance, and the construction of a bastion against fascism after '45, which is what the East German State was intended to be. He also talked about Eluard and Aragon, signed copies of whose books were there on his shelves. He harked back to the good old days of communism and to the Belle Epoque of Stalinism, which had also been a high point for him. In a mocking tone, he commented that, at the rate things were happening with all the repudiations and recantations going on around him, he might well end up being the only survivor of that past. There we were, with this fossil of a man, in his rather elegant drawing room, furnished in an old-fashioned style, which was, I suppose, typical of the privileges granted by the regime to its grandees. From time to time we set him off again, and at one point he told us, without appearing in the least perturbed, that for him communism had represented, first and foremost, a new aristocracy. As I listened to him, one simple idea came into my mind, which, were it to be taken literally, verified, and perhaps generalised, would, I realised, have called into question everything I had thought and written about communism up to that point.

Basically, what did Hermlin say and how did he express himself? Not surprisingly, he spoke with fervour, passion and pride. His life, as he described it, had been full of incident, epic almost. If we were to believe him, it had been full of courageous martyrs and splendid heroes, like the characters in a Malraux novel, as he went from the

International Brigades to occupied France, and from the anti-Nazi resistance to the reconstruction of the new Germany. At the same time, we were struck by the fact that, though his tone was epic, it wasn't really lyrical. Though he spoke of the battles he'd been involved in and readily talked about the time when young communists confronted armed Nazis in broad daylight on the streets of Berlin, and though he was nostalgic about the spirit, bravery, and iron will of Stalinists who didn't crack under torture, not once in our two-hour conversation did he utter the words "hope", "renaissance", "revolution" or "new man", which form part of the vocabulary you expect to hear, idiotic though it is. I pointed this out to him and expressed my surprise at his grim and unrelievedly sombre account. But when I referred to the heroic anti-fascist struggle of his brave comrades and asked if they weren't also inspired by hope and some minimal faith in the future which I had thought was an integral part of true communism, Hermlin looked me up and down with an air of incredulity, mockery, and slight disgust. "I suppose you believe in all those stories about hope?" he said. "Do you really think that people like me believe for a second in such childish nonsense?"

There were two possible interpretations, I told myself. The first was that he had once believed in communism and now no longer did. He had dreamt of revolution and of the new man, but something within him had been destroyed and he was disillusioned. It was a plausible hypothesis, yet it didn't square either with the style and imperturbable nature of the man or with the fact that he seemed from the outset to have been living in some kind of eternal present. The second – and obviously the correct hypothesis – was that he had never believed in communism or accepted its "childish nonsense". Never for one moment had he believed in a break with history or in changing man, either back in the period of the street battles in Berlin or now that the wall had come down which might have produced certain feelings of melancholy within him. That meant, therefore, that when he used the word "communism" or spoke of the "ideal" to which he had remained hopelessly faithful for sixty years, what he had in mind was not what we had described in our books as totalitarianism. He was a cold, cynical communist, without any kind of messianic vision or eschatology. His was a view of communism which had absolutely nothing in common with that "will to purity" which I have constantly referred to in this book.

One might, for convenience sake, describe this second type of communism as "faithless" or "atheistic". As I left him, reflecting on his pessimism compared with the utopian vision and promises of the first type and on his strangely disillusioned view of things, I was surprised to find myself thinking that his communism was not so much Marxist as in the style of Aron! The truth is his postulates and philosophical hypotheses concerning the ultimate end of history (or rather the *absence* of an ultimate end) were closer to good old-fashioned liberal philosophy than to totalitarian-inclined Rousseauism. Those who subscribe to ideas of this kind believe that society is always bad and the world always imperfect. History, which for Marxists was sacred and always seen as offering the possibility at least of fulfilment if not of a second coming, was for them nothing but turmoil and chaos. As a consequence, the goal which they secretly sought to attain above all others, and in the name of which generations of little Herm-lins had fought and sometimes died, was a peculiarly modest one. Rather than seek to save or even transform mankind, they accepted it in all its wretchedness and at the very most tried to tame it a little.

Communism had been reduced to training and discipline; it was a way, amongst others, of herding people, though to them the best way. In this respect it was "Platonic". Hermlin was no Pol Pot. He had realised, long before me, that dreams of utopia, of making a break with past history, were exceedingly dangerous. In his view, men were nasty creatures, always ready to show their hatred and to destroy each other. He had believed – known perhaps – that, left to their own devices, they would create something like Nazism, and that even if one defeated it and, at least officially, expunged the memory of it amongst those who had survived, the German people – was it only them? – would still retain, deep inside them, certain evil passions. Communists like Hermlin were therefore unusual in that they had only one effective means of controlling man, of suppressing his desire to kill, of stilling the inner rumblings of his obsession with Nazism. So as to quieten and contain those emotions, to impose a minimum level of law and order, and to do it more effectively than the demo-cratic regimes whose weakness they despised, they resorted to a mix-ture of cynicism and lies, of worker power and bureaucracy. In addition, they used the collective appropriation of the means of pro-duction against a background of official culture and a determined drive to achieve widespread literacy. In Germany, as elsewhere, this is what was done in the name of communism.

In conclusion, I have three observations to make, the first of which concerns methodology. Whenever in future I return to the subject and to the fact that four or five generations of intellectuals were rendered powerless as a consequence of this political adventure, I shall try not to confuse those who were like Pol Pot and those who resembled Hermlin, the optimists and the pessimists, those who believed in the future and those who did not. This is a fundamental distinction of crucial importance, rather than a matter of detail. It is a question of two different ideologies, though both go under the same name of "communism". They are, in fact, as different as chalk from cheese. Moreover, both past and future histories of communist despotism will be totally misunderstood if we don't begin by drawing a clear distinction between the two. We must beware of simple ideas and simple terms, and of words which express contradictory ideas. More than ever, we need to respect that "concern for complexity" for which I've been calling for ten years.

My second observation concerns the substance of these two forms of communism. As far as I am concerned, both are equally objectionable and can be treated with equal disdain. All the same, the question should perhaps be raised as to which is the more objectionable and also whether it is better to be an optimist rather than a pessimist. How does one choose between "love of the human race", with its crazy dreams, bloody promises, and alluring perspectives which end in nightmare, and the dark, despairing, and slightly jaded vision of someone who has realised that history always goes wrong and that to believe in an ideal is a joke? It will be clear by now, I presume, that I have made my own choice. Confronted by a likeable idealist who, as the saying goes, does at least believe in something, and the gloomy bastard who only believes in his position, his signed copies of Eluard's poems, his house, his furniture, and the privileges he has lost, paradoxically I would choose the latter. Impurity is always preferable to purity, just as the pessimist who wagers that the worst will happen is more acceptable than the person who seeks to alter the course of history and to transform men for their own good. As Baudelaire would have said: the enemies of mankind are always preferable to those who claim to be its friends.

My third observation concerns the future. I have, I believe, already suggested that the initial version of communism, with its ideals, its purity, and its messianic vision of a new man, had more than one trick up its sleeve, and that its cult of purity and youth could still have a certain appeal. It could gradually and discreetly begin to seduce people again and, God forbid, reverse all the changes which have taken place. What I would now add, however, is that the pessimistic communist, who seems so much less appealing and therefore less threatening, also has his weapons and resources. To start with, he claims to offer people a form of social cohesion and a way of managing their interests. Yet it cannot be disputed that his vision of the world has been declared null and void. Furthermore, at the very moment we were talking to Hermlin, the Germans were declaring quite forcibly that they didn't want it at any price. But let us see what happens as a consequence of the awakening of liberal and democratic forces. Let us hope that in these countries which have been ravaged and ruined by dictatorship, that amongst these peoples who have been bruised and broken, and for whom it is not even certain that the word "freedom" still has a meaning, siren voices will not be heard. Let us hope that in the face of all the upheavals and of the surge of feelings which had been blocked by totalitarianism and were now being expressed, the old refrain will not be heard: better socialism than chaos, better socialism than the absolute barbarism of tribes and nations. Socialism or barbarism – does that mean anything to you or remind you of anything? I wouldn't rule out the possibility that it might again one day become a terrible reality, though that is indeed a nightmare vision.

14

"The last of those intellectual leaders, Louis Althusser"

A CONVERSATION WITH JEAN GUITTON

Our conversation took place a few months before the death of Louis Althusser. Jean Guitton, a Christian and a philosopher, had known Louis since adolescence and had never completely lost touch with him. His view of the author of *Pour Marx* is, to say the least, unusual.

You met Althusser before the war.

Yes, in '36 or '37. I got to know him over a period of two years when he was in "hypokhâgne" and then "khâgne".

What memories do you have of him as a student? What is your first memory?

Oh, the first memory. If I close my eyes I can see him quite clearly. He was in the second row on the left. When I looked at him, I noticed his forehead. That's what captivated me, as well as his handsome head of hair. He had golden hair which suggested enormous sensibility and intelligence.

Do you remember conversations you had, essays he wrote?

Of course. When he produced his first essay, I said to him: "You'd better be careful, Althusser! it reads like Lamartine! Remove all those epithets and adjectives and make your writing as spare as a tree in winter."

Did he listen to you?

Yes, I think so. His initial style was Lamartinian and Romantic. There was – is – a romantic streak in Althusser. Perhaps I helped him to shed his romantic skin and to discover his true style.

It's said that as a young man Althusser was a fervent Catholic . . .

Certainly. He was a fervent and troubled Catholic. He came to tell me he suffered a great deal because he felt he was insincere when he held forth about Catholicism. He was troubled and he had doubts. He told me: "If I followed my own instincts, I would become a Trappist in order to love God all my life. To talk about God isn't to love

392

him." I thought at the time that he had a vocation as a great mystic – and I told him so.

It's hard to imagine.

It's true. He is by nature a mystic. His mysticism developed in a different direction, around Lenin and communism, but it was a form of mysticism. I remember a conversation I had with John Paul II, who said to me: "Your friend Althusser is a logician." I replied by saying that he was a logician who found in Marxism a hidden form of mysticism. Personally speaking, that's why I liked him so much. It was a very unlikely combination of logic and mysticism.

When did you break with him? Do you remember the moment when this young Catholic became the Marxist-Leninist we all know?

Of course. It was at the end of the war. Althusser and I met up again in Avignon. We had lunch together in a little restaurant, and he said to me: "I'm going to introduce you to the person who has had the greatest impact on my life. Her name is Hélène, and she has enabled me to become an atheist and a communist. I shall have nothing more to do with you and your teaching, since I now believe the opposite of what you taught me. I have abandoned Pascal and Bergson for Karl Marx." If I'm to be totally honest, I should add that he also said to me that day: "I have a feeling inside which makes me fond of you. In my heart I feel attached to you. Whenever I'm depressed and feel the need to escape from people for a rest, I shall get you to come and see me."

Is that what he did?

Over a period of forty years, that's exactly what happened. Whenever he was ill, or tired or suffering in some way, he would send for me, and I would go and visit him. We never talked about religion and philosophy. Do you understand what I'm saying?

Of course. What about Hélène, do you have memories of her?

The first time I saw her she put me in mind of an ant, and then very quickly of the person now referred to as Mother Teresa. There was something of Mother Teresa about her. Opposite the Ecole normale at the time, there was a street which was called the Rue Pierre Thuillier. Is it still there?

I presume so!

Well, in the Rue Pierre Thuillier, there were some nuns that I knew who belonged to the order of Père de Foucauld. Althusser was very fond of them, and Hélène was also very very attached to them. I met her once when I was visiting them.

That's strange . . .

393

The third time I saw her was in this room where we are now. She had come with Louis to ask me to make arrangements for him to meet Pope John Paul II. I told her it would be difficult; that it would have been easy with Paul VI, as I had been friendly with him. But I didn't know John Paul II well enough to be sure of arranging an audience. However, I told them I'd try, and that's what I did. I said to the Pope: "Holy Father, I have a friend who is a communist and an atheist to whom I'm very attached. His name is Louis Althusser." John Paul replied: "I've heard of Althusser. He's a logician." – "Yes", I said. "He's a logician. But this logician would like to meet your Holiness." – "Well, let him come, then. I'll receive him."

Why did Hélène – and I suppose Althusser as well – so much want to meet him?

Hélène was very clear about that. Both of them felt that John Paul had been chosen by destiny to be the Pope who would bring about a reconciliation between communism and Catholicism. We think, she said, that the day will come when it will be possible to establish common ground between the ideas of John Paul and those held by Leninists, and that this will herald a new era.

Why, in the end, did the meeting never take place?

I don't know . . . I don't know . . . I think it was at the time when Althusser . . . I think it was at the time of the terrible drama in Althusser's life . . .

What were your thoughts concerning this drama?

I knew them both. I think it was a crime of love.

Did Althusser ask to see you after the crime?

Of course.

Did you see him again?

Yes, often. I remember him saying to me: "Listen. When I was seventeen, I told you I wanted to be a Trappist. Do you remember? The first time I saw you, I told you I wanted to enter the Trappist order. Well, I've entered it now. I've been caught by the Trappists at Sainte-Anne."[1]

And after Sainte-Anne?

He was at Les Eaux Vives, which was a sort of convalescent home for the mentally ill, where I saw him five or six times. Then he went back home to the Rue Leuwen near the Père Lachaise cemetery, where I visited him quite often. The room where he worked was extremely shabby. He sometimes asked me to bring him cakes, so I used to buy little shortbreads in a cake shop in the Rue de Fleurus and take them to him. He loved those. On a shelf, he had the twenty volumes of Lenin's works and also works by Teresa of Avila. His great idea was to reconcile the ideas of Lenin and Saint Teresa.

Did he talk to you about the crime?

No. How could he talk about it? There are things you don't talk about because you live with them constantly. The death of his wife was a sort of hole in his life which we didn't talk about.

So your conversations were strictly about religious matters?

The great issue we discussed was death and how it was linked to love.

Did he talk to you about his work?

Rarely. But on one occasion I remember he'd discovered I was writing my memoirs and he said to me: "That's good. Someone will perhaps write about your life after you're dead, but it's good that you are doing so. I'm also in the process of writing the story of my life, but it's terrible. I've already consumed a lot of ink and paper on this project."

Did you see what he'd written?

He showed me a sort of memoir, but I didn't read it. I didn't read any of it. I'm not sure he could have written about his own life. You need a certain brazenness which he didn't have.

So he was working? Is he still?

Listen. When you visit him in the Rue Leuwen, there are books everywhere, on the shelves, on the tables, on the floor. It's a bit like here, you get the same sense of total disorder. He certainly is working, and reading.

Can we return for a moment to what you referred to as the "drama". You told me that you used your influence to get Althusser's case dealt with at a psychiatric level.

As it happens I've known Jacques Chirac² a long time, from the Corrèze, and I've stayed with him a number of times. Mme Chirac came to visit me on my eightieth birthday. I introduced Chirac to the man who was the head of his private office at the time, Bernard Billaud. It is true that when I heard that Althusser was likely to be punished, I turned to Bernard Billaud and Jacques Chirac for help. It's through them that I succeeded in getting Althusser treated as insane rather than as a criminal.

What did Chirac think about it all?

Chirac is generous by nature. He thought what he was doing was right. The fact that Althusser was a Marxist didn't inhibit him at all.

What are your own thoughts on this crime?

Like Saint Teresa and Descartes, I think we are all capable of the greatest crimes and the highest virtues. I say again, Althusser had a vocation for saintliness, as Catholics would describe it. And so did Hélène. It all happened in five or six seconds. The point at which he tightened the handkerchief around her neck had been part of both their destinies from the beginning of time. That's all I can say about it. That's all I know.

I also sometimes saw Althusser and Hélène together. I certainly didn't have the same impression of them as you did.

There's no doubt they were communists. But they thought that true communism involved poverty, absolute selflessness, and saintliness. They shared an ascetic, mystical view of communism. I say again, he and Hélène were mystics.

Who does he see now? Who do you think is close to him?

There's a priest, I think, who goes to see him frequently. He belongs to a congregation based in Rome called the Passionists. He sometimes comes to see me, and I gather from him that Althusser is still preoccupied with questions of a religious nature. I myself haven't seen Althusser for some time.

To conclude, may I revert to the subject of the nuns in the Rue Pierre Thuillier? To me, it's absolutely unbelievable.

It is indeed unbelievable, in the ecclesiastical sense of that word.

So we have to imagine Althusser teaching us about Das Kapital, *the science of "epistemological divergence", and "the dictatorship of the proletariat" by day at the Ecole normale, and going to visit these nuns in the evening . . .*

That's right . . . That's right . . . I also saw these nuns of Père de Foucauld and knew them well. I've told you I was very friendly with Pope Paul VI. He had a secretary called Macchi who often used to visit me here. Macchi stayed with the nuns of Père de Foucauld in the Rue Thuillier and heard about Althusser and Hélène. He knew these Sisters had instructed them.

I have to say again, it would have been inconceivable to his students at the time.

You have to understand that Althusser really was an ascetic mystic. That explains his communism. I don't think he changed fundamentally from the outset.

A CONVERSATION WITH FATHER STANISLAS BRETON

My conversation with Stanislas Breton, who is also a philosopher and a Christian, took place a few months after Louis's death. He recognised that he was the "Passionist priest" referred to above, and, after the publication of part of my interview with Guitton in the *Corriere della Sera*, he asked to see me to set the record straight.

So you were shocked when you read the text of my conversation with Guitton?

You heard what he said. "There was a priest who was a member of a Roman congregation (that's not correct, the Roman congregations are different). It was a Passionist congregation. He saw Althusser regularly and he came to talk to me about him. I know they discussed religious matters." Well, I reacted when I read that. Firstly because the description could only apply to one person, and secondly because I wasn't the only one to take an interest in Louis. Michèle Loi did, amongst others. Thirdly, during that whole period, I only saw Guitton once at a meeting about Paul VI and artists at Unesco. That just shows he's prepared to say anything.

What about the religious nature of your conversations?

That was completely crazy. It's true that at a certain point Louis did ask me about liberation theology, but only insofar as it had a *political* impact. Much earlier, when Louis had his viva in Amiens, he was friendly with Madame Barthélemy-Madaule. One day she sent him a book in which there was something about him and liberation theology. As it was a student of mine in Lyon who had initiated this particular theology, I had an idea. I produced a text for him, and he typed it out. It was one of the last occasions he was on form. He altered parts of the text as he typed it.

I don't understand.

I produced a paper about liberation theology which Louis corrected. I told him I didn't know all the texts on the subject, but that if theology of that kind were to be created that's how I would construct it. The text I dictated to Louis was short, and he changed certain things. Obviously it had a political dimension, which is what interested him. It was never a religious issue in the existential sense of that term.

Nonetheless, he was very close to Guitton . . .

Yes, that's true. Louis liked him, and I think it was mutual. But for Guitton to say he'd seen various people and that as a result Louis had been spared the worst – that's to say prison – is a bit much! In any case, the psychiatrists were quite clear that it had all happened in a moment of madness and that article 64 could be applied. Hence, the decision taken at the time by the judges and the fact that Louis was taken into care. Did you know he was in care for a long time? Guitton's account is very garbled.

But did . . .

It was just like him! I'd warned people. Did you know he interviewed Pope Paul VI? He had a talent for prompting both the questions and the answers. He made the Pope look like an idiot. Guitton was egocentric. There's a theological name for that, it's called ego-theology. I'd warned the Pope's brother who talked to me about him. I'd also warned the Pope's sister-in-law, Camille, that he was trying to take over Catholic doctrine. You saw too how poor Hélène was brought into the whole thing. Everybody was a mystic . . .

What are your views on the story about the nuns in the Rue Thuillier?
I know nothing about them.

Did you see Althusser latterly?

You're aware that he didn't die either in Paris or at the Marcel Rivière Institute, but at the Denis Forest home at La Verrière which was linked to the Institute. I visited him there towards the end. Things had definitely got worse. I'll give you an example. He said to me: "I can't swallow my saliva any more." He was quite definite: "If I swallow my saliva, my hand closes." I said to him: "What are you talking about?" He said: "It's true, the two things are connected; if I swallow my saliva, my hand closes, they're totally inseparable."

What did you talk about in that final period?

We didn't hold a conversation. He let me do the talking, and said very little himself. He talked a little about the crisis in the Gulf. He had had a phone call from Derrida before he set off on his travels. That's all.

Was he still working?

The very last conversations we had of any interest were about the convergence between liberation theology and the uprisings in Madagascar, in Africa, etc. He seemed to think that things were moving towards some kind of convergence. His view was that philosophers ought to be thinking about the global situation.

When was that? A year before he died?

Oh no! Three years. After that he was reading Michaux. There were certain experiences which he felt he could identify with. But that's all. There was not much else, and conversation gradually dwindled.

Did he read the papers?
Very little.

Didn't you mention the Gulf?

He did show a little interest in that. Towards the end, I once saw a copy of *Le Monde* in his room. He still had his radio, but he didn't turn it on very often. He loved music. I've seen him lying on his back for hours on end at Marcel Rivière.

How was he physically speaking?

He had great difficulty in walking, which had nothing to do with his psychological state. He also found it very difficult to swallow. You know he'd had an operation for the removal of his oesophagus, though he didn't have cancer. Latterly, they gave him compounds in a glass which were rich in vitamins to supplement his very meagre diet. Even so, he was very weak. My last memory of him was at Saint-Louis Hospital, where I'd gone to see him with Etienne Balibar. His voice was a little clearer and he still had that handsome look about him. Those are my last memories, his voice and the way he looked. I saw him again after that, but he was in a completely different state.

When you saw him . . .

He was lying on his bed, and I sat beside him. We didn't say much. He was fading away. He had been a giant of a man, but he was worn out. He was taking so many pills and potions! It seemed to me he was obsessed with his suffering towards the end, trapped inside his own body.

Did he read? I don't mean at the very end, but during his final years.

He sometimes went to the library. In his better moments – three years or so ago – he would occasionally go to the library at Marcel Rivière. There was a reading room there. He also read the papers a bit.

But no books?

No, he didn't read books. He had a few books that people had brought him. For example, the young Comte-Sponville was one of the last. You know who I mean? He took him a copy of his book, but he didn't open it. He had gradually lost interest.

Moulier showed me a book this morning written by an American called Eliott. It's a book about Althusser, which was published two years ago in the States. Louis had obviously read about a third of it, because there were notes in the margin in his writing . . .

What year was that?

'87.

Written in the margin in '87?

Yes. It was called Althusser *and it was published in '87. It's clear that the first third of the book had been read. Things had been underlined with a brown felt-tip, and there were notes as well. At one point there was a*

399

capital "H" with an arrow pointing out from the text. At another point he'd written "nouveaux philosophes". There were things like that.

You astonish me. The last time I saw him make any corrections was in his flat. It was when the Mexican woman, Fernanda, interviewed him. I remember Louis altering certain things and making a number of remarks. But I'm going back at least five years.

Was he still excited by his own philosophy at the time?

At that time, he was. But it was at least five years ago. We discussed things. He even wrote a little.

He did?

A few thoughts about himself, about his own life. It was quite a long text.

Was it an autobiography?

Sort of.

Where is that text?

Unfortunately, I can't tell you, because I don't know. I did have it, but I don't know what's become of it. Anyway, we'll see . . .

Do you have any letters from him?

I've got a very fine letter. I looked for it two months ago when he died. I needed to know where he was to be buried. It was a letter he sent me in '75 when his father died. He talked about his father's death, and said how much he liked that spot in the Ile-de-France where his mother was also buried.

When he was still reasonably well in '84–'85, what did he hope to do? Go back to writing books, rediscover . . . ?

He had moments of exhilaration during his illness. That was normal. During those moments, he had various projects. He talked to me about working on Machiavelli, and I got the feeling he was definitely planning a book.

He was working then?

I'm talking about pre-'85. His last good period. After that, Michèle Loi, his nephew, and Derrida felt he ought to go into the Marcel Rivière Institute.

Did Derrida take a great deal of interest in him?

Derrida was magnificent. He was often away. But he was magnificent.

That was all before '85?

That's right. After that, we had a few conversations about Michaux and talked about Gorbachev a bit. But our conversations were very brief, as he got tired very quickly. He was like one of the peripatetic philosophers. We talked as we walked slowly round the paths at

Marcel Rivière. But the conversations were nothing like those we'd had at an earlier stage.

Was he still aware of being Althusser, of having written books and influenced people?

No. Latterly, he wasn't interested. There were colloquia on him held in Germany and the United States. I don't think . . .

Didn't it matter to him any more?

Perhaps that's not quite the right way of putting it. It no longer meant anything to him . . .

Guitton said he was very taken up with theological concerns, religious matters at that time . . .

That's what I'm protesting about. Because he implied there was only one priest, me as it happens. That's false. There was Michèle Loi, Moulier-Boutang, Etienne, and others. There were a number of us, though slightly fewer than at the beginning, obviously. After all, it went on for a period of ten years from '80 to '90. You know how it is, there are always less at the end than at the beginning. But to claim that the priest concerned, an old friend of his, was practically the only one and that we discussed religious matters which he'd always been a bit inclined to do, and then to say that I talked to him, Guitton, about it is wrong. It gives the impression that I was there as a priest, just to be with him at the end of his life, and that's the most appalling part of the whole story. It was as if I were taking advantage of Althusser's distress, because he certainly was in distress. I myself have too great a respect for the freedom of faith and for philosophy to take advantage of that kind of distress and to suggest that someone's distant past had dramatically reasserted itself. That's what hurt me. And that's why I wanted the whole business put right.

So Guitton . . .

Guitton's account is very coherent. There were the Sisters of Foucauld, the letters which Louis had sent him in the past, when he was young etc. He was therefore destined or predestined to be a mystic, and the outcome was inevitable. The best bit is that Hélène was involved in the whole thing. [laughter] Frankly no! So if you could quietly set the record straight.

Did he talk to you about Hélène?

Hélène? Obviously, Hélène . . . He spoke about her from time to time, but less as time went on.

What did he say?

He had a few memories . . . a few memories . . . All of a sudden he asked me: "Did you know Hélène?" I said: "Yes, you know . . ."

You did know her of course?

Of course. At the Ecole ... and then at Clamart, where I was living at the time. Out of the blue she questioned me about Roman Congregations. She wanted bits of information. I think she had a diary.

She kept a diary?

Yes, yes, I believe so ...

Did he talk to you about the murder?

No, no. He knew of course. He knew he'd killed Hélène. It would be wrong to think ...

Obviously ...

It may have been a moment of madness, but he knew. He knew quite well he had strangled her. But he didn't talk about it out of a sense of shame. Perhaps he felt it so strongly that he couldn't talk about it. I myself was rather guarded about it too. Whenever he recalled a memory, I quickly changed the subject.

But he did talk about her?

Odd memories ... little outbursts ... But I couldn't say they occurred very frequently. From time to time, the subject of Hélène cropped up in the course of our conversations. When I used to go for walks with him early on, in '82–'83, when he was in Choisy. It was the period when Foucault used to visit him.

Foucault?

Yes. It was rather touching. That's how I met Foucault. I admired his devotion. Louis sometimes said to me when he was feeling very anguished: "Call Foucault."

That was at the time when ...

Yes, he remembered all sorts of things. He had a fantastic memory. He remembered you, for example. I said to him: "Lévy, Bernard-Henri Lévy, I haven't read anything of his." He talked to me about you. He quite liked you ... I shouldn't say so but it's true ... [laughter]

So he told you to "Call Foucault"?

That's right. On one occasion Foucault said to me: "Listen, Father, I'm going to give you a special phone number. You'll be able to reach me wherever I am." I kept it in my diary to remind me. I don't know what it was, probably an international number. Anyway, I could reach him, even if he was in America or elsewhere, and give him the news about Louis.

Did he come often?

He came to see Louis. I saw him with someone else you knew,

Alexandre Adler, who was a specialist on the Soviet Union. You know who I mean?

Very well.

He came to see Louis from time to time. But work and other commitments everyone has . . .

What were his conversations with Foucault like?

I was only present at one real conversation, which took place at Choisy. There was Adler, Louis and myself. We were sitting on a bench in a huge green space between two woods. Foucault asked me about my memories of monastic life, and I was telling him about it. I remember it was on that occasion he said to me: "Father, Christianity has a great deal to say about love, but it has never understood friendship." The conversation lasted about two hours.

Did Louis say anything?

He was suffering a lot at the time. He was, however, still able to follow a conversation. He followed our conversation about friendship and Christianity. I said to Foucault: "People have only recently found out about men in monasteries." That made him laugh.

THE MYSTERY SURROUNDING ALTHUSSER

Who of my generation can really boast that they followed one of Althusser's lectures? Maybe the previous generation could, people like Balibar and Rancière, who were among the first of his followers and who "happened on" a year when he was in better health and miraculously able to give his course. But could it truly be called a course? There would be one session, perhaps two; a group seminar for which he set aside one or two hours. And that was it. Nothing more. My generation found him to be in a strange state of exhaustion. Althusser was a professor who didn't give any lectures. It was the opposite of the usual situation, where the lecturer had something to say which no one wanted to hear. We wanted to hear him, but he didn't perform. Thousands of us claimed to be disciples of Althusser, and we were watching and waiting for him to speak. We speculated endlessly about the positions he might or might not adopt. A single word, a fragment was all we wanted. When, by chance, one of us discovered an unknown article by him in some old review, there were great celebrations. Dozens of photocopies were made and passed round as if it were a Samizdat text. It was venerated like a relic! But though he announced courses, real courses, at the beginning of each year – he was after all our philosophy tutor – each year passed without him giving a single class. I spent four years at the Ecole normale without once hearing my professor speak.

Did his teaching and his influence therefore stem from his books? Yes and no. There again, there are no books by Althusser. There are lots and lots of titles, certainly. He was a genius at thinking up titles. No one else could toss out titles as he did, which you then brandished. But if you looked behind these titles, if today you were to examine these books closely, you would discover a collection of articles (*Pour Marx*), a text written to order (*Lénine et la philosophie*), and an article which had been "expanded", as publishers put it, and turned into an opuscule (*Réponse à John Lewis*). His main book, *Lire le Capital*, was in fact a collective work, and if you removed the pieces written by his disciples, you would be left with the equivalent of a few meagre lectures. He didn't really produce a book as such, that's to say something with a beginning, a middle and an end that had a controlling idea and an internal structure. Not that he disliked or rejected the idea. It simply wasn't the right moment, but it would come, was coming. "One day, I must" ... "I ought to decide to" ... "For the moment we only have the cornerstones of the theory concerning this or that" ... Those famous "cornerstones" which were to be the basis of his triumphant success! The endless "foundations" he was constantly reinforcing, on which nothing was ever erected! He seemed sure of himself when he told us of these things. He knew what he was saying and where he was going. We imagined this was the prolegomenon and that the system would follow. But Louis Althusser died, and all he left behind were prolegomena.

Was it simply because his ideas were in gestation, changing, that they were vigorous, living ideas which scorned systematisation and were directed at the infinite? Yet again, I'm not sure. After all, the chief characteristic of Althusser's work was its stability. It was fixed, as if illness had arrested its momentum and prevented it from opening out. One detail struck me. His little office, which became something of a legend, was on the ground floor of the Ecole normale. There were books everywhere, as well as papers, a jumble of press-cuttings, and manuscripts on the radiator. It was the classic setting for an active intellectual. Except that when you looked more closely, noticed the date of the cuttings, the colour of the covers on the manuscripts, the page at which a book of Marx lay open, or the sheet in his little typewriter, you became aware of something untypical. From one visit to the next, from one week to the next, nothing ever really changed in this decor which suggested activity. It was a frozen state of disorder. Time stood still. In *Le Diable en tête*, I spoke of a "frozen landscape", of a "Pompeii of the mind". The image is somewhat forced, but the idea is correct. When I knew him, Althusser had stopped writing and perhaps stopped reading too. His thought was still robust, but no longer dynamic. It didn't progress. When an idea came to him, it was like a muffled explosion, without echo. If, for example, you had listed the phrases of Marx he quoted, you would have realised they were always the same and that he lived on his "reserves" (another of his favourite words) which were definitively fixed. That was another sign.

Was it the spoken word which gave him his authority, as well as direct contact with everyone? Was he a kind of Socratic figure or rather a modern Lucien Herr, to whom he has often been compared? Again I'm not sure. Lucien Herr was a talker. He argued his case. He spent hours convincing Jaurès, Blum, Péguy of the innocence of Dreyfus or of the merits of socialism. Whereas if you visited Althusser, he spoke as rarely as he wrote. When you knocked, he would open the leather covered door very quickly, as if he had been waiting behind it just for you. His handshake was brief and his first glance was slightly sidelong, but fixed and somewhat insinuating. He wore a pair of corduroy trousers and a woollen shirt. He had the heavy step and anxious expression of someone whose work had been interrupted but who just happened to want to see you urgently. "Excuse me, am I disturbing you? – Yes, I was writing . . . but come in . . . you've arrived just at the right moment . . ." Without saying a word, he would point to the armchair on the left and sit down in the one on the right. He looked like an old conspirator who might express himself with abrupt gestures, nods, and pouts. You were obliged to do the talking, to avoid having to sit there in silence. During the whole of the "conversation", he would sit slumped in his chair without saying a word, looking at you pensively with his terribly intense, fine blue eyes.

Did he listen to you at least, and was he as attentive as he appeared? You thought so, of course, otherwise how could you explain his performance, the knowing looks and pensive air? You stammered a little as you began to speak. Not surprisingly, you felt intimidated by the gaze of the man who, let's not forget, was the purest Marxist theoretician on the planet. Oh dear! you're making a mistake . . . you aren't pure or orthodox enough . . . he's going to think you understand nothing about "divergence" or the difference between historical and dialectical materialism . . . he'll think you're frivolous, a socialite . . . he'll say to himself: who is this person? he doesn't really seem like one of us ... I remember my embarrassment in the first years when I left him my vacation address. I remember women I didn't mention and books I read without telling him. I remember feeling awkward in 1973 at having to tell him I was leaving university – worse still four years later when I published *La Barbarie*. I'm convinced now he had forgiven me in advance. Because deep down he was feeling anguished and terribly alone – which few of us suspected – he wasn't bothered whether his followers were orthodox or not. The frown, the sudden angry look, the less than friendly handshake when you said goodbye had no special significance. It was like the face in the famous story of Kuleshov which seemed randomly to express hunger, fear or desire depending on whether it was shown above a picture of a bowl of soup, a wild animal, or a naked woman. Althusser was profoundly unconcerned about one's potentially heretical views. Why should he have been concerned when he had only one thought on his mind? In an hour's time, when you decided to leave for fear you might be inconveniencing him, he would find himself alone again in his unhappy and sick state of mind.

So, did we know or was it apparent that he was ill? Did we talk about it amongst ourselves and refer to the fact that our professor was insane? How did someone like me, who considered himself a disciple, view that "madness" which today is used to define him almost as much as his re-reading of Marx? Strange as it may seem, I don't think I noticed it. I sometimes found him odd and slightly comical. He had his phases of intense excitement, his mad enthusiasms, and then he would be away for weeks or months on end and one would knock in vain on his door. There were strange scenes as well, like the famous evening in the Midi, which belonged to a much later period when I realised there was no risk in telling him about my holiday haunts. The air was soft, the girls were pretty (which he liked), and the evening was drawing to a close. He was amused by Jean-Paul Dollé making a play on words on his name and suddenly decided to join in by "doing a Khrushchev" and banging his shoe on the table. The young woman who was with him seemed very upset at this and burst into tears. She was obviously aware of his illness, whereas, yet again, we didn't want to know. Why, you may ask? Because he put us off the scent by being Althusser, which meant that he gave himself a protective shell with words like "rigour", "scientism", "intransigence", which were key words in the system. Althusser was mad, but he had cloaked his madness with logic and so cauterised the wounds that one would have genuinely said he was in good health. Poor old

Louis, who loved nothing better than having a laugh with Dollé and who on almost every occasion (apart from evenings such as this which always went wrong) would have pretended to be the very serious and stern author of *Pour Marx*.

This brings us to the final question, that of Althusser's influence. How was it that this man, this intellectual who no longer read, didn't talk, barely listened and thought in silence, exercised the extraordinary influence he did? For me, the explanation is clear. It was his language and wonderful rhetoric. His philosophy and thought had a military or warlike tone which pervaded his most minor texts and left an indelible mark on us. In my own case, there is a whole series of concepts and ways of thinking which clearly come from him and which led me to observe in the preface to my first book that "I owed him almost everything". I could mention, for example, a certain anti-naturalism, an anti-historicism, and a mistrust of all philosophies of history – including the Marxist one. But above all else, and notwithstanding individual cases, there was one essential reason for the influence he had. You are doubtless aware of the theory held by some ethno-psychiatrists that every epoch establishes simultaneously the criteria of normality and a pattern of madness. Althusser could be seen in those terms, since his madness was of its period. It had the same structure, the same fundamentally equivocal nature, and the same mixture of pessimism and impatience. It was also reflected in his desire for revolution, at once impossible and urgent, unthinkable and desirable. It combined structuralism of the mind and messianism of the will. It relinquished the illusions of a stultifying humanism whilst at the same time attempting to think the great upheaval. Althusser might be seen as the ultimate example of the will to purity.

Althusser is now dead, and, as everyone knows, he died twice. The first time was when he strangled his wife Hélène at the end of a night which neither judges nor psychiatrists ever really understood. The second time was his actual death, after years of suffering and minimal existence. I try to imagine what those years were like for him, spent in sickness and isolation, in hospitals and old people's homes. The great Althusser had become an invalid, his body slightly swollen. His life was a succession of visits, distractions, empty hours, and horrible dreams. His face coarsened and there was a defeated look in his eyes. He was astonished at his own physical suffering, the bedsores, his failing body, which he couldn't comprehend; and he was surrounded by malign presences, including that of Hélène. Was it true that some nights he woke with a start, crying out "Hélène" as he wandered around his flat? But he had finished with "theory", with "scientificity" and was just a pitiable old man who was a little too stiff to sit in a chair, which is what he had to do when he had a visitor. On top of that, there was his wretched illness which was ever-present; a cycle of euphoria and depression which was accelerating and becoming like a series of contractions which occurred ever more frequently, giving him no respite. There were sudden starts and flashes too, short-circuits in his mind which shook his startled body. I'm sure he had moments of intuition and illumination as well, but only intermittently. His reason had been reduced to mere spasms, to its ultimate fears. I heard that he was interested in Gorbachev and the end of communism, in the reawakening of Islam and in the world which was turning upside down around him. It was at that precise moment that he died. The man who had embodied the extreme delirium of his age disappeared at the very moment when the delirium itself was changing. A coincidence?

One last word. I had not seen Althusser again after Hélène's death, out of a sense of decency, certainly, but also out of tact. I didn't like the idea of playing a voyeuristic role by going to see what had happened to my mentor. Perhaps I was also waiting for a sign from him, some sort of invitation. Every time I met one of his old disciples who had remained in touch – Dominique Lecourt, Yann Moulier-Boutang . . . – I vaguely hoped for a some sort of message from him, however stupid that might have been. No message ever came, or rather it came too late, as was seen above in my conversation with Father Stanislas Breton. One day I was fed up, as I was finishing this book. I was immersed in the whole business of the end of communism and the turnabout in the course of history. It was the end of one world and the beginning of another. There was a sense of upheaval in the air and all our bearings had lost their certainty. I said to myself: "This is stupid, I must see Althusser. He's the best witness there is of this whole adventure." So I asked a friend to call Yann Moulier-Boutang and get him kindly to pass on my request. Moulier-Boutang replied: "It's too late. Althusser died this morning."

NOTES

1. The Asile St-Anne is the mental hospital in Paris where Althusser was confined.

2. Jacques Chirac, Gaullist politician; Mayor of Paris in 1977, President of the Republic in 1995.

Biographical Notes

ALAIN (1868–1951): Pen-name of Emile-Auguste Chartier. Essayist and philosopher. Influential teacher and mentor of André Maurois. Famous for his short articles (*Propos*) which he began publishing in newspapers in 1903. A humanist and a republican idealist.

ALTHUSSER, Louis (1918–1990): Active in Catholic youth organisations as a young man. Captured in 1940 and spent the rest of the war in a POW camp. Joined the Communist Party in 1948. Taught philosophy at the Ecole normale supérieure from 1948. Attempted in *Pour Marx* (1965) and *Lire "le Capital"* (1965) to redefine Marx's historical materialism.

ARAGON, Louis (1897–1982): Poet, essayist, novelist and journalist. One of the originators of surrealism. Joined the Communist Party in 1932 and was a lifelong member. Directed communist paper *Ce Soir* for five years in the thirties and edited *Les Lettres françaises* after the war. His novels include *Le Paysan de Paris* (1926) and *Les Clochers de Bâle* (1936, trans. *The Bells of Basel*). As a popular Resistance poet he published two patriotic collections *Le Crève-coeur* (1941) and *La Diane française* (1945).

ARON, Raymond (1905–1983): Sociologist, philosopher and political commentator. Joined De Gaulle after the fall of France. Wrote for the leftist *Combat* and then for the conservative *Le Figaro* and for *L'Express*. In *L'Opium des intellectuels* (1955, trans. *The Opium of the Intellectuals*) he criticised his former friend Sartre and other Marxists for their support of the USSR.

ARTAUD, Antonin (1896–1948): Actor, director and theorist of drama. Hostile to realism and naturalism, he wanted to return to a primitive, ritualistic form of theatre and to restore to it a passionate and convulsive conception of life. His ideas are expressed in *Le théâtre et son double* (1938, trans. *The Theatre and its Double*). He was associated with surrealism from the beginning.

BARRÈS, Maurice (1862–1923): Novelist, essayist and Deputy for Nancy in 1889. A dilettante and aesthete as a young man. Roused by the Boulangist movement, he became very patriotic and began to emphasise the importance of race and blood ties. During the 1914–1918 war and for a while afterwards, he was President of the League of Patriots. He chronicled his times in three series of novels: *Le Culte du Moi* (1888–1891), *Le Roman de L'Energie nationale* (1897–1902) and *Les Bastions de l'Est* (1905–1909).

BARTHES, Roland (1915–1980): Literary critic and Professor of Semiology at the Collège de France. Challenged orthodox views of literature and was associated with "New Criticism". Analysed texts as a system of signs in order to discover the "meaning" of the work. Made great use of paradox and frequently changed his theoretical position. His writings include *Le Degré zéro de l'écriture* (1953, trans. *Writing Degree Zero*), *Essais critiques* (1964, trans. *Critical Essays*) and *Le Plaisir du texte* (1973, trans. *The Pleasure of the Text*).

BATAILLE, Georges (1901–1962): Essayist and novelist. Trained as an archivist and worked as a librarian in Orléans and at the Bibliothèque nationale in Paris. Founded the literary review *Critique* in 1946. Wrote several erotic novels, including *Le Bleu du Ciel* (1957) and *L'Abbé C.* (1950), as well as a study of literature and evil and another on eroticism.

BERNANOS, Georges (1888–1948): Novelist and writer of polemical essays. The most celebrated of his novels, all of which introduce the supernatural and depict the struggle between good and evil, is *Journal d'un curé de campagne* (1936, trans. *The Diary of a Country Priest*). He condemned Franco and the Spanish church during the Civil War and left France in disgust after Munich, returning in 1945.

BLANCHOT, Maurice (1907–): Novelist and critic. His work is a sustained reflection on the activity of writing and its implications and on the way in which language moves towards silence. His novels, which include *Thomas l'obscur* (1940) and *Aminadab* (1941), are written in a somewhat abstract language and his characters are haunted by death.

BRASILLACH, Robert (1909–1945): Novelist, critic and political commentator. Associated with the fascist press in the thirties. Collaborated with the Germans during the war. Was found guilty of treason and shot. The impact of Nazism on him can be seen in his novel *Les Sept Couleurs* (1939).

BRETON, André (1896–1966): Poet, essayist and chief theoretician of the surrealist movement. Was involved in early Dadaist publications and happenings in Paris. Uncompromising in his defence of surrealism, his views are expressed in the *Manifeste du surréalisme* (1924) and the *Second manifeste* (1929). His poetry includes *Les Champs magnétiques* (1919), an experiment in automatic writing in which he collaborated with Philippe Soupault. He published the autobiographical "novel" *Nadja* in 1928.

CAILLOIS, Roger (1913–1978): Sociologist and writer. Founded the French Institute in Buenos Aires, edited the human sciences review *Diogène* and has worked for UNESCO. Has published works on aesthetics and artistic and literary creation – see *Puissance du roman* (1941). Seeks to create links between different branches of knowledge.

CAMUS, Albert (1913–1960): Novelist, dramatist, essayist, journalist and moralist. Active in the Resistance movement "Combat", he edited the paper of the same name from 1944. Elaborated a doctrine of the "absurd", exploring the themes of happiness and suffering. Developed his ideas on the concept of rebellion in *L'Homme révolté* (1951, trans. *The Rebel*) which gave rise to the quarrel with Sartre. His best-known novels are *L'Etranger* (1942, trans. *The Outsider*) and *La Peste* (1947, trans. *The Plague*). He won the Nobel Prize for Literature in 1957.

CÉLINE, Louis-Ferdinand (1894–1961): Novelist and physician. He was an admirer of Nazism. His novels, written in a fractured, hallucinatory style, include *Voyage au bout de la nuit* (1932, trans. *Journey to the End of the Night*).

CLAVEL, Maurice (1920–1979): Novelist, playwright, journalist, Christian philosopher. Active in the Resistance. Founded a theatre festival in Avignon with Jean Vilar in 1948. Analyst of the events of May '68 which he saw as an expression of resurgent spiritual needs. Denounced the Gulag and Marxism.

COCTEAU, Jean (1889–1963): Writer, artist and film-maker. Published collections of poems as well as plays and novels which include *La Machine infernale* (1934, trans. *The Infernal Machine*) and *Les Enfants terribles* (1929, trans. *Children of the Game*). Produced ballet sketches for Diaghilev and encouraged the group of musicians known as "Les Six" (Honegger, Poulenc, Milhaud, etc.) Films include *Le sang d'un poète* (1932) and *Le testament d'Orphée* (1959).

DRIEU LA ROCHELLE, Pierre (1893–1945): Novelist, literary and political journalist. Deeply affected by his experiences in the First World War. Reacted strongly to what he thought of as the decadence of France and corruption of the Third Republic in the twenties and thirties. Edited the literary review *La Nouvelle Revue*

Française during the Occupation. His fiction includes the collection of stories about the 1914–1918 war *Comédie de Charleroi* (1934), *Le feu follet* (1931) and the panoramic novel of the inter-war years *Gilles* (1939).

FOUCAULT, Michel (1926–1984): Philosopher. Taught in various universities and became Professor of the History of Systems of Thought at the Collège de France in 1970. Concerned with changing historical assumptions about the nature of knowledge. His influential writings include *Histoire de la folie* (1961, trans. *Madness and Civilisation*) and *Histoire de la sexualité* (1976, trans. *The History of Sexuality*).

GARY, Romain (1914–1980): Novelist and diplomat. Joined De Gaulle in London during the war and served as a pilot in the Free French Forces. Was French Consul in Los Angeles from 1956–1960. His best-known novel, *Les Racines du ciel* (1956), won the Prix Goncourt.

GENEVOIX, Maurice (1890–1980): Novelist. He described the experience of combat during the 1914–1918 war in a series of four novels *Ceux de Verdun* (1915–1922). He subsequently wrote novels about rural life depicting the countryside in a lyrical manner. He was elected to the French Academy in 1946.

GIDE, André (1869–1951): Novelist, critic, essayist and diarist. Marked by his strict Protestant upbringing to which he reacted strongly after visiting North Africa as an adolescent. The tension between puritanical and "pagan" values underpins his work. Helped found *La Nouvelle Revue Française* in 1908. His fiction includes *L'Immoraliste* (1902, trans. *The Immoralist*), *La Porte étroite* (1909, trans. *Strait is the Gate*) and *Les Caves du Vatican* (1914, trans. *The Vatican Cellars*). He won the Nobel Prize for Literature in 1947.

GIRAUDOUX, Jean (1882–1944): Novelist, playwright and career diplomat. Made considerable use of classical themes in his plays – *Amphityon 38* (1929), *La Guerre de Troie n'aura pas lieu* (1935, trans. *Tiger at the Gates*) and *Electre* (1937, trans. *Electra*). Was Director-General of Information, 1939–40.

HERR, Lucien (1826–1926): A brilliant student who became Librarian of the Ecole normale supérieure. He supported Dreyfus and helped found the daily paper *L'Humanité* in 1904. An ardent socialist, he influenced Jaurès and Blum as well as countless students at the Ecole normale.

JAURÈS, Jean (1859–1914): An "agrégé" of philosophy who taught briefly before taking up journalism and politics. Became a Deputy in 1885. A great orator and fervent democrat. Founded and edited the socialist newspaper *L'Humanité*. Assassinated a few days before the outbreak of the First World War.

KLOSSOWSKI, Pierre (1903–) Essayist, novelist and translator of various Latin authors. Published studies of Nietzsche and Sade. His erotic novels, which include *Roberte ce soir* (1950) and *La Révocation de l'Edit de Nantes* (1959), have a philosophical and theological dimension.

LACAN, Jacques (1901–1981): Trained as a doctor in Paris and became involved with the psychoanalytic movement in 1936. Expelled from the International Psycho-analytical Association in 1959. Founded the Ecole Freudienne in Paris in 1964. Taught at the University of Vincennes. Most of his published work consists of seminar and conference papers and reports – see *Ecrits* (1966, trans. *Ecrits: A Selection*).

LAZARE, Bernard (1865–1903): Novelist and critic. He challenged the anti-semitism of Drumont and took up the cause of Dreyfus. He was a messianic socialist.

LEIRIS, Michel (1901–1990): Anthropologist, novelist, poet, autobiographer. Has published a number of anthropological studies. His most significant work has been a mythological and poetic exploration of his past in several volumes of autobiography – *L'Age d'homme* (1939), *La Règle du jeu* (4 volumes, 1948–1972).

LEFEBVRE, Henri (1901–1991): Marxist philosopher and sociologist. He was a founder member of the "Philosophes" group in the 1920s. Joined the Communist Party in 1927 and became something of a theoretician. He helped supervise anthologies of Marx and Hegel for the Gallimard publishing house in the 1930s. He was expelled from the Party in 1957.

LÉVI-STRAUSS, Claude (1908–): Social anthropologist influenced by structuralist linguistics. Taught at the University of Sao Paulo, Brazil, 1935–1939, where he also did field-work. Became Professor of Social Anthropology at the Collège de France in 1959. His numerous published works include *La Pensée sauvage* (1962, trans. *The Savage mind*) and *Le Cru et le cuit* (1964, trans. *The Raw and the Cooked*).

MALRAUX, André (1901–1976): Novelist, essayist, philosopher of art and "man of action". Helped to found a revolutionary newspaper in Indo-China (1925–1926), having previously been sentenced to three years imprisonment for removing statues from a ruined Buddhist temple. Organised the International Air Squadron during the Spanish Civil War. Minister of Information in De Gaulle's Provisional Government in 1945. Minister of Culture (1959–1969). His fiction includes *Les Conquérants* (1928, trans. *The Conquerors*), *La Condition humaine* (1933, trans. *Man's Estate*) and the novel about the Spanish Civil War *L'Espoir* (1937, trans. *Days of Hope*). He published his *Antimémoires* in 1967 (trans. *Anti-Memoirs*).

MAURIAC, François (1885–1970): Novelist, biographer, critic and journalist. Published clandestinely during the Occupation under the pen-name "Forez". Elected to the Académie française in 1933. Won the Nobel Prize for Literature in 1952. He sought to make the Catholic universe of evil palpable in his novels, most of which are set in the Bordeaux region where he grew up. Amongst the best-known are *Le désert de l'amour* (1925, trans. *The Desert of Love*), *Thérèse Desqueyroux* (1927, trans. *Thérèse*) and *Le noeud de vipères* (1932, trans. *The Knot of Vipers*).

MAURRAS, Charles (1868–1952): Poet, essayist and journalist. A polemical writer, he helped to found the "Action française" movement and newspaper (1899) to promote the restoration of the monarchy. He admired the restraint and order of classical culture and was hostile to Romantic individualism. These and other themes are dealt with in *Anthinéa* (1901) and *L'Avenir de l'Intelligence* (1905). He was a supporter of Pétain.

MOUNIER, Emmanuel (1905–1950): Essayist, critic and "agrégé" of philosophy. Founded the review *Esprit* in 1932 to promote the ideas of a new movement of Christian moral and social philosophy known as Personalism, based on the individual's sense of responsibility. *Esprit* was suppressed in 1941 and Mounier was imprisoned for a while by the Vichy Government.

NAVILLE, Pierre (1903–1993): Writer and sociologist. He was one of the first joint editors of *La Révolution surréaliste* in December 1924. He joined the Communist Party but was expelled in 1928 and became a Trotskyist. He worked at the Centre national de la recherche scientifique, a government-funded research establishment, from 1947 to 1974.

NIZAN, Paul (1905–1940): Novelist, essayist and journalist. Met Sartre at the Lycée Henri IV. Visited Aden, 1925–1926. Became a member of the Communist Party in 1927. Wrote for various communist publications and was a member of the Association of Revolutionary Artists and Writers. Visited the USSR in 1934. Broke with the Party over the Nazi-Soviet Pact in 1940. Killed at Dunkirk in May 1940. His writings include the vehement pamphlet *Aden Arabie* (1932) and the novels *Antoine Bloyé* (1933) and *La Conspiration* (1938).

ROLLAND, Romain (1866–1944): Novelist, playwright, essayist and musicologist. Taught history at the Ecole normale supérieure and music at the Sorbonne. Appealed to French and German intellectuals to cooperate in the interests of peace (*Au-dessus de la mêlée* (1915)). Became interested in communism and Buddhism. His best-known novel *Jean-Christophe* (1906–1912), is the study of a German musical genius who moves to France. He won the Nobel Prize for Literature in 1915.

SARTRE, Jean-Paul (1905–1980): Philosopher, novelist, playwright, critic. Principal exponent of existentialism whose influence on intellectual life in the post-war years was considerable – see *L'Etre et le Néant* (1943, trans. *Being and Nothingness*). Founded the review *Les Temps Modernes* (1945) and became an active supporter of numerous moral and political causes. Declined the Nobel Prize for Literature in 1964. His most celebrated novel is *La Nausée* (1938, trans. *Nausea*) and his plays include *Les Mouches* (1943, trans. *The Flies*) and *Huis Clos* (1944, trans. *In Camera*).

SIMON, Claude (1913–): Novelist. Initially aspired to be a painter. Published his first novel in 1945 but came to prominence in the 1950s with a group of writers associated with the "New Novel". Seeks to render the flux of consciousness in which chaos constantly threatens to overwhelm the individual – *La Route des Flandres* (1960, trans. *The Flanders Road*). Later novels include *Histoire* (1967) and *Les Géorgiques* (1981).

VALÉRY, Paul (1871–1945): Poet, essayist and critic. Moved to Paris in 1894 and was a regular member of the group which met in Mallarmé's flat. Worked as a civil servant for the Havas News Agency. Became Professor of Poetry at the Collège de France in 1937. His best-known works are the long poem *La Jeune Parque* (1917) and the collection *Charmes* (1922).

Bibliography

L. Althusser, *The Future Lasts a Long Time* and *The Facts* (trans. Richard Veasey), Chatto & Windus, 1993.

Pierre Andreu & Frédéric Grover, *Drieu La Rochelle*, Hachette, 1979.

Pierre Assouline, *Gaston Gallimard*, Balland, 1984.

Jacques Baynac, *La Terreur sous Lénine*, Le Sagittaire, 1975.

Pierre de Boisdeffre, *Malraux*, Editions universitaires, 1969.

Dominique Bona, *Romain Gary*, Mercure de France, 1987.

Jean-Denis Bredin, *L'Affaire*, Julliard, 1983.

François Broche, *Maurice Barrès*, Lattès, 1987.

Colette Capitan-Peter, *Charles Maurras et l'idéologie d'Action française*, Le Seuil, 1972.

David Caute, *Communism and the French Intellectuals*, Deutsch, 1964.

Christophe Charle, *Naissance des "intellectuels"*, Minuit, 1990.

Annie Cohen-Solal, *Sartre: A Life*, Minerva, 1991.

Martine de Courcel, *Malraux: life and work*, Weidenfeld & Nicolson, 1976.

Stéphane Courtois & Adam Rayski, *Qui savait quoi?*, La Découverte, 1987.

Pierre Daix, *Aragon, une vie à changer*, Le Seuil, 1975.

Régis Debray & Jean Ziegler, *Il s'agit de ne pas se rendre*, Arléa, 1994.

Jacques Delperrie de Bayac, *Les Brigades internationales*, Fayard, 1968.

Ramon Fernandez, *Gide ou le courage de s'engager*, Klincksieck, 1976.

Bernard Frank, *La Panoplie littéraire*, Flammarion, 1980.

Hervé Hamon & Patrick Rotman, *Les Porteurs de valises*, Albin Michel, 1979.

Gherard Heller, *Un Allemand à Paris*, Le Seuil, 1981.

Julien Hervier, *Deux écrivains face à l'histoire*, Klincksieck, 1978.

Denis Hollier, *College of Sociology, 1937–1939*, University of Minnesota Press, 1990.

John Lechte, *Fifty Contemporary Thinkers, From Structuralism to Postmodernity*, Routledge, 1994.

Jean Lacouture, *Léon Blum*, Holmes and Meier, 1982.

Jean Lacouture, *André Malraux*, Deutsch, 1975.

Jean Lacouture, *François Mauriac*, Le Seuil, 1977.

Monique Lange, *Cocteau, prince sans royaume*, Lattès, 1989.

Bernard Legendre, *Le Stalinisme français*, Le Seuil, 1980.

B-H. Lévy, *Les Aventures de la Liberté*, réalisé par Alain Ferrari, La Sept/Vidéo, 1992. Cassette 1, 1900–45, Cassette 2, 1945 – à nos jours.

Herbert Lottman, *Albert Camus*, Weidenfeld & Nicolson, 1979.

Maurice Nadeau, *The History of Surrealism*, Penguin, 1978.

Pierre Naville, *Mémoires imparfaites*, La Découverte, 1987.

Pierre Pélissier, *Brasillach, le Maudit*, Denoël, 1989.

Michael Richardson, *Georges Bataille*, Routledge, 1994.

Jean-François Sirinelli, *Intellectuels et passions françaises*, Fayard, 1990.

Manès Sperber, *Les Visages de l'histoire*, Odile Jacob, 1990.

Zeev Sternhell, *La Droite révolutionnaire*, Le Seuil, 1978.

Zeev Sternhell, *Naissance de l'idéologie fasciste*, Gallimard Collection Folio Histoire, 1994.

Michel Surya, *Georges Bataille*, Séguier, 1973.

Robert Thornberry, *André Malraux et l'Espagne*, Droz, 1977.

Micheline Tison-Braun, *La Crise de l'humanisme*, Nizet, 1967.

Acknowledgements

I would like to thank all those whom I consulted for the film and the book. Some of the interviews have been included, others – the majority even – have not. Those concerned are as follows: Maurice Bardèche, Philippe Bauchard, Jacques Baumel, Jean Bénier, Jean-Denis Bredin, Georgette Camille, Philippe Muray, Jean Daniel, Régis Debray, Dominique Desanti, Jean-Toussaint Desanti, Roger Garaudy, Marek Halter, Christian Jambet, Elie Kagan, Klaus Croissant, Claude Lanzmann, Emmanuel Levinas, Claude Mauriac, Maurice Nadeau, Henriette Nizan, Joe Nordmann, Louis Pauwels, François Ponchaud, Emmanuel Robles, Edouard Roditi, Daniel Rondeau, David Rousset, Yvonne Sadoul, Guy Scarpetta, Philippe Sollers, Jacques Soustelle, André Thirion, Jean Bruller – alias Vercors.

B.-H. L

Index

Abetz, Otto, 167, 236, 261
"Acéphale", 25, 192, 195, 196–7, 198–9, 200
L'Action française, 8, 18n, 153, 154n, 224; Cahiers gris, 8
Adler, Alexandre, 403
Adorno, Theodor, 209
Agathon survey (1911/12), 74, 80n
Alain (Emile-Auguste Chartier), 99–100, 208n, 411; Citoyen contre les pouvoirs, 99; Mars ou la guerre jugée, 99; Propos, 99, 411
Algeria/Algerian War, 38–41, 42n, 60–1, 81, 286–94, 300–1, 302, 306–12, 314, 315–16, 317, 318, 319, 329, 355, 373n, 374, 380
Alsace-Lorraine Brigade, 28, 162, 277, 280
Althusser, Hélène, 51, 393–4, 395, 396, 398, 401–2, 407–8
Althusser, Louis, 1, 2, 45, 51, 334, 344, 345, 392–408, 409; Father Stanislaw Breton's view of, 396–403; Guitton's view of, 392–6, 397; Lénine et la philosophie, 404; Lire "le Capital", 345, 404, 411; the mystery surrounding, 403–8; Pour Marx, 345, 392, 404, 407, 411; Réponse à John Lewis, 345, 404
Amiel, Denys, 75
Amsterdam-Pleyel Committees (1932–3), 192, 293n
Anouilh, Jean, 178
Apollinaire, Guillaume, 11, 106
Aragon, Louis, 1, 3, 7, 11, 12, 14, 17, 18, 28, 34–5, 36, 38, 41, 46, 72, 94, 106, 111, 117, 123, 159, 171, 173, 201, 247, 249, 254, 256, 259–70, 275, 333, 354, 356, 387, 411; Aurélien, 247–8, 259, 261–2; breaks with USSR over Prague spring (1968), 269; Les Clochers de Bâle, 411; as co-author of Un Cadavre, 110; Cocteau's relations with, 174–5; Communist Party member, 14, 16, 104, 115–16, 174–5, 241, 257, 259–61, 263–9, 271, 409; Le Crève-coeur, 411; Défense de l'infini, 119, 257, 260; La Diane française, 411; Edmonde Charles-Roux's view of, 262–9; "Fou d'Elsa", 174; "Front rouge", 241; Hourra l'Oural, 259, 270n; Kharkov affair (1930), 265, 268, 270n, 354; and Naville, 101–3, 104, 105; "Le Prix de l'esprit", 105; La Semaine sainte, 267; and surrealism, 12, 105, 110, 112, 128, 132, 159, 260, 261, 265, 266–7, 268–9
Aron, Raymond, 27, 36, 39, 94, 183, 275, 283, 290–9, 346, 389, 411; and Algeria, 39, 40, 290–4; Clausewitz, 298; Dix-huit leçons, 346; L'Introduction à la philosophie de l'histoire, 291, 297; Mémoires, 183, 297; L'Opium des intellectuels, 346, 411; Paix et guerre entre les nations, 297; portrait of, 294–7; and Sartre, 27, 36, 297, 298, 299; La Tragédie, 290–1
Artaud, Antonin, 11, 12, 101, 107, 111, 120, 122, 128, 259, 409; Le Pèse-Nerfs, 101; Le Théâtre et son double, 411
Association of Revolutionary Artists and Writers (AEAR), 192, 193n, 352, 414
Auffret, Dominique 92
Aurore littéraire, artistique, sociale, L', 55
Auschwitz camp, 183; Carmelite monastery, 318–19

Baader, Andreas, 47, 48, 360
Balibar, Etienne, 399, 401, 403
Balzac, Honoré de, 63, 69–70, 119, 190, 249, 348, 352; La Comédie humaine, 70; La Physiologie du mariage, 249
Le Banquet, review, 73
Barbusse, Henri, 11, 15, 16, 24, 30n,